Sue Allison

NURTURING CHILDREN'S SPIRITUALITY

NURTURING Children's SPIRITUALITY

*Christian Perspectives
and Best Practices*

EDITED BY
Holly Catterton Allen

CASCADE *Books* · Eugene, Oregon

NURTURING CHILDREN'S SPIRITUALITY:
Christian Perspectives and Best Practices

Copyright © 2008 Wipf and Stock Publishers. All rights reserved. Except for brief quotations in critical publications or reviews, no part of this book may be reproduced in any manner without prior written permission from the publisher. Write: Permissions, Wipf and Stock Publishers, 199 W. 8th Ave., Suite 3, Eugene, OR 97401.

Cascade Books
A Division of Wipf and Stock Publishers
199 West 8th Avenue, Suite 3
Eugene, Oregon 97401

www.wipfandstock.com

ISBN 13: 978-1-55635-558-5

Bible translations quoted in this text: English Standard Version, Fox Translation, New American Standard Bible, New International Version, New King James Version, New Living Translation, The Chumash, Today's New International Version, New Life Version

Modified versions of the following chapters appear in *Christian Education Journal*, Fall 2007. The Fall 2007 issue of *CEJ* was a mini-theme issue focusing on children's spirituality. The chapters are reprinted here with permission from *CEJ*:

Chapter 2 by Donald Ratcliff
Chapter 5 by Mara Lief Crabtree
Chapter 10 by Linda V. Callahan
Chapter 13 by Judy Harris Helm, Stacy Berg, and Pam Scranton
Chapter 18 by MaLesa Breeding & Dana Kennamer Hood

Portions of chapter 8 by T. Wyatt Watkins were previously published in the *What Our Kids Teach Us About Prayer* (Crossroad, 2005) by T. Wyatt Watkins. This material is reprinted here with permission from Crossroad.

Portions of chapter 11 by Michael Anthony were previously published in the Introduction to *Perspectives on Children's Spiritual Formation: Four Views* (Broadman & Holman, 2006) edited by Michael Anthony. This material is used by permission of Broadman & Holman.

Cataloging-in-Publication data:

Nurturing children's spirituality : Christian perspectives and best practices / edited by Holly Catterton Allen.

xvi + 400 p.; 23 cm.
ISBN 13: 978-1-55635-558-5
Includes bibliographical references.

1. Children—Religious life. 2. Christian education of children. Spiritual life—Christianity. I. Allen, Holly Catterton. II. Title.

BV4571.3 N85 2008

Manufactured in the U.S.A.

To my children

David, Daniel, and Bethany

whose spiritual journeys

I have been privileged to share

Contents

*Preface: The Children's Spirituality Conference—
Christian Perspectives: 2003, 2006, 2009 xi*

Kevin Lawson

Acknowledgments xv

PART I	Definitional, Historical & Theological Issues of Children's Spiritual Development
Introductory & Definitional Concepts	1. Exploring Children's Spirituality from a Christian Perspective 5 *Holly Catterton Allen* 2. "The Spirit of Children Past": A Century of Children's Spirituality Research 21 *Donald Ratcliff* 3. Children's Spiritual Development: Advancing the Field in Definition, Measurement, and Theory 43 *Chris J. Boyatzis*

•

Historical & Theological Understandings of Children's Spirituality

4. The Christian Nurture of Children in the Second and Third Centuries 61

   James Riley Estep Jr.

5. "Forbid Not the Little Ones": The Spirituality of Children in Celtic Christian Tradition 78

   Mara Lief Crabtree

6. Theological Perspectives on Children in the Church: Reformed and Presbyterian 93

   Timothy A. Sisemore

7. Theological Perspectives on Children in the Church: Anabaptist/Believers Churches 110

   Holly Catterton Allen

PART II Best Practices for Nurturing Children's Spiritual Development

Prayer, Storytelling & Reading

8. Unfettered Wonder: Rediscovering Prayer through the Inspired Voices of Children 131

   T. Wyatt Watkins

9. Making Stories Come Alive 146

   Jeffrey E. Feinberg

10. Turning Down the Noise: Reading and the Development of Spirituality in Children 164

    Linda V. Callahan

For Churches & Schools

11. Children's Ministry Models, Learning Theory, and Spiritual Development 183

    Michael J. Anthony

12. Equipping Children for Ministry 198

    Jane Carr

13. Documenting Children's Spiritual Development in a Preschool Program 214

    Judy Harris Helm, Stacy Berg, and Pam Scranton

•

For Families

14. Parenting Styles and Children's Spiritual Development 233

    Sungwon Kim

15. A Qualitative Understanding and Application of the Deuteronomy 6 Commandment for Parents 252

    Marcia McQuitty

16. God Across the Generations: The Spiritual Influence of Grandparents 267

    Holly Catterton Allen with Heidi Schultz Oschwald

•

For Specific Populations

17. The Place of Forgiveness in the Reintegration of Former Child Soldiers in Sierra Leone 289

    Stephanie Goins

18. Voices Unheard: Exploring the Spiritual Needs of Families of Children with Disabilities 305

    MaLesa Breeding and Dana Kennamer Hood

19. The African American Church and Its Role in Nurturing the Spiritual Development of Children 320

    La Verne Tolbert and Marilyn Brownlee

PART III Facing the Challenges for the Future

20. Reimagining the Spirit of Children:
    A Christian Pedagogical Vision 341

    Karen Crozier

21. The Church's Contemporary Challenge: Assisting Adults
    to Mature Spiritually *with* Their Children 355

    John H. Westerhoff III

22. THE Story and the Spiritual Formation of Children
    in the Church and in the Home 366

    Catherine Stonehouse and Scottie May

23. "The Spirit of Children Future" 380

    Donald Ratcliff

    Contributor List 393

Preface: The Children's Spirituality Conference—
Christian Perspectives: 2003, 2006, 2009

IN THE SUMMER OF 2000, SEVERAL CHILDREN'S MINISTRY PROFESSORS FROM North America attended the first International Conference on Children's Spirituality held in Chichester, England. Following that experience, a half dozen of those who attended the international conference gathered informally at the North American Professors of Christian Education (NAPCE) conference in Toronto, Canada, to discuss the experience and explore the possibility of a North American gathering of Christians doing research and teaching in the area of the spiritual life and nurture of children.

With the help of a planning grant from The Louisville Institute, the first conference was held in June 2003 at Concordia University in River Forest, Illinois. Some of the plenary speakers addressed a range of biblical and theological issues regarding the spiritual life of children. Others focused on church history and recent social science research, different cultural contexts, and ways of encouraging a healthy and growing spiritual life for children. Scores of seminars were offered and a dozen ministry models were presented. Local groups of children shared their gifts of music in the plenary sessions and led worship. Over three hundred Christian educators, researchers, children's ministers, professors, and Sunday school directors from the States, from Canada, and from overseas attended; it was an excellent experience. The question quickly arose regarding when the next conference would be held, with many attendees requesting that it become an annual event. The next year a collection of papers from the 2003 conference was published, titled *Children's Spirituality: Christian Perspectives, Research, and Applications* (edited by Donald Ratcliff).

After the first conference, the planning team was expanded slightly, and the team decided to make the conference a triennial event in order to allow time for new research and writing to be completed and new ideas and models to emerge. The second conference was held in June 2006, again at Concordia University in River Forest, and over 350 attended this time. The plenary speakers explored the concept of children and the kingdom of God, views of children in Genesis and the New Testament, and the spiritual needs of children around the world. The opening keynote address by John Westerhoff III and the closing plenary presentation by Catherine Stonehouse and Scottie May appear in part 3 of this text. Again, dozens of seminars were offered at the conference, several of which make up the chapters of this book.

Now, as this second book goes to press, the planning team for the conference is expanding again and exploring incorporation as a non-profit organization. The plans are to prepare a similar conference for June 2009. The goals for the coming conference are three-fold: (1) to network Christians who are doing research and writing on children's spiritual development and formation; (2) to provide a forum for integration of biblical, theological, and social scientific perspectives on children's spiritual experiences, development, and formation; and (3) to explore innovative approaches in children's ministry and to provide encouragement to those in this important area of ministry. The planning team members for the 2009 conference are listed below:

Holly Catterton Allen, John Brown University, Arkansas
Chris J. Boyatzis, Bucknell University, Pennsylvania
Marcia J. Bunge, Valparaiso University, Indiana
Shelley Campagnola, Children's Ministry Partnership, Canada
Elizabeth Jeep, Siena Center of Dominican University, Illinois
Kevin Lawson, Talbot School of Theology, California
Scottie May, Wheaton College, Illinois
Lisa Milligan Long, Lee University, Tennessee
Shirley Morgenthaler, Concordia University, Illinois
Donald Ratcliff, Wheaton College, Illinois
Gene Roehlkepartain, Search Institute, Minnesota
Cathy Stonehouse, Asbury Theological Seminary, Kentucky
William Summey, Belmont University and Lifeway Christian
    Resources, Tennessee

La Verne Tolbert, Crenshaw Christian Center and Haggard School of
 Theology, California
Karen Marie Yust, Union-PSCE, Virginia

We encourage you to consider joining us for the upcoming and future conferences. Conference information can be found at our website: www.childspirituality.org.

Kevin E. Lawson
Planning Team Chair
Children's Spirituality Conference: Christian Perspectives
August 2007

Acknowledgments

OVER THE PAST TWELVE MONTHS, MANY PEOPLE HAVE CONTRIBUTED TO shaping this book. Their insight and encouragement have helped to bring it to completion. First, I would like to thank the twenty-six contributors to the book. They willingly transformed their originally oral presentations into written form; along the way, they responded positively to deadlines and graciously to editing suggestions.

Donald Ratcliff, editor of *Children's Spirituality: Christian Perspectives, Research, and Applications*, the book from the first Children's Spirituality Conference in 2003, helped me shape the introductory chapter, as well as publicize and promote this book on the Children's Spirituality website. Throughout the project, he offered sound advice and encouragement from his own expertise from shepherding edited books to press. His support and assistance have been invaluable.

I also appreciate Kevin Lawson's vision that provided the initial impetus for the first Children's Spirituality Conference, as well as his gift for organization that has sustained the necessary momentum for the 2006 conference and the upcoming 2009 conference. His confidence in me to complete this task has been encouraging.

I also thank Grace Bentley, my student worker, for transcribing John Westerhoff's opening keynote address for chapter 21, Steve Paschold (librarian *extraordinaire*) for aid in locating several obscure sources, and Crystal Perry for her excellent proofreading skills and attention to detail.

John Brown University provided a summer stipend and travel funds (through a Shipps Research Grant) for the research and writing of the Anabaptist chapter, as well as a course release to encourage writing. I am very grateful.

And especially, I thank my husband, Leonard Allen—theologian, author, and my partner for over three decades—for listening patiently to various emerging versions of the book. Over a period of many months, he read and critiqued my chapters, as well as several others, and he encouraged and supported me in the decisions and choices made along the way.

PART I

Definitional, Historical &
Theological Issues of Children's
Spiritual Development

Introductory & Definitional Concepts

1 Exploring Children's Spirituality from a Christian Perspective

Holly Catterton Allen

EXPLORING CHILDREN'S SPIRITUALITY FROM A CHRISTIAN PERSPECTIVE IS a rich cross-disciplinary endeavor. Educational psychologists, theologians, child development specialists, church historians, pedagogical experts, spiritual formation leaders, and biblical scholars all bring important perspectives to the table. The social scientists, especially educational and developmental psychologists, weigh in heavily, calling for rigorous empirical research to support hypotheses; they bring the great theorists Jean Piaget, Erik Erikson, Lawrence Kohlberg, and James Fowler to the conversation, keeping the focus on children. The church historians and theologians note that theological conundrums involving children have been part of the ecclesial mix since the first century and that others before now have had much to say regarding the spiritual nurture of children. Spiritual formation gurus direct the discussion toward the spiritual disciplines that have impacted adults, and they offer their ideas to those who nurture children; they also reiterate that God is Spirit, gently reminding that mystery is inherent in this undertaking. Biblical scholars elucidate those scriptural passages that reveal the heart of God for children as well as exegeting those difficult passages about children and sin. And the Christian educators, ministers, and parents keep the discussion real.

Therefore, given the cross-disciplinary nature of this enterprise, it is evident that these twenty-three chapters—though the authors include psychologists, professors of Christian education, theologians, early childhood specialists, spiritual directors, and ministers, as well as other practitioners—will not (and cannot) surface all of the issues, much less answer all the questions that Christian educators and parents pose regarding the spiritual development of the children in their care. However, this text will make a bold effort to address an impressive list of their concerns.

The first question that must be raised is, What is meant by the phrase, "children's spirituality from a Christian perspective"? To respond to this question, first, I will examine definitions of spirituality in general, then Christian spirituality specifically, and finally children's spirituality in general. There are dozens of definitions of these three concepts; however, few definitions address the concept of children's spirituality from within the explicitly Christian community. Thus, I start with definitions of the first three constructs in working toward an operational definition of children's spirituality from a Christian perspective.

Defining Spirituality

When I speak in various venues on children's spirituality, I ask the audience the following question: What is meant by the term "spirituality" in general conversation? The responses are quite varied—"living beyond the self," "inner peace," "in touch with the sacred," or "a sense of otherness."

Eugene Peterson (2003) comments, "Spirituality is like a net that, when thrown into the sea of contemporary culture, pulls in a vast quantity of spiritual fish" (p. 30). Once exclusively used in traditional religious contexts, the word "spirituality" is now broadly used in a variety of circumstances and with diverse meanings.

Because of the current and growing interest in spirituality, there have been myriad attempts in recent years to give spirituality a concrete, functional definition. In the last decade many books and articles have been published on spirituality, and it seems there are as many definitions as there are authors. At this point, the academic world appears to be dividing generally into two strands or streams of thought on the subject: non-religious spirituality and religious spirituality or, as Sandra Schneiders (2000) says, "an anthropological position providing a 'definition from below'" and "a dogmatic position supplying a 'definition from above'" (p. 252).

Non-Religious Spirituality

Dallas Willard, philosophy professor at the University of Southern California, notes the two strands of spirituality and addresses the secular form in this way: "Much modern thinking views spirituality as simply a kind of 'interiority'—the idea that there is an inside to the human being, and that this is the place where contact is made with the transcendental" (Ortberg, 1995, p. 16).

Non-religious spirituality "often refers vaguely to some interior state or heightened awareness or perhaps to participation in a project, however conceived, greater than oneself" (Collins, 2000, p. 10). Jeff Lewis (2000) defines it as "an orientation towards ourselves and our relations with all other things" (p. 274). David Hay of the University of Nottingham is a scholar who has spent his academic career looking at spirituality. Hay and Nye (2006) describe spirituality in this way: "Each of us has the potential to be much more deeply aware both of ourselves and of our intimate relationship with everything that is not ourselves" (pp. 21–22).

Two common themes in all of these secular or anthropological definitions are self-transcendence and relationality—that is, relationship with self, others, the world, and perhaps with the transcendent.

Religious Spirituality

Religious spirituality also has been described in multiple ways. The editors of a recent volume on spirituality and world religions offer the following working definition of religious spirituality as their "definitional assumption" for their book:

> Spirituality is the intrinsic human capacity for self-transcendence in which the individual participates in the sacred—something greater than the self. It propels the search for connectedness, meaning, purpose, and ethical responsibility. It is experienced, formed, shaped, and expressed through a wide range of religious narratives, beliefs, and practices, and is shaped by many influences in family, community, society, culture, and nature. (Yust, Johnson, Sasso, & Roehlkepartain, 2006, p. 8)

Some religious spiritualities are more monistic (seeing all things as coming from one substance), such as the spirituality of Buddhism; and others are more theistic, such as Judaism, Christianity, and Islam (Collins, 2000, p. 13). One definition of theistic spirituality would be Haddad's (1986): "The whole of human life in its efforts at being open to God" (p. 64). Christian spirituality, though it lies comfortably within this theistic definition, is a smaller subset. Yet, even within the realm of Christian spirituality, a plethora of descriptions abounds.

Christian Spirituality

Collins (2000) gives the etymology of the English word spiritual in the introduction to his edited book on Christian spirituality; he says it is from the Latin word *spiritualitas* and is a "translation of the original Greek terms *pneuma* and *pneumatikos*" (p. 10). It appears that it was a new word in the first century, "a Christian neologism, coined apparently by St. Paul to describe that which pertained to the Holy Spirit of God" (Schneiders, 1986, p. 257). Some scholars adhere to this narrow definition with the single focus on the Holy Spirit; for example, William Lehmann (1998) says, "Spirituality is to be moved by the Holy Spirit" (p. 83).

Other Christian scholars refer to God, not the Holy Spirit per se, in their definitions. For example, Thomas Groome (1988) offers this moving description:

> Spirituality is our conscious attending to God's loving initiative and presence in our lives and to the movement of God's spirit to commit ourselves to wholeness for ourselves and for all humankind by living in right relationship with God, ourselves, and others in every dimension and activity of our lives. (p. 10)

Groome's definition also highlights what many consider to be a crucial component of spirituality—its outward evidence in the Christian life.

Scholars who want to differentiate Christian spirituality from other forms of theistic spirituality often focus on the Trinitarian nature of Christian faith. For example, Sandra Schneiders (1986), professor of New Testament studies and Christian spirituality at Jesuit School of Theology at Berkeley, says that Christian spirituality is the "capacity for self-transcendence that is constituted by the substantial gift of the Holy Spirit establishing a life-giving relationship with God in Christ within the believing community" (p. 266). Philip Sheldrake (2000), professor of practical theology at the University of Durham, England, explores several descriptions of Christian spirituality in his chapter in Collins's recent book on the subject. Ultimately, he creates a definition with a Trinitarian emphasis, saying that it is "a conscious relationship with God, in Jesus Christ, through the indwelling of the Spirit and in the context of the community of believers" (p. 40). Both Schneiders's and Sheldrake's definitions echo the relational nature of spirituality mentioned earlier; both also note the importance of the believing community.

Defining Children's Spirituality

Is children's spirituality qualitatively different from adult spirituality? That is one of the fundamental questions addressed in this volume. And the burgeoning literature on child and adolescent spirituality grapples with this question as well.

Not surprisingly, scholars working in the field of children's spirituality offer definitions that also fall into the two broad camps mentioned earlier—non-religious and religious. The editors of the text, *The Handbook of Spiritual Development in Childhood and Adolescence* (2006), a social scientific (and generally non-religious) perspective on the topic, provide the following definition as the "starting point" for the book:

> Spiritual development is the process of growing the intrinsic capacity for self-transcendence, in which the self is embedded in something greater than the self, including the sacred. It is the developmental 'engine' that propels the search for connectedness, meaning, purpose, and contribution. It is shaped both within and outside of religious traditions, beliefs, and practices. (Roehlkepartain, King, Wagener, & Benson, pp. 5–6, quoting Benson, Roehlkepartain, & Rude, 2003)

Once again the idea of self-transcendence appears.

Two leading scholars in the area of children's spirituality are Barbara Kimes Myers and David Hay. Both Myers and Hay, who work in secular educational settings, attempt to carve out a place in education for children's spirituality to be fostered without reference to religion—though both explicitly acknowledge Christian faith.

Myers (1997) is a prominent American educator who advocates intentional spiritual development in preschool children. She defines spirituality as a socially constructed, "inexhaustible web of meaning interrelatedly connecting self, other, world, and cosmos" (p. 109). She believes that "spirit is a biological condition of being human" and that "all human beings in every culture have spirit as a life-giving force" (p. 101).

Britisher David Hay and his (at the time) research assistant Rebecca Nye are the authors of the current seminal book on children's spirituality on the international scene, *Spirit of the Child* (2006), originally published in 1998. One basic premise of the book is that every human being possesses a biological "spiritual awareness" (p. 22). In locating the origin of spirituality in biology, Hay not only establishes its universality, but he also somewhat distances the discussion from religion. Ultimately, he seeks a definition apart from God, a more inclusive one that atheists and agnostics can embrace (p. 21). Hay finds such a definition in Elaine McCreery's work: "Spirituality is an awareness that there is something Other, something greater than the course of everyday events" (p. 60).

Eventually, Hay and Nye's (2006) research conclusions offer the idea of "relational consciousness" as the phrase they prefer to describe spirituality. Nye explains relational consciousness as the child's consciousness or perceptiveness about how the child relates to other people, to self, to things, and to God—"'I-Others,' . . . 'I-Self,' 'I-World,' 'I-God'" (p. 109); this is similar to Myers's (1997) "self, other, world, and cosmos" (p. 109). (Though Hay prefers a definition without reference to God, the children in the research almost universally referred to the idea of any transcendent being as "God," thus the retention of that term in the description.)

Both Hay and Myers argue that young children, even before receiving any formal religious training, possess a spiritual awareness that should be fostered and not hindered. Many Christian scholars seem to share the conviction that children, indeed, possess this spiritual awareness; however, Christian scholars would argue that this awareness is directly related to God.

Shirley Morgenthaler (1999) of Concordia University, River Forest, Illinois, edited *Exploring Children's Spiritual Formation*, a book that brings together Lutheran scholars from the fields of philosophy, theology, psychology, and sociology on issues concerning children's spirituality. Essentially, this book attempts to address the same problems Hay mentions—lack of agreement on what spirituality is and a shortage of information about the spiritual life of children—albeit from a Lutheran perspective.

Scholars offer scores of definitions of spirituality in general, dozens of definitions of Christian spirituality, and a few definitions of children's spirituality, but Morgenthaler (1999) offers the rare definition of children's spirituality within the Christian framework: "The child's development of an awareness of the relationship which has been initiated by God in and through baptism, the role of the child's community in fostering that relationship, and the child's understanding of, and response to, that relationship" (p. 6).

Another important book on children's spiritual development within a Christian context is Catherine Stonehouse's *Joining Children on the Spiritual Journey: Nurturing a Life of Faith* (1998). Stonehouse develops the theme of children's spirituality slowly and circuitously throughout the book. Though she does not give a concise definition, she describes the concept in enlightening ways: "children think deeply about God" (p. 133); "a genuine knowing of God is open to children" (p. 174); and "they grasp the reality of the transcendent and are even more open to God than many adults" (p. 181).

At this juncture, there is not a definition of Christian spirituality, or of children's spirituality, that is widely accepted. Definitions of Christian spirituality sometimes focus exclusively on the Spirit, sometimes on God, and sometimes on the Trinity. Others add the importance of the believing community or outward evidence of commitment. A prevailing motif in most current definitions is the idea of relationality—for example, Mead and Nash (1997) say that "spirituality is properly defined as the creation and cultivation of an intimate relationship with God" (p. 54).

To create a working definition of children's spirituality with a Christian focus, Don Ratcliff and I considered the major definitional concepts discussed thus far. We were charged in 2005 with constructing a working definition of the concept for the 2006 Children's Spirituality Conference: Christian Perspectives.[1] Our current definition derives mainly from Sheldrake's (2000) description of Christian spirituality and from Morgenthaler's (1999) depiction of children's spirituality:

> the child's development of a conscious relationship with God, in Jesus Christ, through the Holy Spirit, within the context of a community of believers that fosters that relationship, as well as the child's understanding of, and response to, that relationship.

As mentioned, this is a working definition; it is subject to modification as future conferences are convened. The field of children's spirituality is a relatively new one, and concepts and definitions are still emerging.

The definition above is posted on the conference website (www.childspirituality.org), and those who read papers at the conference and wrote chapters for this book had access to the definition; however, conformity to this definition was not required. Some might prefer a definition that is not explicitly Trinitarian; others might wish to incorporate

---

1. See Kevin Lawson's background on the Children's Spirituality Conference: Christian Perspectives in the Preface of this book.

the concepts of relationality with self, others, and the world, as well as with God. Consequently, some authors offer other working definitions.

Overview of the Book

The remaining chapters of this book are composed of material that was first presented at the 2006 Children's Spirituality Conference: Children's Perspectives, at Concordia University in River Forest, Illinois. Over sixty-five papers were presented at the conference; the chapters for this book were selected from these papers because they offered historical or theological ideas pertinent to the understanding of children's spirituality, or as they presented research, literature, or empirical support for a variety of ways to nurture children's spirituality in homes, schools, and churches. The following section offers brief synopses of each of the remaining chapters.

Part One

The first part of the book offers introductory and background information on children's spirituality, including definitional concerns as well as a historical overview of social scientific research and methodological insights into the field of study. Part one also explores historical and theological understandings regarding children from four standpoints—second- and third-century Christianity, Celtic Christianity, the Reformed perspective, and Anabaptist views.[2]

Don Ratcliff (2004), editor of the first Children's Spirituality Conference book, has studied children's spirituality and religious development for thirty years and is the author of chapter 2. Ratcliff notes in his chapter that children's spirituality has roots in more than a century of research conducted around the world. He provides an overview of some of this research, reflecting several phases that emerged over time, each with its distinctive emphasis. Tracing children's religious and faith development research through holistic periods, cognitive phases, and the recent spiritual emphasis lends a rich, textured understanding to current research and generates stimulating possibilities for the future. Essentially, his chapter addresses the question: How did the field of children's spirituality emerge?

---

2. Wesleyan, Orthodox, Lutheran, and Catholic theological perspectives were also presented at the conference.

In chapter 3, Chris Boyatzis—a developmental psychologist who is an expert on current social scientific approaches to children's spirituality research—offers keen insight on how future research can more clearly and skillfully address the central questions that continue to arise in the field. Specifically, he discusses the value of a social-ecological approach to investigating various contexts of spirituality, as well as the importance of using multiple measures of related constructs for a more valid understanding of a central concept. Boyatzis responds to the question: How can this be done better?

James Estep Jr. opens the section that examines how theological issues have impacted current views of children in the church. Chapter 4 addresses Christian nurture of children in the church between the second and fourth centuries AD, specifically focusing on the nature of children, children's place in the church, and the church's responsibility to children. Ultimately, he explores implications for the contemporary church. Estep asks: What can be learned about nurturing children from the second- and third-century church fathers?

Mara Crabtree, in chapter 5, focuses on a later era of church history. She asks: What can be learned from Celtic Christians about nurturing children's spirituality? Rather than hindering the participation of children in various spiritual life practices and pursuits, the Christian Celts welcomed their presence and their contributions. Crabtree's exploration of Celtic Christian beliefs and practices regarding children's spirituality yields perceptive insights into the contemporary nurture of children and the spiritual wholeness of families and communities.

Timothy Sisemore's chapter in the book from the first conference (Ratcliff, 2004) explains the concept of original sin from the Reformed perspective. In chapter 6 of the current book, Sisemore further explores Reformed theology, insightfully and cohesively explicating infant baptism and covenantal theology, particularly as these concepts relate to children's spirituality.

The Anabaptist view of children stands in unmistakable contrast to the predominant view in church history (since Augustine) that children are born with inherited sin and guilt of Adam (the view described by Sisemore in chapter 6). Chapter 7 describes a theological perspective of children espoused by those who believe that children, though born with a sinful nature, are not guilty of Adam's sin, and are not lost until they choose to sin. This chapter examines the historical and theological development of this basic view as it has been understood and practiced among various "Believers' Churches" for the past several centuries. It concludes with spiritual implications for this view of children within Believers' Churches today.

Part Two

Part 2 offers a robust assortment of answers to the question: How can parents, Christian schools, and churches encourage, promote, and cultivate spiritual development in the children in their care? In chapter 8, Wyatt Watkins narrates his journey back to authentic prayer practice via an unusual conduit—listening to his children pray. Watkins shares some of his children's prayers, such as his daughter thanking God for "the gift in the heart," and Wyatt ponders what that might be. This beautifully written chapter is devoted not merely to the theoretical but also to the experiential wonder of engaging children at prayer.

Jeffrey Feinberg, a Messianic Jew, asks and answers: What makes a story come alive? In chapter 9, Feinberg reminds the reader of the power of story—and that Jewish methods of storytelling have developed over thousands of years. Then he shares several techniques storytellers can utilize to impart stories that influence attitudes, alter worldviews, and change behaviors. Feinberg combines his research on story schema with his thoroughgoing familiarity with Torah to offer a unique perspective.

Linda Callahan asks a challenging question in chapter 10: What is the impact of technology and electronic media on the spirituality of children? Callahan says that enchantment with the Noise (technology and electronic media) begins early, citing familiar (and depressing) statistics about the number of hours preschool and school-age children spend using screen media. Her premise is that children who use the media as their frame of reference often ignore their spirituality and experience emptiness and alienation. As an antidote, Callahan offers a variety of fresh ways that reading to and with children can counter the influence of the media and foster spirituality in children.

The next subsection of part 2 examines how churches and Christian schools can improve their programs to enhance spiritual growth of the children in their care. Michael Anthony considers an important ministry question: How can children's ministry models encourage the nurture of children's spirituality? In chapter 11, Anthony describes contemplative models such as Godly Play; pragmatic-participatory approaches such as Promiseland and KidStuf; media-driven, active-engagement programs such as KIDMO; and instructional models such as Awana. He explains that each of these models offers unique ways to build on children's learning styles to foster spiritual development. This chapter provides a needed framework to assist children's pastors as they assess and choose a ministry model that fits their settings.

In chapter 12, Jane Carr considers how children grow spiritually when given opportunities to serve. Carr explores what the Bible says about serving, its implications for spiritual formation, and ways in which churches are encouraging children to serve. The chapter concludes with findings from a recent study of sixty-five children who are actively serving in their churches and communities. She explores the spiritual impact that serving has on children's lives. Carr asks an incisive question: What has prevented churches from providing opportunities for children to serve?

Judy Helm, Stacy Berg, and Pam Scranton engage the question: How can we document spiritual growth and development in children? In chapter 13, they describe how the teachers of Northminster Learning Center, a faith-based, early childhood educational program, do exactly that—they photograph children involved in Godly Play and religious activities, record what children say and do, and engage children in conversation about spiritual issues. This chapter includes four of the display panels the authors use to graphically communicate how Christian formation occurs in their program. Helm, Berg, and Scranton also share fascinating data from a study (involving their documentation panels) that reveals attitudinal change in adults regarding children's spiritual development.

The next subsection of part 2 is designed to help families foster spiritual awareness in their children. Sungwon Kim, a doctoral student, asks the vital question: How do parenting styles impact children's spiritual growth and development? In chapter 14, Kim offers a comprehensive literature review that examines the effect of various parenting approaches on children, beginning first with an explanation of four basic parenting styles: authoritative, authoritarian, indulgent, and uninvolved or neglectful. She then summarizes research that describes specific parenting behaviors and attitudes that can enhance (or hinder) children's healthy spiritual development. Kim concludes by overviewing biblical principles of parenting based on God's role as the heavenly Father.

In chapter 15, Marcia McQuitty reports the results of a qualitative study that explored how parents of contemporary adult believers nurtured their children's spiritual development. Graduate students at Southwestern Baptist Theological Seminary conducted the field research for the study, asking seminary professors how their parents instructed them in the spiritual disciplines of Scripture reading, prayer, giving, and outreach. McQuitty's study describes several specific approaches and methods those parents employed to cultivate the spiritual growth of their children.

The basic question, How can grandparents uniquely foster their grandchildren's spiritual growth? is addressed in chapter 16. Heidi Oschwald and I revisit the field data from my 2002 dissertation on children's spirituality and survey relevant literature to surface evidence of grandparents' spiritual influence on their grandchildren. In this chapter, we offer anecdotal support for the idea that grandparents nurture children's relationships with God through their frequent prayers, their wonderful stories, their clear example, their quiet witness, their availability to share experiences of wonder, and especially their ability to lavish love, grace, and mercy on grandchildren who are in deep need of such gifts.

The last subsection of part 2 looks at unique populations of children and their spiritual needs. Stephanie Goins, in chapter 17, explores an unusual situation: recovery for children who recently served as soldiers in armed groups, becoming victims, and ultimately perpetrators, of horrific violence. Their participation elicits a troubling question: How is it possible for such children to move on to whole and healthy lives? This chapter focuses on the restorative process of forgiveness. Sierra Leonean children (the child soldiers in Goins's study) describe forgiveness as an enacted language that is inclusive and hope-filled. Goins says that former child soldiers feel burdened by the offenses they have committed, understanding they have transgressed moral and cultural values. Goins believes that recovery is promising for these children, their families, and their communities because of the restorative and renewing power of forgiveness.

MaLesa Breeding and Dana Hood, in chapter 18, ask: What are the needs of families who have children with disabilities and how can the church better serve these families? In their interviews with several adults and older siblings of children with special needs, Breeding and Hood found that, as a general rule, faith communities struggle in their response to this growing population. The chapter addresses the spiritual implications for families of children with disabilities and how faith communities can provide support to them.

In chapter 19, La Verne Tolbert and Marilyn Brownlee ask: How well does the African American church nurture the spiritual development of children and youth? To respond to this question, Tolbert develops a new model of spiritual nurture that she calls the Luke 2:52 Triad, based on the passage, "And Jesus increased in wisdom and stature, and in favor with God and man." Tolbert and Brownlee then profile and evaluate four ministries that serve primarily African American children, utilizing Dallas Willard's spiritual disciplines of abstinence (e.g., solitude and silence) and engagement (e.g., study, worship, and service) as well as the Luke 2:52 Triad. Lastly, Tolbert shares insights from her interview with a teenager who participated as a child in one of the profiled ministries.

Part Three

Part 3 considers future challenges for the children's spirituality movement. It asks: Where do we go from here?

Karen Crozier, in chapter 20, questions how leaders, teachers, and even parents have received children into the adult Christian world. She challenges adults to see children's spiritual depth and knowledge through different lenses that can lead to improved adult-child interaction in the family, community, church, and educational ministries of children. Crozier speaks clearly for more inclusive pedagogy.

John Westerhoff III, the opening keynote speaker of the conference, reflected decades of thought and expertise concerning children and spiritual formation. He spoke with few notes, but with a wealth of knowledge and expertise at his behest. His contribution to this book, chapter 21, is a transcription of his speech (which he approved). It captures the depth of wisdom that only a lifetime spent with the germane issues can bring. He asks, and answers: How can adults grow *with* their children?

Catherine Stonehouse and Scottie May, the closing speakers of the conference, asked two penetrating questions: At a time of major change in culture and the church, what are the essentials for nurturing the faith of children? And: What is necessary if children are to become whole-hearted disciples of Jesus? In response to these questions, chapter 22 explores the formative power of the biblical story and of the faith communities of church and home. Stonehouse and May point out that children are profoundly influenced by how the community tells and lives the story; the authors perceptively note that story will be a key theme in the spiritual formation of the current generation of children. They also provide guidelines for readers to evaluate how well they are doing at nurturing children in their faith communities.

The concluding chapter of the book, chapter 23, is an expanded version of the conclusion to Don Ratcliff's conference presentation. He examines issues likely to be important in future years related to the study of children's spirituality, particularly emphasizing Christian perspectives. First, he examines the often-heard question of whether or not there might be a new journal devoted to this area in the near future. He then considers the adjective "Christian" in relation to children's spirituality, examining both the benefits and limitations of a broad comparative approach that includes multiple religious perspectives. Next, Ratcliff encourages dialogue between researchers and practitioners related to children's spirituality, and offers practical means to mutual understanding, appreciation, and benefit among researchers, teachers, and parents. Finally, the author explores the possibility for new classes and programs in children's spirituality at the college and seminary level. Ratcliff's long familiarity with the principal issues pervades his writing.

Concluding Remarks

Despite a bold attempt to address pressing questions about children's spiritual development, and an effort to bring a multiplicity of perspectives to the task, this work will inevitably fall short. And, indeed, it is a remarkably audacious task—helping children seek the ineffable. The hope of the twenty-six contributors to this book is that it will offer biblical, theological, historical, empirical, pedagogical, and experiential support for the idea that every child is on a spiritual journey and that adults can impact that journey.

I close with a poignant vignette. Kathleen O'Connell Chesto, a Roman Catholic who has written intergenerational religious educational materials over the last decade, offers several stories about children and religious understanding. Perhaps nothing better makes the connection between children, spirituality, and theology than the following illustration from Chesto's (1987) dissertation:

> I remember coming across Elizabeth at two years of age, celebrating Eucharist in her room with a brass candlestick and a small white disk. Over and over again she repeated, "This is my Body." When I asked her later if she had hoped to change the disk into Jesus, she responded, "Oh no. I change Wizbef [Elizabeth] into Jesus." (p. 29)

Chesto remarks about her own feelings after this conversation:

> It only took a moment to realize how much better her theology was than mine. What does it matter if the bread and wine are changed if the people who celebrate with bread and wine are not transformed into Jesus? Six graduate credits in sacramental theology had failed to teach me what my child had grasped at two. (pp. 29–30)

Chesto's story shows that children, even very young children, exhibit a spiritual awareness and begin life with a sense of the inexpressible mystery of God. What can adults do to nurture that sense of the holy?

Adults sometimes unintentionally discourage and hinder children in their spiritual journeys. Whether this tendency is due to lack of understanding and expertise, or simply a lack of focus, the result is the same. To counteract that propensity, this book suggests dozens of way for adults to encourage children in their spiritual development. What could be more important?

References

Allen, H. (2002). A qualitative study exploring the similarities and differences of the spirituality of children in intergenerational and non-intergenerational Christian contexts. Doctoral dissertation. Talbot School of Theology, Biola University, La Mirada, CA.

Collins, K. J. (2000). Introduction. In K. J. Collins (Ed.), *Exploring Christian spirituality*. Grand Rapids, MI: Baker.

Groome, T. H. (1988). The spirituality of the religious educator. *Religious Education*, 83, 9–20.

Haddad, F. (1986). Orthodox spirituality: The monastic life. *The Ecumenical Review*, 38, 64–70.

Hay, D., & Nye, R. (2006). *Spirit of the child* (Rev. ed.). London: Kingsley.

Lehmann, W., Jr., (1998). The philosophic roots of research into children's spirituality. In S. K. Morgenthaler (Ed.), *Exploring children's spiritual formation: Foundational issues* (pp. 81–96). River Forest, IL: Pillars.

Lewis, J. (2000). Spiritual education as the cultivation of qualities of the heart and mind: A reply to Blake and Carr. *Oxford Review of Education, 26*, 263–83.

Mead, L. B., & Nash, R. N. (1997). *An eight-track church in a CD world: The modern church in a postmodern world.* Macon, GA: Smyth and Helwys.

Morgenthaler, S. K. (Ed.). (1999). *Exploring children's spiritual formation: Foundational issues.* River Forest, IL: Pillars.

Myers, B. K. (1997). *Young children and spirituality.* New York: Routledge.

Ortberg, J. (1995). What makes spirituality Christian? [interview with Dallas Willard]. *Christianity Today, 39*(3), 16–17.

Peterson, E. H. (March 22, 2003). Why spirituality needs Jesus. *The Christian Century, 120*(6), 30–37.

Ratcliff, D. (Ed.). (2004). *Children's spirituality: Christian perspectives, research, and applications.* Eugene, OR: Cascade.

Roehlkepartain, E. C., King, P. E., Wagener, L., & Benson, P. L. (Eds.). (2006). *The handbook of spiritual development in childhood and adolescence.* Thousand Oaks, CA: Sage.

Schneiders, S. (1986). Theology and spirituality: Strangers, rivals, and partners. *Horizon, 13*, 253–74.

Schneiders, S. (2000). Spirituality in the academy. In K. J. Collins (Ed.), *Exploring Christian spirituality: An ecumenical reader* (pp. 249–69). Grand Rapids, MI: Baker.

Sheldrake, P. (2000). What is spirituality? In K. J. Collins (Ed.), *Exploring Christian spirituality* (pp. 21–42). Grand Rapids, MI: Baker.

Stonehouse, C. (1998). *Joining children on the spiritual journey: Nurturing a life of faith.* Grand Rapids, MI: Baker.

Yust, K. M., Johnson, A. N., Sasso, S. E., & Roehlkepartain, E. C. (Eds.). (2006). *Nurturing child and adolescent spirituality: Perspectives from the world's religious traditions.* Laham, MD: Rowman and Littlefield.

2   "The Spirit of Children Past": A Century of Children's Spirituality Research[1]

Donald Ratcliff

THE STUDY OF CHILDREN AND RELIGION HAS A LONG HISTORY, INCLUDing numerous comments in the Bible and more than might be expected by theologians in church history (Bunge, 2001). In contrast, if the topic is delimited to study in which current research methods are employed, and "spirituality" is understood to be deeply significant experiences marked by awe, wonder, and transcendence, then there are only about twenty years of work to consider. For the purposes of the present analysis, research will be considered that makes use of social science research methods—and research-informed analysis by scholars—that examines religious concepts and beliefs as well as spiritual experiences. Defined thus, the relevant research spans approximately a century, beginning in 1892, when the first identified research study of children's spirituality was published.

During those early years, it seems, religion and the daily lives of children were less dichotomized than today. It was common for a research study of some aspect of development—language, for example—to include data and responses that were religious in nature. Thus, in describing a child's vocabulary, children's religious words were cited in studies as frequently as other words were cited.

With time, research methodologies became increasingly sophisticated, as quantitative statistical studies became more common. During the 1920s, the number of research studies of religion and children in the

---

1. This chapter in an earlier version appeared in the Fall 2007 *Christian Education Journal* and is reprinted here with permission from *CEJ*.

standard journals decreased, with a simultaneous increase in such articles appearing in religious journals, particularly *Religious Education*. Over the next several decades, researchers gave less attention to mystical and experiential aspects of religion in their study of children.

By the early 1960s, a highly cognitive approach to the study of children's religious understandings predominated, to the near exclusion of the experiential dimensions of spirituality. An emphasis upon cognitive stages flourished for another thirty years, perhaps best exemplified by the work of David Elkind and James Fowler.

Scholars seemed to tire of the study of children's religious concepts by the late 1980s, and an increased emphasis on children's spiritual experiences moved to the foreground. Research participants often included children of religions other than Christianity, a rare practice prior to 1990. The spiritual experience of both religious and non-religious children gained in prominence in the last decade of the twentieth century and the beginning of the new millennium.

Thus, four phases in the scholarly study of children's spiritual and religious development are identified and considered in this chapter. The first phase is an early holistic period (1892 to 1930); the second phase is an era marked by a decreased emphasis on experience (1930 to 1960). Then three decades follow with of emphasis on cognitive stages (1960 to 1990); and this brought a metamorphosis to the fourth phase, with a current emphasis on children's spirituality (1990 to the present).

These dates are approximate and there is some overlap in emphases. A major publication marked the transition into each era: Earl Barnes in 1892, Hartshorne and May in 1928, David Elkind in 1961, and Robert Coles in 1990. Just as with any study of historical trends, alternative descriptors and transition points might fit as well as those described above, yet these four eras of thirty years each are particularly salient.

Early Holism (1892 to 1930)

During this first period of interest in children's religion by scholarly journals, children's religious comments were recorded and analyzed, even when the research topic was not religious in nature. Religious concepts and experiences were as likely to be explored as other characteristics, and were not significantly differentiated from other aspects of life (see e.g., Hall, 1891). This practice suggests that a more holistic, integrated perspective of children predominated among the researchers; religion exemplified the life of the child as much as other areas of existence, and thus, faith was unlikely to be ignored or considered irrelevant.

The Earliest Studies of Children and Religion

G. Stanley Hall was a key person in psychology and education at the turn of the twentieth century. He received the first PhD in psychology in the United States, founded the American Psychological Association, and initiated the first American psychology journal, *The American Psychologist*. While not espousing a conservative theology, he did study for a short time at Union Theological Seminary, and affirmed the value of studying religion.

In 1891 Hall founded the research journal *Pedagogical Seminary* (which later became the *Journal of Genetic Psychology*), the first journal to focus on children and educational psychology. Developmental studies of children and teenagers were prominent in the journal from the beginning, as well as school-related topics. In its second year, the journal published "The Theological Life of the California Child" (Barnes, 1892; Barnes with Boring, 2003). Barnes' work was only the first of several research studies over the next three decades that reported or described religious thought, church-related beliefs, and religious experience of children. More often, and perhaps more significantly, the journal included religious examples in research of "secular" developmental and educational topics.

It is difficult to imagine a mainstream educational or psychological journal publishing similar articles today. It was a different time, with different children and different readers from today, but the early psychologists apparently affirmed emergent religious insights and comments about secular topics in scholarly journals.

Research and Scholarly Analysis of Children and Religion

Over the next twenty-five to thirty years, journals continued to publish articles that explored children's understandings and experiences of religion. George Dawson (1900), who later wrote a book based upon his own research of children and religion (1909), considered the degree of interest children had in the Bible. Tanner (1906) reflected upon the development of religious concepts of children. Mary Calkins (1896), the first female psychologist in the United States, considered the implications for religious education of new methods for studying children. Koons (1903) examined the innate "religious nature" of children. Stephens (1905) edited a volume of eleven essays on the relationship between religion and children, and Weaver (1913) surveyed the general religious development of children. Hugh Hartshorne, who would later shake the religious education world with *Studies in Deceit* (1928), emphasized character and religion in children's lives (1919), while Pierre Bovet, Director of the Jean Jacques Rousseau Institute, described religion during childhood and "the development of the religious sentiment" (1928). Examples of secondary applications of previous research include Ellis's (1896) and Hall's (1901) review of methods and approaches to teaching Sunday school and biblical content. Adult religious education was also regularly considered.

During this era it was also a common practice for scholars and educators to write essays on children and religion that were opinion pieces rather than the results of systematic observation. Like Freud's work of this era, these were "clinical" reflections on children's faith and practice, and the esteemed views of these experts were conveyed in journals as essentially equal to the published research.

Between 1910 and 1920 the venue for the publication of research related to children and religion shifted. Although earlier work was published in journals that could be deemed "secular," such research increasingly shifted to religious journals. For example, *Religious Education* published Hartshorne's (1915) study on children's religious concepts; and *The Biblical World* published a series on the relationship between the child's mind and religion (Starbuck, 1907a, 1907b, 1907c, 1907d, 1908, 1909), and later it published the more general topic of childhood religion (Robins, 1917a, 1917b, 1918a, 1918b, 1918c, 1918d). Why this shift occurred is not altogether clear, although it may be related to the increasing prominence of behaviorism and related theories that began to displace the authorities of church and Bible (Johnson & Jones, 2000, p. 29). Also, the growing perception that science and faith were enemies—a view fueled by the Scopes Trial—may have made religious research in general less palatable to the mainstream journals.

Declining Emphasis on Religious Experience (1930–1960)

Near the end of the 1920s there were several studies, such as Bovet (1928), Bose (1929), and Fahs (1929), that marked the emergence of increasingly complex and statistically-oriented research on children and religion. But perhaps more than any other work, Hartshorne and May's (1928) *Studies in Deceit* exemplified advanced quantitative research that attempted to speak objectively, even when what was spoken was problematic for the discipline. Though Hartshorne was a professor of religious education at the University of Southern California, and was later a president of the Religious Education Association, the book said little about children's religious education. What it did say about deceit, children, and religion was devastating, and was recalled countless times in the decades to come: "Apparently . . . the tendency to deceive is about as prevalent among those enrolled in Sunday school as it is among those who are not" (p. 359). For example, in one school, 31 percent of Protestant children who attended Sunday school cheated at school, in contrast with 29 percent of Protestants who did not attend Sunday school. Furthermore, the researchers found no correlations between deception and years of church attendance or deception and regularity of attendance.

During the subsequent decade, published research considered the emergence of religion in babies (Fahs, 1930), the lack of religious content in children's literature (Fahs, 1932), religious education for younger children (Murray & Tyler, 1937), and the emergence of religious consciousness (Fahs, 1939). Acheson (1944) reported a group of studies related to children's religious needs.

A significant review of the literature (Smith, 1941) and innovative research at Columbia University (Mathias, 1943) were followed by three important studies all released one year before the end of World War II. R. M. Loomba (1944) summarized a three-stage progression in the religious development of children in India, as the child moves from "supernaturalist" explanations in the preschool years, to naturalistic explanations for the sun, wind, and "other grand phenomena of nature" in adolescence, separated by the elementary school years that were described as a time of transition between these stages. That same year, Harms (1944) explored children's religious development by tracing the child's imaginative thinking expressed artistically in drawings and paintings. Similarly to Loomba, he found three phases in the child's understanding of God: the "fairy-tale" God between the ages of three and six, the "realistic" phase during the elementary years where God, angels, and saints are portrayed as human beings, and the more individualistic phase associated with adolescence. In a third study that year, Wheeler and Wheeler (1944, 1945) found that children who attend church in a college town often have more sophisticated religious beliefs than similar children in an industrial town.

These studies, just as those of the previous decade, tended to downplay the importance of spiritual experience, as an increasingly rationalistic framework became predominant. The next decade continued the trend with noteworthy Yeaxlee's (1952) work at Oxford. Yeaxlee highlighted the emergence of the concept of God as part of the infant-parent relationship, linking the spiritual experience of children to Otto's (1950) concept of the numinous, much as Loomba had done. American studies of this decade included an analysis of the children and worship (Fahs, 1950; Brown, 1956), the theology of children (Curry, 1956) and teaching religion to mentally challenged children (Silver, 1957).

Cognitive Period (1960 to 1990)

During the second half of the twentieth century, behaviorism continued to have a powerful influence in psychology and education, but increasingly, it shared the spotlight with emphases on cognitive development. While B. F. Skinner's philosophy and methods—which were never as inherently related as people thought (Bufford, 1981)—continued to influence some researchers, Jean Piaget's perspectives applied to the study of children's religious thinking soon trumped behaviorism, both conceptually and methodologically. The influence of Piaget is significant in most of the research of children's religion from this time on.

The foundational premise of the Piagetian-influenced research of the time was that cognitive development is integrally connected to religious development in children. Though there were critics (Murphy, 1977, 1978), most researcher-theorists of this era embraced the cognitive emphasis, as well as the importance of stages. Hundreds of studies were conducted between 1960 and 1990 related to children's understanding of religious concepts and practices, and at least one researcher—Kalevi Tamminen (1991) at the University of Helsinki—spent almost an entire career studying these topics.

Rather than attempt a systematic survey of this immense literature, already accomplished in a stellar manner by Kenneth Hyde (1990), this chapter will summarize the relevant work of three major researcher/theorists who contributed significantly to this literature and influenced many others who did subsequent research.

Though the study of children's religious concepts had been at the margins of developmental psychology in the United States since the early decades of the twentieth century, such research was highly respected by school and church educators alike in the United Kingdom, much of Europe, and Scandinavia. There were probably twenty research studies on children's religion on the York side of the Atlantic Ocean for every similar study on the New York side at this time, primarily the consequence of governments that supported not only the state church but also funded research to inform and improve religious education in the public schools. In spite of limited funding, two Americans contributed significantly to this literature—David Elkind and James Fowler—but it would be a serious omission to overlook the great work of that controversial Brit, Ronald Goldman.

David Elkind: Children's Understanding of Faith Traditions[2]

In the early 1960s, David Elkind introduced an aspect of religious development largely unexplored in previous research—the child's religious affiliation. Using Piaget's semi-clinical interview approach (1964), he interviewed eight hundred Jewish (1961), Catholic (1962), and Protestant (1963) children to determine the level of understanding they had of their faith tradition.

Elkind (1978) assumed children comprehend religion in fundamentally the same manner in which they understand concepts in other areas, such as science or math—an assumption later questioned by Oser and Gmunder (1991). He also focused on their comprehension of *institutional* religion rather than *personal* religion. Consistent with Piaget's theory, he categorized children's responses in stages.

During the early elementary years (ages five to seven) each child reflected a general understanding of faith—for each child, his or her understanding of faith was not fully developed. When Elkind pushed them to go beyond their general understandings, children tended to use ethnic or national descriptors, or to refer to a denomination as a concrete object. The second stage corresponds with middle childhood (ages seven to nine), when particular actions of members of a religious group were considered

---

2. Portions of the sections on David Elkind and Robert Coles were reprinted with permission from "How Children Understand Religious Concepts," taken from the journal *Religion and Public Education* (vol. 19, no. 2–3, 1992, pp. 162–72), which has now changed its name to *Religion and Education*.

the basis for membership. Between ten and twelve years of age their understanding of religion changed dramatically; inner belief predominated over external behavior as the basis for religious group membership (Elkind, 1978).

Elkind concluded that children younger than eleven or twelve do not understand religious concepts in the abstract manner of an adult; instead they understand religion in concrete terms. He further explored this idea in subsequent research related to children's concepts of prayer (Elkind, Spilka & Long, 1968), and the relationship between religious education and play (Elkind, 1980). Although Elkind's work in this area did not become widely known to the American public, the Piagetian base for his research did influence most of the next three decade's research on children's religious concepts.

Ronald Goldman: Religious Instruction for Children Questioned[3]

As with Elkind, Goldman's early 1960s research yielded a three-stage developmental rubric for children's understanding of the Bible and religion. However, Goldman (1969) drew one recommendation from his research that produced a firestorm of controversy in the United Kingdom: formal religious instruction was not recommended—and could indeed be counterproductive—until ten or eleven years of age. Goldman later said that his conclusions were misinterpreted. He was quoted as saying, "No child under twelve is capable of understanding a religious concept" (p. 48). But Goldman responded,

> I have never made this statement either verbally or in print. . . . I do not question the capacity of children 'to feel their way into religion' and indeed advocate this as part of the program of worship and exploration with young children. The main difficulty is in communicating at a verbal level. (p. 48)

Goldman (1964/1968) described how difficult it is for children, especially for small children, to communicate theology, and he provided considerable evidence for this from his study.

---

3. The section on Ronald Goldman is in part taken from "Teaching the Bible Developmentally," reprinted by permission from the *Christian Education Journal* (vol. 7, no. 2, 1987, pp. 21–32).

Goldman's research involved telling children three stories from the Bible, followed by questions to probe the child's comprehension of the stories. Building on Piaget's concepts, as well as some of his research techniques, Goldman found a developmental pattern consistent with stage theory, although not all of Goldman's interpretations and conclusions are consistent with Piaget's (Wilhoit, 1982).

Goldman summarized the stage progression of a child's religious thought using Piagetian terminology: intuitive religious thinking was marked by oversimplification, fragmentation, and magical thought (age two to six); later, concrete logic was applied to religious thought and physical descriptors of spirituality (age eight to twelve); and finally, abstract religious thinking developed in which children use verbal propositions and symbolic terminology (generally beginning about age fourteen). Between each of these is a transitional phase of about two years each (ages six to eight and twelve to fourteen). A decade later, John Peatling (1973) found a similar stage progression in American children.

Methodologically, Goldman's research surpassed any previous work in the area. But his approach—like that of Piaget—could mask cognitive abilities of children by ignoring receptive or expressive language limitations (Ratcliff, 1988). Are stages a clear indication of mental abilities or a mere reflection of language capabilities? Is it possible for a child to intuit an understanding of faith from a religious experience that surpasses the supposed stage-related limitations that Goldman—and Piaget—suggested?

James Fowler: Faith in Phases

Of the many stage theories related to religious and spiritual development, the most enduring has been James Fowler's (1981). His research built upon a broader theoretical formulation than most researchers of this period, including not only Piaget but also Erik Erikson and Lawrence Kohlberg. Fowler identified phases in the development of faith that often, though not always, correspond with age. His theory suggests that faith is not confined to religion, but involves whatever an individual deems most important. Family, career, recreation, and other possibilities can be objects of faith. His emphasis is more on the structure of, rather than the object of, faith. This is similar to Kohlberg, who highlighted the reasoning behind moral decisions more than the decisions themselves. Key to his theory—yet often ignored—are spirals by which the person moves through the stages, in contrast with the linearity of most stage theories.

The infant has primal faith or "undifferentiated faith," where the development of trust—or lack thereof—tends to be fostered by relationships with the primary caretakers. In the preschool years, the first actual stage of faith is "intuitive-projective" in which the imagination rather than logic controls the child's faith. Prayers are magical and "banked" for the future. Fantasy plays a prominent role, as the child develops mental images of powers that protect or threaten, such as God and Satan. These images are to some extent influenced by family, church, and the media.

Fowler's second stage, corresponding with the school years for most people, is "mythic-literal faith," where stories become an important source of meaning. The child distinguishes speculation and fantasy from the real world. God is perceived as rewarding good actions and punishing evil. Community belongingness, conformity, and the centrality of the symbols and language of that community are underscored. Stories bring coherence to life. This stage concludes with a move towards forming a coherent identity, reflecting Erik Erikson's views of adolescence.

Fowler's theory continues to influence researchers, scholars, and lay persons, perhaps because it is research-based but also because it resonates with many different faiths, including non-religious faith. Fowler's concept of faith is broader than that of historic Christian theology and Scripture. His work remains a rich resource that can inform the understanding and experience of children's spirituality.

For thirty years the Piagetian/stage approach to children's religious development predominated, with the research of Elkind, Goldman, and Fowler probably being the most influential. Developmental research did not end in 1990—indeed stage theories of religious and spiritual development continue to be explored in research studies (see e.g., Smoliak, 1999).

Children's Spirituality (1990 to the Present)

While several hundred research studies in the United Kingdom and United States were conducted over the previous thirty years that emphasized a cognitive developmental view of children's religious and spiritual development, spiritual experience was rarely given much direct attention. When experience was considered, it was often in response to a pre-formulated question such as, "Have you ever sensed God or an unusual presence close to you?" but rarely was spiritual experience the focus of attention in such studies. Almost inevitably, descriptions of spiritual experiences were subjected to cognitive stage categories.

An important exception to this tendency was the work of Edward Robinson (1977) who examined adult retrospective accounts of their religious experiences as children. Robinson built upon the earlier work of Sir Alister Hardy who collected thousands of accounts of people's spiritual experiences, some (though not all) being religious. Hardy, a zoologist at Oxford, was convinced that experiences of a spiritual nature were inherent to being human and were based biologically in the evolutionary process.

Robinson succeeded Hardy as director of the "Religious Experience Research Unit" at Oxford University, founded by the latter, and took a special interest in the many accounts of such experiences in childhood. Excerpts and insightful analysis of these accounts were recorded in his book *The Original Vision: A Study of the Religious Experience of Childhood* (Robinson, 1977). While retrospective accounts of childhood experience sometimes fall short because of the selective and sometimes inaccurate memory of childhood by adults, this work significantly influenced the next director of the research centre, David Hay, and his protégé Rebecca Nye who would introduce perhaps the finest theory—supported by excellent research—in the area of children's spirituality to date (Hay & Nye, 1998/2006). The biological basis for human spirituality continues to expand through the use of neurological study and other methods (Hay, 2007) in the attempt to discover how people are "hard-wired" for spirituality.

Problems with Stages and Cognitive Development

In the 1990s, researchers of children's religion and spirituality—especially researchers in Europe—began to note difficulties with the research of the 60s, 70s, and 80s. The most obvious weakness was that the research seemed to be *too* closely linked with Piaget's stage theory; beginning with Piagetian assumptions and using Piagetian methods of research, the studies led almost inevitably to Piagetian results. As noted in the previous section, studies often revealed a three-phase developmental progression corresponding to Piaget's preoperational, concrete operations, and formal operations stages. The stages were often creatively re-named to reflect the religious concepts being described; the average age for stage acquisition might vary two or three years (often less than that); and some theorists suggested transitional phases between stages. Yet religious development appeared to progress essentially like cognitive development in general (Ratcliff, 1985, 1987).

A second problem was that while stage theory seemed to provide guidance for religious instruction, it was rather inept at that task: that is, a descriptive account of what *is* does not automatically lead to a prescriptive account of what *can* or *should be*. Curriculum that emerged during the cognitive era built heavily on the assumptions of Piaget's stages—that is, that children in each stage thought and behaved in certain ways; such curriculum may have discouraged insights and exploration outside the expected stage parameters. However, Stonehouse's (2001) work suggests that even preschool children can offer comments that are characteristic of formal operational thought when more open-ended curricula are utilized.

Third, it has long been recognized that researchers can unintentionally encourage or elicit statements from children that may not reflect their actual thoughts (Vianello, Tamminen, & Ratcliff, 1992), perhaps not unlike the induction of false memories of abuse that have been reported in recent years (Robbins, 2004). Are stage characteristics merely the product of researcher expectations?

A fourth concern was that the research seemed sterile, removed from the real world of the spirit. Even young children—some would say particularly young children—can have experiences that transcend everyday experience. These might indeed be encounters with the Holy Spirit that transcend a cognitive explanation, or they might be deeply moving experiences of nature and people that are not merely cognitive, but also emotional, affective, even involving perceptions that transcend the physical realm. While belief and understanding are important—theologically essential, some would say—it is possible to have cognition without associated behavior, attitudes, and experience. Religion that is only cognitive is not only sub-scriptural, it is also subhuman. God cares about the whole child, not just the intellect. There needed to be a shift of perspective; the spirit of the child, and the transforming Spirit of God, deserved the attention of theorists and researchers.

The Spiritual Life of Children: Robert Coles

That shift in perspective, while beginning earlier in other areas of the world, came to center stage in the United States in brilliant new research by Robert Coles (1990) and his associates, who interviewed five hundred children, most of whom were between eight and twelve years old—a few as young as six and as old as thirteen were also studied—from many parts of the world. His approach involved detailed discussions within a phenomenological framework, highlighting the value of the child's experience and the meaning given to that experience. Thus he purposely avoided stage-oriented analysis as an oversimplification of the child's world. Children do not think of their spiritual experiences in terms of stages, Coles suggested, so he attempted to enter the world of children's first-hand experiences of life and faith. He was highly respected for his prior work with at-risk children and his prominence among the Harvard faculty, and thus was taken seriously by scholars and the public alike. He took a largely narrative approach, providing few generalizations, in order to help the reader feel what it is like to be a child within a particular faith tradition.

Coles compared the accounts of children who were Christians, Jews, Muslims, and non-believers. The central message of faith for the Christian children studied was God's "visit" to earth in the form of Jesus, who was described as a guide and Savior, as well as an adult who was able to survive childhood. The emphasis upon Savior may reflect the personal vulnerability of children, Coles suggested. Surrender to Allah was a central concept for Islamic children studied, as the terms "submission" and "obedience" were used far more often by these children than their Christian or Jewish peers. Personal devotion and purity were also important concepts to them. Righteousness was the central theme of Jewish children, while perfectionism was also underscored in many comments. God was seen as a guide and judge by many Jewish children, who also described heated discussions and arguments provoked by religion.

Unlike many previous researchers, Coles also investigated the religious remarks of children who came from non-religious backgrounds and who, at best, rarely attended church. These kids also struggled with religious topics, such as wondering about life's meaning and what mattered most in life. "Soul-searching" by these children of little or no religious faith involved attempting to find ideals and values that reflected who they were. Questioning one's personal faith and beliefs was found to be common among religious and non-religious children alike. Coles concluded ". . . with respect to faith and doubt, belief and unbelief, we are all 'on the edge'" (Coles, 1990, p. 301).

Perhaps it was the Harvard credentials, or perhaps it was his earlier work with migrant children and youths in the Civil Rights movement, that brought Coles' work into the spotlight of public opinion. It is also possible that Coles' video, "Listening to Children," which included spiritual accounts by at-risk children and their parents, made his work stand taller than previous work. Or, quite possibly, scholars in the United States had a sense that something was missing in the developmental literature; that "something" came to be termed "the spirit of the child." Scholars in the United Kingdom had been moving in this direction for some time, but few Americans who studied human development appeared to be aware of their work.

Rebecca Nye: Relational Consciousness

Over the last decade of the twentieth century, there was a surge of interest in the spiritual, with dozens, if not hundreds, of books describing the human spirit and sometimes the transcendent Spirit. Yet most of them lacked the careful research and nuanced conclusions that characterized Coles' work. Though some of the books included insightful thoughts and helpful suggestions, it was often hard to tell which books could be trusted; some were clearly tapping into the latest fad for profit and personal acclaim. Confusing things further, definitions of "spirit" and "spiritual" were often missing, or were vague. Many who spoke of children's spirituality were clearly not talking about the same thing as others; often it was difficult to tell exactly what *was* being described.

Midway through the last decade of the century, doctoral student Rebecca Nye initiated her ground-breaking study of children's spirituality under the guidance of David Hay, at that point still directing The Religious Experience Research Centre at Oxford. Nye collected accounts of spiritual experience provided by children who were somewhat hesitant to share their experiences due to fear of ridicule or disbelief from adult researchers. One of Nye's goals was to construct an adequate definition of children's spirituality, using a research approach rarely attempted by previous researchers: a qualitative approach to analysis termed "grounded theory." Through ongoing analysis of the children's stories and comments, a theory was constructed, "from the ground up" so to speak, rooted in the data, consisting of the words and thoughts of the children themselves. The day of imposing stage-oriented assumption on children was clearly passed.

The highly esteemed *British Journal of Religious Education* carried the initial report of the research, emphasizing the need for an adequate definition of spirituality in the title, "Identifying Children's Spirituality: How Do You Start Without a Starting Point?" (Nye & Hay, 1996). The premier issue of the new *International Journal of Children's Spirituality* reiterated the concern (Hay & Nye, 1996). The details of the definition, and the children's comments from which it was created, were elaborated in *The Spirit of the Child* (Hay & Nye, 1998), now in its second edition (2006).

Hay and Nye (2006), as in the earlier work by Coles, indicated that religion should not be equated with spirituality. Religion and spirituality could overlap in the form of a religious experience, but religion could also include non-experiential content such as creeds and theology. In contrast, spirituality encompassed the wonder and heightened attentiveness of an exquisite sunset, as well as a deeply moving experience of God. Hay and Nye outlined three categories of spiritual sensitivity: awareness-sensing, mystery-sensing, and value-sensing.

Awareness-sensing involves the immediate experience, often emphasized in meditative experiences, as well as "focusing" in which a holistic awareness of the body is present. Concentration that is intense and undivided is sometimes referred to as the "flow" experience, or "tuning" which is a special awareness arising from aesthetic experiences.

Mystery-sensing, the second category of spiritual sensitivity, is marked by an imaginative state that moves beyond everyday living. Awe and wonder reflect the ultimate mystery in life, Hay and Nye (2006) offered.

Third, value-sensing is related to what is worthwhile or valuable to the person, a trusting in life, and expressions of delight or despair. A quest for ultimacy and meaning in life can be related to one's identity.

These three categories are all related to the central category of spirituality, which Hay and Nye describe as "relational consciousness." The first term, "relational," refers to the context of spirituality, that of relating to people, things, self, or divinity. The second term, "consciousness," emphasizes a heightened state of awareness, perception, and reflection.

When children lack spiritual nurture, the likely result will be meaninglessness. This meaninglessness can be manifest in negative forms of spirituality, such as drug abuse, violence, and corruption. In contrast, a fostering of spirituality is likely to result in altruism, a desire for justice, and ecological sensitivity.

Subsequent research has not always affirmed every aspect of the Hay and Nye definition, but often their ideas serve as a key reference point. My own work on the emergent spirituality of children in an American public school hallway (Ratcliff, 2001) is but one of many studies that can be cited here. Many other research studies on children's spirituality are summarized in three fairly comprehensive summaries: *The Handbook of Spiritual Development in Childhood and Adolescence* (Roehlkepartain, King, Wagener, & Benson, 2006), *Children's Spirituality: Christian Perspectives, Research, and Applications* (Ratcliff, 2004), and the present volume.

Conclusion

Examining more than a century of research on children's spirituality is an overwhelming task. Attempting practical applications of this literature is also difficult, or rather, it is impossible, as the varying perspectives suggest conflicting recommendations. The wide variety of theories, methods, and specific issues involved presents a virtual kaleidoscope of possible lenses on children's spirituality. Several major points, however, deserve additional consideration.

I am impressed with the similarities between the first period of research and recent developments in the field. Researchers during that early time attempted a more general understanding of the child, often considering both the parts and the whole of the developmental phenomenon or characteristics of a child. Religion was not marginalized for several decades. Today's qualitative methods are not unlike some of the procedures used a century ago, although there certainly have been advancements in methods of observing, interviewing, and analysis. The parallels are fascinating, yet it must be admitted that the current approach to human development is far from the holism of a hundred years ago.

The classic Hartshorn and May (1928) study that concluded what is taught in Sunday school may not influence daily behavior, is also intriguing to consider 75 years later. There are weaknesses in the study, but it would be helpful to see a replication with some of those weaknesses addressed. But even if the conclusion were to still hold, perhaps it would be more constructive to identify the precise implications. One possibility is that verbal teaching alone does not transfer very well to the everyday lives of children. Verbal learning may give us ideals, but what is real can be far from what is ideal. On the other hand, there is something to be said for examining the ideal, particularly the values that help shape children's perspectives in life (though they may not function in a deterministic manner). Stories can have a powerful effect on children, particularly in the areas of values and morality (Coles, 1989). Did Hartshorn and May examine all of the possible areas of potential influence from this form of verbal learning? How are spirituality, ethical behavior, and stories related?

Are stages relevant to children's spirituality? While certain aspects of spirituality are influenced by development in other areas, other aspects may be distinct from development (Feldmeier, 2007). While some features of stage theories may be questioned, there *are* systematic differences corresponding with age that can be identified, such as the major shift between five and seven years of age. Hundreds of years ago, theologians noted this significant shift, and it is not accidental that Roman Catholics offer first communion at this time. In non-Western countries, children often begin to take on adult responsibilities at this point, such as caring for younger siblings. In the West, children begin formal education about this time. Stages may be just another way to conceptualize this change.

Similarly, the Jewish bar mitzvah and Roman Catholic confirmation are implicit recognition of a stage shift near the beginning of the teen years. In non-Western countries, initiation rites mark this transition. The corollary to this stage change, as well as the previous one, can be found in studies of brain structures that undergo a localized metamorphosis at this time, which accounts for age-related changes of perception, thought, and behavior. Perhaps a second look at stages is warranted, using neurological studies, cross-cultural studies, and even theological perspectives as comparison points. Not all of what Piaget said about the stages holds up to recent scrutiny (Ratcliff, 1988), yet some of his analysis reflects brilliant insights with theological parallels (Loder, 1998).

The final section of this chapter highlighted the importance of interdisciplinary study in children's spirituality. Studying a multiplicity of perspectives produces a more comprehensive understanding of spirituality as well as spawning a variety of approaches to the *nurture* of that spirituality (see, for example, Ratcliff, 2007). All aspects of children are important in understanding their spirituality, including the emotional, verbal, social, behavioral, and perhaps most important, the imaginative, creative, and inner aspects of life. To pretend that one, or even some combination, of these is sufficient to explain spirituality is overly reductionistic. Spirituality within a Christian reference—because it relates to God—transcends the conceptual boxes made for it, because it involves "God with us" (Christ within) and the Holy Spirit in communion with the human spirit. Research is invaluable in the quest to understand children's spirituality, but even the most sophisticated investigation will produce only a partial reflection of reality (1 Cor 13:12).

References

Acheson, E. L. (1944). Religious needs of tomorrow's children. *Religious Education, 39,* 111–14.

Barnes, E. (1892/2003). The theological life of the California child. *Pedagogical Seminary, 2,* 442–48. Reprinted with the addition of Miss Ora Boring as coauthor in D. Ratcliff (Ed.), *Children's spirituality: Christian perspectives, research, and applications* (pp. 409–17). Eugene, OR: Cascade.

Bose, R. G. (1929). Religious concepts of children. *Religious Education, 24,* 831–37.

Bovet, P. (1928). *The child's religion: A study of the development of the religious sentiment.* New York: E. P. Dutton.

Brown, J. P. (1956). Children and worship. *Religious Education, 51,* 346–52.

Bufford, R. (1981). *The human reflex: Behavioral psychology in biblical perspective.* San Francisco: Harper & Row.

Bunge, M. J. (2001). *The child in Christian thought.* Grand Rapids: Eerdmans.

Calkins, M. W. (1896). The religious consciousness of children. *New World, 5,* 705–19.

Coles, R. (1989). *The call of stories.* Boston: Houghton Mifflin.

Coles, R. (1990). *The spiritual life of children.* Boston: Houghton Mifflin.

Curry, R. E. (1956). Theology and children. *Religious Education, 51,* 355–56, 358–60.

Dawson, G. E. (1900). Children's interest in the Bible. *Pedagogical Seminary, 7,* 151–78.

Dawson, G. E. (1909). *The child and his religion.* Chicago: The University of Chicago Press.

Elkind, D. (1961). The child's conception of his religious denomination: I. The Jewish child. *Journal of Genetic Psychology, 99,* 209–25.

Elkind, D. (1962). The child's conception of his religious denomination: II. The Catholic child. *Journal of Genetic Psychology, 101,* 185–93.

Elkind, D. (1963). The child's conception of his religious denomination: III. The Protestant Child. *Journal of Genetic Psychology, 103,* 291–304.

Elkind, D. (1964). Piaget's semi-clinical interview and the study of spontaneous religion. *Journal for the Scientific Study of Religion, 4,* 40–47.

Elkind, D. (1978). *The child's reality: Three developmental themes.* New York: Lawrence Erlbaum.

Elkind, D. (1980). The role of play in religious education. *Religious Education, 75,* 282–93.

Elkind, D., Spilka, B., & Long, D. (1968). The child's concept of prayer. In A. Godin (Ed.), *From cry to word* (pp. 51–64). Brussels: Lumen Vitae.

Ellis, A. C. (1896). Sunday school work and Bible study in the light of modern pedagogy. *Pedagogical Seminary, 3*, 363–412.

Fahs, S. L. (1929). How childish should a child's religion be? *Religious Education, 24*, 910–17.

Fahs, S. L. (1930). The beginnings of religion in baby behavior. *Religious Education, 25*, 896–903.

Fahs, S. L. (1932). Should Peggy and Peter pray? *Religious Education, 27*, 596–605.

Fahs, S. L., (1939). When should come a consciousness of God? *Religious Education, 34*, 208–15.

Fahs, S. L. (1950). The beginnings of mysticism in children's growth. *Religious Education, 45*, 139–47.

Feldmeier, P. (2007). *The developing Christian: Spiritual growth through the life cycle*. New York: Paulist.

Fowler, J. (1981). *Stages of faith*. San Francisco: Harper and Row.

Goldman, R. (1964/1968). *Religious thinking from childhood to adolescence*. New York: Seabury.

Goldman, R. (1969). Dr. Beeching, I Presume? *Religious Education, 64*, 47–52.

Hall, G. S. (1891). The contents of children's minds on entering school. *Pedagogical Seminary, 1*, 139–73.

Hall, G. S. (1901). Some fundamental principles of Sunday school and Bible teaching. *Pedagogical Seminary, 8*, 439–68.

Harms, E. (1944). The development of religious experience in children. *The American Journal of Sociology, 50*, 112–22.

Hartshorne, H. H. (1915). Religious development of children. *Religious Education, 10*, 481–92.

Hartshorne, H. (1919). *Childhood and character: An introduction to the study of the religious life of children*. Boston: Pilgrim.

Hartshorne, H., & May, M. (1928). *Studies in deceit*. New York: Macmillan.

Hay, D. (2007). *Something there: The biology of the human spirit*. Philadelphia: Templeton Foundation.

Hay, D., & Nye, R. (1996). Investigating children's spirituality: The need for a fruitful hypothesis. *International Journal of Children's Spirituality, 1*, 6–16.

Hay, D., & Nye, R. (2006). *The spirit of the child* (Rev. ed.). Philadelphia: Jessica Kingsley.

Hyde, K. E. (1990). *Religion in childhood and adolescence*. Birmingham, AL: Religious Education.

Johnson, E. L., & Jones, S. L. (2000). *Psychology and Christianity: Four views.* Downers Grove, IL: InterVarsity.

Koons, W. G. (1903). *The child's religious life: A study of the child's religious nature.* New York: Eaton & Mains.

Loomba, R. M. (1944). The religious development of the child. *Indian Journal of Psychology, 17,* 161–67.

Loder, J. E. (1998). *The logic of the spirit: Human development in theological perspective.* San Francisco: Jossey-Bass.

Mathias, W. D. (1943). *Ideas of God and conduct.* New York: Teachers College, Columbia University.

Murphy, R. (1977). The development of religious thinking in children in three easy stages? *Learning for Living, 17,* 16–21.

Murphy, R. (1978). A new approach to the study of the development of religious thinking in children. *Educational Studies, 4,* 19–22.

Murray, B. F., & Tyler, D. (1937). A study of religious education for young children. *Religious Education, 32,* 55–61.

Nye, R., & Hay, D. (1996). Identifying children's spirituality: How do you start without a starting point? *British Journal of Religious Education, 18,* 144–54.

Oser, F., & Gmunder, P. (1991). *Religious judgment.* Birmingham, AL: Religious Education.

Otto, R. (1950). *The idea of the holy* (2nd ed.). London: Oxford University Press.

Peatling, J. (1973). The incidence of concrete and abstract religious thinking in the interpretation of three Bible stories. *Dissertation Abstracts International, 34* (12A), 7604. (UMI No. AAG7412859).

Ratcliff, D. (1985). The development of children's religious concepts: Research review. *Journal of Psychology and Christianity, 4,* 35–43.

Ratcliff, D. (1987). Teaching the Bible developmentally. *Christian Education Journal, 7,* 21–32.

Ratcliff, D. (1988). The cognitive development of preschoolers. In D. Ratcliff (Ed.), *Handbook of preschool religious education* (pp. 7–29). Birmingham, AL: Religious Education.

Ratcliff, D. (2001). Rituals in a school hallway: Evidence of a latent spirituality of children. *Christian Education Journal, 5NS,* 9–26.

Ratcliff, D. (Ed.). (2004). *Children's spirituality: Christian perspectives, research, and applications.* Eugene, OR: Cascade Books.

Ratcliff, D. (2007). Four approaches to encouraging children's spirituality. Adapted from a seminar presented at Nazarene Theological Seminary, April 10, 2007. Retrieved June 15, 2007 from http://www.childspirituality.org/don/approaches.htm

Ratcliff, D., & Nye, R. (2006). Childhood spirituality: Strengthening the research foundation. In E. Roehlkepartain, P. E. King, L. M. Wagener, & P. L. Benson (Eds.), *Handbook of spiritual development in childhood and adolescence* (pp. 473–83). Thousand Oaks, CA: Sage.

Robbins, S. P. (2002). Wading through the muddy waters of recovered memory. In B. Slife (Ed.), *Taking sides: Clashing views on controversial psychological issues* (13th ed., pp. 199–210). Guildford, CN: McGraw-Hill.

Robins, H. B. (1917a). The religion of childhood I. *The Biblical World, 50,* 292–99.

Robins, H. B. (1917b). The religion of childhood II. *The Biblical World, 50,* 353–62.

Robins, H. B. (1918a). The religion of childhood III. *The Biblical World, 51,* 31–37.

Robins, H. B. (1918b). The religion of childhood IV. *The Biblical World, 51,* 96–98.

Robins, H. B. (1918c). The religion of childhood V. *The Biblical World, 51,* 159–63.

Robins, H. B. (1918d) The religion of childhood VI. *The Biblical World, 51,* 216–26.

Robinson, E. (1977). *The original vision: A study of the religious experience of childhood.* Oxford: The Religious Experience Research Centre.

Roehlkepartain, E. C., King, P. E., Wagener, L. M., & Benson, P. L. (Eds.). *Handbook of spiritual development in childhood and adolescence.* Thousand Oaks, CA: Sage.

Silver, D. J. (1957). The retarded child and religious education: A case study. *Religious Education, 52,* 361–64.

Smith, J. J. (1941). Religious development in children. In C. E. Skinner & P. L. Harriman (Eds.), *Child psychology, child development and modern education* (pp. 273–98). New York: Macmillan.

Smoliak, W. G. (1999). What children's narratives tell us about their developing thoughts of God. In K. H. Reich, F. K. Oser, & W. G. Scarelette (Eds.), *Psychological studies on spiritual and religious development.* Lengerich, Germany: Pabst Science Publishers.

Starbuck, E. D. (1907a). The child-mind and child-religion: I. The child-consciousness and human progress. *The Biblical World, 30,* 30–38.

Starbuck, E. D. (1907b). The child-mind and child-religion: II. The nature of child consciousness. *The Biblical World, 30,* 101–10.

Starbuck, E. D. (1907c). The child-mind and child-religion: III. The method of evolution of consciousness. *The Biblical World, 30,* 191–201.

Starbuck, E. D. (1907d). The child-mind and child-religion: IV. The development of spirituality. *The Biblical World, 30,* 352–60.

Starbuck, E. D. (1908). The child-mind and child-religion: V. Stages in religious growth. *The Biblical World, 31,* 101–12.

Starbuck, E. D. (1909). The child-mind and child-religion: VI. The regimen of adolescence. *The Biblical World, 31*, 8–22.

Stephens, T. (Ed.). (1905). *The child and religion: Eleven essays.* London: Williams & Norgate.

Stonehouse, C. (2001). Knowing God in childhood: A study of Godly Play and the spirituality of children. *Christian Education Journal, 5NS*, 27–45.

Tamminen, K. (1991). *Religious development in childhood and youth: An empirical study.* Helskini: Suomalainen Tiedeakatemia (Finnish Academy of Science).

Tanner, A. E. (1906). Children's religious ideas. *Pedagogical Seminary, 13*, 511–13.

Vianello, R., Tamminen, K., & Ratcliff, D. (1992). The religious concepts of children. In D. Ratcliff (Ed.), *Handbook of Children's Religious Education* (pp. 56–81). Birmingham, AL: Religious Education.

Weaver, R. M. (1913). *The religious development of the child.* New York: Revell.

Wheeler, L. R., & Wheeler, V. D. (1944). Religious ideas of children in communities of two different cultural patterns. *Journal of Educational Sociology, 17*, 563–71.

Wheeler, L. R., & Wheeler, V. D. (1945). Differences in religious ideas and attitudes of children who go to church and those who never attend. *Religious Education, 40*, 149–61.

Wilhoit, J. (1982). Memory: An area of difference between Piaget and Goldman. *Journal of Christian Education, 2*, 11–14.

Yeaxlee, B. A. (1952). *Religion and the growing mind.* Greenwich, CN: Seabury.

3 Children's Spiritual Development: Advancing the Field in Definition, Measurement, and Theory[1]

Chris J. Boyatzis

IN RECENT YEARS THERE HAS BEEN A DISTINCT SURGE OF INTEREST IN children's spirituality. This sudden growth comes with many challenges in definition, measurement, and research design. In this chapter, I explore several such challenges and offer suggestions for dealing with them that may help advance the field. First, I offer evidence of the historical neglect and recent attention by scientists regarding children's spirituality and religion. Second, I explore the definitional challenges inherent in studying children's spirituality. Third, I use several recent studies of youth to show the value of utilizing a social-ecology approach to investigate multiple social contexts of spirituality. Fourth, I suggest that researchers should use multiple measures of related constructs for a more valid understanding of their topics. Fifth, I offer a critique of traditional developmental stage theory.

SCHOLARS HAVE NEGLECTED CHILDREN'S SPIRITUAL DEVELOPMENT

The emerging field of children's spiritual development is now playing catch-up, as scholars have long neglected this dimension of development. As prior studies have shown, a conspicuously small percentage of scholarly work on children has examined spirituality (Benson, Roehlkepartain, & Rude,

---

1. Portions of this paper were presented at the Spirituality of Children and Youth Matters Conference, Hunter College, April 2007. Address correspondence to Dr. Chris J. Boyatzis, Dept. of Psychology, Bucknell University, Lewisburg PA, 17837; boyatzis@bucknell.edu.

2003) or religion (Boyatzis, 2003a). A more recent (March, 2007) search on PsycINFO was conducted to update those investigations. Using "child*" in the subject term, roughly 375,000 entries appeared. However, of that massive total, less than half of 1 percent (.0049 percent) also addressed religion, and far fewer (.0007 percent) addressed spirituality. Thus, one challenge facing this field is its newness; time is required for scholarly maturity in definition, measurement, theory-building, and empirical foundations.

Fortunately, there are ample signs that scholars are now heeding the call to "honor spiritual development as a core developmental process that deserves equal standing in the pantheon of universal developmental processes" (Benson, 2004, p. 50). Major handbooks and volumes on children's spirituality and religion have been published, for example, *The Handbook of Spiritual Development in Childhood and Adolescence* (Roehlkepartain, King, Wagener, & Benson, 2006), *The Encyclopedia of Religious and Spiritual Development* (Dowling & Scarlett, 2006), *Nurturing Child and Adolescent Spirituality: Perspectives from the World's Religious Traditions* (Yust, Johnson, Sasso, & Roehlkepartain, 2006), and *Children's Spirituality: Christian Perspectives, Research, and Applications* (Ratcliff, 2004). In addition, many special issues of journals have recently appeared, such as in *The International Journal for the Psychology of Religion* (Boyatzis, 2006), *Review of Religious Research* (Boyatzis, 2003b), and *Applied Developmental Science* (King & Boyatzis, 2004). A conspicuous example appeared recently in the prestigious *Handbook of Child Psychology*, long viewed as the "bible" of child development theory and research. In the most recent edition (Damon, 2006, 6th ed.), there is now an entire chapter on religious and spiritual development (by Oser, Scarlett, & Bucher, 2006). This coverage is in stark contrast to the prior edition from 1998 that had only three index listings on religion or spirituality. Taken together, all of this very recent scholarly productivity demonstrates clearly that religious and spiritual development is exploding in interest and entering the mainstream.

Other evidence of this growth comes at the other end of the scholarly pipeline, in the form of dissertations. As figure 1 shows, a 2006 PsycINFO search discovered that there have been more dissertations on the subject of children and religion from 2000–2005 than in the decade of the 1990s, and the 1990s had more such dissertations than the previous two decades combined. In addition, a search of dissertations on children and spirituality revealed that 53 percent of them have appeared since 2000. This dissertation activity promises that scholarly attention to religious and spiritual development will continue to burgeon.

Figure 1: Historical Trends in Dissertations on Children and Religion
Dissertations on Child* and Religio*
PsycINFO (Feb. 2006)

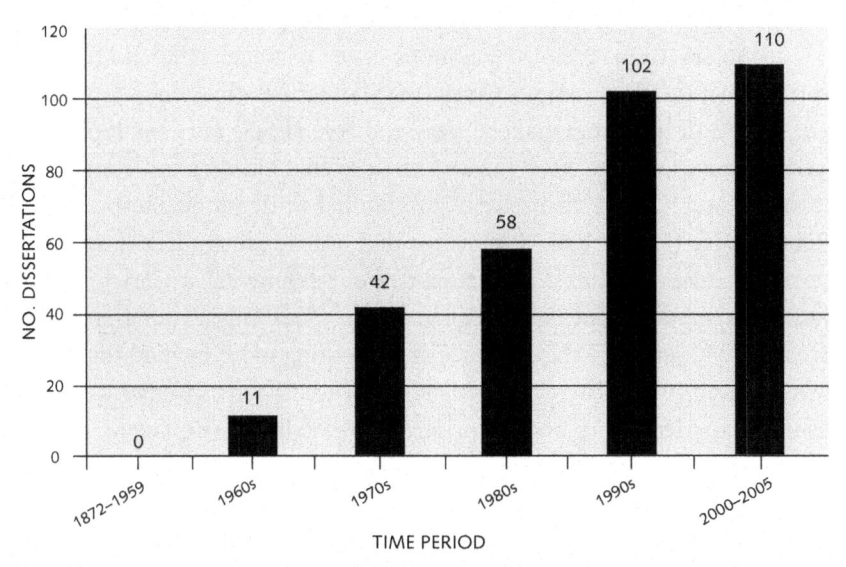

Time Period	No. Dissertations
1872–1959	0
1960s	11
1970s	42
1980s	58
1990s	102
2000–2005	110

Defining Spiritual Development Is Difficult

A fundamental task for our field is to generate valid, comprehensive definitions of our terms. This is all the more important for two reasons: One, the study of children's spirituality is relatively novel, and two, "spirituality" is a term that many have criticized as overly imprecise, New-Agey, fuzzy. In these embryonic times for the field of spiritual development, articulating what we mean and do not mean by "children's spirituality" is a necessity for mature growth in the field. There are, however, many challenges ahead.

First, there are long-standing conceptual and semantic tensions between "spirituality" and "religion." Scholars may safely assume that any attempt to define spirituality will evoke questions of its overlap and distinctions from religion. There are many works on this issue and I will not attempt to chart again those waters. Second, and perhaps more pressing for those who study children, is the need to clarify what we mean by "spiritual *development*." As others have argued (Roehlkepartain, Benson, King, & Wagener, 2006), there has been more effort to define "*spirituality*" than "spiritual *development*." If development is the object of our study, *what* is it that develops? Wrestling with this question will provide energy to sustain the field for years to come. The organizers of the landmark volume, *Handbook of Spiritual Development in Childhood and Adolescence,* have concluded that "there is no consensus about what 'this domain' (of children's spirituality) really is" (Roehlkepartain, Benson, et al., 2006, p. 4), though this is not to say there have been no attempts.

Scholars from various traditions have characterized children as spiritual beings. For example, Coles (1990) describes children as "spiritual pilgrims" and "meaning makers." Hay and Nye (1998) offer the term "relational consciousness" to represent the idea that children are connected to something beyond themselves. Through her in-depth qualitative work, Rebecca Nye (Hay & Nye) also claims that individual children have their own "spiritual signatures." The cognitive-developmentalist Carl Johnson (2000) suggests that in their frequent "why" questions, "young children are already oriented to the existence of 'something more' beyond the given world" (p. 208). In Alister Hardy's database of adults' retrospective accounts of such experiences, 15 percent occurred in childhood (Robinson, 1983). These and other studies (Farmer, 1992; Robinson, 1983) have concurred that children have many spiritual experiences and these are typically characterized by wonder, awe, and a sense of connectedness to something greater than the self.

I believe one major reason for our current difficulty in defining children's spirituality is the long-standing dominance of cognitive-developmental models of growth that posited an invariant march toward logical, rational thought and away from other modes of thought. The post-Enlightenment, Piagetian emphasis on rational thought brought along a dismissive attitude toward other forms of knowing. However, many scholars have argued for a more inclusive approach that, I believe, helps us think in ways that may better accommodate children's spirituality. In his classic, *Will Our Children Have Faith?* John Westerhoff (2000) wrote: "Two modes of consciousness are possible. . . . One is intellectual. . . . The other is intuitional . . . experiential, and is characterized by nonverbal, creative, nonlinear, relational activities. The development and integration of both modes of consciousness is essential to the spiritual life" (p. 70). Robinson (1983) also makes this point in his collection of children's spiritual experience, *The Original Vision:* "What I have called the original vision of childhood is no mere imaginative fancy, but a form of knowledge and one that is essential to the development of any mature understanding" (p. 16).

These more inclusive views are consistent with claims by many contemporary cognitive-developmentalists who no longer accept a Piagetian model of development (see Boyatzis, 2005; Johnson & Boyatzis, 2006). As prominent developmentalist Jacqui Woolley (2000) said, "Children's minds are not inherently one way or another—not inherently magical nor inherently rational" (pp. 126–27). Indeed, many scientists now embrace a *co-existence* model of cognition in which magical thinking *and* rational thinking, "ordinary" reality *and* "extraordinary" reality co-exist in the minds of children (and adults) (Subbotsky, 1993). The decline of Piagetian assumptions and the ascent of this more inclusive, flexible co-existence model will, I believe, help us move toward a better understanding of children's spirituality.

Qualitative work can help give rise to definitions of spiritual development. One definition that offers promise comes from scholars at the Search Institute: Spiritual development is growth in "the intrinsic capacity for self-transcendence, in which the self is embedded in something greater than the self, including the sacred. . . . It is shaped both within and outside of religious traditions, beliefs, and practices" (Benson, Roehlkepartain, & Rude, 2003, pp. 205–6). This definition seems fruitful because it recognizes spirituality as (a) a natural propensity, (b) characterized by connection and relationality to what is beyond the self, and (c) socialized through multiple experiences (i.e., both within and outside organized religion). Some fundamental questions generated by this definition are: What trajectories and developmental pathways does this "intrinsic capacity" reveal and follow? What forces and entities beyond the self engage or attract the child in meaningful relationality? Which experiences inside and outside religion impede and which foster this self-transcendent growth? And each of these questions, of course, gives rise to many other more refined versions. As the study of children's spiritual development evolves, it will be crucial to examine how development in this domain is related to and/or distinct from development in other domains (cognition, emotion, neurology, social skills, etc.). The research agenda is a full one!

The Benson et al. (2003) definition offered above is not restricted to a particular formal religious doctrine or sacred entities. Their definition reflects a broad approach to children's spirituality. Their definition also posits a natural inclination toward spirituality, what some have named the "biological argument" (e.g., Hay, Reich, & Utsch, 2006). Hay and Nye (1998) claim that their version of the biological argument posits the existence of a relational consciousness that emerges prior to religious and ethical beliefs. From this view, children are spiritual beings first, and then are socialized and acculturated (or not) into a religious tradition. Those who would work from this view would support the idea that God is not predetermined to be the only transcendent entity with whom a child can grow in relationship. While this view may be uncomfortable to some with a particular faith-based starting point (e.g., Loder, 1998), it creates more room for understanding the spiritual growth of more (rather than fewer) children, in more (rather than fewer) cultural, religious, and ideological contexts.

One example of this attempt to capture a more universal approach to children's spirituality is work coming out of the Search Institute's Center for Spiritual Development in Childhood and Adolescence (www.spiritualdevelopment.org), which is studying children's spirituality in diverse cultures and religions around the globe. However, it will also be fruitful for some scholars to approach children's spirituality from specific faith-based perspectives while other scholars operate from a broader framework. For example, other chapters in this book offer examples of Christian scholars investigating children's spirituality as it evolves in relation to God and Jesus Christ. In other venues, for example, Islamic scholars may study children's spirituality as it develops in relationship to Allah and Muhammed. These distinct bodies of knowledge could then be aggregated at some point to learn of fundamental differences and commonalities. Such a step would help move toward a more comprehensive appreciation of children's spiritual development as a general human phenomenon.

It is clear there is much work to be done in these basic components of our field. Perhaps because of these complexities, some scholars warn that we should proceed with caution. Some say it is "premature—and potentially dangerous—to propose that a single definition could capture the richness, complexity, and multidimensional nature of spiritual development" (Roehlkepartain, Benson, et al., 2006, p. 6). Of course, the field should heed these caveats but continue to work toward clear definitions of children's spirituality. One helpful guideline for scholars is to state as clearly as possible what one's working definition is in any published or presented piece of scholarship. Another helpful guideline is for scholars to interrogate their own work and others' by asking, what are the implications of my (your) definition of spirituality? What might be systematically excluded or overlooked by one's particular definition? In short, intellectual honesty and humility regarding our own definitions will help the field advance through these definitional challenges.

A Social-Ecology Approach to Children's Spirituality

A social-ecology model (Bronfenbrenner, 1979) illuminates the many influences on children's spiritual development by analyzing diverse social contexts of growth. If scholars embrace this model, we would assess different microsystems that have immediate and proximal impact (e.g., family, church, peer group, school) and the interactions (or mesosystems) between them. Beyond these immediate contexts, broader macrosystem influences would be examined (culture, historical era). (For fascinating discussions of the links between macro-level culture and spiritual development, I refer the reader to Gottlieb, 2006; Mattis, Ahluwalia, Cowie, & Kirkland-Harris, 2006.) This approach raises many crucial questions. For example, the most studied social context is surely the family. But beyond the family, how are children and youth influenced by the beliefs, rituals, transcendent entities, and involvement in a religious community? There has been (ironic) neglect of worship institutions as settings for spiritual development; a recent paper referred to congregations as "unexamined crucibles" of spiritual development (Roehlkepartain & Patel, 2006). Fortunately, a few scholars have offered in-depth analyses of children's experience in congregations (e.g., Allen, 2004; Mercer, Matthews, & Walz, 2004), although much more work is needed. From a social-ecology view, the mesosystem or linkage between microsystems must be studied. That is, how does development in one social context (say, the home) interact with development in other contexts (say, the congregation)? To illustrate the interplay of several different social contexts, I review several recent studies.

A recent study on adolescents illustrates the value of studying religious and spiritual development in such a model. American youth who live in high-poverty areas are more likely to stay on track academically if they are also high in church attendance, whereas those youth in the same high-poverty areas who are low in church attendance are likely to fall behind academically (Regnerus & Elder, 2003). Thus, religious involvement can be a crucial behavioral variable that ameliorates broader risk factors such as community and poverty.

A superb study by Schwartz (2006) measured adolescent spirituality in relation to parent and peer religiosity. Data were collected at a large ($N =$ 4600) international denominational Christian youth conference in Canada; the youth campers were sixteen years old on average. In group sessions, data were collected on standardized surveys of religious belief and commitment and "perceived faith support" from parents and friends, with items such as "my parents (friends) and I talk about how we are doing as Christians" and "my parents (friends) show me what it means to be an authentic Christian." Analyses showed that, not surprisingly, the teenagers' own religiosity was predicted by their parents' and friends' religiosity; teens with stronger faith also had parents and peers with stronger faith. But the more interesting finding was that friends' religiosity mediated the influence of parents: After controlling for friends' faith support, parents' faith support predicted teens' religiosity less strongly. Therefore, the Schwartz study illustrates that our understanding of adolescent spirituality is enriched by measuring the interplay and different contexts of parents and peers. A theoretical interpretation may be that while peers are potent agents in adolescent spirituality, just as models of adolescent development predict (e.g., Fowler, 1981), peer influence may also reflect the indirect influence of parents who "channel" (Cornwall, 1989) their children toward peer settings and friendships that support the parents' values and faith orientations.

Another recent study shows the power of a social-ecology approach. Regnerus, Smith, and Smith (2004) analyzed data from the National Longitudinal Study of Adolescent Health, a large database of youth from grades seven through twelve. The surveys included two religiosity outcomes for the youth: worship attendance and importance of religion. Regnerus et al. computed the relative influence of the religiosity of parents, peers, the youths' schools, and the local county norms (of worship attendance). As expected, teenagers' worship attendance was related most strongly to their parents' attendance, but peers and local county norms also had strong relations to youth attendance. The outcome of importance of religion was strongly related to the importance religion held to both their parents and their friends, but the importance of religion in the youths' schools turned out to have the strongest relationship to importance of religion for the youth.

Taken together, these studies confirm the value of a social-ecology approach that assesses the religiosity of multiple social contexts. Such an approach allows not only for analyses of the direct links between youth spirituality and these multiple social forces, but also of the interplay between the social contexts. Although this approach has value, we should remind ourselves that "the map is not the territory." That is, analyzing structural relations between variables in large data sets is one thing, but truly knowing *how* and *why* these variables affect each other is another matter. Large-scale survey studies are invaluable for charting out the basic relationships between constructs, but deeper work—ideally, in-depth qualitative work with multiple informants within these multiple social contexts—will be needed to more clearly understand the dynamics between the constructs and contexts.

The Need for Multiple Measures

Our research is grounded in measurement of constructs. One issue, then, is whether a sufficient number of constructs are operationalized and measured in our work. One review of work on religion and family published in the past few decades raises concerns, showing that fully 83 percent of studies examining links between religiosity and family life used only one- or two-item measures of religiosity (Mahoney, Pargament, Swank, & Tarakeshwar, 2001). Such an approach will help lay out whether simple relationships exist between these general variables, but clearly more detailed measurement is needed. In a recent study on parent-child communication about religion (Boyatzis & Janicki, 2003), researchers used both a survey measure and a qualitative diary measure to assess the frequency, content, and structure of parent-child conversations about religious issues. The two measures converged in some ways yet diverged in others, showing that even when studying the "same" variable, different methods will arrive at somewhat different conclusions. To further illustrate the value of measuring multiple constructs related to a topic of interest, I will describe recent research on parents' use of spanking in relation to different measures of religiosity.

Many reports have found that parents who are affiliated with a conservative Christian religion also approve of spanking and actually use it more often with their children (see Gershoff, Miller, & Holden, 1999). However, later research (see Gershoff et al., 1999) discovered that a stronger predictor of spanking (than religious affiliation *per se*) was the parents' theological conservatism (e.g., thinking that children possess original sin, wrongdoing must be punished, etc.). This personal belief was more related to actual spanking than was mere affiliation. This is not surprising, as categorical variables such as affiliation (gender, political party, etc.) explain very little by themselves. This advance, however, shows the value of measuring a religious belief rather than denominational affiliation alone.

This religiosity-spanking link has been further elucidated by a superb recent study. Murray-Swank, Mahoney, and Pargament (2006) measured several indices of religious belief in midwestern mothers including their theological conservatism (vs. liberalism) and their sanctification of their roles as parents. Theological conservatism scores were based on responses to two survey items: "The Bible is God's Word and everything will happen exactly as it says" and "The Bible is the answer to all important human problems." Sanctification refers to how much mothers imbue their roles with sacred and holy qualities and see themselves as doing "God's work" as parents. The results directly illuminated the value of measuring multiple constructs. Neither conservatism nor sanctification was related independently to the mothers' use of spanking. However, regression analyses showed that spanking was predicted by the *interaction* between the mothers' conservatism and sanctification scores. Specifically, mothers who were theologically conservative were *more* likely than other conservative mothers to spank their children if they also viewed their parent role as sacred and holy; in contrast, mothers who were theologically liberal were *less* likely than other liberal mothers to spank their children if they also viewed their role as sacred and holy. Thus, "the link between sanctifying one's role as a parent and using corporal punishment . . . was moderated by how conservative or liberal a mother was in her interpretation of the Bible" (p. 283).

I have chosen this complicated and controversial topic of spanking in my discussion here to demonstrate that our scientific understanding of complex behavior is enriched by our use of multiple measures of relevant religious constructs. In this research, scholars should move beyond a "main effects" emphasis that focuses on between-group differences (e.g., conservative vs. liberal) and examine the *interactions* between multiple variables. Fortunately, many scholars are calling for the use of multiple methods in this burgeoning field of spiritual development. I concur with the proposal for the "need for qualitative and quantitative studies that go both deep and wide" (Roehlkepartain & Patel, 2006, p. 333).

Once More Into the Breach: The Problem With Stage Theory

Although stage theories have dominated the study of development for a very long time, it is possible that our understanding of spiritual development has been impeded by a reliance on stage models. Developmental psychology has, in many ways, outgrown stage theory (see Overton, 1998). My hope is that the scientific study of children's spiritual development moves forward without the encumbrances of old ideas that should not be too venerated. For example, for decades the paradigm of cognitive-developmentalism dominated the study of children's religious and spiritual development (Spilka, Hood, Hunsberger, & Gorsuch, 2003), with a focus on distinct cognitive processes within different stages. But it is clear now that the "obsession with stages" impedes our understanding of the gradualness and the "complexity and uniqueness of individual religious development" (p. 85). Our understanding of young children's spirituality, and certainly our work with children in applied/educational settings, has been constrained by assumptions of young children's cognitive limitations and immaturity. It is also safe to say that our notions of older children's spirituality may have been exaggerated due to our assumptions of their relative cognitive maturity.

Another problem is that there is probably substantial variability within individuals at any given age or stage. Individuals experience sudden gains and spurts due to experiences or insights, as well as regressions due to trauma or despair; and then long seasons of stillness or plateaus seem to characterize the experience of many. Surely, different individuals experience a wholly different mix of these different experiences—growth, loss, stasis—at different times, in different ways, due to different causes, and with different consequences. Data from the most famous stage theory in our field, Fowler's (1981) stages of faith, confirm that variability within a single age is common. Drawing from Fowler's data (his Table B.3, "Distribution of stages of faith by age," p. 318), one can see that while 72 percent of children in middle childhood possessed a mythic-literal faith, children actually scored in *four* different stages or combined adjacent stages. In the subsequent stage of synthetic-conventional faith, 50 percent of adolescents scored in this "normal" stage, yet *five* different stages or substages were scored across the entire subsample of teens.

Another intellectual imposition of stage theory is the implicit notion that development entails "forward progress." As others have noted, there are religious and philosophical traditions that disagree with this assumption (Roehlkepartain, Benson, et al., 2006; Yust et al., 2006). While these issues cannot be resolved in these brief pages, the field will need to wrestle with these fundamental beliefs and assumptions if we are to genuinely mature as a field.

Of course, development entails change, and some change will seem stage-like. But my point is that we have oversold (or overbought) stage theory and in the process have pigeonholed too much of children's development into its constraints. While it may be convenient to focus on the average and modal, a true understanding of children's spirituality will require closer consideration of the varieties of religious and spiritual thinking and experience as they occur naturally and organically within a given child and across large numbers of children within any age group.

Conclusion

Children's spirituality is receiving attention from scholars like never before. This is a good thing for many reasons, not the least of which is that it will help us understand what some believe to be the core dimension of human development and, indeed, of human life. However, this emerging field has growth pangs to suffer as it matures. I have attempted to lay out some of the basic challenges facing our field. These include definitional challenges, the design of our studies (e.g., using multiple measures of constructs and employing a social-ecology design in our studies), and the consequences of relying on traditional stage theory for understanding spiritual development. As scholars wrestle with these and other issues, the field will mature over time and provide us with a deeper understanding of a dimension of life that, though challenging to understand, may be most central to our humanity.

References

Allen, H. C. (2004). Nurturing children's spirituality in intergenerational Christian settings. In D. Ratcliff (Ed.), *Children's spirituality: Christian perspectives, research, and applications* (pp. 266–83). Eugene, OR: Cascade.

Benson, P. L. (2004). Emerging themes in research on adolescent spiritual and religious development. *Applied Developmental Science, 8,* 47–50.

Benson, P. L., Roehlkepartain, E. C., & Rude, S. P. (2003). Spiritual development in childhood and adolescence: Toward a field of inquiry. *Applied Developmental Science, 7,* 205–13.

Boyatzis, C. J. (2003a). Religious and spiritual development: An introduction. *Review of Religious Research, 44,* 213–19.

Boyatzis, C. J. (2003b). Religious and spiritual development. *Review of Religious Research, 44*(3).

Boyatzis, C. J. (2005). Children's religious and spiritual development. In R. F. Paloutzian & C. L. Park (Eds.), *Handbook of the psychology of religion and spirituality* (pp. 123–43). New York: Guilford.

Boyatzis, C. J. (Ed.) (2006). Unraveling the dynamics of religion in the family and parent-child relationship. *The International Journal for the Psychology of Religion, 16*(4).

Boyatzis, C. J., & Janicki, D. (2003). Parent-child communication about religion: Survey and diary data on unilateral transmission and bi-directional reciprocity styles. *Review of Religious Research, 44*, 252–70.

Bronfenbrenner, U. (1979). *The ecology of human development.* Cambridge, MA: Harvard University Press.

Coles, R. (1990). *The spiritual life of children.* Boston: Houghton Mifflin.

Cornwall, M. (1989). The determinants of religious behavior: A theoretical model and empirical test. *Social Forces, 68*, 572–92.

Dowling, E., & Scarlett, W. G. (Eds.). (2006). *Encyclopedia of religious and spiritual development in childhood and adolescence.* Thousand Oaks, CA: Sage.

Farmer, L. J. (1992). Religious experience in childhood: A study of adult perspectives on early spiritual awareness. *Religious Education, 87*, 259–68.

Fowler, J. (1981). *Stages of faith: The psychology of human development and the quest for meaning.* New York: HarperCollins.

Gershoff, E. T., Miller, P. C., & Holden, G. W. (1999). Parenting influences from the pulpit: Religious affiliation as a determinant of corporal punishment. *Journal of Family Psychology, 13*, 307–20.

Gottlieb, A. (2006). Non-Western approaches to spiritual development among infants and young children: A case study from West Africa. In E. C. Roehlkepartain, P. E. King, L. Wagener, & P. L. Benson (Eds.), *The handbook of spiritual development in childhood and adolescence* (pp. 150–62). Thousand Oaks, CA: Sage.

Hay, D., & Nye, R. (1998). *The spirit of the child.* London: Fount.

Hay, D., Reich, K. H., & Utsch, M. (2006). Spiritual development: Intersections and divergence with religious development. In E. C. Roehlkepartain, P. E. King, L. Wagener, & P. L. Benson (Eds.), *The handbook of spiritual development in childhood and adolescence* (pp. 46–59). Thousand Oaks, CA: Sage.

Johnson, C. N. (2000). Putting different things together: The development of metaphysical thinking. In K. S. Rosengren, C. N. Johnson, & P. L. Harris (Eds.), *Imagining the impossible: Magical, scientific, and religious thinking in children* (pp. 179–211). Cambridge, UK: Cambridge University Press.

Johnson, C. N., & Boyatzis, C. J. (2006). Cognitive-cultural foundations of spiritual development. In E. C. Roehlkepartain, P. E. King, L. Wagener, &

P. L. Benson (Eds.), *The handbook of spiritual development in childhood and adolescence* (pp. 211–23). Thousand Oaks, CA: Sage.

King, P. E., & Boyatzis, C. J. (Eds.) (2004). Exploring adolescent religious and spiritual development: Current and future theoretical and empirical perspectives. *Applied Developmental Science, 8*(1).

Loder, J. E. (1998). *The logic of the spirit: Human development in theological perspective.* San Francisco: Jossey-Bass.

Mahoney, A., Pargament, K. I., Swank, A., & Tarakeshwar, N. (2001). Religion in the home in the 1980s and 90s: A meta-analytic review and conceptual analysis of religion. *Journal of Family Psychology, 15,* 559–96.

Mattis, J. S., Ahluwalia, M. K., Cowie, S. E., & Kirkland-Harris, A. M. (2006). Ethnicity, culture, and spiritual development. In E. C. Roehlkepartain, P. E. King, L. Wagener, & P. L. Benson (Eds.), *The handbook of spiritual development in childhood and adolescence* (pp. 283–96). Thousand Oaks, CA: Sage.

Mercer, J. A., Matthews, D. L., & Walz, S. (2004). Children in congregations: Congregations as contexts for children's spiritual growth. In D. Ratcliff (Ed.), *Children's spirituality: Christian perspectives, research, and applications* (pp. 249–65). Eugene, OR: Cascade.

Murray-Swank, A., Mahoney, A., & Pargament, K. I. (2006). Sanctification of parenting: Links to corporal punishment and parental warmth among biblically conservative and liberal mothers. *The International Journal for the Psychology of Religion, 16,* 271–88.

Oser, F., Scarlett, G. W., & Bucher, A. (2006). Religious and spiritual development throughout the life span. In W. Damon & R. M. Lerner (Eds.), *Handbook of child psychology: Vol. 1: Theoretical models of development* (6th ed., pp. 942–97). New York: Wiley.

Overton, W. F. (1998). Developmental psychology: Philosophy, concepts, and methodology. In W. Damon & R. M. Lerner (Eds.), *Handbook of child psychology: Vol. 1. Theoretical models of development* (5th ed., pp. 107–88). New York: Wiley.

Ratcliff, D. (Ed.) (2004). *Children's spirituality: Christian perspectives, research, and applications.* Eugene, OR: Cascade.

Regnerus, M. D., & Elder, G. H., Jr. (2003). Staying on track in school: Religious influences in high- and low-risk settings. *Journal for the Scientific Study of Religion, 42,* 633–49.

Regnerus, M. D., Smith, C., & Smith, B. (2004). Social context in the development of adolescent religiosity. *Applied Developmental Science, 8,* 27–38.

Robinson, E. (1983). *The original vision: A study of the religious experience of childhood.* New York: Seabury.

Roehlkepartain, E. C., Benson, P. L., King, P. E., & Wagener, L. (2006). Spiritual development in childhood and adolescence: Moving to the scientific mainstream. In E. C. Roehlkepartain, P. E. King, L. Wagener, & P. L. Benson (Eds.), *The handbook of spiritual development in childhood and adolescence* (pp. 1–15). Thousand Oaks, CA: Sage.

Roehlkepartain, E. C., King, P. E., Wagener, L., & Benson, P. L. (Eds.) (2006). *The handbook of spiritual development in childhood and adolescence.* Thousand Oaks, CA: Sage.

Roehlkepartain, E. C., & Patel, E. (2006). Congregations: Unexamined crucibles for spiritual development. In E. C. Roehlkepartain, P. E. King, L. Wagener, & P. L. Benson (Eds.), *The handbook of spiritual development in childhood and adolescence* (pp. 324–36). Thousand Oaks, CA: Sage.

Schwartz, K. D. (2006). Transformation in parent and friend faith support predicting adolescents' religious faith. *The International Journal for the Psychology of Religion, 16,* 311–26.

Spilka, B., Hood, R. W., Jr., Hunsberger, B., & Gorsuch, R. (2003). *The psychology of religion: An empirical approach* (3rd ed.). New York: Guilford.

Subbotsky, E. (1993). *Foundations of the mind: Children's understanding of reality.* Cambridge, MA: Harvard University Press.

Westerhoff, J. W., III. (2000). *Will our children have faith?* (Rev. ed.). Toronto: Anglican Book Centre.

Woolley, J. D. (2000). The development of beliefs about direct mental-physical causality in imagination, magic, and religion. In K. S. Rosengren, C. N. Johnson, & P. L. Harris (Eds.), *Imagining the impossible: Magical, scientific, and religious thinking in children* (pp. 99–129). Cambridge, UK: Cambridge University Press.

Yust, K. M., Johnson, A. N., Sasso, S. E., & Roehlkepartain, E. C. (Eds.). (2006). *Nurturing child and adolescent spirituality: Perspectives from the world's religious traditions.* New York: Rowman & Littlefield.

Historical & Theological Understandings of Children's Spirituality

4 The Christian Nurture of Children in the Second and Third Centuries[1]

James Riley Estep Jr.

THE CHRISTIAN COMMUNITY SINCE IT INCEPTION HAS ALWAYS GIVEN ATtention to the faith needs of children (Matt 18:1–6; Mark 10:13–16; Eph 6:1–4; Col 3:20–21). Over the centuries the church has demonstrated a variety of opinions on the nature of children and the appropriate pastoral response to them. Though often considered irrelevant, voices from church history are still valuable for contemporary pastoral ministry with children. G. K. Chesterton (1959) once wrote:

> Tradition means giving a vote to the most obscure of all classes, our ancestors. It is the democracy of the dead.... Tradition refuses to submit to the small and arrogant oligarchy of those who merely happen to be walking about [alive]. All democrats object to men being disqualified by the accident of birth; tradition objects to their being disqualified by the accident of death. Democracy tells us not to neglect a good man's opinion, even if he is our groom; tradition asks us not to neglect a good man's opinion, even if he is our father. (p. 45; cf. Lewis, 1946, pp. 5–7)

---

1. I would like to thank Shawn Smith and Beth Ragan for their assistance in completing the research for this paper. Shawn Smith (MA, History; MDiv, Theology) served as my teaching assistant from 2003–2004 and returned to aid in the location of primary sources in the patristic writings. Beth Ragan, an MDiv student (Christian Education), was my teaching assistant 2005–2006, and likewise located primary sources in the patristic writings, as well as conducting subsequent research required for the completion of this paper.

It is with this appreciation of history and tradition that this chapter approaches the issue of childhood nurture in the ante-Nicene church.[2]

Importance of This Period

Why focus on the church of the second and third centuries AD? There are three important reasons that this chapter focuses on these early centuries:

1. These centuries are generally poorly represented in the precedent literature. Marcia Bunge's edited volume, *The Child in Christian Thought* (2001), contains one chapter on the New Testament (chapter 1), and two on the latter early-church era, focusing on Chrysostom and Augustine (chapters 2 and 3 respectively). No connecting materials cover the two hundred years between the close of the New Testament and the beginning of the latter patristic period in the early church. This gap typifies the omission of this period from many histories.

2. These centuries are a crucial formative period in the early church. Focused attention has been given to children of the church of the fourth and fifth centuries through examining the writings of Jerome, Chrysostom, and Augustine, but the work of these later theologians was built around the issues and debates of the second- and third-century authorities on infant baptism, the Eucharist, and original sin. Hence, the ante-Nicene period offers insight into the historical precedents that influenced the latter church fathers.

3. These two centuries provide insight into the post-apostolic, pre-Nicene formation of theological traditions that influence even our current discussions regarding, for example, original sin and childhood salvation.

This chapter explores the idea of childhood in the second- and third-century church, with specific attention given to the nature of childhood in the ante-Nicene church, the ecclesiastical status of children in that period, and the ante-Nicene church's responsibility to children. Ultimately, the purpose of this article is to discern the early church's concept of nurturing childhood faith from its theology of and pastoral practices with its children, as well as to glean insights for today's ministry with children.

2. "Ante-Nicene" (i.e., before Nicaea) refers to the time period after the first century and before the First Council of Nicaea produced the Nicene Creed in AD 325.

As one surveys the precedent literature of the second- and third-century Christian community, one realizes rather readily that a search for the term *child* (and any of its derivatives) will yield thousands of references, though many of them are metaphorical in nature. Once the texts addressing children in a more literal sense are isolated, only a few dozen surface as being significant treatments of the idea of childhood in the early church. However, even though the idea of children or childhood was often used metaphorically or illustratively by the early church fathers, their insights are valuable and valid, as Bakke (2005) observes:

> They [the early church fathers] construct an ideal child or an ideal picture of childhood in ways that suit their argumentative strategy.... We may assume that their constructed pictures of childhood related to or reflected points of connection with real images of childhood. It is reasonable to assume that the qualities they ascribe to children are not much different from those their audience associated with childhood. (pp. 57–58)

As such, the writings of the ante-Nicene church authorities provide a window into their concept of the child in the church, whether those writings metaphorically or literally address childhood.

What ages comprised childhood in the second and third centuries? Roman literature seems to indicate that at the age of seven (about the time a child would begin attending the *ludus*, elementary school), a child's adult journey began (Wiedemann, 1989, p. 154; Ariès, 1962). While this was the beginning of the child's journey into adulthood, it was indeed not the completion of it, which was symbolized by the exchange of the *toga praetexta* for the *toga virilis* by one's father upon the completion of formal schooling (Bonner, 1977, pp. 84–85, 137). Christians seem to have adopted this understanding as well, as reflected in this Christian child's prayer from the fourth century, "Today, dear God, I am seven years old, and must play no more. Here is my top, my hoop, and my ball: Keep them all, my Lord" (Wiedemann, p. 153).

In a Greco-Roman context, children were valued primarily for socioeconomic reasons. This is not to suggest that parental love did not exist, but children were seen as heirs (cf. Gal 4:1–4), a means of continuing the family name and economic endeavors. Hence, "childhood was viewed largely negatively as a state of immaturity to outgrow.... Children occupied a low rung on the social ladder" (Gundry-Volf, 2001, p. 32; cf. Francis, 1996, p. 72).

In the literature of the early Christian community, ideas about children centered around three critical issues: 1) the nature of children and childhood, typified by the debate over original sin; 2) the ecclesiastical status of children, typified by the debate over infant baptism; and 3) the early church's responsibility to children, as typified by the debate over education and schooling.

The Nature of Children in the Ante-Nicene Church

Graham Gould (1994) comments that the "anthropological problem of childhood" had "three interrelated factors":

1. The development of a child's soul in terms of its possession, or lack, of faculties such as reason and desire

2. The extent to which a child's soul is open to the same temptations, desires, or passions as that of an adult, [and]

3. The extent to which children are capable of understanding ideas and precepts or may be held to deserve reward or punishment for their actions. (pp. 39–40)

All of these factors hinge on the notion of the spiritual status of the child, that is, the child as good, innocent, or depraved. As one reads the ante-Nicene patristic writers, one is struck by the absence of a clear and authoritative statement of original sin. However, during the second and third centuries, the nature of children was not yet as definitively stated as it was in the fourth and fifth centuries when original sin was fully delineated in light of the debate between Augustine and Pelagius. As Berkhof (1937) comments, "Greek anthropology also influenced the West . . . in the second and third centuries, but in the third and fourth centuries the seed of the doctrine that was destined to become prevalent in the West [Augustinian original sin], especially the works of Tertullian, Cyprian, Hilary and Ambrose," was planted and gave rise to Augustine's doctrine of original sin in the fifth century (p. 129; cf. Wright, 1987, pp. 58–63; Olsen, 1999, pp. 267–74).

Similarly, Klotsche (1945) speaks of "two great tendencies" in the church of the East and West, with the West emphasizing human depravity and the East, human freedom (p. 83); however, this distinction was not obvious during the second and third centuries. While some authorities did speak of original sin in this early period, it was not fully defined until the fifth century. According to Bakke (2005), "In the West, a striking discontinuity occurred at the beginning of the fifth century with regard to the idea of children's innocence"—innocence was replaced by Augustine's doctrine of original sin (p. 281). During the second and third centuries children were described far more frequently as innocent than as sinful.

Early attention on children focused on Jesus' allusion to children as models for Christian maturity and faithfulness, particularly in Matthew 18:1–4 and 19:13–14 and parallel passages (Carroll, 2001, pp. 127–32). In these passages, Jesus contradicts the prevailing Greco-Roman view of childhood, placing those with limited social status as the paradigm for Christian maturity (Gundry-Volf, 2001, pp. 38–39). What quality did children possess that we are to emulate? What is it that Christ saw in them so as to use them as a Christian paradigm? While it must be acknowledged that Jesus himself never directly affirms the innocence of children, their innocence, according to the earliest understandings, is what Jesus intended to convey in his child metaphor.[3]

The theme of child-innocence, in contrast to the corruption of adult-evil, is carried into the early church fathers of the latter second and the third centuries. The Christian philosopher Aristides (d. 133/134) perhaps makes the most direct affirmation of this understanding in his *Apology*, 15, "And when a child has been born to one of them, they give thanks to God; and if moreover it happen[s] to die in childhood, they give thanks to God the more, as for one who has passed through the world without sins."[4] In fact, childhood innocence was so predominant that imagery of children and nakedness (as in the Garden of Eden) occurs on occasion (Hill, 2003, p. 28).

Other authorities from this period likewise emphasized the innocence of children by hearkening back to the garden imagery from the creation accounts, for example, the *Gospel of Thomas*, 37, and Irenaeus' *Demonstrations of Apostolic Preaching*, 14. Similarly, Clement of Alexandria (ca. 150–215) likewise highlights the positive attributes of children, such as their "simplicity," "innocence," and "loyalty" as the mark of Christian maturity (*The Instructor*, 1.5–6), contrary to the common perception of Greco-Roman culture (Bakke, 2005, p. 63) and his Gnostic counterparts (Gould, 2004,

---

3. cf. Shepherd of Hermas, *Commandments* 2.1; *Similitudes* 9.29.1–3; *Epistle of Barnabas* 6.11;

4. cf. also Athenagoras, *Resurrection* 14.

pp. 40–41). Clement's pupil, Origen (ca. 185–254), accepts his mentor's ideal image of childhood, explaining that these qualities of a child stem from a lack of adult sexual desire and an incomplete rational function. He notes that the child's lack of desire for power/prestige/position associated with adulthood is likewise a mark of childlike simplicity (*Commentary on Matthew* 13.16; cf. Tertullian, *On Monogamy*, 8).

Tertullian (ca. 150–220) perhaps makes the most startling statement regarding childhood innocence, depicting children as not needing remission of sin, and even arguing for a delay in baptizing children (*On Baptism*, 18; cf. Wright, 1987, pp. 47–50). While Tertullian affirms original sin elsewhere in his writings (Bakke, 2005, p. 69), for him original sin does *not* include guilt or condemnation, since he questions the need of even baptizing infants and young children (unlike Augustine). Louis Berkhof (1937) observes, "Infant baptism was evidently quite current in the days of Origen and Tertullian, though the latter opposed it on the grounds of the inexpediency of placing young children under the heavy responsibility of the baptismal covenant" (p. 248).

In this period, Cyprian (ca. 200–258), acknowledging that children are guilty of no sin of their own, introduces the notion of original sin through Adam as a justification for infant baptism. "How much more should we shrink from hindering an infant, who, being lately born, has not sinned [unlike those baptized as adults], except in that, being born after the flesh according to Adam, he has contracted the contagion of the ancient death at its earliest birth, who approaches the more easily on this very account to the reception of the forgiveness of sins—that to him are remitted, not his own sins, but the sins of another" (*Epistle* 58.5). With Cyprian, the anthropological debate makes a significant new departure, one that will reach its fullness in the early church with Augustine's response to Pelagius in the late fourth century (McGrath, 1998, p. 35).

In general, the ante-Nicene authorities more often affirmed the innocence of children, not merely from their own sins, but even from the complete culpable effect of "original sin" as later promulgated by Augustine (Hill, 2003, pp. 78–79, 89–90; cf. Klotsche, 1945, p. 83).

THE ECCLESIASTICAL STATUS OF CHILDREN IN THE ANTE-NICENE CHURCH

What was the child's "place" in the church? Though Greco-Roman society marginalized children, the church seems to have been more open to their presence and place within their community. Three practices illustrate the ecclesiastical status of children: their presence in the faith community, the practice of infant baptism, and their participation in worship/Eucharist.

Presence Within the Community of Faith

Children were not marginalized or alienated within the Christian community of this period. Ignatius (ca. 35–107) concludes one of his epistles with "I salute the families of my brethren, with their wives and children, and the virgins who are called widows" (*Epistle to the Smyrneans*, 13.1). Similarly, Aristides (d. 133/134) comments that even the children of slaves who accept Christ are equal members of the church: "Further, if one or [the] other of them have bondmen and bondwomen or children, through love towards them they persuade them to become Christians, and when they have done so, they call them brethren without distinction" (*Apology* 15).

Whether the children are those of the head of the household or those of the servants, children were regarded of an equal status within the community of faith. Irenaeus (ca. 120–200) also saw this child-adult equality and rooted it in the person of Christ, emphasizing that Jesus, too, was once an infant and child (*Against Heresies*, 2.22.4; cf. Bakke, 2005, p. 237).

Childhood presence was not merely acknowledged, but, on occasion, children were called to service. Cyprian (ca. 200–258) informs his readers of the appointment of a boy, age unknown, to serve as lector (*Epistles* 32), demonstrating not only the equivalent standing of adults and children in the church, but also the capacity to assume an active role in the ministry of the congregation, in spite of questionable educational level (Bakke, 2005, pp. 252–53; cf. Weidemann, 1989, pp. 186–87). This practice was not as isolated as it may seem, since Pope Siricius (ca. 334–98) later decreed "that one who devotes himself to the service of the church from his childhood must begin as lector" (Wiedeman, p. 101, 186). While some distinction may have been made due to age (and hence some natural and social-cultural limits evident), children were apparently valued in the early church as full members.

The Practice of Infant Baptism

The subject of infant baptism is central to determining the relationship of the child to the community of faith. In the ante-Nicene era one observes the formation of the practice and theology of infant baptism. The earliest *direct* reference for infant baptism is in the third century; earlier references, for example, household baptisms in the New Testament (e.g., Acts 16:15, 31; 18:8; 1 Cor 1:16; 16:15) and in the writings of some second century fathers, are only inferential. Perhaps the earliest direct reference to infant baptism may be found in Hippolytus's (ca. 180–235) *Apostolic Traditions* 21.3, "First you should baptize the little ones. All who can speak for themselves should speak. But for those who cannot speak, their parents should speak or another who belongs to the family."[5]

Tertullian, early in the third century, questioned the practice of infant baptism, urging that the practice be examined and stating that

> the delay of baptism is preferable; principally, however, in the case of little children . . . the Lord does indeed say, "Forbid them not to come unto me." Let them "come," then, while they are growing up; let them "come" while they are learning, while they are learning whither to come; let them become Christians when they have become able to know Christ. (*On Baptism*, 18; cf. Wright, 1987, pp. 47–50)

It is critical to note that Tertullian seems to be questioning an accepted practice, indicating that infant baptism is not a new innovation; he is simply questioning the rationale for it. Other early church voices, likewise, seem to indicate that baptism is for older children and adults.[6]

However, Cyprian (ca. 200–258), fifty years after Tertullian in North Africa, questioned how long following birth the holy kiss and baptism should be performed (*Epistle 58*). Cyprian advances the notion that baptism is the New Testament's equivalent to Old Testament circumcision (*Epistle* 58.4). Based on this sacramental view of baptism, it was determined that "no one ought to be hindered from baptism and from the grace of God,

---

5. Textual difficulties exist regarding the legitimacy of this sentence—that is, the Greek text has been lost in its entirety and the earliest Latin text does not contain the sentence; however, all other editions of the text contain parallel statements (Strange, 1996, p. 89).

6. cf. Justin Martyr, *First Apology*, 61; *Didache* 7.1–4; also cf. *Martyrdom of Saints Perpetua and Felicitas*, 3, 14–15; Strange, 1996, p. 87, wherein the births of Christian children are curiously absent of any mention of their baptism.

... [especially] infants and newly-born persons" (*Epistle* 58.6). Cyprian's writings indicate that infant baptism seems to be an accepted practice, possibly normative, at least for the churches of northern Africa of the mid-third century (Bakke, 2005, p. 70). This indication is historically significant because it represents a shift in degree of acceptance over the fifty years between Tertullian and Cyprian, from a questioned practice, probably initiated by parents, to an affirmed preference of the ecclesiastical authorities (Strawbridge, 2005, pp. 8, 12).

In regard to the place and presence of children in the church, as John Francis (1996) concludes, "the development of infant baptism in the church surely also meant the crossing of another frontier in marking the full acceptance of the child within the Christian community" (p. 83).

Children in Worship and Participation in the Eucharist

Hippolytus notes that it was typical to administer the Eucharist after receiving the sacrament of baptism. Whereas he provides specific instruction to children and adults, even men and women, in regard to baptism, he gives only one set of instructions for those receiving the Eucharist (*Apostolic Traditions*, 21, 23), suggesting that children and adults partook equally in the Eucharist (Strawbridge, 2005, pp. 4).

Likewise, Cyprian notes the participation of children in the Eucharist in *On the Lapsed*, 25.[7] In this account, a female child is left in the custody of a wet nurse while her Christian parents fled persecution; but the nurse turned the child over to the magistrates who in turn involved her in a pagan rite. When the child was later recovered, the Christian mother brought the child to a Christian gathering, presumably worship, where the child's behaviors became problematic; the child was "impatient of our prayer and supplications," "weeping," "tossed about . . . by the violent excitement of her mind," and when offered the Eucharist, the child "turned away its face, compressed its mouth with resisting lips, and refused the cup." Eventually the Eucharist was "forced on her," which led to "sobbing and vomiting," which was interpreted as the child's conflict between the pagan rite and the

---

7. The term "lapsed" refers to Christians who had returned to paganism for a period of time, but then returned to the Christian faith. This presented a substantial theological and practical issue for the early church, particularly under the persecution of Decius, which forced Cyprian into exile. Upon his return to Carthage after Decius' death, he faced a many instances of lapsed Christians. Cf. Cyprian, *On the Lapsed*, 20; Strawbridge, 2005, p. 14; and González, 1984, p. 88–90, 245.

Christian Eucharist. Regardless of what one may make of the episode, the point for our purposes is the child's participation in the Eucharist and the subtle affirmation of the child's spiritual discernment.[8]

Once again, the participation of children in the Eucharistic celebration further indicates their acceptance in and by the community of faith, even as infants.

The Ante-Nicene Church's Responsibility to Children

Beyond the provision of baptism and the Eucharist, what was the church's responsibility toward children's maturing in the faith? The community of faith's commitment to children rested in its affirmation of parental instruction, combined with corporal discipline, as well as care provided for orphans and disadvantaged children.

Instruction and Discipline

In the New Testament, Paul seems to lay the responsibility for Christian instruction and growth of children on parents, especially the father as head of the household (Eph 6:1, 4; Col 3:20–21) as well as leaders of the Christian community (Titus 1:6–9; 1 Tim 3:4).[9] This theme is also prevalent in the Old Testament and the literature of Judaism (Carroll, 2004, p. 125). This view is undeniably reflective of the notion of *patria potestas* and the *paterfamilias* pervasive throughout Roman culture (Stamps, 2000, p. 197). "This hierarchical order [father-mother-child] conformed to the cultural expectation of the times" (Strange, 1996, p. 77).

Gundry-Volf (2001) writes that "although Ephesians [6:4] agrees with other ancients about children's need for education and the role of fathers in this task, it nevertheless gives the education prescribed a specifically Christian character: 'the discipline and instruction of the Lord'" (p. 57). In fact, the notion of associating Christian education with children occurs in possibly the earliest extra-canonical Christian writing. Clement of Rome's *First Epistle to the Corinthians* contains the injunction, "Let your children be partakers of true Christian training [*en Christō paidias*]" (*First Epistle to*

---

8. cf. Cyprian, *On the Lapsed*, 9.

9. cf. Gundry-Volf, 2001, pp. 58–59; *Didascala Apostolorum*, 4, makes instruction of children mandatory for those aspiring to become bishops.

the Corinthians, 21.8).[10] Other apostolic fathers make similar injunctions regarding the teaching of children.[11]

Familial education of children in the faith continued into the later second and third centuries.[12] Perhaps one of the more dramatic portrayals of success of such familial education in the faith is seen in the literature of the martyrs. "And many, both men and women, who have been Christ's disciples *from childhood*, remain pure at the age of sixty or seventy years; and I boast that I could produce such from every race of men" (emphasis mine) (Justin Martyr, *First Apology*, 15). A portion of the *Martyrdom of Justin and His Companions*, 4 (ca. 165), reads:

> A man called Paeon stood up and said: "I also am a Christian."
> The prefect Rusticus said: "Who taught you?"
> Paeon said: "I received from my parents this good confession."
> Euelpistus said: "I listened indeed gladly to the words of Justin, but I too received Christianity from my parents."
> The prefect Rusticus said: "Where are your parents?"
> Eulpistus said: "In Cappadocia."
> Rusticus said to Hierax: "Where are your parents?"
> He answered, saying: "Our true father is Christ, and our mother our faith in him. My earthly parents are dead, and I was dragged away from Iconium in Phrygia before coming hither." (Stevenson & Frend, 1987, p. 33)

This brief account attests both to the influence of parents on the faith of their children and to the fact that the earliest Christian communities acknowledged this powerful influence.

The Schooling Controversy

As previously noted, Christian education was predominantly home-based, that is, familial, in the early centuries of Christianity. General education was provided by the educational system of the Roman Empire, the elementary school or *ludus*. The exposure of Christian children to non-Christian learning, specifically Roman religious practices and literature, for some was appalling and intolerable. Chapter 10 of Tertullian's treatise *On Idolatry*

---

10. Marrou (1956, p. 314) believes this to be the first actual use of the phrase *Christian education*, dating to ca. AD 95.

11. Polycarp, *Epistle to the Philippians*, 4.2; Shepherd of Hermas, *Vision* 1.3.2; 2.2; *Epistle of Barnabas*, 19.5; and the *Didache* 4.9.

12. cf. Clement of Alexandria, *Instructor*, 5; *Didascalia Apostolorum*, 22.

cautions Christian parents about schooling their children in the Roman system (Bromiley, 1978, p. 31). Though Tertullian makes allowance for a Christian student in a Roman school, he does not do so for a Christian teacher, since the teacher would have to espouse and affirm the pagan content of the Roman *ludus*, which is different from simply learning the literature taught in it (Barclay, 1959, pp. 239–41). Hence, instruction that was distinctively Christian in content and character seems to have been the purview of the home and Christian family. While Christian education through schooling was in its formative stages at this time, it was principally through familial instruction, fostered by the community of faith, that children became disciplined followers of Christ.

Care for the Underprivileged[13]

The church institutionalized the concern for widows and orphans that is expressed in James 1:27. The *Shepherd of Hermas* (early second century) instructs its reader:

> Having fulfilled what is written, in the day on which you fast you will taste nothing but bread and water; and having reckoned up the price of the dishes of that day which you intended to have eaten, you will give it to a widow, or an orphan, or to some person in want, and thus you will exhibit humility of mind, so that he who has received benefit from your humility may fill his own soul, and pray for you to the Lord. (*Similitudes* 3)

The *Didascalia Apostolorum* 14 addresses the care of widows and orphans. The responsibility for orphans falls to the bishop, who is instructed to "bestow care upon these," but also provide care to widows who "are in need of help through want or sickness or the rearing of children." Furthermore, it specifies the level of care to be provided to orphans. The following itemizes the care provided:

1. Childless Christian adults should adopt male or female orphans.
2. Christian parents of a son should adopt a female orphan to be his wife "when her time is come."
3. Adopted male orphans should "learn a craft" so as to become a productive member of society once grown.

---

13. For a more thorough treatment, see my forthcoming chapter in *Hope for Children in Poverty: Profiles and Possibilities* (Judson Press, 2007, H. Upchurch, Editor).

4. In both instances, male or female orphans are to be adopted so as to not place "a burden upon the love of the brethren."

5. No one receiving church support due to being an orphan should be shamed, "for he is esteemed at the altar of God, therefore shall he be honored of God. (17.4.1–3)

The first mention of such endeavors on behalf of orphans is made in time of Arian bishop George of Cappadocia (d. 361) by the church historian Socrates (*Ecclesiastical History* 2.28), but probably existed earlier (Miller, 2003, p. 46).

As previously noted, it was assumed and expected that Christian parents would provide instruction in the faith to their children. Orphans, having no parents, Christian or otherwise, would not have such opportunities unless Christian adults adopted them. This was a means of evangelism of children, providing Christian instruction to those without a means of receiving it otherwise.

Summations and Conclusions on Children in the Ante-Nicene Church

First, children are both actually and metaphorically described as being in a state of innocence, the absence of sin. While this was soon to change in the West with the Augustine vs. Pelagius debate, during this period innocence seemed to receive the greater emphasis. In the anthropological paradox of innocence and depravity, the earliest witnesses seem to favor innocence to the virtual exclusion of any depravity, particularly those church authorities in the East. However, during the third century, the Christian community began to shift this depiction as children being innocent of committing any sins themselves, toward being stained by the sin of Adam (though not necessarily the guilt of Adam's sin).

Second, Christian nurture was provided both by the church, through actual and ritual inclusion of the child, and by the Christian family through instruction. As such, children were nurtured in the context of family and church. Christian nurture of the child was primarily the responsibility of Christian parents. The community of faith continually provided injunction and direction for the child's parental instruction in the faith. Even in the case of orphans (those without parents, Christian or otherwise), adoption into a Christian family was a means of providing instruction in the faith.

The Christian family provided a continual context of nurturing relationships, instruction, and also discipline, which was closely associated to instruction.

Unlike Roman society, children were valued as full members of the Christian community. While the church of the second and third centuries did not engage in formal schooling of children on a large scale (a practice that became more common in the fourth century), it did provide direct opportunities for Christian nurture beyond that of instruction. Inclusion and spiritual nurture within the community of faith was facilitated by initiation (infant baptism), liturgy (Eucharist), participation in the congregation (presence and service), as well as through instruction in the faith through the liturgy and familial education. By way of the parents' joint participation with the child in infant baptism, Eucharist, and liturgy, the church accentuated parental influence on a child's life and faith.

Finally, how would a child manifest growth or maturity in the faith? What would be the general benchmarks of a child's growth in the faith? The ante-Nicene church called for a faith that was living, evident in the life of the child. The authorities of the second and third centuries indicated that a child's relationship with God was to be evident in perhaps three ways: acceptance of Christian beliefs, that is, faithful to the teachings of the church (cognitive); living a disciplined life, that is, values and behaviors (affective); and service within the church, that is, continued participation in the Christian community, possibly even serving as a lector (behavioral). The church's high view of the status of children in the church as described in this chapter contributed extensively to the child's growth and maturity.

Contemporary Ministry Implications from the Ante-Nicene Church

First, pastoral ministry with children must be predicated on theological rationale, not *vice versa*. Developing a theology in light of practice is a case of the proverbial cart-before-the-horse or the tail-wagging-the-dog. While there is no doubt that our pastoral and educational practice does influence our theologizing about it, we should place a priority on theology, and perceive practice as an expression of it.

Second, children's faith capacity should never be underestimated. Opportunity for growth in every dimension of faith should be afforded to children. Opportunity for service within the faith community should be offered as soon as the child demonstrates the desire and capacity for service.

Third, learning in childhood is built around experience in the Christian faith; for example, participation in the Eucharist can lead to the teaching of its meaning as the children grow. Their participation and witnessing of the ethos and practices of the church will lead them to a deeper understanding of it than mere classroom teaching can impart.

Fourth, the church needs a renewed commitment to support familial education in the Christian faith. While the church since the third century has developed an extensive network of educational venues for children as well as the accompanying resources, family life is still a significant factor in their spiritual formation. Yet, while churches often encourage families to participate in the Christian nurture of their children, rarely are families equipped to do so.

Fifth, the church must remain committed to children in need. What is our responsibility to children in the congregation and community who live in poverty? The Christian community must be willing to see the unique needs of such children, facilitate their presence within the congregation and community, and be willing to take measures beyond the typical programming of the congregation to nurture them.

Finally, children should not be marginalized in the Christian community, but openly included as members of God's family and citizens of God's kingdom. Children's ministry and education must become a vital part of the church's idea of congregational ministry, not an appendix to the pastoral concerns of the congregation.

In conclusion, G. K. Chesterton was right. The contemporary church can learn from history, tradition, old books—even from the fathers of the ante-Nicene church. We need to listen to our faith-fathers, though they have long been deceased; their example, commitment, and teachings are still relevant to those of us serving in their legacy of ministry to children. We must not forget that our present was their future, and our present will soon be another's past.

REFERENCE LIST

Ariès, P. (1962). *Centuries of childhood: A social history of family life*. New York: Random House.

Bakke, O. M. (2005). *When children became people: The birth of childhood in early Christianity* (B. McNeil, Trans.). Minneapolis: Fortress.

Barclay, W. (1959). *Educational ideals in the ancient world.* Grand Rapids: Baker.

Berkhof, L. (1937). *The history of Christian doctrine.* Grand Rapids: Baker.

Bonner, S. F. (1977). *Education in ancient Rome.* Los Angeles: University of California Press.

Bromiley, G. W. (1978). *Historical theology: An introduction.* Grand Rapids: Eerdmans.

Carroll, J. T. (2004). Children in the Bible. *Interpretation,* 55(2), 121–34.

Chesterton, G. K. (1959). *Orthodoxy.* New York: Image/Doubleday.

Francis, J. (1996). Children and childhood in the New Testament. In S. C. Barton (Ed.), *The family in theological perspective* (pp. 65–85). Edinburgh: T. & T. Clark.

González, J. (1984). *The story of Christianity: The early church to the dawn of the Reformation* (Vol. 1). San Francisco: HarperSanFrancisco.

Gould, G. (2004). Childhood in eastern patristic thought: Some problems of theology and theological anthropology. In D. Wood (Ed.), *Studies in church history: The church and childhood* (Vol. 31). Cambridge, MA: Blackwell.

Gundry-Volf, J. M. (2001). The least and the greatest: Children in the New Testament. In M. Bunge (Ed.), *The child in Christian thought* (pp. 29–60). Grand Rapids: Eerdmans.

Hill, J. (2003). *The history of Christian thought.* Downers Grove, IL: InterVarsity.

Klotsche, E. H. (1945). *The history of Christian doctrine* (Rev. ed.). Grand Rapids: Baker.

Lewis, C. S. (1946). Introduction. In Athanasias, *The incarnation of the word of God: Being the treatise of St. Athanasius.* New York: MacMillan.

Marrou, H. I. (1956). *A history of education in antiquity.* New York: Ward and Sheed.

McGrath, A. E. (1998). *Historical theology: An introduction to the history of Christian thought.* Oxford: Blackwell.

Miller, T. S. (2003). *The orphans of Byzantium: Child welfare in the Christian empire.* New York: Catholic University of America Press.

Olsen, R. E. (1999). *The story of Christian theology.* Downers Grove, IL: InterVarsity.

Stamps, D. L. (2000). Children in late antiquity. In C. Evans & S. Porter (Eds.), *Dictionary of New Testament backgrounds* (pp. 197–201). Downers Grove, IL: InterVarsity.

Strange, W. A. (1996). *Children in the early church: Children in the ancient world, the New Testament, and the early church.* Eugene, OR: Wipf & Stock.

Strawbridge, G. D. (2005, November). *Eucharist participation in the early centuries: Biblical and historical evidence for paedocommunion*. Paper presented at the Annual Conference of the Evangelical Theological Society, Valley Forge, PA.

Wiedemann, T. (1989). *Adults and children in the Roman Empire*. New Haven, CT: Yale University Press.

Wright, D. F. (1987). How controversial was the development of infant baptism in the early Church? In J. E. Bradley & R. A. Muller (Eds.), *Church, word, and Spirit: Historical and theological essays in honor of Geoffrey W. Bromiley* (pp. 45–63). Grand Rapids: Eerdmans.

Patristic Sources

Bradshaw, P. F., Maxwell E. J., & Phillips, L. E. (2002). *The apostolic traditions: A commentary*. Hermeneia. Minneapolis: Fortress.

Connolly, R. H. (1929). *Didascalia Apostolorum*. Oxford: Clarendon.

Niederwimmer, K. (1998). *The Didache: A commentary*. Hermeneia. Minneapolis: Fortress.

Patterson, S., & Meyer, M. (1994). *The complete Gospels: Annotated scholars version*. Santa Rosa, CA: Polebridge.

Roberts, A., & Donaldson, J. (1951). *The ante-Nicene fathers*. (Vols. 1–5, 10). Grand Rapids: Eerdmans.

Schaff, P. (1954). *The Nicene and post-Nicene fathers*. (Series 2, Vol. 2). Grand Rapids: Eerdmans.

Scheck, T. P. (2001). *Origen: Commentary on the epistle to the Romans* (Books 1–5). Washington, DC: Catholic University of America Press.

Stevenson, J., & Frend, W. H. C. (1987). *A new Eusebius: Documents illustrating the history of the church*. London: SPCK.

5   "Forbid Not the Little Ones": The Spirituality of Children in Celtic Christian Tradition[1]

Mara Lief Crabtree

CHRISTIAN CELTIC TRADITION, IN THE CONTEXT DATING FROM ROUGHLY the fourth century to the twelfth centuries A.D., and encompassing the geographical areas represented by the modern nations of Ireland (Eire), Scotland (Alba), Wales (Cymru), Brittany (Briezh), Cornwall (Kernow), and the Isle of Man (Mannin),emphasized a practical, lived theology that embraced both the reality and the validity of children's spirituality (see e.g., Culbreath, 2004, ¶ 1). Unlike various other Christian cultures of that and other periods, Celtic faith tradition reflected an understanding similar to the Synoptic Gospels and the Gospel of John in recognizing the humanity and spirituality, as well as the unique attributes, abilities, giftings, and expressions of personality that were consideredthe God-given possessions of children (Mitton, 1996).

    Children's place in the overall Celtic Christian community was one of honor and esteem, due to the Celts' understanding of certain biblical passages (e.g., Matt 19:14). Within the context of Celtic Christian faith development, the religious culture was deeply influenced and daily molded by the spirituality evident in various types of faith-based communities. Rather

---

    1. At the Children's Spirituality Conference, Dr. Crabtree's original paper, on which this chapter is based, was presented by Patricia Mercier, Doctor of Ministry candidate at Regent University School of Divinity and children's pastor. This chapter is dedicated in memory of Deborah Marie Mercier (2003–2007), daughter of Patricia and Edwin Mercier.

    This chapter in an earlier version appeared in the Fall 2007 *Christian Education Journal* and is reprinted here with permission from CEJ.

than forbidding the participation of children in many spiritual life practices and pursuits, the Christian Celts were careful to "forbid them not"[2] (Matt 19:14; Mark 10:14; Luke 18:16, NKJV), but rather to acknowledge and to encourage children's spirituality and their capacity to minister to others (Newell, 1999).

Studying the spirituality of children in Celtic Christian tradition yields knowledge that has vital implications for the contemporary understanding of children's spiritual, emotional, relational, and vocational formation. A study of this tradition provides information that addresses important questions relating to Christian holistic formation in contemporary faith cultures. Understanding the spirituality of children in Celtic Christian context informs the process of addressing and responding to the following questions: How, specifically, did this religious faith tradition contribute to molding the holistic formation of children? What areas of children's spiritual development were most influenced by the beliefs and practices inherent in Celtic Christian tradition? How did the Celtic Christian faith community's attitude toward and treatment of children impact the spiritual development of both children and adults? How did the spiritual contributions of children impact the wider community and the developing religious culture? How does children's spirituality in this tradition inform the present Christian ecclesial community in regard to the catechesis, holistic formation, and overall spiritual health and well-being of children? Children's spirituality in Celtic Christian tradition informs, empowers, and encourages the present-day ecclesial community'scontribution to the spiritual nurture, overall holistic formation, and the development of children's ministerial capacities.

Attitudes Regarding Children

Christian Celtic tradition embraced a spirituality that recognized the realities of this present, temporal and earthly realm, as well as the eschatological promise of Jesus Christ for a perfected, eternal age to come. Celtic

2. "Forbid not the little ones" is a partial paraphrase of Matthew 19:14; Mark 10:14; and Luke 18:16 as included in the New King James Version translation of the New Testament. Matthew 19:14: "But Jesus said, 'Let the little children come to me and do not forbid them; for such is the kingdom of heaven.'" Mark 10:14b: "'Let the little children come to me and do not forbid them; for such is the kingdom of God.'" Luke 18:16: "But Jesus called them to him and said, 'Let the little children come to me, and do not forbid them, for such is the kingdom of God.'"

Christians viewed faith and spiritual practice as gifts from God, giving meaning, purpose, and power to individual lives as well as to the community. The Celts viewed faith as integral to thetypically mundane needs and practices of daily life (Cahill, 1995).

The Realities of the Present and the Eternal

Celtic Christian faith did not compartmentalize or separate beliefs of faith from the realities of everyday life (Leidel, 2004). Daily life was not simply a time to be endured until, at life's end, one would be transported to a perfect, heavenly existence. Celts viewed eternity as present here and now: Christ in their midst, to guide, protect, and sustain them through the difficulties and vicissitudes of life. Indeed, there was the "already" of the kingdom of God—Christ living in their hearts in the here and now. There was also the reality of, and longing for, life in the perfect kingdom of the future, but the "already" of present life and the "not yet" of eternal life were not in opposition. Earthly life prepared one for the perfection of heaven; present life was eternal also, in that earthly life and the coming heavenly existence represented a continuum of living with God. Now, in this life, we are being prepared for the life ahead; then, we will be in the near presence of God where our hearts' most profound spiritual longings will be fulfilled (Adam, 1994).

The Sacredness of God's Creation

This sense of life as the "eternal now" gave Celtic Christians a belief in the sacredness of all that lives—of all people and of all living things created by God. Everyone and everything was created with a sacred purpose and was understood as purposeful and meaningful additions to this present life. Indeed, all persons and things were created for the purpose of allowing one to live for God in the present and to prepare for the perfected eternal life of the future (Sellner, 1993).

This sense of the sacredness of all persons and things is very important to understanding children's spirituality within Celtic Christian tradition. Since all of life was sacred, all people, even to the youngest, smallest, and weakest, were miraculous gifts from God. One's appropriate response was to rejoice in these gifts, to honor them as given by God, and to relate to them with joy and even wonder. Every created person was a resource—a gift from God clothed in humanity, and created to glorify God. The spiritually aware person would grow in understanding and faith, by rightly relating to God's created beings. All individuals and faith communities had a holy purpose, and it was the responsibility of those who loved God to discover those purposes and live responsibly as God's stewards of every good gift (Newell, 1999).

Certainly God's "good gifts" included children. These "little ones" were holy, meaning "set apart," consecrated by God for God's holy purposes, and not to be taken lightly, dishonored, or dismissed due to their vulnerabilities and seeming lack of certain abilities or powers. Indeed, it was the very vulnerability and weakness of the young that tested the moral probity of their elders. One must love and cherish God's gift of children, if one was to love and cherish God (Mitton, 1996).

Holy Gifts from God: The Blessing of Children

Since children were considered holy gifts from God, their arrivalwas greeted by theirparents and community with much celebration—with a sense of great joy that life was good, for God had blessed the world with another child (Newell, 1999). From the poorest to the wealthiest families, the arrival of a new child was far from an ordinary event. Indeed, it marked a time when present earthly life met with the coming perfected eternal life, for after all, the conception, gestation, and arrival of children pointed to one of the greatest of life's mysteries. God himself came from heaven to earth as an infant, eventually to provide humankind's salvation from sin and the gift of eternal life. It is fair to state that for Christian Celts, each new birth brought remembrance of the Incarnation since the Sacrament of Baptism refers to the Incarnate Christ (Davies & Bowie, 1995). In contrast, the loss of a child in utero, by stillbirth, or in childhood by an accident or disease, brought the greatest of sorrows. With the loss of a child came the loss of the hope and promise of that life—that is, the continuing joy that the child, in youth and as a mature son or daughter, would have brought to his or her parents, family members, and the community. As is common in most cultures, no burial was sadder than the burial of a child.

The Desire for Many Children

The birth of children was welcomed. The possession of a large family was cause for great pride and joy. To have one's supper table full of children of varying ages was the hoped-for picture of family life for those in Celtic tradition. Indeed, the rigors of life in the Celtic Isles were very difficultto endure without a strong family unit. For farmers and dairymen, for shepherds of sheep and goats, and for fishermen on the coasts, a large family provided the means for livelihood since everyone could share in the responsibilities of making a living.[3] In farming families with several children, the numerous dailychores could be shared by all family members, and children had the opportunity to learn responsibility and the values of shared family life and community, while learning life skills (Newell, 1999).

Yet children were not viewed in any sense as employees, that is, asvaluable primarily for the purpose of helping their parents succeed economically. They were enjoyed primarily as people in their own right. Their antics, their playfulness were enjoyed, yet not without the stern discipline that might be needed to eventually train strong wills to react in life's situations with mature actions of morality and responsibility (Mitton, 1996).

The Role of Prayer

Celtic Christian tradition is strongly characterized by the commitment to a prayerful life; not merely set, liturgical prayers at times of formal worship with family or community, but spontaneous prayer, characterized by various charisms: the gifts of God for various kinds of prayer. Upon rising each day, one would say the *caim*, praying for the Holy Trinity to encircle and protect one's life (Doherty, 2003). Blessings were prayed at table before meals; prayers were offered for good weather; prayers of praise and thanksgiving were part of daily life; prayers for protection and for physical healing were common; and prayers were offered at children's morning rising and before every child's nightly rest (Adam, 1994).

Prayers that Shaped Lives

It was not at all uncommon for children in Christian households to participate in family prayer and to be encouraged by their parents to express spoken prayers. Prayer shaped the lives and spirituality of Celtic Christian children since they heard prayer and participated in prayer very often. Children heard words of prayer invoking God the Holy Trinity—Father, Son, and Spirit. They heard prayers that mentioned various saints, and

---

3. The desire for a large family was also connected to Celtic faith in the Roman Catholic tradition. Teachings of the Church encouraged the raising of large families.

prayers that interceded for family members and friends. There were prayers at home, prayers at church, prayers heard in the homes of playmates, prayers in the morning, prayers at work, prayers at meals, prayers at night. The spirituality of prayer for Celtic children was not only expressed as a formal tradition of liturgical prayer, as one might expect in the celebration of the Mass. To the prayers of liturgical tradition were added the informal prayers of mother and father, sisters and brothers, so that, for Celtic children, prayer was often the primary communication of the home, the first heard language at the baptismal font and at the cradle (Newell, 1999).

The sounds of prayer so often heard by children no doubt had a profound effect on how these children viewed life and faith. Daily prayers shaped their understanding of the world and their responses to others and to life events. They were made aware at very early ages that reality existed beyond this world, yet was a reality that touched the world, and was interwoven with this present existence (Denham & Caan, 1998). For Christian Celts, the spiritual was not a "virtual reality" but a "lived reality" (Hunter, 2000). God, although not seen, was understood as always present throughout the day, not merely at special times or special ceremonies.

An Integrated Spirituality

Because prayer in everyday contexts was very natural—a frequent, spontaneous offering of thoughts, feelings, confessions, and intercessions to God—children had the opportunity to view spirituality as an integrated part of every aspect of life. Thus, worship and the whole experience of spiritual life was not confined to formal religious practices such as daily or weekly attendance at Mass or other religious practices. God was understood as present at all times and open to hearing the words and conversations of even the smallest child (Earle & Maddox, 2004).

The rugged visual beauty of the Celtic Isles was an additional element in the spirituality of children. Celtic children were surrounded daily by the beauty of the land, the sky, and the ocean—a pervasive beauty that encouraged their interest in, and expression of, artistic endeavors, and they would often learn various arts (e.g., weaving, knitting, wood sculpting, metalworking, and playing musical instruments) at an early age (Power, 2001).

These children developed an integrated spirituality. Their developing belief in God andtheir understanding of faith was not something removed, different, or separate from mundane life, but faith was surely present at all times in every question, need, joy, and sorrow of this earthly life (Davies & O'Loughlin, 2000).

Holistic Formation of Children

The Christian Celtic worldview integrated the real and unseen with the real and seen. God was real and present, yet unseen. People were real, present, and seen. The Celts embraced this irony, not viewing it as difficult, but simply as a glorious fact that emphasized the wonder and mystery of God (Adam, 1987). This aspect of worldview and theology affected children in a positive way since their parents understood the presence of God's angels to be ever with their little ones. Children would be rocked to sleep with sung prayers and lullabies to comfort them. The oft-heard prayers at home and in church encouraged a formative spirituality that was connected with every context and phase of life (DeWaal, 1999).

Celtic *Cairdeas* and Children's Sense of Belonging

The strong sense of community and the value placed on sharing generous hospitality combined to allow children the inner strength and peace of heart that comes from emotional stability and a sense of belonging, a feeling that one was loved and that one was important to the community. Life may be hard, but life was also very good, for God was present in the *cairdeas*,[4] that is, the fellowship, kinship, and friendship of the community of faith.

Spirituality and God's Gift of Nature

Another important aspect of Celtic Christian spirituality that had much impact on the spiritualityof children was the Celts' appreciation for, and stewardship of, nature. Nature was not worshiped, but the sky, the sea, the trees, the fields, and the weather all pointed to the glory of the Creator. The Celtic respect for nature, as experienced in the context of the Isles, with their unique formations of mountains, crags, brilliant green fields and trees, lakes, and magnificent cliffs, inspired a love for the land (Sellner, 1993).

The beauty and power of nature served as moment-by-moment reminders of the surpassing greatness of God who created these things.

---

4. *Cairdeas*: friendship, from the Old Irish *carides*, as translated by McBain (2007).

One did not take God for granted, for living in theCeltic Isles set one face-to-face with many powerful and changing aspects of nature. The sea was always close by with its winds, waves, and storms; the fields may or may not yield their fruit, depending on conditions; animals must be carefully tended. This close connection with all of nature prevailed among Celtic people (Mitton, 1996). No earthly fortune was as prized as owning land that entailed caring for the land, tending its crops, defending it, and stewarding its resources. Sitting on one's porch, looking out at the sun-kissed fields dotted with black and white sheep, was pure joy and reason to praise God (Davies & Bowie, 1995).

This sense of connectedness with nature served to encourage children in enjoying nature, in appreciating the power, beauty—and even dangers—of nature. They were taught that "bidden or unbidden God is always present."[5] Therefore, their spirituality was holistic—not confined to a building or to a ceremony, but present in all of life, open and waiting for the worshipful heart to be reverent, prayerful, and praising in the presence of God.

Celtic Arts and Children

The Celts, historically, were known as very gifted in the arts. The *Book of Kells*, a collection of illuminated Scriptures, gives evidence of the breathtaking beauty, skilled artistic work, and the embedded humor inherent in Celtic art. Common to the culture were Celtic metalwork, including gold and silver jewelry made with intricate knotting patterns, excellence in weaving the high quality wools of the Celtic Isles into very unique patterns on sweaters, shawls, and other items, and skilled glassblowing to make very delicate artistic works for everyday use and as museum-quality artifacts. The artistic excellence of Celtic design continues to be popular today (Power, 2001).

Children's spirituality was impacted by this love of beauty and the dedication to skilled craftsmanship. It was not at all uncommon for every family to have a gifted person who made some form of artistic contribution to the family or community, perhaps even using the artistic gift to make a living for the family. Closely associated with artisanship was the Celtic love for music—the making of harps, violins, bagpipes, drums, horns, and other instruments. Nearly every family would have an instrument or two, for the

5. From the writings of medieval scholar Erasmus.

Celtic home would have been considered a dreary place without the gift of music. Children were encouraged to learn an artistic skill, were trained in music and the dance from an early age, and were allowed to join with the adults in sharing these gifts (Sawyers, 2005).

Rhythm of Daily Life

The structure and rhythm of daily life in the mostly rural Celtic communities affected both children's and adults' understanding of life and faith—how the seasons, and the work associated with each season, were necessary components of living a joyful and meaningful life. The schedule of everyday life pointed to the schedule of the liturgical year including Advent, Christmas, Epiphany, Lent, Easter, Ascension, and Pentecost.[6] Each of these seasons pointed to specific events in the earthly life of Jesus Christ and helped to teach children and to deepen adults' understanding of the meaning of the Scriptures and a life of reflection, prayer, and charitable service to God and to the community. Through the daily experience of living structured lives, both children and adults learned to practice spiritual disciplines such as prayer, work, service, retreat for rest, and set times for celebration (Adam, 1994).

THE SPIRITUAL CONTRIBUTIONS OF CHILDREN

The Celtic Christian culture viewed the presence and contributions of children as essential to the life and faith of the community. Children were not considered as non-contributing members—as those who would *someday*, but not in childhood, become true and valuable citizens of the community. Rather, they were seen as essential to the community, even as families awaited the time of birth. During pregnancy, mothers were praying and planning for the event of a new member of the community who would bring many gifts to the family and the community simply by his or her presence. The essential personality and uniqueness of an individual child were treasured since each child was created in the image of God and given attributes that were mysterious, remaining to be understood and realized. Parents celebrated the existence of a new child as they listened to each nuance of infant sighs and cries: Who is this child that God has given us? We

---

6. The seasons listed are common to the Western liturgical tradition. The Eastern tradition also includes: Feast of the Cross, Nativity Fast, Nativity, Theophany, Great Lent, Pasch, Transfiguration, Dormition, and Intercession.

watch with anticipation the unfolding of this life; we will give ourselves to the nurture of this child—spiritually, intellectually, physically, emotionally, and relationally (Mitton, 1996).

A primary and needed contribution of children to the wider community and the developing religious culture was the gift of hope. Every child born healthy raised the hopes of the child's mother and father and of the wider community: we have another in our midst; the gifts and graces of God in this child will grow daily. Who knows the miracles God will perform through his life? Who knows that she will not grow to build the community, to honor and to save the community in some way? A child, in Celtic tradition, was a symbol of renewed hope. Births were considered as sure evidence that the civilization was prospering, that families would go on and on through the centuries. The Christian religious culture in the Celtic Isles was dependent upon a hopeful attitude. There were many dangers in life; children brought hope that the community would remain strong and become stronger as time progressed. There would be loving children, grown sons and daughters, to take care of them in their old age and see them through to the "other side" of eternity (Davies & O'Loughlin, 2000).

As the Celtic Isles developed religious cultures, primarily based in Roman Catholic and Protestant theologies and practices, the life of individual faith communities, such as city, town, and village churches, monasteries, and other cloistered or vowed communities, developed along the lines of maintaining traditional rites such as liturgies, sacramental observances, various lay ministries of outreach, witness, and other missional endeavors (Doherty, 2003). Still, the Celtic attitude ("forbid not the little children" for they are God's and God's gift to us) remained intact. Though schooling involving catechism classes required children to spend time away from home in academic and ecclesial settings, they were never too far from home, due to the small geographic area of the Celtic Isles.

The love of home and land remained a strong component of Celtic Christian spirituality, and certainly those loves were cherished by children. Children's joy flourished because adults delighted in the young, and accepted them as full members of family and community. The acceptance of children and delight in their presence were sustaining graces in Celtic communities. The belief that every child should be treasured and nurtured, even when discipline was necessary, strongly influenced a joyful spirituality in children. Celtic Christian children were not strangers to the quality of spontaneous abandonment to joy that is evident in children who are carefree and happy.

Perhaps the greatest spiritual impact of Celtic children upon the wider culture was their joy. Even though a certain darkness existed in Celtic culture when the hardness of island life pressed in with its daily challenges and reminders of disasters in the past, and of possibilities for disaster in the future, the Celtic Christian nature was a hopeful and celebratory one (Earle & Maddox, 2004). The naturalness of children, their tendency to spontaneity and joyful play, is reflected in the general Celtic character as seen in their love of dancing, good humor, and the desire to find joyfulness in everyday life.

The Celtic Christian Tradition and Contemporary Christian Faith Formation

Mitton (1996) explains that Celtic Christianity was characterized by the following basic aspects:

- a high value upon relationships in family and community
- prayer, both liturgical and spontaneous, as appropriate and needed practices relating to every aspect of life
- appreciation of nature—specifically a love for the land and commitment to stewarding the land and its resources
- the practice of generous hospitality
- delight in diverse artistic efforts and expression
- dedication to experiencing the joys of daily life, for example, family sharing at table, at hearth and in work, and
- participation in the life of one's faith community

These values were tenaciously held and faithfully practiced as the spiritual bedrock of life's foundation.

The Contrast

The realities of contemporary life contrast sharply with the Celtic Christian world. Life in the Celtic Isles was, for the most part, a slow-paced, rhythmic existence in which one was very in touch with nature, cognizant not just of one's immediate surroundings but of the farther mountain, or farm, or village. One was concerned that those who lived in these "farther" places be blessed with a good life, for the reality was that whatever came *their* way may come also to one's own place (Joyce, 1998).

Socially, the relative smallness of the Celtic Isles served to emphasize the connectedness or kinship of the Celtic peoples. The sense of family was well developed. Relatives far away were still considered an intimate part of the family and one longed to be with them again. Meal times were vitally important to the development of relationships, to the support and nurture of family life, and to the rest and rhythm of everyday life. One may go away, but one always longed to come back to the hearth of home, to hear again mother's prayers in the dimming light of evening, and to hear father's boots on the early morning hearth as he stoked the early day's fire (Joyce, 1998).

The United States is no longer primarily an agrarian economy, but rather is technological and industrial at its economic base. The country's huge land mass does not encourage lifelong family interaction in which people remain primarily in the same or nearby communities for all of their lives. Metropolitan areas continue to grow larger, while rural areas and wide-open spaces are receding. The opportunity to be face-to-face with the natural environment is limited for many.

In families where one or both parents work away from the home, family members are separated physically from one another much of the day. Continuing advances in technology allow for large spans of time to be spent in electronic pursuits or entertainment, where interaction with family members is often limited. Lifestyles often negate the practice of family meal time, or place this time at restaurants rather than in the home. People often marry those who come from far distances, rather than individuals known to the community. Spiritualities are many and diverse; even among the Christian community there is diversity regarding theology, styles of worship, and other practices.

Could it be that the wide popularity and acceptance of the Irish *Riverdance*[7] company with its original interpretations of traditional Celtic music and dance touches a void in the American postmodern spirit that is reaching out for a spirituality that will again connect people with certain

---

7. *Riverdance* is an Irish dance performance company presenting traditional and contemporary forms of Irish dance and original music in the Celtic tradition. The company has enjoyed wide popularity internationally in presenting live and recorded performances.

absolutes and with an integrated passion for God and for life—a passion that has been stifled, if not abandoned?

Implications for Today

Despite vast differences between the contemporary United States and the Celtic Christian world, the Celtic tradition may yet inform our understanding of what is needed for present day spiritual formation and the spiritual health of children. Practicing the Celtic attitude of joyfully receiving and accepting the community's young members as truly being God's gifts contributes greatly to children's sense of personal worth, acceptance of self, and connectedness to the family unit.

The spiritual language of prayer, understood in Celtic tradition as one's "primary speech" (Ulanov, 1982, p. 1), if heard and taught in children's everyday life experience, develops spiritual awareness and the understanding of God as Person—present and active in one's life. The practice of informal, spontaneous prayer contributes to an integrated spirituality in children in which they begin to perceive that all of life connects with transcendent realities; prayer is not compartmentalized but available and appropriate in everyday life needs and situations.

Encouraging children's understanding of, and love for, nature assists in developing the practice of stewarding natural resources and living with an attitude of thankfulness for the gifts of God.

Participating in the accomplishment of daily family life tasks at the level of effort and responsibility appropriate to children's ages and abilities engenders a sense of community. As children work together with siblings and parents to accomplish practical tasks, they begin to understand a family unit's interdependent responsibility to support life; they also gain a sense of self-worth in realizing that their own efforts contribute to the good of all.

The Celtic tradition of gathering at home, hearth, and table models for contemporary culture the idea that the structures of daily tasks, interaction with family, and the rhythm of shared daily life contribute to a "lived theology" that seeks community with others and understands that support from one's family is essential to spiritual growth.

The Celtic tradition's delight in and practice of diverse artistic endeavors inform the need to encourage children's creative expressions as a process vital to the development of spiritual sensitivity, the practice of worship, and an overarching appreciation of life.

What is the primary truth gained from thelessons of Celtic tradition in regard to children's spirituality? What is the truth gained that is potentially applicable in contemporary contexts? The Celtic tradition embraces a practical theology of inclusivity: the truth that children are not merely immature, spiritually unformed, intellectually naive, wholly dependent persons whose spirituality depends, for its viability and wisdom, upon the adults around them. Rather, Celtic theology celebrates the understanding that "the life of God is born anew among us in the birth of a child" (Newell, 1999, p. 13). Therefore a community is blessed, enriched, and ennobled by the gift of children, and is encouraged to go on in faith. Its people are empowered to be and to do—to achieve their goals as a community—because, by embracing and honoring even its youngest members, the community embraces its own overarching purpose and identity as a commonwealth. The ultimate lesson of Celtic Christian spirituality is that encouraging, not forbidding, the spirituality of "little ones" increases the spiritual vitality of families, of faith communities, and potentially, of whole cultures.

References

Adam, D. (1987). *The cry of the deer: Meditations on the hymn of St. Patrick.* Harrisburg, PA: Morehouse.

Adam, D. (1994). *The open gate: Celtic prayers for growing spirituality.* Harrisburg, PA: Morehouse.

Cahill, T. (1995). *How the Irish saved civilization: The story of Ireland's heroic role from the fall of Rome to the rise of medieval Europe.* New York: Doubleday.

Culbreath, S. A. (2004). *The Celtic nations.* Retrieved March 11, 2007, from http://www.Celticgrounds.com/chapters/c-nations.htm.

Davies, O., & Bowie, F. (1995). *Celtic Christian spirituality: An anthology of medieval and modern sources.* New York: Continuum.

Davies, O., & O'Loughlin, T. (Eds.). (2000). *Celtic spirituality.* Mahwah, NJ: Paulist.

Denham, J., & Caan, H. (1998). *A child's book of Celtic prayers.* Chicago: Loyola.

De Waal, E. (1999). *The Celtic way of prayer: The recovery of the religious imagination.* New York: Doubleday.

Doherty, J. C. (2003). *A Celtic model of ministry: The reawakening of community spirituality.* Collegeville, MN: Liturgical.

Earle, M. C., & Maddox, S. (2004). *Holy companions: Spiritual practices from the Celtic saints.* Harrisburg, PA: Morehouse.

Hunter, G. G., III. (2000). *The Celtic way of evangelism: How Christianity can reach the West . . . again.* Nashville, TN: Abingdon.

Joyce, T. (1998). *Celtic Christianity: A sacred tradition, a vision of hope.* Maryknoll, NY: Orbis.

Leidel, E. M. (2004). *Awakening grassroots spirituality: A Celtic guide for nurturing and maturing the soul.* Lincoln, NE: iUniverse.

McBain, A. *An etymological dictionary of the Gaelic language.* Retrieved March 11, 2007, from http://www.ceantar.org/Dicts/MB2/mb06.html.

Mitton, M. (1996). *The soul of Celtic spirituality in the lives of its saints.* Mystic, CT: Twenty-Third.

Newell, J. P. (1999). *One foot in Eden: A Celtic view of the stages of life.* Mahwah, NJ: Paulist.

Power, P. C. (2001). *Timetables of Irish history. An illustrated chronological chart of the history of Ireland from 6000 BC to present times.* New York: Black Dog and Leventhal.

Sawyers, J. S. (2005). *Celtic music: A complete guide.* New York: Da Capo.

Sellner, E. C. (1993). *Wisdom of the Celtic saints.* Notre Dame, IN: Ave Maria.

Ulanov, A., & Ulanov, B. (1982). *Primary speech: A psychology of prayer.* Atlanta: John Knox.

6 Theological Perspectives on Children in the Church: Reformed and Presbyterian

Timothy A. Sisemore

THE MINISTER INVITES DANIEL AND CAITLYN WOLLEN TO COME TO THE front of the sanctuary, bringing with them four-year-old Anthony and three-month-old Anna. The family stands to the right of the baptismal font of First Presbyterian Church as Reverend Linden, flanked by Elder Mills, explains what is about to take place when he baptizes little Anna. Visitors of differing Christian traditions may not fully understand the meaning of baptism for Presbyterians—why they baptize infants and what it means. Baptism is a Christian rite that has been subject to a variety of meanings and, in the case of the Presbyterian/Reformed tradition, those meanings are rooted in a broad theological system.

The answer to these questions lies in the theological system undergirding the practice. For Presbyterians, and others of the Reformed faith (except a subgroup of Reformed Baptists who part company on this particular doctrine), infant baptism is an outflow of an entire approach to interpreting Scripture and viewing persons in light of it. It is my formidable task to introduce this system and show how children fit into it. This position places great value on children even as it stresses their sinfulness apart from Christ. My goal is that, after reading this chapter, the reader will have a fairly clear understanding of what we believe transpires at Anna's baptism.

It is important to point out that there is not one single Reformed perspective on children in the church. In the broad realm of Reformed theology, I would see myself as having a moderately conservative position. This position assumes the Bible to be authoritative and draws from the mainstream of the theological tradition that runs from the apostles through Augustine, John Calvin, John Knox, and lesser-known theologians since.

To cover our topic, I will set the stage with some background issues that are fundamental in understanding the place of children in Reformed and Presbyterian thinking. I will then present an overview of covenant theology, the overarching framework of how we understand Scripture. After this, I discuss where children fit within covenant theology and how that relates to their place in the ministry and sacraments of the church, and in what sense we see children as spiritual. I conclude our brief overview with some implications of the model for ministry to our little ones.

Foundational Theological Issues

How are we to view children as spiritual beings? Much current thought sees them in relation to adults, and as such they appear innocent and naïve. Given this day of vague ideas, it seems best to turn to Scripture, and to consider what it teaches about children before God, rather than before adults. What we learn here will drive much of the discussion to follow. We will see that the Reformed tradition sees Scripture as teaching a complicated view here, not a simple, sentimental one.

Positive Aspects of the Spiritual Nature of Children

There is no doubt that God values children, and that people are to value them as well. In contrast to the world around them, as exemplified by two separate mass murders (Exod 1:15–22 and Matt 2:13–23), followers of God in biblical times were taught to value children, and they did so. Several specific themes from Scripture detail why this was true.

Blessings, not Burdens

One such theme is that children are a heritage from God. This contrasts with the contemporary notion, among some young couples today, that children are expensive and draining, not to mention distracting from career aspirations and leisure pursuits. Psalm 127:3 speaks of children as a heritage from God, and thus as his blessings to us. This was better understood in earlier times when children were valued for their ability to contribute to family life, helping dad in the fields and mom in more domestic tasks. Automation of household tasks decreases workload in the home, but increases the need for parents to labor outside the home to earn the money to purchase these conveniences. Children also drain financial resources whereas in the past they decreased the need for so much income by contributing to the home economy through their labors. Moreover, some shortsighted contemporary couples lose sight of the heritage they leave behind when they die. Without children, little is left to the world and to the service of the church. On a more selfish level, one wonders who will care for our generation when we age and have produced only a small progeny to attend to us.

Gifts from God

If children are blessings, then they are gifts from God. Deuteronomy 32:39 teaches that God ordains each life. Given the high view of God's providence in Reformed theology, this means each new life is an intentional act of God. Thus, in the Bible, children are signs of God's favor. Genesis 3:15 foreshadows the most anticipated of them all, the birth of Jesus (Luke 1:28–38). A promised child (Isaac) is an essential element of God's covenant with Abraham in Genesis 12 and 17. Samson (Judg 13), Samuel (1 Sam 1), the son of the Shunammite woman (2 Kgs 4:8–37), and John the Baptist (Luke 1:5–24) exemplify this principle. As John Calvin, in his commentary on Psalm 127:3, explains, "Children are not the fruit of chance, but ... God, as it seems good to Him, distributes to every man His share of them" (Calvin, 1984, p. 111). If children are gifts from God, they are to be treasured as such.

Adoption Valued

Adoption is another theme that reflects biblical teaching of the value of children. If for some reason the parents of a child cannot care for him or her, others are encouraged to step in to care for this gift from God. Abraham's heir, prior to his biological son's birth, was to be an adopted child (Gen 15:2–3). Moses, of course, was adopted by Pharaoh's daughter (Exod 2:1–10), and Mordecai adopted Esther (Esth 2:7). This practice formed the background of the great doctrine of adoption. In contrast to popular thought, Scripture does not teach that all people are the children of God. Rather, adoption as sons and daughters is the privilege of Christians alone (Rom 8:15; Gal 4:5; Eph 1:5).

This high view of the value of children led the early church to advocate for little ones, and to condemn the evil practices of exposure and abortion.

There is an important precedent for Reformed theology here, where believers play a role in caring for the children of others and not just those who are biologically their own.

Natural Affection

In God's grace to fallen persons, there is still a normative "natural affection" (Greek *storgos*) of parents for children. We see this when it is negated as God withdraws his restraining grace in Romans 1:31 and there is a loss of it (the English Standard Version, 2001, translates this as "heartless"). I find this most interesting in my clinical work as I see so many parents, particularly fathers, who show little love for their children—particularly after a divorce.

The Moral Nature of Children: Made in the Image of God

It is at this point that Reformed theologians typically make a clarification. Children are greatly valued, but *not* because they are innocents. Following the teaching of Scripture, children are valued because they are made in the image of God. This, of course, is true of all persons beginning with the original couple (Gen 1:26). What exactly it means to be made in God's image is a subject of lively discussion among biblical scholars. One reason it is difficult to determine exactly what this implies is because the image was distorted (but not destroyed) when Adam and Eve sinned. As revelation proceeded, we find that the continuing image is an essential reason we respect other persons. Life is valued (Gen 9:6) and we are to speak kindly to others because of it (Jas 3:9).

The Reformed tradition (e.g., the Westminster Confession, 1981/1646, IV.2) largely follows Calvin's approach in his *Institutes* (1559/1960; I.xv.3), which has been called the restoration hermeneutic. If humans originally were perfectly in God's image, then we might consider that to which we are being restored as God works in us. Hints of this are seen in Ephesians 4:24 and Colossians 3:10. Combining the thoughts of the two verses, we see that we are being remade into the image of the Creator by being renewed in righteousness (holiness) and knowledge. We can infer, then, that the image consists, at least in part, in our being without sin as Adam and Eve were, and in sharing to some extent in the knowledge of God. This means that when children act like Christ, they are doing right, and when they do not, they are doing wrong. Knowledge of God aids in telling the two apart. Children, therefore, are moral creatures.

One might ask what relation this has to the modern use of the term "spirituality" when applied to children. Contemporary use of this term is quite nebulous, largely referring to the child's ability to perceive the nonphysical realm in some vague way. Persons of the Reformed faith are disinclined to use the term in that way. Rather, we say that children are spiritual in the sense that, being made in God's image, they have some perception that there is something more than the physical and have a sense that there is right and wrong. There is then a moral element to spirituality as they apprehend in some way that there is a God and we are to be like him. Sin distorts that sense so that we see children distorting right and wrong to meet their selfish needs, but that sense is present nonetheless. Spirituality will have a more specific sense for believing children, as we will see shortly.

Original Sin and Children

We noted earlier that persons of Reformed faith value children highly, but not because they are innocent. In contrast to much current thought, Reformed theology holds firmly to the historic Christian doctrine of original sin. Numerous texts support this belief (Job 14:4; 15:14; Ps 58:3; Eph 2:3; Rom 5:12–19), but the most straightforward statement comes from the pen of David in Psalm 51:5 as he confesses "Behold, I was brought forth in iniquity, and in sin did my mother conceive me."

To grasp the doctrine of original sin, one must get past the behavioral view of sin as specific acts of willful transgression. This is a widespread view that considers children innocent of sin until they reach an age of accountability and not only do something wrong (like steal a playmate's toy) but also do so intentionally. The doctrine of original sin, in contrast, considers sin as part of our fallen nature so that we are sinful before we commit specific sins in our overt behavior. If you plant an apple tree, you know it to be that by its nature. There is no drama as to what fruit it will bear as it matures; it will manifest its character by producing apples. Even so, children, tainted by original sin, are sinful before they inevitably commit specific acts of sin. Calvin explains, "For even though the fruits of their iniquity have not yet come forth, they have the seed enclosed within them" (1559/1960, II.i.8). There is not a period of innocence destroyed by a willful act, but merely a point where the inevitable becomes manifest. This is how David and other biblical writers knew they were sinful from the start.

What does this imply about children? First, they are naturally inclined to do wrong. They need no instruction to be selfish and demanding. Reformed believers are not surprised when children are naughty. As Paul, quoting Psalm 14, observes, "None is righteous, no, not one" (Rom 3:10b). This explains the recurrent biblical theme of the parents' responsibility to train their children. Discipline is not only necessary, it is also required of godly parents, and without it the child is considered illegitimate (Heb 12:7–11). God thus disciplines us as his children, and he expects us to do the same for ours, as we recognize their sinful inclinations and work to train them in righteousness. This also means that children are in need of a Savior. Parents long for their children to profess and live faith in Jesus Christ as the one who died for their sins and adopts them into his family. The doctrine of original sin is the last preliminary doctrine to our seeing specifically where children fit into the manifestation of Reformed theology in the form of covenant theology.

Children of the Covenant

It is vital that Reformed theology is not a buffet where the theology is built on personal choices from a menu of theological tidbits. Rather, it is a systematic way of organizing all of the teachings of the Bible. This is why one does not ask why Anna is baptized without considering the theological context of the doctrine of infant baptism. As it has developed, covenant theology has clarified the predominant theme of Scripture as the Sovereign God covenanting with a people to accomplish his purposes in the world. Horton (2006) summarizes this by affirming that "Reformed theology is synonymous with covenant theology" (p. 11). Its roots lie, of course, in the Bible, but the themes also appear in Augustine and become more apparent in Calvin. Even early Lutherans held a form of covenant theology (Horton 2006), but its fullest development has been in the Reformed churches. (Readers interested in a more detailed history are referred to the excellent work of Schenck [1940/2003]). We will first look at the basic outline of covenant theology and then consider precisely where children fit in it.

An Overview of Covenant Theology

Covenant theology is not monolithic, and there are many variants in it. I will attempt to trace a moderate line through it. Recent summaries such as Golding (2004) are excellent, but I will draw primarily from the work of Horton (2006).

Covenant theology originates in the notion that God in the Trinity is covenantal by nature as the Father, Son, and Holy Spirit are covenanted in a never-ceasing devotion to one another, and who in divine counsel determined to create covenantal creatures to worship and serve the Triune God. Hence, at its root covenant theology is communal and runs contrary to the individualism of our day. Whereas Westerners stress individual rights and self-determination, God is communitarian and calls individuals only to make them part of his covenant people. Just as the Trinity is three persons yet still one God, so covenant theology views God's people as individuals *and* as a community, balancing these two dimensions.

Scripture unfolds in terms of covenant and this concept can be traced though both testaments. Its form is that of ancient treaties based on the suzerain-vassal relationship (Horton, 2006). A suzerain was a great and powerful king whose relationship with vassals (minor rulers) was like that of a knight and his tenants in the Middle Ages, or more recently, like Moscow and the other nations under the USSR's sphere of control. One was powerful, the other weak. Treaties served to protect the vassal on the condition of loyalty to the suzerain. These were struck not just as business ventures, but involved deep affections.

These treaties began with a prologue detailing what the suzerain had done for the vassal, and so biblical versions began by proclaiming what Yahweh had done for his people—Israel in the Old Testament, the Church in the New. This was followed by stipulations and sanctions for violating these, including both blessings and cursings. The oaths were made by the vassal, not the suzerain, as it was the latter's treaty. There would then be regular public readings to keep the terms fresh in everyone's minds. One can easily see how these ideas are found in the Bible as God deals with his "vassals," albeit in a particularly merciful way. Though many covenants are encountered in the pages of Holy Writ, covenant theology subsumes them under two major ones.

The Covenant of Works or Creation

It is important that the two covenants are not coincidental with the Old and New Testaments as both are found in both. God's original covenant with man is summarized in Genesis 2:16 as God commands Adam, "You may surely eat of every tree of the garden, but of the tree of the knowledge of good and evil you shall not eat, for in the day that you eat of it you shall surely die." There is no discussion, the Suzerain announces his terms: obey and you will live; disobey and you will die. The offer still stands, as Golding (2004) points out, in passages such as Matthew 19:16–17. Adam's failure, however, as representative of humanity, plunged all of his descendents into sin and thus failure to keep terms of the covenant. Those who have not found forgiveness in Christ stand condemned by the terms of covenant of works by the original sin inherited from Adam.

The Mosaic Law also stands in this tradition, though only with regard to our earthly life. The law given at Sinai shows what must be done by human effort to earn blessings, just as Hagar and her son demonstrated Abraham's effort to fulfill God's promise of a child by human effort (Gal 4:21–26). Even to our day, the Ten Commandments and the rest of the moral law point us to what is necessary to earn God's favor, and immediately show us how terribly our efforts fail. The provision of sacrifices in the Mosaic law indicate that now provision must be made for our sin, for we will not be restored to God's favor by our obedience to the stipulations of the covenant.

The Covenant of Grace or Redemption

God first hints that he will open a way to restoration in Genesis 3:15 when he promises to bruise the serpent's head, but the covenant of grace was formally established with Abraham in Genesis 15. The "miracle" child born to Abraham by his wife Sarah showed that God will take the initiative to fulfill the conditions and provide a remedy for sin. This takes the form of a royal grant treaty, an outright gift of the suzerain to the vassal. Ancient treaties were sealed by a self-maledictory oath whereby the vassal cut an animal in half, swearing that he would be suffer the same fate should he break the covenant. Thus, the term often used was to "cut" a covenant (Horton, 2006). Yet, in Genesis 15, God passes between the pieces of the halved animals, performing the self-malediction as the maker of a royal grant treaty.

This was strange indeed as typically these did not contain the oaths as the grantor was not one in the position of doing such. Horton explains,

> It is as if, from the divine side, the covenant made with Abraham is a suzerainty treaty in which God swears unilaterally to personally perform all of the conditions and suffer all of the curses for its violation, but from the human side, the same covenant is a royal grant, an inheritance bestowed freely and in utter graciousness on the basis of the Great King's performance. (pp. 41–42)

Therefore, Paul, in Galatians 4:21–26, links the promise with Sarah and Zion, not Moses and Sinai. God gives faith as a gift; and he, in the person of Christ, pays the penalty for our violations of the covenant of creation in accordance with the promise to Abraham. Wonderful truth indeed!

Children in the Covenant

The covenant with Abraham climaxes in Genesis 17 with the birth of Isaac and the introduction of the covenant sign of circumcision. This demonstrated the communal notion of the covenant, for verse 7 specifies "I will establish my covenant between me and you and your offspring after you throughout their generations for an everlasting covenant." Notice that the sign was not "until Jesus comes" but represented an everlasting promise. Circumcision, not coincidentally, was a form of cutting—cutting the boy in a place that was precisely between the man and woman at the time of intercourse to show the promise to the next generation. Note also that this covenant was built on faith (Heb 11:8–12), not physical birth (or else Ishmael, circumcised though he was, would not have been excluded). The primary circumcision was not of the flesh, but of the heart (Deut 30:6). Yet, the primary source of believers of succeeding generations is the children of the previous generation.

This tradition of the covenant blessings being primarily to the offspring of the faithful reappears in the New Testament as Peter announces at Pentecost (Acts 2:39) that the promise is to "you and your children." Stephen also refers to the covenant of circumcision in his sermon in Acts 7, even calling the skeptics "uncircumcised in heart" (v. 51). Paul himself stresses the continuity of God's people in Ephesians 2:11–22 and relates Old Testament promises to believers (2 Cor 6:14—7:1). Peter joins the chorus as he uses Old Testament titles for God's people and applies them specifically to Christians (1 Pet 2:9–10). But if circumcision is a sign of this ongoing covenant of grace, why is it no longer required in the New Testament? We will now consider where infant baptism fits in the matrix of covenant theology.

Salvation and the Sacraments for Children

Covenant theology prepares us to address the relatively scant biblical data on the vital issues of the sacraments with regard to children. One reason for the diversity of views of children in Christian theologies is that the Bible actually says surprisingly little about them, leaving ample room for interpretive freedom. Yet, an overarching theology such as we have developed gives clarity to these biblical teachings and guides us in understanding where children fit in God's plan. We will look at the sacraments, pausing to consider the salvation of children in the covenant conceptualization as it relates to baptism.

Children and Baptism

The Reformed tradition maintains that the church practices two sacraments, baptism and communion. We now consider how these are understood, and how children fit into their practice.

Circumcision to Baptism

In the Great Commission of Matthew 28:19–20, Jesus declares baptism to be the New Testament sign of the covenant, marking those who are Abraham's descendents because of their faith in him. This makes sense because no longer would a bloody sign be needed: God himself has fulfilled the self-maledictory oath by the suffering and death of Jesus on the cross. This is clarified further in Colossians 2:11–12 where the "circumcision of Christ" is based on "having been buried with him in baptism." If this is true, then baptism would be applied to children as circumcision was in the Old Testament, though now the sign can be placed on girls as well. Baptism, indeed, may be the way in which children of believing parents are set apart (made holy) in 1 Corinthians 7:14. It only makes sense that God would provide a sign of the covenant in the New Testament when he provided one in the Old. Not to have one would seem to leave our children at a disadvantage relative to those in the Old Testament.

Meaning of Baptism

In believer's baptism, the act signifies being dead with Christ and raised to new life and thus reflects the experience the person *has already had* when he or she became a Christian. Clearly infant baptism cannot mean the same thing, so what might it mean? It does not mean, in the Reformed tradition, that the infant is made a Christian by virtue of the baptism alone. Rather, various explanations have been offered. I will mention a few.

According to the position we have already developed, baptism can be seen as a sign that the child is a member of the covenant community. Neilands (1980) explains, "We demonstrate our faith in God's covenant promises when in obedience to God's commandment we bring our children for baptism. By faith we claim these promises for our covenant children" (p. 166).

Baptism may also be seen as a sign of membership in the believing community of the church. Calvin (1559/1960, IV.xvi.9) supports this saying, "The children receive some benefit from their baptism: being engrafted into the body of the church, they are somewhat more commended to the other members. Then, when they have grown up, they are greatly spurred to an earnest zeal for God." The Westminster Confession (1981/1646, XXV. ii) concurs that the visible church is comprised "of all those throughout the world that profess the true religion, together with their children." Baptized children are generally considered to be non-communing members of the church until they are admitted to the Lord's Table as we will see shortly.

Baptism also signifies the forgiveness of sin, but does not accomplish it. Rather, it anticipates the promise in earnest hope that the child will make a profession of faith. (Compare this to circumcision, which was given as a sign in hope that the recipient would participate in the faith of Abraham.) How, then, is the child saved? The process is explained with nuances by different theologians, including the notion of "presumptive regeneration" (Schenck, 2003/1940). Given the Reformed emphasis on God's initiating action, the child need not have a dramatic conversion experience. Schenck notes in his survey of the history of the doctrine that the conversion experience was not an issue until the advent of revivalism during the eighteenth and nineteenth centuries. Even some Presbyterians began asserting that the experience defined the believer. But true Reformed doctrine sees grace as God's gift that may, or may not, come by a dramatic experience. Remember, for example, Samuel, who was called from birth with no period of riotous living (1 Sam 1–3). The prayer at baptism is that through the grace of God and the power of the Word taught at home and in church, the child will never know a day where he or she did not believe self to be a sinner and Jesus to have died to save from sin. Thus, baptism anticipates this in earnest hope as it challenges parents and congregation to prayer for, and nurture of, the child. Yet, the grace of salvation may begin at baptism, as much theology throughout history has seen regeneration as gradual, not sudden. Calvin (1559/1960, IV.xvi.19), again is helpful, "I ask, what the danger is if infants be said to receive now some part of that grace which in a little while they shall enjoy to the full." Furthermore, one sees household conversions throughout Acts (e.g., 11:14; 16:14–15, 31–33; see also 1 Cor 1:16). Can we imagine there were no children in any of these households? That seems unlikely. Infant baptism was thus the nearly universal practice of the early church.

In the Presbyterian understanding, the congregation also takes vows at baptism to assist the parents in the Christian nurture and discipline of the child as the child belongs to the community of faith as well. As Anna's head is dampened with the baptismal water, it symbolizes the covenant of grace and the hope (not certainty) she will grow into faith, with parents and congregation vowing to nurture her toward that end.

We can now add to our understanding of children's spirituality that children of believers are partakers of God's grace in some sense, and given a heightened spiritual consciousness that hopefully leads them to a life of following Christ. Recalling how vague the term is, we admit that children of unbelievers can be "spiritual" in a sense that is outside of Scriptural meanings, as they may be drawn to the ideas of a spirit world, some higher power, or even demonism. Yet, this is far from Christian spirituality and it is something we would want to change for these children rather than endorse as an acceptable alternative spirituality. Christian children are spiritual in their being made in God's image and in their having received God's grace and been drawn into a relationship with him that offers comfort, challenge, and growth while the child responds with worship, prayer, and wonder. The believing child is truly spiritual, living in relationship with God who is Spirit. Such a child is indwelt by the Holy Spirit, prompted by God to obedience, convicted of sin when he or she errs, and loves and abides in Christ.

Children and Communion

The other covenant sign in the Old Testament was that of Passover (Exod 12:1–13). Though the Bible does not specify that children were involved in the meal, it is likely they were. Jesus himself made it clear that the Passover was transformed into the Lord's Supper as he declared the wine to be the "new covenant in my blood" (Luke 22:14). Paul was also explicit in teaching that "Christ, our Passover lamb, has been sacrificed" (1 Cor 5:7), so that the remembrance of this replaces the other sacrament of the Old Testament. Once again, the transformation is from a bloody covenant sign to one without blood as Jesus fulfilled the self-maledictory oath.

The lack of clarity about children's participation in Passover has led to controversy in recent days among conservative Reformed believers regarding whether children should partake of communion. A new group holding to paedocommunion (among other doctrines pertaining to children that are beyond our purview) has garnered considerable attention. If the reader has interest, Wikner (2005) has compiled a series of essays that present this position while a balanced mix of pros and cons may be found in Beisner (2004). I concede many in the early church allowed young children to take communion, and the topic has drawn relatively little attention from Reformed theologians until this recent debate. As always, such controversy will serve the church by refining her doctrine.

I offer two primary reasons why I hold, with most Reformed believers, that children should not be admitted to the table until they can clearly profess their faith. First, in Luke 22:19, Jesus specifically commands that the Supper be done in remembrance of him. Young children, of course cannot do that. Thus, part of the significance of the act is lost. Second, and more poignantly, one is commanded to examine oneself before partaking lest he or she commit sacrilege (1 Cor 11:28–29). So the Larger Catechism (*Westminster Confession*, 1646/1981) Question 177 states that communion is to be served "only to such as are of years and ability to examine themselves." This would clearly exclude young ones.

In the Presbyterian tradition, parents use communion as a teaching time for their children who do not partake. As they mature and make a clear profession of faith, they are encouraged to take a class to prepare them to become communing members of the church. Once ready, children go before the elders of the church and offer their Christian testimony. The leaders and members have seen their lives and can draw from that to see whether the testimony given has taken root in their behavior. Once admitted as communing members of the church, children are welcomed to the Lord's Table.

Ministry to Children in Light of the Reformed Perspective

Covenant theology, by its nature, looks to more than the individual, providing clear roles and responsibilities to insure believers are nurtured within a community. This is particularly true of children, who are viewed as an essential part of the covenant community and of particular families.

The Church as Community

I have stressed that covenant theology is communal, viewing God as covenanting with a people, not simply individuals. As such, children of believing parents are offered a place to belong and to be in relationship. The church can serve as a "parallel society" as Dawn (1997) has argued, providing a context where they see the faith lived in contrast to the godlessness of the world around them.

Children are invited into the worship of the church (Bacon, 1993). Psalm 8:2 sees worship as coming from the mouth of babes, and those in my strand of Reformed theology prefer to have children in the main worship service. Why? For they can worship as well (Exod 12:24–27; Deut 29:10–13, 31:10–13; Josh 8:35; 2 Chr 20:13; Neh 12:43; Ps 148:12; Joel 2:15–16; Matt 21:15–16). If God's covenant people in the Old Testament included children in their worship, it follows we should, too. This teaches children that they are valued members of the community who can contribute and it keeps families together while worshipping. This also affords wonderful opportunities for teaching. Our church, for example, prints children's bulletins to aid in their understanding of what is happening during worship. I am touched when I hear very small children join in with liturgical pieces such as the Doxology.

Reformed theology stresses to children that they belong and contribute. This strengthens their fledgling faith, encourages Christian commitment, and inoculates against the lures of the world. Churches are to seek creative ways to involve children in the work and ministry of the church. From handing out bulletins, to helping with cleanup days, to visiting widows with others, children learn to serve God by serving their fellow believers. Reformed theology also stresses that the church leadership is to oversee families, shepherding families as smaller flocks. They are to pray for, and with, families and their children, and to educate parents on how to raise their children as members of the covenant community.

Reformed Families

The stress on biblical doctrine and the importance of children in Reformed theology means there is a legacy of good instruction on parenting based on it. Examples might include my tracing of the role of the doctrine of original sin in Puritan parenting (Sisemore, 2004) and the work of Koelman (1679/2003), which made practical application of doctrine. More recent efforts have included the popular work of Tripp (1995). I offer a few suggestions from this tradition.

In covenant theology parents make vows at baptism because they are spiritually responsible for the nurture of their children. A cornerstone of this has been the practice of family worship, and numerous helps have been written to promote and guide this important ritual. Early manuals include the fine work of Alexander (1847/1990). Typically, the father is encouraged to lead these times that are, indeed, to be worship, with singing, praying, Bible study, and work on the catechism. These regular times, ideally morning and evening, draw the family before the Lord as a small covenant community, and teach while keeping all of life oriented to worship and service to God.

Part of this responsibility, as mentioned, is catechism. The church throughout its history has sought to be systematic in training its children into the truth of Scripture through catechesis. Sadly, many traditions neglect this great opportunity. Recent works such as Van Dyken's (2000), guide modern families in this ancient practice.

Parents train children in godliness in the day-to-day world of mundane life as they teach not only by correcting sinful behaviors, but also by showing children how to seek God in daily activities and to look for his hand in all of life's events. Here, spirituality meets reality as covenant theology draws from the mandate of Deuteronomy 6:7, in which parents are commanded to teach children "when you sit in your house, and when you walk by the way, and when you lie down, and when you rise." Christian parenting is an active, constant process.

The reader can hopefully now see more of what is going on as Anna is baptized. She is being initiated into a community of faith, receiving God's grace to sharpen her spiritual senses, and receiving the commitment of an entire community to nurture her faith as it becomes manifest. This is, indeed, a blessed event, putting a child's spiritual well-being as a focus of the community's gathering. This is not an insult to the child's free will, but a generous outpouring of God's Spirit in the life of the child and community. I conclude with the words of Clement of Alexandria from ca. AD 200 as he hymned about children and beautifully summarized the place of children in worship:

> Shepherd of tender youth,
> Guiding in love and truth
> Through devious ways;
> Christ, our triumphant King,
> We come thy Name to sing
> And here our children bring
> To join Thy praise.
>
> So now, and till we die,
> Sound we Thy praises high,
> And joyful sing;
> Infants, and the glad throng
> Who to Thy church belong,
> Unite to swell the song
> To Christ, our King. (1942, p. 450)

References

Alexander, J. W. (1847/1990). *Thoughts on family worship.* Pittsburg: Soli Deo Gloria Publications.

Bacon, R. (1993). *Revealed to babes: Children in the worship of God.* Audubon, NJ: Old Paths Publications.

Beisner, E. C. (Ed.). (2004). *The Auburn Avenue theology pros and cons: Debating the federal vision.* Fort Lauderdale, FL: Knox Theological Seminary.

Calvin, J. (1984). *Commentaries* (Vol. 6). Grand Rapids: Eerdmans.

Calvin, J. (1559/1960). *Institutes of the Christian religion* (2 vols., J. T. McNeill, Ed.). Philadelphia: Westminster.

Clement of Alexandria. (1942). Shepherd of tender youth (Henry M. Dexter, Trans.). In *The handbook to The Lutheran Hymnal* (p. 450). St. Louis: Concordia.

Dawn, M. (1997). *Is it a lost cause? Having the heart of God for the church's children.* Grand Rapids: Eerdmans.

Golding, P. (2004). *Covenant theology: The key of theology in Reformed thought and tradition.* Ross-shire, Scotland: Mentor.

Holy Bible, English Standard Version. (2001). Wheaton, IL: Crossway Bibles.

Horton, M. (2006). *God of promise: Introducing covenant theology.* Grand Rapids: Baker.

Koelman, J. (1679/2003). *The duties of parents* (M. E. Ostehaven, Ed., J. Vriend, Trans.). Grand Rapids: Baker.

Neilands, D. L. (1980). *Studies in the covenant of grace: The case for baptizing infants.* Phillipsburg, NJ: Presbyterian & Reformed Publishing.

Schenck, L. B. (1940/2003). *The Presbyterian doctrine of children in the covenant: An historical study of the significance of infant baptism in the Presbyterian church.* Phillipsburg, NJ: Presbyterian & Reformed Publishing.

Sisemore, T. A. (2000). *Of such is the kingdom: Nurturing children in the light of Scripture.* Fearn, Scotland: Christian Focus Publications.

Sisemore, T. A. (2004). From doctrine to practice: The influence of the doctrine of original sin on Puritan child-rearing. In D. Ratcliff (Ed.), *Children's spirituality: Christian perspectives, research, and applications* (pp. 219–32). Eugene, OR: Cascade.

Tripp, T. (1995). *Shepherding a child's heart.* Wapwallopen, PA: Shepherd.

Van Dyken, D. (2000). *Rediscovering catechism: The art of equipping covenant children.* Phillipsburg, NJ: Presbyterian & Reformed Publishing.

Westminster Confession of Faith. (1646/1981). Glasgow, Scotland: Free Presbyterian Publications.

Wikner, B. K. (Ed.). (2005). *To you and your children: Examining the biblical doctrine of covenant succession.* Moscow, ID: Canon.

7 Theological Perspectives on Children in the Church: Anabaptist/Believers Church

Holly Catterton Allen

THE ANABAPTIST VIEW OF CHILDREN STANDS IN UNMISTAKABLE CONTRAST to the predominant view in church history (since Augustine) that children are born inheriting the sin and guilt of Adam. A number of Christian groups hold the view that children, though born with a sinful nature, are not guilty of Adam's sin, and are not lost until they choose to sin. Groups that hold this view are found among a subset of churches that tend to view themselves as neither Catholic nor Protestant (Klaassen, 1981); they are known as Believers Churches.

WHAT ARE BELIEVERS CHURCHES?

In 1967 a conference entitled "The Concept of the Believers Church"[1] was held in Louisville, Kentucky at the Southern Baptist Theological Seminary. A variety of Christian groups were present. Over the last four decades, fifteen Believers Church conferences have been held, the last in September 2004.[2] The conferences were attended by representatives from the following Christian groups: Mennonites, Brethren, Friends, Historic Peace Churches, Churches of Christ, Disciples of Christ, Baptists of different affiliations,

---

1. The phrase *Believers Church* is written sometimes with an apostrophe, i.e., *Believers' Church*. In recent years, the conferences have dropped the apostrophe.

2. The sixteenth Believers Church Conference is to be held at Canadian Mennonite University Institute for Theology and the Church, June 11–14, 2008, in Winnipeg, Manitoba, Canada.

Assemblies of God, Church of God (Anderson, IN), and some Methodists (Durnbaugh, 1998).

Brackney (1998) says, included in the Believers Church tradition

> are a wide range of church communions having their roots either in the sixteenth century Anabaptists . . . or seventeenth century English Separatists. Emphases common to these various traditions include . . . an understanding of the Church as a gathered community of believers baptized as adults upon the confession of faith. (p. ii)

John Howard Yoder describes Believers Churches as those "Christian groups which have insisted upon the baptism of believers, on confession of faith, into visible congregations. . . ." (quoted in Durnbaugh, 1998, p. 220). Though all in this tradition practice believer's baptism, not all of these groups would espouse the view that children are innocent until they choose to sin.

Thomas Finger (2004) identifies a number of contemporary theologians who have been influenced by Anabaptist theology, such as Ron Sider, John Howard Yoder, and James McClendon. These theologians generally focus on the life and teachings of Jesus for their theology in contrast to history or tradition (pp. 60–68).

Historical Development of the Anabaptist/ Believers Church View of Children

The Anabaptist view of children is tied directly to their practice of believer's baptism; they do not practice infant baptism. Though the practice of infant baptism has been an accepted tradition in Catholic and many mainstream Protestant churches for centuries, those in Believers Churches claim that the practice was not of first-century origins and that it developed gradually over the first three or four centuries of Christianity. Aland (1963) and Beasley-Murray (1962) present evidence that the early church did not baptize babies. Aland says, "the first unambiguous testimonies of infant baptism emerge in the middle of the first half of the third century" (p. 79), that believer's baptism was the general practice in the earliest years of the church, and that infant baptism began to be practiced in the second century and only became the accepted practice during the time of Augustine, in the 400s (p. 107).

Finger (2004) says that the Anabaptist biblical argument for believer's baptism (as versus infant baptism) revolves around Jesus' teaching in passages such as Mark 16:16: "Whoever believes and is baptized will be saved . . . " (which implies that the person must be old enough to believe), and Matthew 18:19-20: "Go and make disciples of all nations, baptizing them in the name of the Father and of the Son and of the Holy Spirit, and teaching them to obey everything I have commanded you" (which implies that persons must be old enough to be taught and to obey). Also, throughout Acts, adults are called to repentance and faith before being baptized (e.g., 2:38, 16:31). Other New Testament passages imply that baptism entails an understanding of the process that infants and little children could not possess, for example, Paul's long discussion in Romans 6 or Peter's description that baptism is a "pledge of a good conscience toward God" (1 Pet 3:21).

Yet, infant baptism has been an accepted practice of the Catholic Church and many Protestant churches (Anglican, Episcopalian, Presbyterian, Reformed, Lutheran) for hundreds of years. Scholars and theologians find support for this position both in Scripture and in church history. Strange (1996) makes a case for infant baptism, though he calls it a "tentative" case (p. 102), arguing from patristic writings, particularly by Origen (ca. 185-254) and Cyprian (ca. 200-258), from the example of household baptisms in Scripture (e.g., the households of Lydia and of the jailer in Acts 16), and from the influence of the rite of circumcision. However, though scriptural and historical evidence can be gathered, the main discussion regarding infant baptism centers on theological premises regarding the status of children before God. For the purposes of this study of children and spirituality, infant baptism is important mostly as it relates to this underlying issue. Therefore, in dealing with issues related to children as spiritual beings, the complex issue of original sin and the sin nature of persons must be addressed.

Augustine (354-430) developed his theology of original sin over a period of decades, as he debated with those who differed with his ideas (Stortz, 2001). Some who opposed Augustine allowed infant baptism for the purpose of admission into the church, but denied that "in the case of children baptism conferred the remission of sins, because [they] believed that children had no sins to be remitted" (Strange, 1996, p. 95). Chrysostom (c. 347-407), priest of Antioch and bishop of Constantinople, believed "that newborn infants are innocents wholly without sin" (Guroian, 2001,

p. 70), though he did believe that Adam's sin brought death to his progeny and weakened their capacity to grow into God's likeness.

Chrysostom is a representative voice of the Greek patristic writers who interpreted the fall "as an inheritance essentially of mortality rather than sinfulness" (Meyendorff, 1976, p. 144). The Greek patristic theologians' view arises from their translation of Romans 5:12: "Therefore just as sin entered the world through one man, and death through sin, in this way death came to all men because all sinned." Meyendorff explains that they translated the last phrase *eph no pantes hemarton* correctly as "because all sinned" (p. 144). He further says that Latin patristic theologians, for example, Augustine, incorrectly translated this section in Latin as *in quo omnes peccaverunt*, which means "in whom all sinned" (p. 144). Thus, the Eastern Orthodox tradition has seen "death as the punishment of Adam's sin passed on to all his descendants," whereas the Western Catholic and many Protestant traditions have "stressed that sin is passed on by Adam to all of humankind, and with its guilt also" (Guroian, 2001, p. 68). This segment of the church, the Eastern Orthodox, supports the innocence of infants and children, though Orthodox Christians practice infant baptism as entrance into the church.

But in the West, the doctrine of original sin was largely unopposed for a thousand years until the time of the Reformation, when reformers, such as Luther in his plea of *sola scriptura*, led the way for others to reconsider long-held church traditions and reexamine Scripture. Anabaptists were convinced that only persons who could actually believe should be baptized, and their theology regarding the status of children was developed in light of this conviction. Thus, Anabaptists of the sixteenth century moved away from the concept of original sin and guilt, viewing children as having a sinful nature, but not accountable for their sins until young adulthood. They came to be known as Anabaptists, or "re-baptizers," because adults who were baptized at this time were actually *re*-baptized (having already been baptized as infants). Anabaptists refused to baptize infants; consequently they faced immediate and severe opposition from the Catholic Church and from major Protestant reformers. If babies were born in sin, bearing the guilt of Adam (as was believed), they faced eternal damnation if they died unbaptized. Thus, the Anabaptist view of children was considered heretical (Miller, 2001).

Anabaptists developed their beliefs about children around their understanding of Jesus' teaching and treatment of children. Citing Matthew 3:4 and Matthew 19:14, Dirk Philips said (1564/1981):

> Since therefore Christ sets the children before us as an example and says that we should become like children, and humble ourselves, it follows without contradiction: first, that children ... are innocent and judged by God to be without sin; second that there is ... good in children ... which makes them pleasing to God so long as they remain in it. (p. 186)

An earlier Anabaptist, Hans Schlaffer (1527/1981) wrote along the same lines:

> Christ says about the children that the kingdom of heaven is theirs or of such, and that whoever receives one of them receives him. They belong to him. Whatever you do to the least of these my own, says the Lord, you have done it to me. Now if they are his, the dear little children are not lost. (p. 171)

Schlaffer continues:

> You exorcise and cast the devil out of the children before you baptize them. How do you know that the child only just born in all innocence is possessed by the devil? ... Take note that the Lord says concerning the children that their angels always see the face of their Father in heaven. Now if the children have angels that always see the face of God, it is impossible that they have a devil who is excluded from the face of God. That is why they are called children of their Father in heaven. (p. 171)

Pilgram Marpeck (1532/1981), one of the most well-known among the early Anabaptists, offered similar support for this view of children as innocent—as being in God's kingdom:

> In the New [Covenant], the children are pronounced holy without baptism, without sacrifice, without faith or unfaith; they are simply received by Christ. ... Children and the retarded are not required to believe or disbelieve these words. ... Christ has accepted the children without sacrifice, without circumcision, without faith, without knowledge, without baptism; he has accepted them solely in virtue of the Word: "To such belongs the kingdom of heaven." (p. 176)

Menno Simons (1496–1561), a former Catholic priest who became an Anabaptist in 1536, believed that children exhibited a "complex innocence" (Miller, 2001, p. 194), an innocence "tempered with the acknowledgment of an inherited Adamic nature predisposed to sinning" (p. 194). Though

Simons uses some Reformed language, he rejects the idea of total depravity. Miller says, "Simons delineates between a *nature* predisposed toward sin and actual *sinning*, disallowing the former to obliterate childhood innocence and identifying only the latter as that for which believers have responsibility before God" (p. 201). Simons rejects the idea that children are guilty of the sin of Adam, and calls them innocent, yet he uses the same language of the Reformers to describe their salvation—that they are saved through grace, through the blood of Christ. "Children of Christians 'are saved, holy, and pure, pleasing to God, under the covenant and in His church'" (Simons, *Complete Works*, p. 133, quoted in Finger, 2004, p. 169).

Finger (2004) sums up Anabaptist thought on the issue in this way:

> Anabaptists commonly taught . . . that children were in God's safe-keeping until they intentionally sin. This was sometimes based simply on Jesus' acceptance of them (e.g., Mt. 19:13–15). This could lead to regarding children as wholly innocent, as "born with the purity of creation." Moreover, since sin (like salvation) must involve voluntary action, infants could not really bear guilt for it. (p. 169)

Contemporary Groups who Espouse this View

Several denominations may be legitimately regarded as the successors of the Continental Anabaptists—Amish, some Baptists, Brethren, Hutterites, Mennonites, Bruderhof Communities, and Quakers. Sometimes direct lineal descendants (e.g., Mennonites and Amish) are differentiated from spiritual descendants (e.g., various Brethren groups, some Baptists, and Restoration Movement churches).

Lineal Descendants

Among the direct Anabaptist descendants today are the Mennonites. Marlin Jeschke (1983), a contemporary Mennonite, says, "our job . . . is not to counter God in trying to make sinners or saints out of what he has ordained to be innocent" (p. 104). Jeschke says that Christianity has tended either to condemn children as culpable sinners or to neglect their nurture because they are already saved due to infant baptism (p. 104). He says, "We must resist the temptation . . . to place the human race into only two classes, the saved and the lost. We are required to recognize also a third class, the innocent . . . " (p. 104).

Spiritual Descendants

Among the spiritual descendants of the Anabaptists are a variety of Baptist fellowships, various Brethren groups, and Restorationist churches that include the Churches of Christ, Christian Churches, and the Christian Church (Disciples of Christ).

Baptist Groups

The groups who are now our modern-day Baptists were forming in the seventeenth century. One group, now known as the General Baptists, followed closely the teachings of these earlier Anabaptists:

> What chiefly distinguished the two main sorts of English Baptist (each with strong Dutch connections) had to do with the freedom of the unregenerate human will. The Baptist Confession of 1611, drafted in twenty articles by John Smyth, denied any "sin of origin or descent" because all sin is "actual or voluntary," and it affirmed that "men by the grace of God are able . . . to repent," while alternatively they are able to resist the Holy Spirit. (McClendon, 1998, p. 184)

The statement below from the publication, *Treatise of the Faith and Practices of the National Association of Free Will Baptists* (2001), indicates general agreement also:

> We believe that all children dying in infancy, having not actually transgressed against the law of God in their own persons, are only subject to the first death, which was brought on by the fall of the first Adam, and not that any one of them dying in that state shall suffer punishment in hell by the guilt of Adam's sin for of such is the Kingdom of God. (Article VI, p. 8)

Ingle (1970), who was a Southern Baptist seminary professor, says that all persons "are born with a tendency toward sin: all are destined to sin. However, the individual is not responsible for the sins of the [human] race or his inherited nature" (p. 153). Ingle says that the person "becomes an actual sinner in the eyes of God when, as a morally responsible person he chooses sin and rebels against God. Thus there is a time between birth and moral accountability when the child is not guilty for sin" (pp. 153–54).

Utilizing Donald Durnbaugh's criteria, all Baptist churches would be considered Believers Churches; however, many Baptists, though they practice believer's baptism, hold closely to the doctrine of original sin, and would not align themselves with Anabaptist thought regarding the innocence of children.

Brethren

Brethren Churches are among those who trace their ancestry to the Anabaptist movement. There are six branches of the Brethren heritage, one of which is the Church of the Brethren. The following statement appears in the *Church of the Brethren Handbook*:

> All human beings are born with a sinful nature (Psalm 51:5), and in the case of those who reach moral responsibility, become sinners in thought, word, and deed (Isaiah 6:5; Romans 5:12, 19; Romans 1:18–32). When David spoke of being conceived "in sin" (Psalm 51:5), he spoke not of the act of conception, but of the inherited bias to sin that is transmitted at conception. (Basic Beliefs Within the Church of the Brethren, n.d.)

Dale Stoffer, Professor of Historical Theology and Academic Dean at Ashland Theological Seminary in Ashland, Ohio, says Brethren Churches in general follow the Anabaptist teaching concerning children. Stoffer says that all branches of the Brethren heritage "would agree that children are in a state of grace/innocence until the age of accountability" (email communication, 9-13-07), though they might develop the concept of innocence in a different way from modern day Mennonites or others.

Restorationist Churches

Another group of Believers Churches that views children as innocent (yet claims no direct lineage to Anabaptism) is known as the Restoration Movement (or the Stone-Campbell Movement), a nineteenth-century American movement whose goal was to restore the New Testament church. Churches of Christ and Independent Christian Churches are among the churches in this movement. According to Alexander Campbell (1835/1956), the most influential founding leader of this group, "None are punished with everlasting destruction from the presence of the Lord but those who actually and voluntarily sin against a dispensation of mercy under which they are placed" (p. 16).

This view of children was a basic understanding in Restorationist churches throughout the twentieth century. A well-known periodical during the movement, *Christian Standard,* published an article by James Van Buren (1949) in which he says, "Infants do not need to be saved, since they are not lost until they sin against God of their own volition" (p. 13). Recent and current books on children and baptism promote similar ideas (see e.g., Hicks & Taylor, 2004).

A Third Way

A significant difficulty in discussing the Anabaptist view of the innocence of children is that Christians, for the last century or so, have been accustomed to a discussion with only two views of human nature represented. The first view, that children are born in sin, bearing the guilt of Adam, has been the predominant Christian perspective. The second view, Jean-Jacques Rousseau's philosophical teaching that children are inherently good, has prevailed in progressive education circles and, to some degree, the more liberal strand of Christianity has adopted it as well. There has been little room for a third category, the Anabaptist perspective, that upholds a strong view of sin's power and radical dependence upon God's grace for salvation while moving away from the concepts of original sin and total depravity.

Theological Conundrums

Those who view children as innocent face a number of theological concerns. One significant question revolves around children's status in the church. "Repudiating infant baptism does not itself banish the questions that arise on this score. Are unbaptized children within the community to be considered simply as pagans, until they make a positive voluntary commitment?" (Vandervelde, 1998, p. 213).

Age of Accountability

If one decides that children are born with a sin nature, but are not guilty of Adam's sin, that is, they are innocent until some later date when they choose to sin, one is left with the conundrum of discovering what that age is. The phrase that the Believers Church tradition uses to discuss this problem is "the age of accountability."

Not surprisingly, there are a variety of opinions on this concept. Most agree that a specific age cannot be determined, especially since none is designated in Scripture, though many offer suggestions. Among Anabaptist-

Mennonite groups the age of accountability has varied widely. Miller (2001) reports that early Anabaptist leaders such as Hans Hut (d. 1527), Ambrosius Spittelmaier (c. 1497–1528), and Hans Schlaffer (d. 1528) "thought that adults aged thirty and over qualified for believer's baptism" (p. 206), basing this idea on the age of Jesus at his baptism.[3] Simons is reluctant to give a specific "age of discretion" (p. 203), though he does say children need to be old enough to understand the gospel of grace, certainly older than two, three, or four (p. 204). Miller reports that Mennonites today tend to be baptized in their mid-to-late teens (p. 206).

Marlin Jeschke, the contemporary Mennonite mentioned earlier, discusses the concept of age of accountability in his book *Believer's Baptism for Children of the Church* (1983), in which he offers an alternative approach to conversion for children who are raised in a believing community. Jeschke notes particularly that, for children raised in the church, the move from innocence to accountability is usually a process taking place over weeks, months, or possibly years. He makes a strong case for the concept of an "age of accountability," noting that even "pedobaptist churches recognize it in the practice of confirmation ... Judaism has its 'bar mitzvah' or 'bat mitzvah,' [and] secular society makes a definite distinction between juveniles and adults in courts of law" (p. 112). Taking psychological development into consideration, as well as social and cultural norms, Jeschke settles on adolescence as the most appropriate period of life for moving into moral responsibility.

Groups other than Mennonites address the dilemma of the age of accountability. Some identify fairly young ages. Inchley (1976), in *Kids and the Kingdom*, suggests somewhere between seven and eleven (p. 163); Hendricks (1970) recommends nine and above (p. 95); and Zuck (1996) gives examples of some who place the age much earlier, even at three or four (p. 240). In Churches of Christ and Christian Churches the average age for "conversion" is twelve, according to a survey in the 1990s (Lewis, Dodd, & Tippens, 1995, p. 48).

The Role of Baptism

Anabaptists themselves had differing views of baptism: "Marpeck shared with other Anabaptists the view that regeneration began prior to baptism

---

3. This very mature age for accountability may also have been influenced by the fact that during the time of these early Anabaptists, adults who were re-baptized risked martyrdom.

and that baptism was an outer sign of the new birth. However, Marpeck went on to contend that the sign participated in the reality of regeneration" (Miller, 1986, p. 19). Menno Simons's view of baptism has held most sway—"that baptism follows regeneration rather than effecting it" (p. 21). It is a symbol of obedience to Christ's command. Although there were differing views, all agreed it was very important. Miller says the 1527 Schleitheim Articles indicate that baptism should be given to those:

1. Who have been taught repentance and the amendment of life
2. Who believe that their sins have been removed through Jesus Christ
3. Who express their desire to walk in newness of life, namely to take up what came to be called discipleship or following Christ in life
4. Who so understand baptism, desire, it, and ask for it. (p. 17)

Prominent sixteenth-century Anabaptists indicated in their writings a basic pattern of coming to salvation; the pattern included, "preaching/teaching, followed by a response of faith, inner regeneration, a commitment to discipleship, and baptism and a public confession of faith as a sign of obedience to the command of Christ" (Miller, p. 17).

According to Brown (1986), Brethren Churches "have associated baptism with repentance and the forgiveness of sins" (p. 32). Brethren also view baptism as a call to discipleship, a public covenantal act, and an ordination to public ministry (pp. 32–33).

Jeschke (1983) describes baptism in a variety of ways. He says that it is a command of the Lord and a mark of discipleship (p. 35); he furthers says that it signifies "repentance and reception of the word of the gospel, it offers forgiveness of sins and the gift of the Spirit . . ." (p. 36). He quotes Beasley-Murray, saying, "baptism is presupposed as normative for the acceptance of the Christian faith and entrance into the church. . . . The significance attributed to baptism by the apostolic writers shows that they viewed it as a means of grace" (p. 41).

Restorationist churches reflect a similar high view of baptism. John Mark Hicks and Greg Taylor (2004), authors of a recent book on baptism from the Church of Christ perspective, say in the preface: "Baptism is a performative, or effectual, sign through which God works by his Holy Spirit to forgive, renew, sanctify, and transform. It is a symbol by which we participate in the reality that it symbolizes" (p. 11). Furthermore, they say that baptism is also a command, but they add, "While baptism is both a sign and a command, it is more. Baptism points beyond itself and effectually participates in God's transforming work" (p. 11).

Brethren, Mennonites, Restoration churches, and others with a general Anabaptist perspective tend to have high views of baptism, connecting it directly with faith, repentance, God's transforming work, and a sense of entering a community of believers as well as full commitment. Some are concerned that the practice has become attenuated in some Believers Churches—that it is almost an afterthought. Marlin Miller (1986), who wrote the Mennonite chapter in the book from the Believers Church Conference on baptism in 1984, notes that the recent emphasis in American revivalism on crisis conversion "has diminished both the direct relation between baptism and church membership and the understanding of faith as a commitment to Christian discipleship" (p. 23).

Implications for Children's Spirituality

Having described this third way of considering the status of children before God, what would this perspective say about children and their spirituality? If children are innocent, covered by God's grace until the age of accountability—possessing a sinful nature, but not inheriting Adam's guilt—how does this affect their relationship with God?

Developmental Implications

If children are considered "safe," early conversion would not be seen as a pressing goal, and the norm for conversion would be older, not younger. Jeschke (1983) proposes adolescence as an appropriate age, supporting his judgment, particularly for Americans, in this way:

> In a society in which youth are kept in school by law until the age of sixteen, cannot hold a job or get a driver's license until sixteen, cannot vote until eighteen, and are not usually allowed to live on their own until out of high school, we are deluding ourselves if we ask them to make authentic decisions with respect to personal faith at a much earlier age. (p. 113)

Brown (1986) concurs: "Since the age of puberty has been a crucial age in the history of culture, it is reasoned that the church should not ignore it. It has been . . . the time when children aspire to join the adult world, when they are anxious to do what we want them to do. For this reason it is an easy time for us to invite children to become adult members" (p. 36).

Erik Erikson (1963) says that young people ages thirteen to nineteen are in the "Identity vs. Role Confusion Stage"; at this adolescent stage young people are determining identity—struggling to answer questions, such as Who am I? Where do I belong? What groups am I part of? Martin (1981), in *Identity and Faith*, sees this stage as the key time for children to work out "the potential split between 'tribe' and their own personal autonomy. . . . The child wants and needs the love and security of the family, but does not want to sacrifice his or her individuality for it. This is an acute process for the adolescent" (p. 45).

Brown (1986) notes that the age of puberty has been "the time of bar mitzvah, the first communion, confirmation, and baptism in religious communities" (p. 36). Martin (1981) agrees that "adolescence (at or about the age of puberty) is a significant age for religious experience" (p. 73). He also recommends taking cues from the bar mitzvah or bat mitzvah, when the Jewish teen becomes a fully responsible person, noting that from the Jewish perspective the child, before thirteen, may "receive the merits of his father and is also liable to suffer for parents' sin. After that, each one bears his own sin" (p. 82). The point here is that with the focus on a later age, perhaps puberty or adolescence, the Anabaptist view of children as safe removes the need to press on younger children the sense of urgency to "get saved," which may be considered to be developmentally inappropriate.

Dealing with Guilt

Conscience is tied also to development. Avoiding wrong and doing right in childhood usually entails the desire to avoid punishment; there is rarely authentic inner motivation. Infantile guilt is typically based on "fear, shame, and doubt" (Martin, 1981, p. 58). Martin goes on to say that mature guilt is a "poignant suffering, seldom reducible in an adult to a fear of or experience of punishment. It is rather a *sense of violated values,* a disgust of falling short of the ideal self-image" (p. 58). This type of guilt is unusual in a child; it is the type of guilt associated with a mature conscience and mature faith. It goes beyond the "fear of punishment as a motivation for right living" (p. 58).

Kohlberg's (1973) work indicates that someone who has developed this "mature guilt" has reached the "principled level." Development of this principled level appears about the same time as adolescence. Martin (1981) says the age of accountability fits here—freedom of personal choice can actually emerge here: "True freedom of choice comes when the person chooses values without having to link them to reward and punishment alone" (p. 59).

Early conversions may be primarily associated with guilt and fear of punishment (see e.g., May, Posterski, Stonehouse, & Cannell, 2005, p. 64). These types of conversion do not tend to nurture a child's relationship with God; instead they can become an impediment. Children typically do not develop a "principled conscience" in a day—it is a gradual process. This is also often the case with coming to faith. As children move toward a time when they are accountable to God for their disobedience, deeper study concerning Jesus' death and resurrection, salvation, and lifetime commitment to God are needed.

Role of Baptism

Ultimately the relationship that is nurtured between God and the child should yield in the child a desire to commit to Christ. When that time comes, baptism is the sign, the symbol, the event marking that commitment. Some churches hold a high view of baptism; others have relegated its importance to that of a minor event. George (1986), a Southern Baptist, recommends making baptism a significant family occasion, preceded by a period of catechism (serious instruction), including an emphasis on the Trinitarian nature of baptism and "laying on of hands . . . as a kind of universal ordination. It is a liturgical enactment . . . of the priesthood of all believers" (p. 50). He advocates baptizing out of doors to enhance its significance and emphasize its theological importance.

"We need to affirm that while baptism is not a magical rite, it is nonetheless a very important, sacred, and serious act of incorporation into the visible community of faith. Not only are we saying something to God in baptism, but *God is also saying and doing something for us in baptism*" (George, 1986, p. 50, emphasis added). Baptism is a momentous spiritual marker in the relationship that has been growing between the person and God, a time when the person recognizes that relationship with God entails commitment, cost, and a radical lifestyle. George says that baptism needs to be a "central moment of confession" (p. 51). It should carry the sense that this young person has taken on Jesus as personal Savior—yes—but also that he or she is committing to a life of discipleship in this community of believers.

Concluding Remarks

The views about children outlined in this chapter were controversial in the Anabaptists' day and still are today. Yet, the idea that children are safe, covered by God's grace until the age of accountability, offers a unique perspective on children and their relationship with God. Developmental issues regarding guilt and conscience can be reconsidered, as well as children's status in the kingdom of God.

There is one aspect of the Anabaptist view of children that Christians across a wide spectrum can embrace. Christians in the Anabaptist tradition have historically included children intentionally in their church practices, taking their cues from the Old Testament pattern of children's presence at the annual feasts, from the New Testament church where children were present in the house churches, and, most importantly, from Jesus' treatment of children. When the disciples wanted to send the children away Jesus took them, held them, laid his hands on them, and blessed them. He said, "Let the little children come . . . " (Matt 19:14). This particular pericope was a key passage for the early Anabaptists.

Probably nothing will foster children's relationship with God more than their being among adults who hold them, lay hands on them, bless them, and pray for them and with them. Nurturing children of the church toward the time when they will commit their lives to Christ requires, more than anything else, a faith community where children and committed adult believers are regularly and intentionally *together*. As Eddie Prest (1993) says: "the optimal spiritual impact upon children will take place in a warm, belonging, caring, and concerned interaction with the gathered people of God" (p. 20).

References

Aland, K. (1963). *Did the early church baptize infants?* (G. R. Beasley-Murray, Trans.). Reprinted, Eugene, OR: Wipf & Stock, 2004.

Brethren Revival Fellowship. (n.d.) Basic beliefs within the Church of the Brethren, *Church of the Brethren handbook*. Retrieved August 14, 2007, from http://www.brfwitness.org /Articles/1968v3n2.htm

Beasley-Murray, G. R. (1962). *Baptism in the New Testament*. Reprinted, Eugene, OR: Wipf & Stock, 2006.

Brackney, W. H. (Ed.). (1998). *The Believers Church: A voluntary church.* Kitchener, ON: Pandora.

Brown, D. W. (1986). The Brethren. In M. D. Strege (Ed.). *Baptism and church: A Believers Church vision* (pp. 29–37). Grand Rapids: Sagamore.

Campbell, A. (1956). *The Christian system in reference to the union of Christians, and a restoration of primitive Christianity, as plead in the current reformation.* Nashville, TN: Gospel Advocate.

Durnbaugh, D. (1998). Afterword: The Believers Church conference. In W. H. Brackney (Ed.), *The Believers Church: A voluntary church* (pp. 217–25). Kitchener, ON: Pandora.

Durnbaugh, D. F. (1968). *The Believers Church: The history and character of radical Protestantism.* Scottdale, PA: Herald.

Erikson, E. H. (1963). *Childhood and society* (2nd ed.). New York: Norton.

Finger, T. N. (2004). *A contemporary Anabaptist theology: Biblical, historical, constructive.* Downers Grove, IL: InterVarsity.

George, T. (1986). The Southern Baptists. In M. D. Strege (Ed.), *Baptism and church: A Believers Church vision* (pp. 39–51). Grand Rapids: Sagamore.

Guroian, V. (2001). The ecclesial family: John Chrysostom on parenthood and children. In M. J. Bunge (Ed.), *The child in Christian thought* (pp. 61–77). Grand Rapids: Eerdmans.

Jeschke, M. (1983). *Believer's baptism for children of the church.* Scottdale, PA: Herald.

Hicks, J. M., & Taylor, G. (2004). *Down in the river to pray.* Abilene, TX: Leafwood.

Inchley, J. (1976). *Kids and the kingdom.* Wheaton, IL: Tyndale.

Ingle, C. (1970). Moving in the right direction. In C. Ingle (Ed.), *Children and conversion* (pp. 142–57). Nashville: Broadman.

Klaassen, W. (1981). *Anabaptism: Neither Catholic nor Protestant* (Rev. ed.). Waterloo, ON: Conrad.

Kohlberg, L. (1973). *Collected papers on moral development and moral education.* Cambridge, MA: Center for Moral Development and Education, Harvard Graduate School of Education.

Lewis, D., Dodd, C., & Tippens, D. (1995). *The gospel according to Generation X: The culture of adolescent belief.* Abilene, TX: Abilene Christian University Press.

Marpeck, P. (1981). Confession. In W. Klaassen (Ed.), *Classics of the Radical Reformation: Vol. 3. Anabaptism in outline; Selected primary sources* (pp. 176–77). Scottdale, PA: Herald.

Martin, M. (1981). *Identity and faith: Youth in a Believers Church.* Scottdale, PA: Herald.

May, S., Posterski, B., Stonehouse, C., & Cannell, L. (2005). *Children matter: Celebrating their place in the church, family, and community.* Grand Rapids: Eerdmans.

Meyendorff, J. (1976). *Byzantine theology: Historical trends and doctrinal themes.* New York: Fordham University Press.

Miller, K. G. (2001). Complex innocence, obligatory nurturance, and parental vigilance: "The child" in the works of Menno Simons. In M. J. Bunge (Ed.), *The child in Christian thought* (pp. 194-226). Grand Rapids: Eerdmans.

Miller, M. E. (1986). The Mennonites. In M. D. Strege (Ed.), *Baptism and church: A Believers Church vision* (pp. 15-28). Grand Rapids: Sagamore.

Philips, D. (1981). Christian baptism. In W. Klaassen (Ed.), *Classics of the Radical Reformation: Vol 3. Anabaptism in outline: Selected primary sources* (pp. 185-87). Scottdale, PA: Herald.

Prest, E. (1993). *From one generation to another.* Capetown: Training for Leadership.

Schlaffer, H. (1981). A short and simple admonition. In W. Klaassen (Ed.), *Classics of the Radical Reformation: Vol. 3. Anabaptism in outline; Selected primary sources* (pp. 171-72). Scottdale, PA: Herald.

Stortz, M. E. (2001). "Where or when was your servant innocent?": Augustine on childhood. In M. J. Bunge (Ed.), *The child in Christian thought* (pp. 78-102). Grand Rapids: Eerdmans.

Strange, W. A. (1996). *Children in the early church: Children in the ancient world, the New Testament and the early church.* Carlisle, Great Britain: Paternoster.

Strege, M. D. (Ed.). (1986). *Baptism and church: A Believers Church vision.* Grand Rapids: Sagamore. Papers presented at the Seventh Conference on the Believers Church, Anderson School of Theology, Anderson, IN, June 5-8, 1984.

National Association of Free Will Baptists (U.S.). (2001). *Treatise of the faith and practices of the National Association of Free Will Baptists.* Antioch, TN: Executive Office of the National Association of Free Will Baptists.

Van Buren, J. G. (1949, January 1). Why not "baptize" babies? *Christian Standard,* 13-14.

Vandervelde, G. (1998). Believers Church ecclesiology as ecumenical challenge. In W. H. Brackney (Ed.), *The Believers Church: A voluntary church* (pp. 199-215). Kitchener, ON: Pandora.

Zuck, R. B. (1996). *Precious in his sight: Childhood and children in the Bible.* Grand Rapids: Baker.

PART II

Best Practices for Nurturing Children's Spiritual Development

Prayer,

Storytelling

& Reading

8 Unfettered Wonder: Rediscovering Prayer Through the Inspired Voices of Children[1]

T. Wyatt Watkins

I APPROACH THIS CHAPTER FIRST AND FOREMOST AS A FATHER, SECONDLY, as a pastor-theologian, and thirdly, as a pilgrim seeking guidance along my spiritual path. As a father, I have found that no other experience of parenthood surpasses the intensity of satisfaction I derive from the ritual of prayer undertaken with my children. This has come as somewhat of a surprise to me, due in part to the role of prayer in my chosen profession. As a Protestant pastor, I have given in at points to a profound cynicism about the efficacy of communal prayer as practiced in the institutional church, even prayer's very legitimacy as a corporate spiritual discipline. Years of experiencing prayer carried out in an obligatory, ritualistic fashion have taken their toll. Among my colleagues in ministry, I am not alone in this sentiment.

When, for two years, I left pastoral ministry for other pursuits, it dawned on me that for the first time in my adult life no one was "paying" me to pray, and moreover, that the crucible of this daily ritual of the institutional church had, in fact, been an encumbrance to my own spiritual health. I sought to recover an authentic practice of prayer almost in the way a veteran of war seeks to recover the depths of a soul forsaken in the heat of combat. I attempted this through the spiritual disciplines of silence, meditation, journaling, and the like. But it was from an unexpected source

---

1. Portions of this chapter were published in *What Our Kids Teach Us About Prayer* (Crossroad, 2005) by T. Wyatt Watkins. For a further discussion of children's prayer lives, please refer to the Crossroad volume. Reprinted here by permission from Crossroad.

that I gradually reconnected with the richer, deeper contours of my spiritual being. I began to pray nightly with my children, and to do so with an earnestness I had not before allowed myself. And as I invited my brood to speak freely in prayer and to take their utterances to heart, I found my own prayer life revived.

My consideration of the matter of children at prayer arose in part from a Creative Renewal Arts Fellowship, awarded through the Arts Council of Indianapolis. With this grant I explored the thesis that—contrary to the assumption (of some) that spirituality with children entails indoctrination (i.e., teaching the "truths of God") or that the young are functionally incapable of serious engagement in the spiritual disciplines—adults have much to gain from the intentional, but free-flowing, engagement with children in the practice of prayer. When imaginatively rendered, this endeavor can yield a creative harvest of feelings and insights and so lead to spiritual enrichment.

The Given-ness of Spiritual Awareness

Theologian Marcus Borg credits author Parker Palmer with the evocative story of a young girl whose mother has just given birth to a second child, a boy. Shortly after the newborn arrives in the family home, the daughter requests to be alone with her new brother with his nursery door closed. The parents are apprehensive at first, but having just installed an intercom they concede and, listening in, are at the ready should any strange sound emit from the monitor. They hear the door shut, their daughter pad across the room to the crib, and they imagine her standing on tip toes and peering down over its edge at her three-day-old brother. But then they hear through the monitor something they had not anticipated: addressing the baby in a whisper, she says, simply, "Tell me about God—I've almost forgotten" (Borg, 2003, p. 113).

It is difficult not to resonate with this story, not to warm to the thought of a child earnestly inquiring into the mysteries that already at birth begin to slip from our grasp. Indeed, many of us carry a sense of spiritual loss. We harbor the intuition of a holy center we have strayed from, and to which our spirits long to return. Especially in our time of David Elkind's (1983) "hurried childhood" or even of a "childhood lost" (Kegan, 1994, p. 4), this story bespeaks a universal yearning for a depth of holy awareness that penetrates beneath the surface of things. To one degree or another, each one of us is that child, peering back into the crib as if into the Ground of Existence itself.

Christian education and Western Christian culture generally have ignored this pre-religious, pre-rational level of faith in the very young. From the moment religious teachers commence their task, they engage in the careful selection of data pertinent to the cognitively-based curricula they favor. Faith content quickly pushes spiritual awareness to the sideline. Soon children parrot, and eventually think, only within their inherited framework of belief. Faith, as a lively and ongoing encounter with "the More," becomes synonymous with the creeds and propositions of their particular religious tradition. As young people grow to rationally question, or even to reject, the validity of these formulations of truth, they are often left with no alternative for apprehending the spiritual realm of existence. Their spiritual repertoire remains flat and narrow.

This is not to suggest that adults have no role in shaping children's cognitive spiritual pallet in developmentally appropriate ways. It is, however, to say that the risk runs high that our children will be pressed into religious cognition at the expense of intuition, and into rote responses instead of the boundless invention and originality that is theirs by nature and prayer's by design.

Now I Lay Me Down to Sleep

The threat to the young of this "flattening out" of spiritual awareness takes on many forms. Some are as blatant as spoon-fed faith. Others are subtle, as in the case of this vignette from the prayer experience of my son, Seth:

> Someone who loves my son, Seth, bought him a boy doll that prays. The doll stands about ten inches tall, with a plastic head and limbs and a torso of firm fiberfill. His face wears a pasted-on smile, the kind you associate with a politician you don't trust.
>
> Seth's doll is not an action figure. He doesn't punch, kick, or wield weapons, and he isn't borrowed from the movies. He's not dressed to kill, either, but he is wearing sissy clothes—a striped shirt that recalls *Sesame Street* and the style of short pants cut above the knee that Seth calls "Daisy Dukes." If our Seth were a bully, he'd ridicule a kid whose mother dressed him so funny. But this doll talks, and kids are more forgiving of these, so Seth took a shine to him.

The doll's puffy hands stretch in the air, set at the angle of prayer. When you bring those hands together, a voice box in the boy's back is activated, and his twenty-eight-word recitation begins:

> Now I lay me down to sleep,
> I pray the Lord my soul to keep.
> Guide me safely through the night,
> And wake me with the morning light.

Seth found this poem enthralling and immediately set to memorizing it. He began reciting it not only at nighttime but also for breakfast, dinner, and even between meals. Soon, Seth had elevated the praying boy to second-favored status, right behind his stuffed leopard, Lucky, and he had named him Sam. Bedtime became synonymous with Sam and his twenty-eight-word prayer, reverberating from Seth's bed *ad nauseam*.

I disliked the praying doll from the start. To me, it represented a misguided attempt to coax kids into the genteel art of shallow prayer. Or, worse, it was a marketing ploy to make a buck off parents who were too overprotective to let their children cut their teeth on the real thing and too cowardly to make the journey with them. This doll was prayer on training wheels. Now, here was my own son, propping up a stuffed toy at night to do his praying for him.

Seth began to stand Sam against the headboard of his bed like a Black Madonna at a shrine. He'd bring the doll's hands together, pressed into his own, and boy and doll would recite the verse that hangs on bedroom walls in countless languages around the world. But I'd begun to think of some other lines, from Shakespeare, of "a tale told by an idiot, full of sound and fury, signifying nothing."

Some nights Seth would add his own prayers to Sam's. But mostly, during the days of the praying doll, Sam's prayer was it and then Seth's prayers were over. I thought of hiding Sam or removing his batteries. Once I put him up high on a shelf, but Seth spied him there and retrieved him by scaling it bravely—an act that seemed to capture the very spirit that had gone missing from his prayers! After all, wasn't prayer intended to be a little risky, a bit like walking with a blindfold or hang gliding off a cliff? Didn't some of its wonder arise from the experience of not knowing quite where you were going or how you would get there? Wasn't rote prayer, stripped of all mystery or peril, arguably worse than no prayer at all? But these things play out in kid time, not parent time. And so I waited longingly for the return to evenings with that engaging voice of my own flesh and blood.

Then, one night, Sam's prayer simply stopped and Seth's resumed. Maybe Sam's batteries ran low; I'm not sure. Perhaps Seth finally tired of Sam's voice, silly clothes, and pasted-on smile. But Seth began his own habit of prayer again—kindly, audacious, charming. And life seemed fuller again!

Sam ended up in the bottom of the toy chest—the way of all toys. He is there to this day, as far as I know, his batteries likely corroding. Now and then, out of the blue, Seth will recite Sam's prayer by himself. And as he is getting older, he thinks more about its words and what they might be saying.

"What's a soul?" Seth asked not long ago, when he came to the line, "I pray the Lord my soul to keep."

"A soul is that thing that makes you you," I said. But I was thinking, "A soul is that thing Sam didn't have, but which Seth always will. A soul is that thing that dares you to pray—and to live—without training wheels." (Watkins, 2005, pp. 130–33)

Children as Spiritual Pedagogues

Equal to my concern over nurturing a child's innate spiritual awareness is my interest in the potential benefit for adults who take seriously children's unvarnished sense of the Holy, who place themselves at the feet of the very young for a change. As I write in the introduction to *What Our Kids Teach Us About Prayer* (2005),

> To say, "Let's pray!" and then turn children loose on the act is to unleash a rushing stream over a dry, parched spirit; it is to be swept up into prayer's exuberance and imagination; it is to be given over to those ardent spirits that have yet to be ground down by the mill of conformity. (p. 14)

It may be argued that this whole process of discovery about children and prayer is somewhat counter-intuitive. We stand in a long stream of assumptions about children and all things spiritual—for instance, that children cannot be meaningfully involved in spiritual practices before around age twelve, and that young children are incapable of establishing a genuine relationship with God or of being truly awed or moved by God's Word and world. Such notions were never intended to dishonor children. They were, rather, developmental assumptions with spiritual implications.

Consider Jesus' appeal to children, as his disciples debate who among them is the greatest (Matt 18:1ff.; Mark 9:33ff.). Jesus announces to them, "Whoever wants to be first must take last place and be the servant of everyone else" (Mark 9:35, NLT). This would have been no great revelation to the disciples. After all, Jesus' essential *modus operandi* is servanthood. Yet next, Jesus takes into his arms a child, a non-person in the ancient world, who should, by custom, not even have been present with a teacher and his adult pupils. Jesus not only acknowledges but also makes of this child the measure of greatness.

This act would have been scandalous in Jesus' day. Some of its outrage, thankfully, is lost on us. We value children to a higher degree than earlier societies. Yet, two millennia after Jesus, this legacy of spiritual marginalization of children lives on in subtle ways, and some are rooted in church practice. Children are still routinely absent from worship, ignored there, or put on exhibit. Likewise, parents often remain conditioned to chuckle patronizingly over children's spiritual vocabulary and habits, not to greet them with a sense of earnestness and wonder.

A study from the Northminster Learning Center, Peoria, Illinois involving the spiritual development of children at this Presbyterian ministry demonstrates this well. Presented in 2006 at the second Children's Spirituality Conference held at Concordia University, this study examined assumptions about child spiritual development held by sixty-seven observers of the Learning Center program (see chapter 13 by Helm, Berg, & Scranton in this volume, pp. 214–30). The observers' initial assumptions, recorded on pre-observation surveys, were contrasted with their responses on a post-observation survey. The philosophical underpinnings of this study includes the belief that each child is an individual en route to becoming a functioning adult and that each age has distinct developmental characteristics. In other words, every child is on a developmental continuum vis-à-vis spiritual practice. The presenting questions concerned what, in spiritual terms, is possible along this continuum, and when.

Results of the study revealed a shift in thinking away from the view of the very young child's incapacity for meaningful spiritual experience. Specifically, positive responses to the question as to whether children under age six are capable of a meaningful relationship with God increased by 38 percent in the post-observation survey. Likewise, affirmative responses to the question whether children under six might experience meaningful communication with God or apply religious lessons to life increased by

30 percent and 22 percent respectively. In addition, in the post-observation survey, 45 percent of observers agreed or strongly agreed with the statement, "I was surprised how spiritual young children could be" (Helm, Berg, & Scranton, 2003).

Though inconclusive, such findings indicate the persistent habit of underestimating children's spiritual competencies. While spiritually, as in other realms, children are on a developmental curve, children's symbolic faith imagery, inexhaustible inquisitiveness, and characteristic candor alone qualify them for a place at the table of spiritual discourse. In *Real Kids, Real Faith,* Karen-Marie Yust (2004) drives the point home: "If faith is not something we do but something we are given by God, then anyone can be a recipient of faith and respond with faithfulness, even if that person is incapable of rational reasoning" (p. 7).

Why is this perspective not more widely recognized and celebrated? Possible factors include a lingering legacy of marginalizing children's faith aptitude, the intense societal focus on children's cognitive abilities, and the frenetic pace of modern life. In other words, we fail to recognize the spiritual capabilities of the young because we are not looking for them. Perhaps the problem lies as well with accepted spiritual practice among adults, which is arguably spirituality-once-removed. That is to say, adults spend much time and energy conforming to the institutional norms for spirituality, which often seem to involve *talking about talking* to God, not engaging God as if God were really listening or interested.

How does attentiveness to the spiritual sensibilities of children appear in practice? My personal experience herein continues to revolve around an eager alertness to the imaginative habits of my own children at prayer, disclosed, for instance, in the following account of prayer with my youngest daughter.

THE GIFT IN THE HEART

> Every night at prayer, my daughter Sarah leaves me a mystery. It is a riddle, a secret in the dark, and try as I might I can't crack its meaning. Every night, almost without fail, Sarah prays to God for "the gift in the heart."
>
> Usually Sarah tucks this prayer in between other ones for her family and for all the people of the world she has never met. The sentiment of these prayers I can comprehend. The gift in the

heart, on the other hand, is an enigma to me. And so, each time I hear it, I feel like a knight errant on a grail quest. But here, the Holy Grail is the mystical meaning behind my youngest daughter's simple prayer.

Just what sort of magical thing is this gift in the heart? When I ask Sarah, I get her Mona Lisa smile. She either doesn't know or isn't telling. Either way, the prayer continues, and so the gift in the heart has got to be a precious thing, a "heart" thing.

The ancient Egyptians believed the heart to be the seat of the soul and of all consciousness. When they mummified bodies, they removed to jars all the valued organs but the heart; they believed the heart, weighed against a feather, would measure an individual's worth in the afterlife. Brains, on the other hand, were discarded, regarded as virtually without worth. Today we understand the brain to be our conscious center, but there is still something about the heart that causes us to connect it with our essential nature. "Have a little heart," we say, or, "Don't be cold-hearted." "She has a heart of gold," we say of some truly kind soul, and "home," of course, has always been "where the heart is." Sarah is no student of ancient cultures or modern idioms, but she seems to grasp the power of the heart over the human imagination. She appreciates that she is praying at the threshold of mystery.

We adults, on the other hand, seem to favor prayers devoid of mystery. We like mashed-potatoes prayer—hold the chives—renderings that are uniform and bland. We like i's dotted, t's crossed, and God all fleshed out and friendly. We say "just" a lot—I just this, we just that—because we like things just that tame and sociable.

Yet our world is full of mystery. In this world, the smarter you become, the more ignorant you discover yourself to be. In this world, the longer you stand in one place, the further things speed away from you. In this world, prayer is a candle you light under a cloud of unknowing—and children like Sarah hold the matches.

The history of prayer is itself showered with the mystical—from the grandiose visions of John of Patmos to the demons of Martin Luther, from the stigmata of St. Francis to the "second conversion" of Theresa of Avila. Prayer has always included utterances at the border of reason: "Where two or three are gathered in my name, I am there among them" (Matt 18:20); "Whatever you ask for in prayer with faith, you will receive" (Matt 21:22); "Father, forgive them, for they know not what they do . . . " (Luke 23:34).

Sarah's part in such mysteries involves no voices, no specters, no bleeding wounds. Hers is all wrapped tightly in a five-word phrase: the gift in the heart. This is the specialty of children: simplicity absent simple-mindedness.

So just what do I think Sarah's gift in the heart is? It could be the spirit of God, I suppose, "bearing witness with our spirits that we are children of God" (Rom 8:16). It might be an expression of Sarah's sense of well-being—that she is safe in her own skin, that she belongs. Or perhaps the gift in the heart is prayer itself in all its mystery, all its power to quicken our joy for life and hope for living.

But if I were to guess, I'd say it is none of these. I'd say instead that the gift in the heart is love—Sarah's love for God, and for the world, and for everything in it. I'd say that the gift in the heart is her mystic heart, and mine, and yours, whispering our oneness with God and all things at the deepest center of the universe.

But I'm not sure. And I prefer it this way. I'd like to leave the whole matter a mystery. It is, after all, a gift in the heart—and gifts require no explanation. (Watkins, 2005, pp. 40–42)

A Child Theology of Prayer for Our Time

What might be the philosophical-theological underpinnings, as well as implications, of such spiritual engagement with children? How does a positive valuation of children's faith contributions impinge upon the nature of religious experience?

Many of us were raised to believe that "catching faith" is about indoctrination—learning the truths of God. Then one could do spiritual things: take communion, pray in public, and tell others what to believe. I recall my grandmother offering me $100—serious money for a ten-year-old in the early 1970s—if I could memorize the entire Westminster Shorter Catechism. I began and got down to Question 7: "What are the decrees of God? His eternal purpose, according to the counsel of his will, whereby, for his own glory, he hath foreordained whatsoever comes to pass." By then, however, I had concluded that not only was I not up for the effort of rote memorization, but also I had no clue about the meaning behind what I was painstakingly committing to memory. These words had little or no connection with my faith experience. To my grandmother's disappointment I abandoned the enterprise. I often wonder how horrified she would be to learn I had ended up a noncreedal Baptist!

What we believe about God is critical, but not to the exclusion of simple awe and wonder in the face of the mysterious, ineffable quality of what Marcus Borg (2003) has called "the More." In part, this has to do with the very meaning of faith. Borg identifies several senses of faith, each rooted in its Latin vocabulary. In addition to *assensus* (belief, or the assent to certain intellectual propositions, which receives the lion's share of emphasis in the West), faith can also be understood as *fiducia* (trust in God), *fidelitas* (faithful attentiveness to the Holy), and *visio* (seeing reality and the world in such a way that we are able to embrace it as gracious and not threatening). Borg argues that these ancient, pre-modern forms of religious consciousness characterize an emergent Christianity in which assent to certain truths is only one among many avenues to faith. This is not to suggest that systems of belief are unimportant, but rather that these decidedly-*relational* approaches to faith, these ways of the heart, are more vital and crucial at our present moment than ever before.

In her book, *Postmodern Children's Ministry*, Ivy Beckwith (2004) offers a vivid example of this shift in concern by referencing a booklet marketed several years ago by an evangelical college ministry. The booklet was representative of a whole genre of resources presenting similar versions of the "plan of salvation." At the end of the booklet, Beckwith recalls, was a drawing of a train. In this typology, the train's locomotive stood for "truth," the basic facts of Christianity, similar to the "Four Spiritual Laws." The locomotive pulled a train car called "faith"—made possible by understanding the truth. Bringing up the rear was the caboose, which represented "feelings." Beckwith explains that in this analogy, "consigning emotion to the caboose is the warning that we can't trust our feelings and can't possibly know God through an emotional connection" (p. 20). Beckwith then contends that the postmodern mind, less defined by facts than points of view, less by propositions than intuitions, balks at the very hypothesis of this train illustration. Postmoderns, she asserts, lend as much credence to feelings, mystery, and the like as they do to reason.

It is precisely here that the children of our lives can help us. Children easily tap into these non-propositional, open-spirited ways of faith. They offer a transparency to the transcendent that we should nurture, not dampen or deter. There is a dawning connection between this contemporary interest in children and theology on the one hand, and this emergent, "postmodern" approach to Christian faith, associated with the experiential, intuitive, metaphorical side of religious awareness, on the other.

As if to further elucidate this connection, Beckwith (2004) suggests that one challenge facing the postmodern or emergent church involves rethinking "how we help our kids experience the story, how we help our church communities and families experience the story with their children, and how we find in the story new and delightful and unsettling ideas about God and God's relationship to creation and the future" (p. 38).

Caught in the Act

At my children's bedside in the dark, I have been quietly undergoing a Copernican revolution of sorts in my experience of prayer and spirituality. The above insights comprise some of the theoretical underpinnings, the shift in thinking, which accompanies my experience with kids and spirituality. The revolution itself remains underway. The following vignettes attempt to exemplify what this shift means in practice, to shine a light on this process of concrete engagement with children in the act of spiritual meaning-making.

The Miracle of Me: A Child's Lesson in Self-Worth

We are taught early on that self-congratulation is bad manners. Anything that draws undue attention to one's self is considered untoward. Good parents do not raise braggadocios. Yet lately, I have had to consider whether spiritual practice might not comprise most fertile ground for expressions of self-love, self-worth, and—yes—even self-adulation, spurred on by our only son, Seth:

> Our son has lately taken up a new prayer. At first I found it jarring, but gradually it has come to ring a deep chord within me. Seth has been regularly thanking God for himself.
>
> Such a prayer is unprecedented in my experience. At the end of a long litany of thanksgiving for everything from soccer to cinnamon rolls, he will conclude simply, ". . . and thank you God for me!"
>
> Nothing fancy. Just a straightforward expression of satisfaction at his own existence. And yet I've come to view it as nothing short of revolutionary. What possesses my son to thank God each night for himself? Where does he get the nerve? Until Seth uttered those words, it had never occurred to me that anyone could—or should!

Such words had certainly never escaped my own lips. Growing up, I'd have been afraid to pray such a prayer. I'd have thought it more than a shade arrogant. My generation was chastened to resist all urges of self-adulation. Don't fish for compliments, we were taught; let them come to you. Don't act like you're anything special. No one likes a show-off. Isn't this what landed Jacob's son, Joseph, in so much trouble with his brothers? (Gen 37). He claimed God's special favor and almost got himself killed in the process.

Indeed, there is no lack of biblical support for such advice. "I say . . . not to think of yourself more highly than you ought," Paul tells us, "but to think with sober judgment" (Rom 12:3). Jesus says, "When you are invited by someone to a wedding banquet, do not sit down at the place of honor, in case someone more distinguished than you has been invited by your host; and the host . . . may come and say to you, 'Give this person your place . . . '" (Luke 14:8–9a).

Or take Isaiah: "Woe is me. I am lost, for I am a man of unclean lips . . . " (Isa 6:5). Or again Paul: "Christ Jesus came into the world to save sinners—of whom I am the foremost" (1 Tim 1:15). Or Job, even, wishing he had never been born (Job 3:3).

Enter my son, who brings to prayer the audacity to assert his own intrinsic worth before God. He dares to value himself, just as he assumes God does. He affirms this without diminishing the worth of anyone else. After all, isn't each one of us of monumental importance to God? Why not say so at least once a day?

Most of us certainly tell ourselves regularly all that is wrong with us. We whisper our faults and shortcomings, let them seep down into us till they pool like a cancer in the soul. As we pray to the one who cherishes us, why not let echo there as well our own sweet words of approbation: "Thank you, God, for me!"

That my son, Seth, imagines he is lovable, that my son loves himself, that he presumes that God loves him—all this is itself cause for grateful prayer. Indeed, these affirmations may be the truest prerequisites for all prayer.

It has taken me some time, but gradually I've come to see my son's prayer as the most natural act in the world. In fact, lately I've been finding the courage to speak those simple words to God, too! "And thank you," I've been praying, "thank you also, God, for me!" (Watkins, 2005, pp. 37–39)

Praying for God: A Child's Lesson in Theological Audacity

"Kids say the darnedest things"—but to put it this way cheapens the seriousness of their effrontery to the conventions of thought we adults hold dear. Consider, for instance, the striking implications of this peculiar practice of my children at intercessory prayer:

> In mid-sentence of prayers for all the people they love, my children will abruptly turn the whole procedure on its head. Without warning, they'll offer up a prayer to God for . . . God!
>
> "And be with God," I'll hear them say. "And Jesus," they'll throw in. "And watch over and bless them."
>
> It has taken me a while to process this new wrinkle in intercessory prayer. Initially, it struck me as rather quaint and more than a little bizarre. First, there is the simple illogic of it. How can you pray for the one you've been praying to? If God becomes prayer's subject, then who or what has become the object? More than once as they've prayed this prayer, I've formed a mental image of God looking up from the heavenly throne just to be sure there isn't some other being, yet one echelon higher, to whom my children's prayers for God are being directed.
>
> Just who do my kids think they are, praying for God, the Source and the End of our prayers? Isn't God Transcendent Being, First Cause, Creator of everything? Isn't God omniscient? Omnipresent? All those other omnis? Why would God require the solemn prayers of children for God's own well-being? Why not try and teach Tiger Woods how to putt or Fred Astair how to fox trot? Why not loan money to your bank or give your own doctor a physical examination? But my children seem untroubled by such concerns. Indeed, they pray for God without apology, as though it were the most natural prayer in the world.
>
> And so, I've been thinking, maybe it is! Maybe I'm the one who's been missing something. Why, after all, should the one ultimately responsible for everything be alone without a prayer? Why should a relational God shun the heartfelt concerns of children? Perhaps the classical Christian concept of God as aloof and unmoved has wrecked the possibility of human concern for God's well-being. For God to need or even notice our concern would make God open to change. But a perfect being is by definition beyond change or influence, the argument goes.
>
> My children don't worry, though, over doctrines of God's nature and activity in the world. They only wish to let God know

they care! And the more I think about it, the more I can't help but think that this is somehow a blessed thing, this presumption of theirs that God is no more indifferent to their prayers for God than to their prayers for anyone else. I can't prove it, but I'd like to believe these prayers of theirs are a grace, offered back to the author of grace, and that, even if they cause God an occasional look over the shoulder, they bring God some satisfaction and joy.

As to exactly what or whom my children's prayers for God are directed—I'll leave that up to anyone's imagination. (Watkins, 2005, pp. 79–81)

A Bold New Spiritual World with Children Present

As noted at the outset of this chapter, my journey into this new spiritual kingdom with children was first traveled as a father attending to his brood. Thus, it is highly experiential. My reflections on these things are, foremost, attempts to describe and bear witness to these experiences.

Yet, this very admission cuts to the core of my interest in the topic of children and spirituality. We are living at a watershed moment in the history of Christian thought and practice. The modern era of spiritual truth-telling as a largely factual, propositional, and objective enterprise is now understood in many quarters as inadequate for faith. Meanwhile, a decidedly more experience-based, intuitive, relational approach to the apprehension of truth is in ascendancy. Now christened "postmodernism," this emergent way distinguishes between truth and fact, insists upon the perspective of the individual in claims of knowledge, and holds feeling and intuition as data both valid and vital.

At just such a moment we find ourselves exploring with fresh earnestness the spiritual sensibilities of children. My firm belief is that this is no coincidence. Children are our natural partners on the quest for a deeper, more authentic encounter with the things of the Spirit. To engage them openly and expectantly will be to make this journey into a new spiritual land with imagination and grace—". . . and a little child shall lead them" (Isa 11:6).

References

Beckwith, I. (2004). *Postmodern children's ministry*. Grand Rapids: Zondervan.
Borg, M. (2003). *The heart of Christianity*. San Francisco: HarperSanFrancisco.

Elkind, D. (1983). *The hurried child: Growing up too fast too soon.* Reading, MA: Addison-Wesley.

Helm, J. H., Berg, S., & Scranton, P. (2003, June 5). *Documentation of children's spiritual development in a preschool program: What teachers, parents, and the congregation learned.* Paper presented at the Children's Spirituality Conference: Christian Perspectives, River Forest, IL.

Kegan, R. (1994). *In over our heads.* Cambridge, MA: Harvard University Press.

Watkins, T. W. (2005). *What our kids teach us about prayer.* New York: Crossroad.

Yust, K. M. (2004). *Real kids, real faith: Practices for nurturing children's spiritual lives.* San Francisco: Jossey-Bass.

9 Making Stories Come Alive

Jeffrey E. Feinberg

THE JEWISH EXPERIENCE OF NATIONAL REDEMPTION IS GROUNDED IN the story of God's rescue of the Israelites from Egyptian slavery. After the event, God gives guidelines to the Israelites for celebrating the Passover in household festivals (Exod 12), and during the celebration the parents are commanded to tell the sacred story to the children by prompting children to ask questions (vv. 24–26). Various kinds of foods (parsley, horseradish, an unbroken lamb shank) and activities (dipping, reclining) are employed to prompt questions in the midst of a banquet feast. Parents are instructed to answer the children's questions: "We were Pharaoh's slaves in Egypt, but the Lord brought us out of Egypt with a mighty hand. The Lord displayed before our eyes great and awesome signs and wonders . . . to give us the land that he promised on oath to our ancestors" (Deut 6:20–23).[1] The story is to be told in such a way that each one may personally imagine a primary experience of encountering God.

Storytelling principles gleaned from my Jewish heritage, along with the experimental research findings of my dissertation (Feinberg, 1988), have formed the foundation for the Messianic Jewish curriculum[2] my wife and I developed between 1988 and 2004. In our curriculum, both flannel graph figures and puppets are used. The puppet stories illustrate living experiences gleaned from raising our Jewish family. *Vicarious appropriation* of a living heritage is conveyed by flannel pieces, story figures that come

---

1. Scripture quotations in this chapter are taken from the English translation in *The Stone Edition of the Chumash* unless otherwise indicated (Scherman, 1995).

2. Samples of the Feinbergs' curriculum can be downloaded from www.flamefoundation.org.

off the board to touch the forehead of each child in a movingly personal way. Stillness during the appropriation of the flannel piece adds an element of mystery. These storytelling components allow for the possibility of encountering the mystery of God's elusive presence in a memorable way that is foundational for spiritual formation.

Importance of Story Schema Formation as a Construct for Spiritual Growth

Story has played a vital role in human history. Before the advent of the printing press (AD 1450), much of a people group's historical identity was conveyed orally. For the ancient Hebrews, both in the Hebrew Scriptures and in the New Testament times of Jesus, stories have provided a framework for transmitting values, heritage, culture, and traditions of civilization.

Arthur Applebee (1978) found that children use stories to acquire expectations about the world. Such expectations provide a framework or building blocks for organizing incoming information (Sheble, 1984). This framework for organizing information is called *schema* (plural *schemata*). Thus, stories are integral to creating schemata for understanding one's world.

It would appear that enhancing the child's capacity to construct schemata would also increase the child's ability to assimilate and accommodate incoming information from the environment. Schema formation has integral ties to the building of a framework necessary to construct a worldview for problem solving and responding to unfolding events in one's environment. Thus, helping children take in, integrate, and internalize the stories of their lives—in our case, the scriptural master story in particular—helps with their story schema formation, which in turn should ultimately enhance their spiritual growth and formation. The research therefore focuses on assisting schema formation through examining specific storytelling techniques.

Research Design to Assist and Elicit Schema Formation

The experimental design of this research sought to quantify and measure the four- to six-year-olds' formation of story schema. During a week of Kidz Kibbutz (Vacation Bible School), flannelgraph stories were told to children in groups of approximately eight participants each. Groups were stratified by age and gender to minimize effects of these variables between groups. Each story was written with two episodes—the first episode preceding the theme and the second episode centering on the theme. The stories were modeled to fit a construct posited and explored independently by Vygotsky (1962) and Applebee (1978).

Applebee (1978) found that the processes of *centering* and *chaining* function as basic structuring principles in children's conception of story. Centering consists of maintaining a certain focus or core that relates to the story as a whole. Chaining links story elements or events in a way that moves the story along or helps develop the plot. Children with more advanced cognitive capacities could maintain a constant center (e.g., a story character, action, setting, or theme) and a causal flow from one story event to the next, with successive events helping to further develop the core of the story (consistent forward movement). Some of Applebee's terms used in the procedure and results sections are explained in figure 1 entitled "The Structure of Children's Stories" on the facing page.

Educational techniques to assist story schema formation include *distancing* and *appropriation*. *Distancing* promotes differentiation between subject and object, subjective and objective, or action and idea (Sigel & Cocking, 1977; Page, 1983). Distancing can be facilitated by embedding techniques such as narrator comments or summaries that enable the listener to classify, organize, and overview the story from the vantage point of an objective or disinterested observer. Appropriation can be facilitated by embedding a learning task in the story by which the subject makes the meaning and value of a new fact or idea a part of himself (Colson & Rigdon, 1981). In the stories used in the research, flannel pieces introducing a character, action, setting, or theme can literally *move beyond the boundaries of the story*, personally carried by hand to touch a story-listener, who is addressed by name.

Four different stories—God Gives The Promised Land, God Sends Baby Isaac, Grandchildren for our Family, and Room for Everyone in the Family—were told to six treatment groups as follows:

T0: A0, A0, A0, A0 (control group, no appropriation)

T1: A1, A1, A1, A1 (partial appropriation: tactile component embedded in non-thematic episode)

Figure 1: The Structure of Children's Stories*

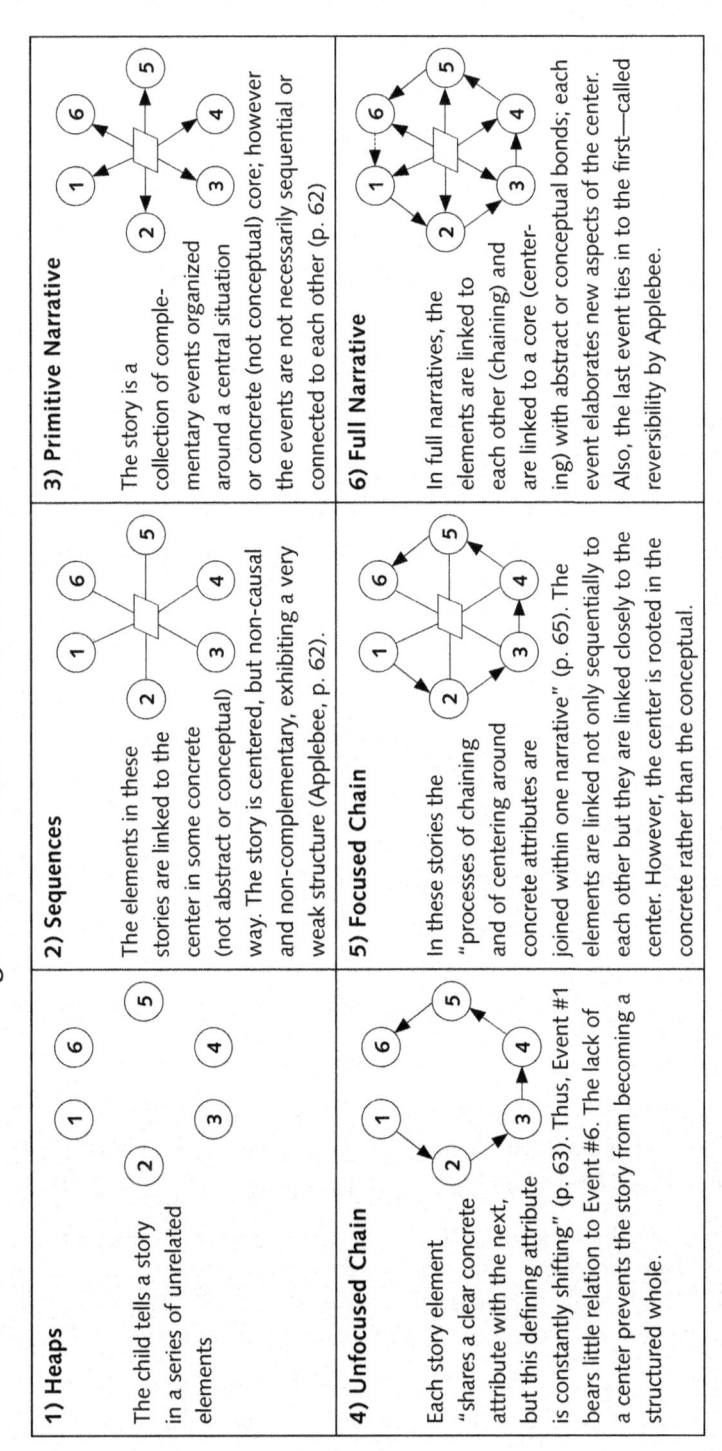

1) Heaps	2) Sequences	3) Primitive Narrative
The child tells a story in a series of unrelated elements	The elements in these stories are linked to the center in some concrete (not abstract or conceptual) way. The story is centered, but non-causal and non-complementary, exhibiting a very weak structure (Applebee, p. 62).	The story is a collection of complementary events organized around a central situation or concrete (not conceptual) core; however the events are not necessarily sequential or connected to each other (p. 62)
4) Unfocused Chain	5) Focused Chain	6) Full Narrative
Each story element "shares a clear concrete attribute with the next, but this defining attribute is constantly shifting" (p. 63). Thus, Event #1 bears little relation to Event #6. The lack of a center prevents the story from becoming a structured whole.	In these stories the "processes of chaining and of centering around concrete attributes are joined within one narrative" (p. 65). The elements are linked not only sequentially to each other but they are linked closely to the center. However, the center is rooted in the concrete rather than the conceptual.	In full narratives, the elements are linked to each other (chaining) and are linked to a core (centering) with abstract or conceptual bonds; each event elaborates new aspects of the center. Also, the last event ties in to the first—called reversibility by Applebee.

Note: In these diagrams, circles represent elements or events in the story; parallelograms represent the center or core of a story; straight lines indicate shared attributes; arrows indicate complementary attributes (similar to Applebee's diagram features, 1978, p. 58).

* Adapted from Applebee, 1978, pp. 58ff.

T2: A2, A2, A2, A2 (partial appropriation: non-tactile embedded in non-thematic episode)

T3: A3, A3, A3, A3 (partial appropriation: non-tactile embedded in theme-related episode)

T4: A4, A4, A4, A4 (full appropriation: tactile component embedded in theme-related episode)

T5: A5, A5, A5, A5 (full appropriation: stories counterbalanced to control for order effects)

To illustrate, several forms of the Baby Isaac story are included below:

Treatment T0: No Appropriation

In Treatment T0, no *tactile* appropriation takes place, though the flannel pieces are placed and moved about. In the following stories, highlighted words represent flannel items that are to be placed.

> Who knows a tiny baby? *(Let children tell about the babies they know.)*
>
> Do you know how your parents felt when you were born? Do you remember your mommy's face? Was she smiling at you? Did her eyes twinkle?
>
> I'm going to tell you a Bible story about a baby. The story is called "God Sends Baby Isaac."
>
> One night, in the land of Israel *(add **palm trees**)*, God spoke to **Father Abram**. God took him outside his **tent** and told him to look at the **stars**. So many stars! "Count the stars, if you can," said God.
>
> Stars were everywhere—far too many for us to count. God told us, "Your family will outnumber the stars." But we didn't have even one child. *(Remove **clouds**, **stars**, and **Abram**.)*
>
> We waited a long time for that first child. **Father Abram** and **Mother Sarai** sat and waited on a **rock**. When **Baby Isaac** was born, Father Abraham was one hundred years old. Mother Sarah said, "God has brought me laughter." Our eyes twinkled with joy!
>
> Baby Isaac became the first star in our family. *(Touch **star** to Baby Isaac and then place in sky.)* Baby Isaac grew up and had a son of

his own. **Father Isaac** named the new baby **Jacob**. Jacob became the second star. *(Touch star to Baby Jacob and then place in sky.)*

When Grandson Jacob grew up, he had more children. Father Jacob had **twelve sons** and **one daughter**—more stars for our family. *(Touch stars to sons and daughter and then place in sky.)*

Much later, **King David** and **Yeshua** became stars in our family. *(Touch stars to King David and Yeshua and then place in sky.)*

The Bible tells us God's promise to Father Abram: "In you all the families of the earth will be blessed" (Gen 12:3). Let's say God's promise together. *(Repeat Gen 12:3.)*

Think how Mother Sarah feels. Her joy grows with every star in our family. When we look at the sky, we can thank God for making us stars in Father Abraham's family.

Let's thank God for keeping His promise to Father Abraham: Thank You, God, for giving Baby Isaac to Father Abraham and Mother Sarah. And thank You for Yeshua, who makes us stars in Father Abraham's family, too. Amen.

Treatment T1: Partial Appropriation; Tactile Component in Non-Thematic Episode

In Treatment T1, a "tactile appropriation, non-thematic episode" means that the flannel piece is *touched to the child* at a point in the story that is *not* connected to the story's theme. Sitting on a rock is *not* part of the theme; the theme is "waiting for the promise." Other themes in this story series are "receiving the Land" or "becoming a child (star) in the family."

We waited a long time for that first child. **Father Abram** and **Mother Sarai** sat and waited on a **rock**, And I sat and waited on a rock, and *(fill in child's name)* sat and waited on a rock *(insert each child's name while touching the* rock *to child's chair)*. Yes, we all sat and waited a long time.

. . . Let's thank God for keeping His promise to Father Abraham: Thank You, God, for giving Baby Isaac to Father Abraham and Mother Sarah. And thank You for Yeshua, who makes us stars in Father Abraham's family, too. Amen.

Treatment T3: Partial Appropriation; Non-Tactile Component in Thematic Episode

In Treatment T3, the focus is on a major theme—becoming a star—but there is no tactile contact. The flannel pieces are not touched to the children.

> ... Much later, **King David** and **Yeshua** became stars in our family. *(Touch stars to King David and Yeshua and then place in sky.)* And through Yeshua, I became a star in Father Abraham's family and *(fill in child's name)* became a star in Father Abraham's family *(insert each child's name while pointing to the child but without holding out any flannel piece).*
>
> The Bible tells us...God's promise to Father Abraham: "In you all the families of the earth will be blessed" (Gen 12:3). Let's say God's promise together. *(Repeat Gen 12:3.)*
>
> Think how Mother Sarah feels. Her joy grows with every star in our family. When we look at the sky, we can thank God for making us stars in Father Abraham's family.
>
> Let's thank God for keeping His promise to Father Abraham: Thank You, God, for giving Baby Isaac to Father Abraham and Mother Sarah. And thank You for Yeshua, who makes us stars in Father Abraham's family, too. Amen.

Treatment T4: Full Appropriation; Tactile Component in Thematic Episode

In Treatment T4, the focus again is on a major theme—becoming a star—and there is tactile contact as well. A flannel piece, in this case, the star, is touched to each child's forehead.

> ... Much later, **King David** and **Yeshua** became stars in our family. *(Touch stars to King David and Yeshua and then place in sky.)* And through Yeshua, I became a star in Father Abraham's family, and *(fill in child's name)* became a star in Father Abraham's family *(insert each child's name while touching a star to each child's forehead).*
>
> The Bible tells us...God's promise to Father Abraham: "In you all the families of the earth will be blessed" (Gen 12:3). Let's say God's promise together. *(Repeat Gen 12:3.)*

Think how Mother Sarah feels. Her joy grows with every star in our family. When we look at the sky, we can thank God for making us stars in Father Abraham's family.

Let's thank God for keeping His promise to Father Abraham: Thank You, God, for giving Baby Isaac to Father Abraham and Mother Sarah. And thank You for Yeshua, who makes us stars in Father Abraham's family, too. Amen.

To further enlighten understanding of the research procedure, see figure 2, a pictogram of the story schema for the Baby Isaac Story on the following page.

Research Purpose and Results

Research questions focused on whether or not the technique of story presentation affected the child's performance. That is, did the tactile appropriation improve the child's performance on a story task? Did the position of an appropriation within the story sequence affect the child's performance on a story task? Finally, did the subject's retelling of the story facilitate schema formation and enable the subject to improve on a subsequent story-retelling task? Subjects were tested for *details* within one day of hearing a story by means of a picture-sequencing task that tested for a spectator mode of story schema understanding. Subjects were tested for *schema formation* within three to five days of hearing four stories by means of a story-retelling task using the flannel pieces to elicit a participant mode of storytelling.

The experimental study found that *spectator modes* (simply hearing a story) and *participant modes* (participating in the story) were independent means of processing information into a story schema. Spectator modes required skills relating to distancing and abstraction, which helped a child to recall a story as an organized whole. In contrast, participant modes better enabled subjects to apply stories to life situations.[3]

The results seem to suggest that schema formation can be assisted and elicited. Tactile appropriation connecting the basic theme throughout the story was helpful to children in attaining *full narrative*, a stage characterized

---

3. Twenty-three of twenty-six subjects were correctly classified within one treatment of the assigned group tested, and fourteen of twenty-six subjects were correctly classified as predicted by the regression results. The quantitative results can be found in Appendices I–U, Tables 9–15, and Figures 5–11 of the doctoral dissertation.

Figure 2: Pictograms of Story Schema
God Sends Baby Isaac

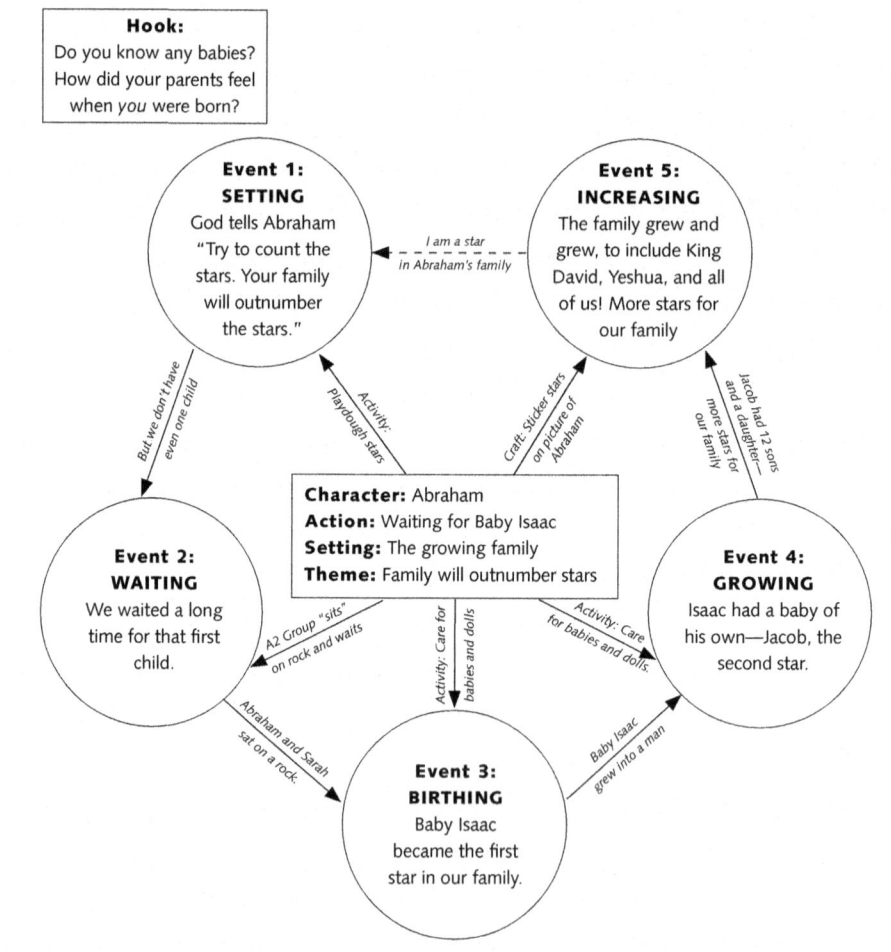

Hook:
Do you know any babies? How did your parents feel when *you* were born?

Event 1: SETTING
God tells Abraham "Try to count the stars. Your family will outnumber the stars."

I am a star in Abraham's family

Event 5: INCREASING
The family grew and grew, to include King David, Yeshua, and all of us! More stars for our family

But we don't have even one child

Activity: playdough stars

Craft: Sticker stars on picture of Abraham

Jacob had 12 sons and a daughter—more stars for our family

Character: Abraham
Action: Waiting for Baby Isaac
Setting: The growing family
Theme: Family will outnumber stars

Event 2: WAITING
We waited a long time for that first child.

A2 Group "sits" on rock and waits

Activity: Care for babies and dolls

Activity: Care for babies and dolls

Event 4: GROWING
Isaac had a baby of his own—Jacob, the second star.

Abraham and Sarah sat on a rock.

Baby Isaac grew into a man

Event 3: BIRTHING
Baby Isaac became the first star in our family.

Note: Complementary bonds can include personal experiences children bring to class (Sigel and Olmsted, 1970), e.g., seeing stars at night, waiting for a baby sibling to arrive, etc.

by *reversibility* or coming full circle in relating the concluding event to the starting event of a story. The limitations of this research (sample size and preliminary, emerging measurement approaches), however, preclude generalizing. Future research should be directed to combining modes and to facilitating advanced aspects of full narrative ("story chunking" or schema formation), including multi-attribute thinking that connects chains (story events) and centers (a main character, action, setting or theme) to forward movement in narrative.[4] (Consult figure 1 again here if needed.)

Further Thoughts on Assisting Schema Formation

Jewish educational methods call upon the parents in a home setting to include the children in participant modes of storytelling at festivals such as Passover (Ratcliff, 1988, p. 264). Spectator modes require increased ability to distance. Without practice and experience, subjects cannot be expected to see the big picture, or even to attempt to construct it using schema. Yet, parents are enjoined that their children will come to *believe* the Passover story themselves on the day that they pass on the story as heads of households. Scripture calls upon parents to employ participant modes in conveying stories as a living heritage—that long unbroken chain of witnesses that have passed on the Torah and inherited stories from generation to generation since the days of slavery in Egypt.

How can the participant and spectator modes be combined in order to pass on these stories as a transcendent experience? Jerome Berryman (1991) cites Edward Robinson's story of a five-year-old girl describing a day in the sun when she became conscious of appearing as a towering giant while she observed a tiny ant on the ground below her. As she wondered whether or not the ant could sense her presence, she found herself sensing the presence of One who was watching her from beyond the clouds and unending blue skies. Berryman calls this kind of religious knowing the "personal intuition" of "compressed, sensorial analogy" (p. 140). Can this knowing be kindled in the space of the stories we tell? Can vicarious appropriation of the Judeo-Christian heritage be conveyed as a present-day

---

4. Applebee schematizes full narrative as characterized by multi-attribute thinking, events linked to one another and also to the story center. Events that are chained by abstract or conceptual bonds progressively elaborate new aspects of the story core. The last event "reverses" or comes full circle to the first event, developing the core in a way that elicits awareness of the story as a whole. See "Full Narrative" on figure 1: "The Structure of Children's Stories."

faith journey that walks in the shadows of future hopes that we glimpse from afar?

Stein and Glenn (1977; 1982) tell an interesting story about a fish and a fisherman that will illustrate several story elements. When the fish story is told, the story-listener initially perceives the story from the fish's perspective. However, the story-listener must move from a *participant mode* of swimming along with a hungry fish (who spots and bites a tasty worm for dinner) to a *spectator's perspective* of watching a hungry fisherman reel in the hooked fish for his own dinner. Both motives and action sequences are useful for organizing this story schema. However, at some point, the setting must be enlarged *(context enlargement)* to see the fishing line and the fisherman on the other end of the worm (fisherman now in the foreground; fish is in the background). Since this comes as a surprise to the fish, the plot reverses direction *(plot reversal)*. The fish switches roles from predator to prey *(grand-scale figure-ground reversal)*. And abruptly enough, the fish changes internal states from happy to sad.

This story demonstrates the schema elements of context enlargement, background/foreground inversions, plot reversibility (coming full circle), and grand-scale figure-ground reversals (surprise endings when content and context invert or enlarge). Applebee (1978) contends that these aspects, especially reversibility, are necessary understandings for attaining full narrative comprehension. Further exploratory work is needed to determine the dynamics of the process of internalizing story schema as one's own. But Berryman (1991) suggests a model that points to context enlargement as a part of the "AHA!" moment of grasping the story as a whole (pp. 152ff.). The child who listens to the story in a spectator mode scans the lake, the sun, and the boat, and takes in the story as a detached, objective observer—who then experiences amusement by the turn of events. In contrast, the child listening in the participant mode identifies with the fish as a hunter stalking its prey until a sudden turn of events shocks him into absorbing the nightmarish experience of becoming dinner for someone else. In the Baby Isaac story, the moment of reversibility comes when event five connects to event one, and "I become a star in the family God promised Father Abraham." (See the pictogram of the Baby Isaac Story in figure 2.)

Implications for Teachers, Tellers, and Writers

By attending to both modes of processing (spectator and participant), teachers can develop a broad range of effective teaching strategies. The elicitation of participant modes can be particularly effective for helping listeners weigh the impact of consequences. With care, such vicarious experiences gained from constructing story frameworks can be assimilated and accommodated into a listener's prior experiences.

In contrast, the elicitation of spectator modes can orient, overview, and embellish content for the generalized "other." Spectator modes focus upon understanding the whole story in context. Special attention to the setting changes in the background as well as the introduction of important secondary characters can help listeners infer and form *chains* to explore the development of the core of a story (see figure 1: "The Structure of Children's Stories"). Constructing abstract or conceptual bonds between the core and the events of the story enables story-listeners to gain a sense of consistent forward movement in the progression of the story. Encouraging multi-attribute chaining of events with the developing core narrative can further enable listeners to organize, process, store, and retrieve information. Perspective with respect to settings, in relation to main and secondary events, leads to a coherent synthesis of the whole story and greater effectiveness in communicating with others (retelling).

Implications for Spiritual Development

So it is with walking in the master story of Scripture. Just as the Israelites were given the Promised Land as their inheritance, Christians today are en route to their inheritance—no longer slaves to sin and death, but set free to live eternally for God. How can the stories we tell create room for the mystery of God's presence? And how can our curriculum move from communicating a story *about* God to a story *of* God?

The *grand-scale figure ground reversal* expands the context and, at the same time, inverts and reverses the relationship. Now, context becomes content, and content becomes context. In other words, the story of the Jewish people in exile becomes the story of God's chosen land, suffering barrenness and depopulation as a result of the sins of the nation.[5] The mas-

---

5. See, for example, Ezekiel 36:8–11,15: "'But you, O mountains of Israel, you will put forth your branches and bear your fruit for My people Israel: for they will soon come. For behold, I am for you, and I will turn to you, and you shall be cultivated and sown. I will

ter story shows that God's mercy to his land and to his creation will cause him to bring the people back to become the nation God swore to give to the patriarchs—Abraham, Isaac, and Jacob. The land will rejoice when its chosen people return, and God will dwell again in the midst of his people. Thus, the master story of primary experience can be seen by looking to yesterday and also to tomorrow. It takes only a flash of primary experience today to see that yesterday and tomorrow connect in the now. For the Jews, the Promised Land is an inheritance of eternal life, secure borders, and households living in peace for a thousand years—it is the Millennium lived under the power and protection of Israel's Messiah.

Suppose you knew that you would die exactly one year before the Messiah returns. Would this awareness transform how you live? Would it change what you say to the children in your care? Would it change how you write or tell a story? After all, you would know for certain that these children would live to see Christ. How then would you prepare them for this primary experience? Could you embed the vicarious appropriation of this living heritage into those small but comprehending minds? How can this consciousness of God's coming breathe life into the stories you pass on to the children?

Implications for Structuring Stories that Live[6]

The Messianic Jewish stories written to use with flannel pieces, which were tested in the research, describe God's promise to Abraham, whose name means "father of a multitude of nations." God shows Abram (before his name was Abraham) the stars in the sky and tells him, "See the stars, if you can count them—so shall your descendants be" (Gen 15:5). As an aside to

---

multiply men on you, and all the house of Israel, all of it; and the cities shall be inhabited and the waste places will be rebuilt. I will multiply on you man and beast; and they will be fruitful; and I will cause you to be inhabited as you were formerly and will treat you better than at the first. Thus you will know that I am the Lord. . . . I will not let you hear insults from the nations anymore, nor will you bear disgrace from the peoples any longer, nor will you cause your nation to stumble any longer,' declares the Lord."

6. Since my original research in the 1980s, *story* has continued to be a key theme in recent and current works. Outstanding contributions to the literature are included in the bibliography, including the works of Egan (1989), Walsh (2003), Erricker and Erricker (2005), Jensen (2005), and Ratcliff (2005). It is hoped that future research will point the way to mapping a dynamic, conceptual understanding of the process by which the story-listener "chunks" story schema. It is believed that such understandings will assist the process of storywriting, storytelling, and story-enacting.

those who tell stories, Abraham lives to see only two grandchildren, who are trading national birthrights as teenagers right under his nose. But the story as told in the curriculum ends with an embedded appropriation, where individual stars come out of the story and touch each child on the forehead, and the words are spoken:

> I became a star in the family of Father Abraham, and *(fill in child's name)* became a star in the family of Father Abraham. *(Insert each child's name while touching a star to each child's forehead.)* Yes, we all became stars in the family that God promised Father Abraham.

Thus, the child appropriates the experience individually and collectively and then leaves the classroom ready to be like his great-great . . . grandfather, counting the stars that night, and thinking of himself as a star and an answer to Father Abraham's prayer life. Fact and fantasy merge in the vicarious appropriation of a living story—that is, heritage.

Internalizing Stories that Live

I will conclude with practical suggestions concerning how picturing and reliving the Last Supper (a Passover Seder) assists participants to appropriate and internalize communion as a "Living Story" of spiritual nurture, transformation, and unity: God amidst humankind, partaking together, in a story without end, now and forevermore.

Living the Torah—Internalizing the Covenant

How does Torah teach Jewish people to pass on, across generations, story-experiences that live? Every morning, millions of religious Jews throughout the globe, literally strap prayer boxes to their arm and forehead and reenact a covenant marriage with the Lord their God. The covenant, a "living story," requires Jews to live in obedience to Torah as God's instruction. In return for Israel's covenant faithfulness, Jews believe God will provide fruitfulness to the wombs of Israel's households and fruitfulness to the land that God swore to give to His people. The nation will prosper, growing in fruitfulness and expanding territory, until all nations worship Israel's God. Inside the prayer boxes (t'fillin), four Scripture passages summarize how God commands the Jewish people to internalize the covenant.

The four Scriptures are code-named (from the Hebrew): "Hearken!" (Deut 6:4–9, Fox trans.), "Now it shall be if you hearken, yes, hearken!" (Deut 11:13–21), "Hallow to me!" (Exod 13:1–10), and "It shall be, when He brings you in" (Exod 13:11–16). What happened more than three thousand years ago must be passed on as a living experience to the next generation. Each of these Scriptures adds movement to a "living story." How the experience in the story of God's covenant with his people is acquired, appropriated, lived, internalized, reenacted, retold, and then passed on across generations is outlined in what follows.

Scriptural Ideas for Passing on Living Stories

At first, the story is told from "I-to-you," in the same way as the celebration of Passover is told to the child before Torah is "in the mouth" (Exod 13:8–9). But once this lesson is internalized as the word of God, the story picks up at a later stage, when the child knows enough to ask a question (and the adult is prepared to answer it). In response to an (elicited) question, the head of the house continues to tell the story, but now the story continues with the *internalized* elements told in an "us-oriented" way, with the child included as a member of the nation, and the *non-internalized* elements told in an "I-to-you" oriented way:

> And it was when Pharaoh hardened (his heart) against setting us free, that the Lord killed every firstborn throughout the land of Egypt, from the firstborn of man to the firstborn of beast. Therefore I myself slaughter-offer to the Lord every breacher of the womb, the males, and every firstborn among my sons I redeem. It shall be a sign on your hand and for headbands between your eyes, for by strength of hand the Lord brought US out of Egypt. (Exod 13:15–16, Fox trans., emphasis added)

Yeshua, the personal "One who saves," clearly understood these methods of Jewish education. At the Last Supper, he continued the story once more. Appealing to the giving of his life as a substitutionary sacrifice (Matt 26:26–28, cf. Exod 13:14–15), he shocked his disciples by taking matzah and wine and instituting a living memorial (*anamnesis*) of his Last Seder as an on-going religious ritual of calling-to-mind: "Take, eat. This is My body. . . . Drink from it, all of you; for this is My blood of the covenant which is poured out for many for the forgiveness of sins" (Matt 26:26–28, NASV).[7]

---

7. cf. John 6:30ff., esp. John 6:60–66 where Jesus shares these ideas with other "fol-

Vicarious appropriation of the Jewish heritage of redemption brings together the eating of the third matzah at the Jewish Passover with a living experience that Yeshua shared with his Jewish followers in Jerusalem. Both stories reenact a redemption that sets partakers apart as a people of God—one promises long life in the land for a people redeemed, the other promises life everlasting for a humbled sinner saved by grace. At story's end, the Passover that gave birth to corporate Israel and immortalizes God's covenant among the nations also gives birth to the redemption of humankind from the enslavement to sin and death to everlasting life in the presence of God the Father. In future times, both Bible stories are destined to come together once again—when Messiah sits on his throne in Jerusalem, but that is the rest of the master story (another grand-scale figure ground reversal) designed to shock Jew and Gentile alike (Matt 23:37–39, cf. Matt. 21:15–16, Zech 9:10, 14–17). Both themes converge with the drinking of the fourth cup of the Passover, the cup called, "I will be your God and you will be my people" (Exod 6:7). Adding an element of mystery, drinking that cup is reserved for that day when "all Israel is saved" (Rom 11:25–26). Of course, Yeshua knew about this cup too, because after instituting the Last Seder, he added, "But I say to you, I will not drink of this fruit of the vine from now on until that day when I drink it anew with you in my father's kingdom" (Matt 26:29 NIV).

Living stories that can transform teller and listener alike are structured as full narrative accounts characterized by reversibility (coming full circle), grand-scale figure-ground reversals (surprise endings when content and context invert or enlarge), and transcendent new beginnings (for example, the rush of emotion and changed internal response that come from transcendent understandings in the silences, or even a primary experience with the living God who bursts into present life and writes new story scripts).

Living the Story—Communion, Re-Creating Messiah's Body

For Jews, Passover has always meant telling a living story to the next generation. Upon completion of a tasty banquet feast of lamb, the children search for and find the afikomen (a piece of matzah that is broken and hidden). Its name is rendered "I am the coming one" (cf. John 12:15; Zech 2:10). Thus, we eat the hidden "bread of life" that is revealed, broken into pieces, and distributed to all believers at the Passover Seder (1 Cor 11:23–24). We pour

---

lowers," who then abandon him in shocked disbelief.

the third cup, also called the cup of redemption: "I will redeem you" (Exod 6:6; 2 Cor 5:21). Jesus (Yeshua, "the One who saves") takes this cup in the presence of the disciples (and their families) in Jerusalem and declares, "This cup is the new covenant in My blood; do this as often as you drink it in living memory of Me" (1 Cor 11:25–26). Jew and Gentile, male and female, rich and poor partake communally and appropriate his living memorial (Gal 3:28). The mystery of communion unites the body of Messiah; we enter together the space that is reserved for God.

Passover enlarges the story context of communion as we proclaim His coming again and the community breaks out singing, "Eliyahu haNavi" (Elijah the Prophet who announces Messiah). Then the fourth cup, the cup of completion, is poured: "I will take you for my people and I will be your God" (Exod 6:7). The Seder concludes, "Next year in Jerusalem!" In this story, God reigns and radiates his holiness from Jerusalem, Judea, and Samaria to the ends of the earth. Will the story shock us once more by leaping out of the pages of history and coming full circle into lived experience? When our stories merge with spiritual realities here and now, our primary experience of life with God can reveal the elusive presence of God in our lives. And in the stories that we tell to one another, the dreams of the prophets merge present-day hopes with biblical stories yet to be fulfilled in the world to come.

References

Applebee, A. N. (1978). *The child's concept of story.* Chicago: University of Chicago Press.

Berryman, J. (1991). *Godly play.* New York: HarperCollins.

Colson, H. P., & Rigdon, R.M. (1981). *Understanding your church's curriculum.* Nashville: Broadman.

Egan, K. (1989). *Teaching as story telling.* Chicago: Chicago University Press.

Erricker, J., Ota, C., & Erricker, C. (Eds.). (2005). *Spiritual education: New perspectives for the 21st century.* Brighton: Sussex Academic.

Feinberg, J. (1988). Measuring story schema: Assisting and eliciting story schema in children. Doctoral dissertation, Trinity International University, Deerfield, IL.

Fox, E. (1995). *The Schocken Bible: The five books of Moses* (Vol. 1). New York: Schocken.

Jensen, D. H. (2005). *Graced vulnerability: A theology of childhood.* Cleveland: Pilgrim.

Page, A. (1983). Children's story comprehension as a result of storytelling and story dramatization: A study of the child as spectator and participant. Doctoral dissertation, University of Massachusetts, Boston, MA.

Ratcliff, D. (1988). Stories, enactment, and play. In D. Ratcliff (Ed.), *Handbook of preschool religious education* (pp. 247–69). Birmingham, AL: Religious.

Ratcliff, D. (2005). *Experiencing God and spiritual growth with your children.* Retrieved June 9, 2007 from www.childspirituality.org

Scherman, N. (Gen. Ed.). (1995). *The Stone Edition of the Chumash: The Torah, Haftaros, and Five Megillos with a commentary anthologized from the rabbinic writings* (Artscroll Series). Brooklyn: Mesorah.

Sheble, J. R. (1983). Relationships of the age and sex of preschool children to their performances on tasks of story schema: Sequence, inconsistencies, story. Doctoral dissertation, University of Maryland, Baltimore, MD.

Sigel, I. E., & Cocking, R. R. (1977). *Cognitive development from childhood to adolescence: A constructivist perspective.* New York: Holt, Rhinehart, and Winston.

Stein, N. L., & Glenn, C. G. (1977). An analysis of story comprehension in elementary school children. In R. Freedle (Ed.), *Multidisciplinary approaches to discourse comprehension* (pp. 53–120). Hillsdale, NJ: Ablex.

Stein, N. L., & Glenn, C. G. (1982). Children's concept of time: The development of a story schema. In W. J. Friedman (Ed.), *The developmental psychology of time* (pp. 255–82). Oshkosh, WI: Academic.

Vygotsky, L. S. (1962). *Thought and language.* Cambridge: M.I.T. Press.

Walsh, J. (2003). *The art of storytelling: Easy steps to presenting an unforgettable story.* Chicago: Moody.

10 Turning Down the Noise: Reading and the Development of Spirituality in Children[1]

Linda V. Callahan

MEDIA AND TECHNOLOGICAL INNOVATIONS OF THE MODERN WORLD command immense power in today's society. A time capsule of the early twenty-first century would not be complete without a cache of paraphernalia. American youth could toss any number of technological wonders into the capsule since their pockets, backpacks, and homes are literally stuffed to overflowing with personal TV screens, digital music players the size of a pack of gum, cell phones with incredible technological capacities, satellite radios that beam down multiple channels from around the world, and video games that provide experiences that are (ostensibly) better than reality. There are so many technological wonders today it would be impossible to successfully encapsulate them all, and many would be obsolete before the time capsule was closed.

For the purposes of this chapter, all of the technological media just described will be referred to as "the Noise." The Noise is undeniably integrated into the fabric of American life. However, most adults who are actively involved with children do not realize the extent of American youth's interaction with the Noise. In 1999 and again in 2004, a nationally representative sample of third- to twelfth-grade students, ages eight to eighteen, was surveyed to determine the practices and trends of their media use (Roberts, Foehr, Rideout, & Brodie, 1999; Rideout, Roberts, & Foehr, 2005). The average amount of time students spent in using all media (the

---

[1]. This chapter in an earlier version appeared in the Fall 2007 *Christian Education Journal* and is reprinted here with permission from *CEJ*.

Noise plus reading apart from schoolwork) remained constant from 1999 to 2004 at forty-four hours per week, or the equivalent of a full-time job! A key change from 1999 to 2004 was that more electronic media migrated from the common areas of the home into students' bedrooms.

Perhaps the most significant change was in the nature of media usage. Over the five-year period there was a 10 percent increase in the amount of time young people spent using two or more media simultaneously. For every hour of media used by these multitasking youngsters, they were actually exposed to one and a quarter hours of media content. Therefore, the total amount of media content to which students were exposed daily increased by about one hour over the five years—from just under seven hours to eight hours. And in those eight hours, students spent only an average of forty-three minutes reading books, magazines, or newspapers (Rideout, Roberts, & Foehr, 2005).

The enchantment with the Noise begins before children even learn to walk or talk. Parents of children ages six months to six years reported that the average time their children spent being read to or reading alone was forty minutes per day, while 83 percent of their young children spent an average of 117 minutes per day using all screen media (TV, video games, videos or DVDs, and computers). Parents of babies under age two reported that almost two-thirds (61 percent) of these children used screen media daily (Rideout & Hamel, 2006).

Impact of the Noise on Connectedness and Spirituality

Family, schools, and churches once heavily contributed to, and influenced, the development of values and relationships, and they were the basis of connectedness in our culture. Ravitch and Viteritti (2003) point out that an estimated one-fourth to one-third of American parents "are not even minimally involved in their children's lives, including what goes on in their schools" (p. 4). The popular media has assumed a major role in the development of youth. The time school-age children spend with the media exceeds the time they spend with their parents or teachers.

From birth through age two, the rapidly developing human brain is stimulated by creative problem-solving activities, exploration, and manipulation, of things in the environment, and most importantly, by interaction with parents and other people. Because screen media does not provide these types of stimuli, the American Academy of Pediatrics (AAP) recommends *no* screen media use for children from birth to two years of age, and no more than one to two hours of media use per day for children over the age of two (Kaiser Family Foundation [KFF], 2005). The vast majority of parents has not heard of the AAP recommendations and shows little concern about the negative effects of the Noise. Instead, they may value what they consider to be the most important effects of exposing their children to the media: some peace and quiet for the parents, an opportunity to watch their own adult programs, and uninterrupted time for chores (Rideout & Hamel, 2006). The importance of connecting with their children is drowned out by the Noise.

From a very early age, infants and children are exposed to computer games and media that infiltrate their creativity and imagination so that their play is a reflection of the images and actions they have absorbed. "Their role as passive viewers increases the prospect of [their] becoming imitators rather than original, inventive, and inspired doers and actors" (De Souza, 2003, p. 271). Older youth live vicariously by watching surreal "reality" programs.

Unfortunately, the roles that many young people imitate are in direct contrast to biblical Christian roles. There is compelling evidence that repeated exposure to media violence contributes to aggressive behavior, anxiety, and desensitization to violence (KFF, 2005). Pardun, L'Engle, and Brown (2005) link middle-school youths' exposure to the sexual content of media (particularly in movies and music) with adolescent sexual activity.

In discussing contemporary influences on the spirituality of young people, De Souza (2003) states:

> We constantly find ourselves caught up in the "doing" of things and we rarely ever find time to just "be." Sometimes many of us have this hollow feeling—a feeling that we have become so distracted, we've forgotten the Self at the core of who we are. (p. 269)

Rossiter (1999) suggests that television and film provide young people basic "source material for the building of their spirituality and identity" (p. 212). Television commercials are specifically aimed at creating values and a self identity that are based on purchasing particular material goods. Pop singer Jewel, in her song "Satellite," exposes the tarnished side of Hollywood's tinsel culture and laments that Americans are very knowledgeable about the Noise but know very little about their inner spirituality:

California's sure lovely, it's the home of the stars and everbody is a nice body but their souls are like shadows, they are hollow inside . . . We understand a lot of things about modern technology but not about dreams. Our hearts are on the shelves. We can't fix ourselves but we can fix a satellite. (Kilcher, 2006, Track 5)

For many Americans, the Noise has become a god. Allender (2003), in describing the media as a cultural godhead, states: "The media, considered as a conglomerate, bear the attributes of God in that they are everywhere (omnipresence), inform us about everything (omniscience), and seemingly can accomplish anything (omnipotence)" (p. 78). Often, film and television imply that there is no spiritual dimension to life, or that spirituality is a negative influence in life. Both in subtle and in not so subtle ways, television and film contribute to the indifference to Christian spirituality and to the high levels of alienation and purposelessness that are common in children, youth, and adults today.

Turning Down the Noise through Reading

The thesis of this chapter is that one approach to countering the devastating effects of the Noise on the spiritual development of children is through reading. Forming connectedness between children and adults through reading may, in turn, foster spiritual formation in children.

In *Hardwired to Connect: The New Scientific Case for Authoritative Communities* (Commission on Children at Risk, 2003), the authors concluded that the deteriorating mental and behavioral health of American children is caused by a lack of connectedness to other people, and a lack of deep connections to moral and spiritual meaning. "Primary nurturing relationships influence early spiritual development—call it the spiritualization of attachment—and spiritual development can influence us biologically in the same ways that primary nurturing relationships do" (p. 27). Specifically, the resilience that is associated with spirituality is the same kind of resilience associated with effective early parental nurture. A child attributes traits to God that the child first attributed to one or both parents. Trust and a sense of security and peace are key aspects of spirituality that develop as the child first associates God with his father or mother.

Spiritual Formation, Spiritual Disciplines, and Reading

Spiritual formation involves the development of a transforming relationship with God as one practices the disciplines of the Holy Spirit. The disciplines that most directly relate to reading and its contribution to spiritual development in children are solitude, silence, study and meditation, and fellowship.

Solitude involves deliberately choosing to withdraw from human interaction and the bondage of things in order to draw closer to God. In this discussion, solitude involves withdrawing from the Noise. Silence, the absence of speech, is always a component of solitude (Tan & Gregg, 1997). Russell Hart (2003b) points out that one does not have to be in a particular place or completely alone to encounter solitude. "Paradoxically, solitude actually enables us to connect to others in a far deeper way than does mere attachment to others. Solitude is a oneness of mind and heart" (p. 254). Hart reflects further on silence, stating,

> Silence is imagination's habitat. It is also, according to Herman Melville, the voice of God. . . . God called the world into being through the Word—a Word that punctuates the silence but does not obliterate it. . . . Our industrial, technological world depends upon machines, and machines make noise. While the background noise cannot be obliterated, it can be reduced if we have the will to do so. (Hart, 2003a, p. 251)

Hart encourages persons to seek silence and actively engage in silence because God's first language is silence. Reading includes periods of both solitude and silence.

Study and meditation on Scripture allow God to speak directly to the reader and also strengthen the disciplines of solitude and silence. The truth of God's character and purpose is revealed in the Bible. All of mankind's personal experience and spiritual understanding can be tested, and confirmed or rejected by God's Word (Tan & Gregg, 1997).

Mercer (2003) defines spiritual reading as a discipline that promotes the formation of conscience and results in mankind's conformity to God's will. "We read to be changed. A deliberate, unrushed, reflective reading . . . can help us overcome the anxiety of self-discovery in the face of the reality of God" (p. 234).

Fellowship, a discipline of service, is described as an opportunity for persons to "become agents of the Holy Spirit to one another's growth and transformation, helping one another to surrender to God's will and reach out to others in loving service" (Tan & Gregg, 1997, p. 159). Parents provide the initial fellowship in an infant's life. And the infant's trust in his parents provides security and peace—the beginnings of spirituality. First, the infant learns that his parents will meet his physical needs, and that he can rely on them to provide care when it is needed. Loving touch is particularly important in the early years of life because touch meets emotional and social needs in addition to physical needs. Rocking and reading to an infant can promote feelings of security and peace.

Withdrawing with a child to a quiet place and reading a book together can result in a one-ness of heart and mind, and can allow both the child and adult to hear the voice of God. The child can begin to conform to God's will and also experience God through fellowship with his parents.

Selecting Reading Material for Specific Stages of Faith

It is important to choose reading materials that are appropriate for the individual child's stage of faith development. Table 1 briefly delineates James Fowler's *Stages of Faith* (1981) for children from birth to age twelve and includes the general types of reading materials that correspond to each stage.

In Fowler's *Stages of Faith* (1981), infants from birth to about age two are said to be in a pre-stage of undifferentiated or primal faith. These foundations for faith, laid down as trust, courage, hope, and love, join together and become the framework for all that comes later in faith development. Reading to an infant involves touching and holding, which promote trust, security, and peace. Parents should begin by reading a book that the infant can safely explore with her senses as she pats, smells, and sees the pages. Numerous secular and religious books made of cloth, plastic, or hardboard are available for this purpose. First published in 1940, *Pat the Bunny* (Kunhardt, 2001) is one such book that allows a baby to pat the fur on the bunny, feel father's rough whiskers, smell flowers, look in a mirror, and play peek-a-boo.

Books that create feelings of trust, love, and peace in the adult reader as he reads to the child are also excellent to read to children in the pre-stage of primal faith. Munsch's *Love You Forever* (1986) tells the story of a little boy as he experiences his mother's love through childhood, adolescence, and into adulthood. One spiritual message that can be drawn from the book is that God's care for his children is similar to the care that parents show for their children. The infant will not understand the words at first, but he will understand the effect that the words have created in the adult who is reading the book.

Fowler's stage one, the intuitive-projective faith stage, develops from approximately ages two to six. The child begins to express herself verbally as thought and language converge. She still cannot discern cause and effect or see another's perspective. Magical thinking and clusters of images make up her perceptions of reality. The child realizes that sounds and words refer to objects, and she begins to understand symbols as the shared representation of meaning.

She loves to listen to stories. Participating with others in rituals and repeated patterns of action become important to her, as well as imitating parents and other adults. The rituals and imitation might take the form of the parent and child enjoying a favorite book together, or the child holding the songbook during worship and "reading" the words as mom or dad point them out. As parents, older siblings, and other significant adults speak the language of their faith tradition, this faith language begins to gain value and significance (Yust, 2003). Books with repeated words, word patterns, and sounds are excellent choices at this stage, as are materials that include fantasy and wonder, such as classic fairy tales and nursery rhymes.

Children begin to internalize the images and values of their family and its faith. For better or worse, these images and values are powerful sources of orientation for the child (Fowler, 1992). The experiences of internalizing family values and faith traditions can be described as experiences of filiation. Children are experiencing being related or being filiated to their families just as they begin to experience the brotherhood or sisterhood of their faith tradition and their human filiation to God (Champagne, 2003). Picture Bibles, simple Bible story books, and other reading materials that put language to the child's faith tradition and rituals are important as the child forms stronger bonds with his faith community.

Kirk (2004), in reviewing literature for toddlers, focuses on separation anxiety and the development of the concept of object permanence in toddlers from ages eighteen to twenty-four months. Kirk says that object permanence allows a young child to begin to believe in the reality of a

Table 1: Fowler's (1981) Stages of Faith in Children and Types of Reading Materials for Each Stage

STAGE	APPROXIMATE AGES	CHARACTERISTICS	TYPES OF READING MATERIAL TO SELECT
Pre-stage (Primal faith)	Birth to 2 years	Foundations for faith are laid down through the joining of trust, hope, and love	Books (cloth, plastic, hardboard) that the child can safely explore with her senses Print materials that create feelings of trust, love, and peace in the *adult reader*
1 Intuitive-Projective Faith	2 years to 6 years	Child realizes the relationship between language and thought Rituals and imitation The images and values of the family and faith beliefs begin to be internalized Child experiences being related to other families and God	Materials that put language to her faith traditions and rituals including picture Bibles, and simple Bible stories Materials that include repeated patterns, words, and actions that he can imitate Materials that include a sense of magic/ wonder/ fantasy such as classic fairy tales & nursery rhymes Picture books that allow the child to perform exercises in object permanence, and to believe in a God who is unseen
2 Mythic-Literal Faith	7 years to 11–12 years	Child very open to spiritual transformation and studying God's Word Child can distinguish fantasy from reality, and connect events into a story over a time period	A child-friendly Bible in an easy to read and understand translation Materials involving real life situations—action and adventure—especially those that encourage thought about spiritual beliefs

God who is unseen.[2] Many picture books for young children provide opportunities for them to carry out exercises in object permanence, and such

---

2. "Object permanence" is the term used to describe the awareness that objects continue to exist even when they are invisible.

exercises foster a child's spiritual development. Kirk notes: "Many of the best remembered and most successful picture books center on searches for . . . caretakers in the context of a confusing and sometimes frightening chaos of objects" (p. 193). An example of one such book is *Make Way for Ducklings* (McCloskey, 1941/1999), a classic tale of parents (who happen to be ducks) who are searching for a safe place to raise their ducklings in downtown Boston. Each of the classic picture books ends with the main character surviving a separation or disaster as the character is welcomed and cared for in a safe place—much like the prodigal son. One spiritual message that can be extrapolated is that even though God cannot be seen, he was, is, and always will be present to care for his children.

Fowler's stage two of faith development is described as the period when children are able to construct a sense of time and to connect events into meaningful patterns. This mythic-literal faith begins around age seven when concrete operational thought allows children to identify cause and effect and to distinguish fantasy from reality. Stage two of faith development typically lasts until ages eleven to twelve. During this stage the child is fascinated with stories and is very much open to spiritual transformation as he begins to read and study the Bible for himself. "Action, adventure, and stories that relate to concrete life situations begin to replace fairy tales and fantasy as preferred fare. The stage two person projects himself or herself into the myths and stories which he or she creates" (Moseley, Jarvis, & Fowler, 1992, p. 47).

Rudyard Kipling's *Just So Stories* (1902/1987) and *Alexander and the Terrible, Horrible, No Good, Very Bad Day* (Viorst & Cruz, 1974) are two books that are good reading for children in the seven to twelve age range who are in stage two of faith development. The *Just So Stories* explore how many things were created, from the long trunk of the elephant and the spots on a leopard to the origin of the alphabet. Children have an opportunity to consider how Kipling's representations relate to their faith tradition's beliefs about creation.

The title of *Alexander and the Terrible, Horrible, No Good, Very Bad Day* (Viorst & Cruz, 1974) describes the subject of the book. Everything that can go wrong does go wrong in Alexander's day. He is so discouraged that he is eager to escape his life and move to Australia. This book allows children to reflect on their strengths and the spiritual disciplines they can use to make it through an awful day. Parents might also use the book as a springboard to discuss the fact that being a Christian does not guarantee a trouble-free world, but that God does promise that he will not give us more problems than we can handle.

GETTING THE BATTLE STARTED

Children are very much open to spiritual transformation as they begin to read and experience the other spiritual disciplines that relate to reading. However, many parents and other adults involved with children may perceive that the authority that the Noise commands is insurmountable. "Parents need to do something they've never been required to do before perhaps at any time in history: deliberately and consciously counter many of the dominant messages of their own culture" (Hymowitz, 2003, p. 233).

On the Home Front

Many parents have little experience with books. Gitlin (2003) says, "The pleasures of serious literature will come as a surprise to students who grow up—as the vast majority do—in homes with parents who themselves lack acquaintance with serious literature" (p. 35). She laments that "most have not heard anyone read well aloud. In a nonstop, fast-food culture they do not have the experience of the pleasures of slowing down" (p. 35).

To get started, the entire family should go to the library. Everyone— even young toddlers and *parents*—should choose at least one book of interest. An excellent resource on reading is *Honey for a Child's Heart* (Hunt, 2002), an annotated list of books that can help children grow spiritually and develop in other areas of their lives. *Take & Read: An Annotated List* (Peterson, 1996) is a resource for adults who wish to pursue their own spiritual reading. When the child is old enough, parents should help the child acquire a personal library card.

At home, the family should read aloud. Many elementary and middle school children enjoy reading to others, and even a preschooler can "read" a book based on the pictures. Noise-free reading times should be a part of each day. Parents should honestly take stock of, and limit, their own use of the Noise by asking questions such as:

- Have I ever used my PDA (Personal Digital Assistant) to access the Internet during a worship service?
- Do I spend a large amount of time using the Noise while on a family vacation?

- Have I ever refused to read with my child because I was checking my email, watching my favorite program, or playing my video game?

Parents should establish family rules that promote a healthy, balanced use of the Noise until children learn to do the balancing themselves.

Children also enjoy reading alone in a comfortable place away from the hustle and bustle of the household. Organizations that promote literacy offer many suggestions for setting up a quiet book nook, and for turning a home into a literacy-rich environment (Reading is Fundamental [RIF], 2007). Children will soon discover the pleasures of silence and solitude.

Children should own their own books. If prices are cost prohibitive at bookstores, parents should shop yard sales, used book outlets, and discount superstores for high-quality books at reduced prices. Parents can set up a book swap and allow their children to trade books with other children at no cost. Children should be encouraged to use their own money to buy a special book, and should be praised when they select a book instead of a toy or the Noise. Parents should give books as treats or as rewards for good behavior instead of candy, toys, or more of the Noise. Books are also excellent choices as gifts for birthdays and holidays, and are particularly appropriate choices for Christian holidays.

In the Pews

The church is the perfect place to inform adults about the effects of the Noise on the spirituality of its youth. The church youth group could present the facts during a skit that included as much Noise as possible. Christians must deliberately counter the effects of the Noise *within* the church.

One of the earliest forms of fellowship a child encounters is in the church nursery—which may be viewed as merely a babysitting service by many Christians. In contrast, Ratcliff (1992) believes that "the nursery ... may be one of several factors that helps set the framework for life-long spiritual development" (p. 11). It is tempting to play a Christian cartoon on DVD to entertain babies and toddlers. With only a little more effort, the nursery worker can foster spiritual development by looking at a picture book with a baby or reading a Bible story to a group of toddlers.

Some churches focus on entertaining children during religious activities instead of nurturing their spirituality, and entertainment often takes the form of Noise. Each church member needs to take the initiative to find out how much Noise has infiltrated the children's ministry. If the ministry has been taken over by Noise, then each adult must act to bring balance back into children's activities. For example, the pastor might read a few pages from a children's book as part of the children's sermon. Pictures from the book can be scanned into the computer and projected on the big screen so everyone can "read" along.

Griggs (1990) acknowledges that the Bible is alive and well in the United States but *studying* the Bible is being neglected by youth and adults. Unfortunately, many parents and religious teachers are not equipped to lead children in biblical study and meditation because they have not studied the Bible themselves. A renewed commitment to studying and meditating on Scriptures is needed by all Christian *adults* in order to promote a child's spiritual development.

When a child begins to study the Bible, it is important that adults select a version that is appropriate for her developmental level and reading ability, as well as congruent with a family's faith beliefs. Rather than waiting to present a Bible to an adolescent, each church should present an age-appropriate Bible to their young readers. Children experience great joy when they have their own Bibles.

Stumbling Blocks

Children often ask to read the same book over and over again. Many parents view such requests as annoyances in a busy day. However, repeated reading of stories offers children the nurturing of self and consciousness because it not only challenges the intellect but also returns attention to the contemplations of issues of the soul. Witte-Townsend and DiGiulio (2004) further propose:

> Many needs of the mind, heart, and body intertwine and grow within the child as these stories are experienced over and over again and social, practical, moral, ethical and philosophical dimensions are explored, including those which are explicitly stated as well as those which are implied. (p. 133)

Some adults are uncomfortable with the silence that is common at the end of reading a book. Witte-Townsend and DiGiulio (2004) share the following experience that occurred after reading to a group of children: "Silence emerges as a sense of wholeness from the circle of small bodies arranged on the floor around my chair. It is here in the silence, waiting together at the end of a story, that the read-aloud experience is transformational" (p. 134). Such silence mirrors the spiritual transformation of the disciplines of solitude and silence discussed earlier.

As an adult, it is easy to rush children to end the silence with the adult's own interpretation of a story. In doing so, children get the impression that there is only one correct response to the complex issues the story raises. It is important that adults allow a child to express his own response to a story—"the hushed response born of the spirit, mind, and heart" (Witte-Townsend & DiGiulio, 2004, p. 136).

Similary, Trousdale (2004) recommends that adults encourage children to express their own spiritual insights about the things they read by posing questions such as "Where are you in this story?" or "What part of the story is most important to you?" Trousdale reminds adults that "children's interpretations of stories are very likely to be quite different from those of adults" (p. 181).

Reading materials do not have to be explicitly Christian to have a spiritual impact. For example, Shel Silverstein's (1981) secular poem "Almost Perfect" describes a person who finds fault with everything in her life, describing each item or circumstance as "almost perfect . . . but not quite" (p. 163). After reading this poem a parent might discuss with the child how to deal with an individual who is always demanding perfection, and going even deeper, how grace might be extended to someone such as the character in the poem.

Some Christian parents forbid their children to read secular materials that they believe undermine their beliefs or promote ideas that go against biblical teaching (Robinson, 2001). There are, of course, secular materials that are definitely *not* appropriate for children, and parents are responsible for protecting their children from clearly harmful materials. However, it is important that Christian parents prepare their children to deal with the real world before they leave home. Christian parents may want to read controversial secular materials with their children and then discuss those aspects that are counter to the faith beliefs of the family. Christian youth need to develop critical thinking skills so they can learn to discern between right and wrong, and choose the best path to take in life.

Finally, as parents try to limit Noise in their child's life in order to focus on reading, they should proceed carefully as some directives may backfire and increase a child's *resistance* to reading. RIF (2007) cautions parents to avoid nagging the child who is not reading, setting unrealistic goals that require dramatic increases in reading, and turning reading into a power struggle so that a child reads only to please a parent rather than himself or eventually refuses to read at all.

The Challenge

It is difficult for a child to find community and connectedness with another human being while playing video games alone, watching television, and surfing the Internet. The Noise also limits opportunities to sit in silence and withdraw from the bondage of material things in order to grow closer to God. Pike (2004), in an editorial for a special issue of the *International Journal of Children's Spirituality* that focused on spiritual development and reading, says that he believes reading is a spiritual gift and also a spiritual discipline that must be practiced. Pike includes a personal account of a spiritual experience he and his four-year-old son shared:

> One evening, a few months ago, after finishing a particular story, there was quite a lengthy pause, after which Luke made a statement that was so profound and full of spiritual insight that I shall never forget it. Quite clearly, Luke informed me: "I'm the boy that God has chosen for you, Daddy." I didn't quite know what to say but I believe he is right: we have been put together. And it is my responsibility to nurture the boy God has chosen for me. (p. 126)

We have acknowledged that the Noise is deeply integrated into the fabric of American life and that it has a negative impact on the development of spirituality in children. However, the Noise is not insurmountable. As Christians who minister to children, we must encourage parents and others in the faith community to embrace their responsibility to nurture connectedness and spiritual development in children. A first step is to deliberately turn down the Noise and pick up a book.

Pike's (2004) closing remarks serve as an encouragement to all adults who foster children's spiritual development: "As educators committed to children's spiritual development, we need to foster the spiritual sensibilities of the children we, too, have been given. Teaching them to read (as a spiritual gift) is a good place to start" (p. 126).

REFERENCES

Allender, D. B. (2003). *How children raise parents*. Colorado Springs: Waterbrook.

Champagne, E. (2003). Being a child, a spiritual child. *International Journal of Children's Spirituality, 8,* 44–53.

Commission on Children at Risk. (2003). *Hardwired to connect: The new scientific case for authoritative communities*. New York: YMCA of the USA, Dartmouth Medical School and Institute for American Values.

De Souza, M. (2003). Contemporary influences on the spirituality of young people: Implications for education. *International Journal of Children's Spirituality, 8,* 269–79.

Fowler, J. W. (1981). *Stages of faith*. San Francisco: HarperCollins.

Fowler, J. W. (1992). Perspectives on the family from the standpoint of faith development theory. In J. Astley & L. J. Francis (Eds.), *Christian perspectives on faith development* (pp. 320–44). Leominster, England: Gracewing.

Gitlin, T. (2003). Teaching amid the torrent of popular culture. In D. Ravitch & J. P. Viteritti (Eds.), *Kid stuff: Marketing sex and violence to America's children* (pp. 19–38). Baltimore: John Hopkins University Press.

Griggs, D. L. (1990). The Bible: From neglected book to primary text. *Religious Education, 85,* 247–54.

Hart, R. M. (2003a). Silence. In K. Beasley-Topliffe (Ed.), *The Upper Room dictionary of Christian spiritual formation* (p. 251). Nashville: Upper Room.

Hart, R. M. (2003b). Solitude. In K. Beasley-Topliffe (Ed.), *The Upper Room dictionary of Christian spiritual formation* (p. 254). Nashville: Upper Room.

Hunt, G. (2002). *Honey for a child's heart: The imaginative use of books in family life* (4th ed.) Grand Rapids: Zondervan.

Hymowitz, K. S. (2003). The contradictions of parenting in a media age. In D. Ravitch & J. P. Viteritti (Eds.), *Kid stuff: Marketing sex and violence to America's children* (pp. 214–39). Baltimore: John Hopkins University Press.

Kaiser Family Foundation. (2005, January). The effects of electronic media on children ages zero to six: A history of research (Issue Brief #7239). Retrieved January 26, 2007, from http://www.kkf.org/entmedia

Kilcher, J. (2006). Satellite. On *Goodbye Alice in Wonderland* (CD). New York: Atlantic.

Kipling, R., & Gleeson, J. M. (1987). *Just so stories* (Reprint ed.). Stamford, CT: Longmeadow.

Kirk, P. (2004). Mapping the contours of faith in the land of separation: Spiritual geographies for children. *International Journal of Children's Spirituality, 9,* 189-202.

Kunhardt, D. (2001). *Pat the bunny* (Reissue ed.). New York: Golden.

McCloskey, R. (1999). *Make way for ducklings* (Reprint ed.) London: Puffin.
Mercer, J. L. (2003). Reading, spiritual. In K. Beasley-Topliffe (Ed.), *The Upper Room dictionary of Christian spiritual formation* (p. 234). Nashville: Upper Room.
Moseley, R. M., Jarvis, D., & Fowler, J. W. (1992). Stages of faith. In J. Astley & L. J. Francis (Eds.), *Christian perspectives on faith development* (pp. 29–57). Leominster, England: Gracewing.
Munsch, R., & McGraw, S. (1986). *Love you forever*. Willowdale, Ontario: Firefly.
Pardun, C. J., L'Engle, K. L., & Brown, J. D. (2005). Linking exposure to outcomes: Early adolescents' consumption of sexual content in six media. *Mass Communication and Society, 8,* 75–91. Retrieved February 22, 2006, from PsycInfo database.
Peterson, E. H. (1996). *Take and read—spiritual reading: An annotated list*. Grand Rapids: Eerdmans.
Pike, M. A. (2004). Editorial: The spiritual gift of reading. *International Journal of Children's Spirituality, 9,* 123–26.
Ratcliff, D. (1992). Baby faith: Infants, toddlers, and religion. *Religious Education, 87,* 117–26.
Ravitch, D., & Viteritti, J. P. (2003). Toxic lessons: Children and popular culture. In D. Ravitch & J. P. Viteritti (Eds.), *Kid stuff: Marketing sex and violence to America's children* (pp. 1–18). Baltimore: John Hopkins University Press.
Reading is fundamental (RIF). (2007). Creating literacy-rich homes. And How to lead reluctant readers age 9–13 back to books. Retrieved January 30, 2007, from http://www.rif.org/.
Rideout, V. J., & Hamel, E. (2006, May). The media family: Electronic media in the lives of infants, toddlers, preschoolers and their parents (KFF Report #7500). Retrieved January 27, 2007, from http://www.kkf.org/entmedia
Rideout, V. J., Roberts, D. F., & Foehr, U. G. (2005, November). Generation M: Media in the lives of 8-18-year-olds (KFF Report #7251). Retrieved January 27, 2007, from http://www.kkf.org/entmedia.
Roberts, D. F., Foehr, U. G., Rideout, V. J., & Brodie, M. (1999). Kids & media @ the new millennium. Menlo Park, CA: Kaiser Family Foundation.
Robinson, B. A. (2001). The Harry Potter™ books: Efforts to ban the books. Ontario Consultants on Religious Tolerance. Retrieved January 31, 2007, from http://www.religioustolerance.org/potter3.htm.
Rossiter, G. (1999). The shaping influence of film and television on the spirituality and identity of children and adolescents: An educational response (Part 3). *International Journal of Children's Spirituality, 4,* 207–24.
Silverstein, S. (1981). *A light in the attic*. New York: Harper Collins.

Tan, S. Y., & Gregg, D. H. (1997). *Disciplines of the Holy Spirit*. Grand Rapids: Zondervan.

Trousdale, A. M. (2004). Black and white fire: The interplay of stories, imagination, and children's spirituality. *International Journal of Children's Spirituality, 9*, 177–88.

Viorst, J., & Cruz, R. (1974). *Alexander and the terrible, horrible, no good, very bad day*. New York: Atheneum.

Witte-Townsend, D. L., & DiGiulio, E. (2004). Something from nothing: Exploring dimensions of children's knowing through the repeated reading of favourite books. *International Journal of Children's Spirituality, 9*, 128–42.

Yust, K. M. (2003). Toddler spiritual formation and the faith community. *International Journal of Children's Spirituality, 8*, 133–49.

For

Churches

& Schools

11   Children's Ministry Models, Learning Theory, and Spiritual Development[1]

Michael J. Anthony

MORE AND MORE CHURCHES ARE REALIZING THAT AN IMPORTANT FACTOR in church growth is a well-staffed, well-trained children's ministry team. Many ministries have professionals leading the team due to the heavy demands of programmatic designs. Bible colleges and seminaries are experiencing resurgence in demand for training and preparation in this career specialization.

Reconciling theory and practice is one of the tensions between theologians who explore children's spirituality issues and pastors who do the work of children's ministry. Theories are not easily condensed into neatly packaged, descriptive paradigms. One effective means of exploring the theological, philosophical, and theoretical foundations of children's spiritual formation is to critically examine prominent children's ministry programs and their underlying rationale. The focus of this chapter is to examine each of the four prominent programs for children's spiritual formation.

Connecting theory to practice has been a challenge for ministry leaders for generations, especially for those in the age-level specializations of children, youth, and singles. Although programs exist in each of these avenues, it is sometimes difficult for successful ministry practitioners to articulate just *why* their programs are successful. Without this descriptive

---

1. Portions of this chapter have been published in the Introduction to *Perspectives on Children's Spiritual Formation: Four Views* (Broadman & Holman, 2006) edited by Michael Anthony. For a fuller discussion of the four models described in this chapter, please refer to the Broadman & Holman volume. This material is used by permission of Broadman & Holman.

analysis, it is challenging to determine whether or not their success is based on carefully considered theological or philosophical reasoning, or just plain good luck. In some cases, the success may be based on the "fad of the day" approach to ministry experience.

As both a theoretician and practitioner, my goal is to connect theory to practice by developing a paradigm for children's spiritual formation that utilizes learning theory, and then analyzing four major models of children's spiritual formation in light of this paradigm. The purpose is not to *assess* the models *per se*, but rather to describe each model's unique goals, methods, typical elements, and important practices in terms of children's desire and need to know, and to know about, God.

A Paradigm of Children's Spiritual Formation

For this discussion, I will illustrate a paradigm of children's spirituality utilizing an integrative model based on two helpful typologies. The first is Urban Holmes's (1980) illustration in his book, *A History of Spirituality*. His illustration suggests a scheme for visualizing what patterns of Christian spirituality have looked like down through the ages. The graphic in figure 1 below is adapted from Holmes's diagram that depicts a helpful typology for the spiritual life (p. 4).

Figure 1. Holmes's Phenomenology of Prayer (Adapted)

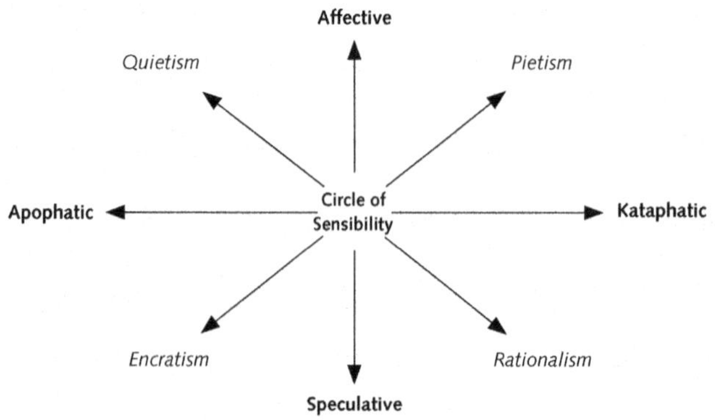

```
                    Affective
                       ↑
       Quietism        |       Pietism
            ↖          |          ↗
              ↖        |        ↗
                ↖      |      ↗
                  ↖    |    ↗
  Apophatic ←———— Circle of ————→ Kataphatic
                    Sensibility
                  ↙    |    ↘
                ↙      |      ↘
              ↙        |        ↘
            ↙          |          ↘
       Encratism       |       Rationalism
                       ↓
                   Speculative
```

The horizontal axis represents the apophatic/kataphatic scale. At the right end of the continuum is the piety that Holmes calls *kataphatic*. The term is Greek and literally means, "pertaining to speech." This type of spirituality is comfortable with forms such as ritual gesture, hymns, and prayers from a book, and it would cherish doctrine, creedal statements, and liturgical forms in worship.

At the left end of the same axis, Holmes locates an *apophatic* piety, a term that means "against speech" or "away from speech." This type of spirituality is suspicious of forms; it is an emptying spirituality, one that stands open and exposed before God, without mediating forms or structures.

The vertical axis of the diagram represents the speculative/affective continuum. (In this diagram these two ends are opposite Holmes's version to integrate this typology more easily into the discussion of the second typology that follows.) The vertical axis depicts the degree to which one's methods of fostering spiritual formation emphasize the illumination of the mind (speculative or *rational*) or the illumination of the heart or emotions (affective). By comparing these two axes it is possible to define spiritual practice and its immediate objectives with some degree of clarity. This "circle of sensibility," Holmes (1980) suggests, provides a "phenomenology of prayer" that depicts a way of understanding various strands of Christian spiritual traditions (pp. 4–5).

The resulting typology contains four schools of thought on spiritual formation: affective-kataphatic, speculative-kataphatic, speculative-apophatic, and affective-apophatic (Holmes, 1980, pp. 4–6). Westerhoff (1994) processes and explains Holmes's typology in his excellent book, *Spiritual Life: The Foundation of Preaching and Teaching*. Westerhoff describes the schools of spirituality that would exemplify each quadrant; he also states that each of these schools "is subject to a natural heresy, [that is] ... a truth that has gone too far" (p. 53).

According to Westerhoff (1994), practitioners in the affective-kataphatic school (the northeast quadrant) are concerned primarily with holiness in life. This spirituality is a "sensate, feeling spirituality" (p. 56) and is typically characterized by "verbal-sensate prayer" that involves the whole body as well as the emotions. This group would focus on the joys of liturgy and hymns with the express purpose of teaching the heart. A danger for this group, according to Holmes's diagram, is pietism (in italics on the chart), a disproportionate concern for right feelings that can lead to emotionalism.

In the southeast quadrant, the speculative-kataphatic school would center primarily on the illumination of the mind, using forms provided by words and gestures and traditions. The heretical danger for this group is rationalism, "an excessive concern for right thinking that leads to dogmatism" (Westerhoff, 1994, p. 54).

Those in the southwest quadrant, the speculative-apophatic, would form ascetic, self-disciplined—but vibrant—spiritual communities. Perhaps social gospel supporters would also find their place in this quadrant. The heresy that might befall this group is encratism, "an excessive concern for right behavior" (Westerhoff, 1994, p. 54).

According to Westerhoff (1994), Quakers and Mennonites and others like them would be found in the northwest quadrant, the affective-apophatic. These Christians tend to be uncomfortable with forms that are typically found in more liturgical, creedal traditions, but are concerned with emptying the self. They could be subject to quietism, an "excessive concern for right interior experience that leads to escapism" (Westerhoff, p. 54).

The second matrix that is insightful to our understanding of spiritual formation is David Kolb's "Model of Learning" (Kolb, 1984, p. 42; Kolb, 1981, p. 235; Kolb & Fry, 1975). It allows for both teachers and learners to account for individual differences found in the process of learning. Much like developing spiritual maturity, learning is highly personal, and no one description fits all individuals. Kolb's model (see an adapted version in figure 2) accounts for these students' individual differences. This model

Figure 2. Kolb's Model of Learning (Adapted)

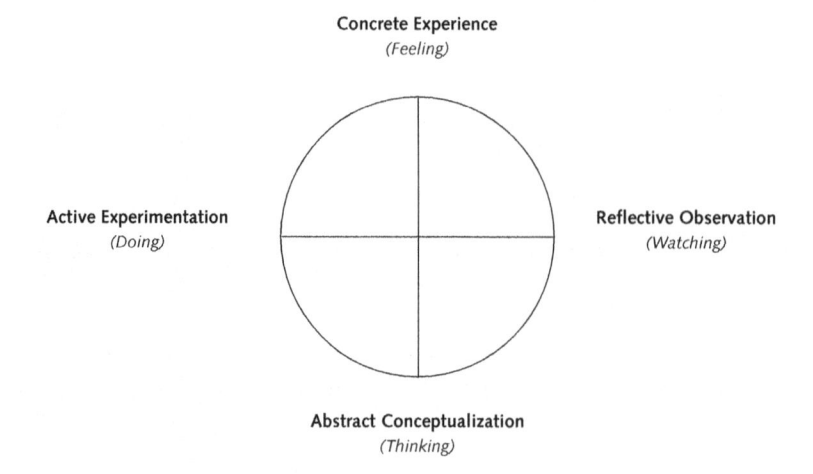

Concrete Experience
(Feeling)

Active Experimentation
(Doing)

Reflective Observation
(Watching)

Abstract Conceptualization
(Thinking)

employs a double axis typology that describes how individuals come to *experience* and *process* new information in their world. Since spiritual formation is a learned process, and requires considerable development across one's lifespan, a comprehensive look at how one develops spiritually should consider the different learning styles.

Kolb's vertical axis describes how the student perceives new information. One end of the axis depicts concrete experience (feeling) and the other end is abstract conceptualization (thinking), similar to Holmes's affective/speculative continuum. According to Kolb's learning model, students *perceive* new information on a continuum from intuitive feeling to cognitive reasoning. The horizontal axis depicts the manner in which students *process* new information. At one end is active experimentation (doing) and at the other end is reflective observation (watching). In essence, students process new information either by getting personally involved through hands-on interaction or by watching others interact with the information.

Holmes's typology provides useful insights as to how one develops spiritually, while Kolb's approach offers beneficial understanding regarding how one learns experientially and cognitively. What I am proposing is not a new theory *per se* but more of an integration of these models to describe this complex process of spiritual formation, particularly in the life of a child—although it might apply to adults as well.

People come to experience, and learn about, God in unique and personal ways; and spiritual formation is an interactive relationship between these two variables: *experiencing* and *knowing*. We *experience* God in profound and personal ways when we sense him drawing us into a relationship with him. It can occur at the oddest of times—perhaps while staring out into the vastness of an ocean or gazing into the simple beauty of a handpicked, backyard flower. At some point, we realize that there is something to life that is much bigger than ourselves and we sense that God is real. It is hard to define, but we know that voice within us is real and alive. Something or someone is beckoning us to explore a new way of thinking about what life is all about. Slowly, we are drawn into a relationship with an eternal God. We experience his gentle voice and recognize his influence. But this is not the same for everyone. Why would a creative God limit himself to formulaic actions? It is uniquely personal—but experienced nonetheless.

We know God as we build a relationship with him. He beckons us to come and we have accepted his invitation. Along the way, we interact, dialogue, and commune. Some days are filled with excitement and discovery, while others are quiet and contemplative; our relationship is anything but predictable. We pass through a season of remarkable growth as we study Scripture or other books that open our soul and speak to our heart's need. Or we may pass through a season where our growth accelerates because of the depth of personal relationships we enjoy with others who are on a similar journey; as we "do life together," we feel alive and encouraged. Another season may emerge, and we come to know the ways of God through times of reflective journaling and self-analysis. Throughout life, the means may be varied, but all believers can deepen and uniquely enrich their relationship with God. Again, knowing God in these ways may be difficult to define and dissect, but that does not negate its reality.

Building on Kolb's ideas, experiencing, and knowing about, God can be displayed as a matrix. We come to *experience* God (vertical axis), and we come to *know about* God (horizontal axis) in dynamic interface.

Figure 3. Experiencing God

Affective Expression
(Feeling)
↑
│
How we
***experience* God**
│
▼
Cognitive Reasoning
(Thinking)

Regarding the vertical axis (see figure 3), there have always been two outcomes of the spiritual life. The first attends an affective spirituality that focuses on the engagement of one's affective expression (i.e., feelings, emotions, inner impressions, etc.). The second is a less emotional spirituality that is housed in cognitive reasoning (i.e., thinking, reasoning, rational thought, etc.). Viewed this way, we experience God on a continuum somewhere between how we feel about God (a function of our affect, or feeling) and what we believe to be true about God (a function of our mind, or thinking).

The horizontal axis describes how people come to *learn* about God (see figure 4). At one end of the axis are those who prefer to learn about

God by reflective observation. They watch closely the faith of their parents, Sunday school teacher, camp counselor, pastor, and peers. Their faith is developed through less-kinesthetic means such as study, group prayer, and small group interaction.

Figure 4. Learning about God

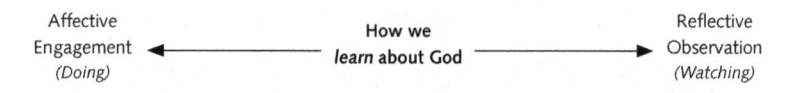

```
Affective                    How we                    Reflective
Engagement   ◄──────────  learn about God  ──────────►  Observation
(Doing)                                                 (Watching)
```

At the other end of the axis are those who prefer to learn about God through hands-on activities. They are busy testing the biblical principles to see if they are valid. They like action-oriented activities with real-life application. Bible study to these individuals is dry and lifeless. They would rather volunteer for a day serving in a soup kitchen than sit for an hour and listen to someone preach about servant hood. They might not be able to quote chapter and verse for why they do what they do, but they know it is what Jesus would do if he were in their shoes today, and that is all the information they need before acting. In essence, they prefer doing to watching.

Overlapping these two axes creates a typology that combines the personal manner in which people come to experience a relationship with God and how they learn about him to further develop the relationship. Both are needed for spiritual formation. To experience God without sustaining that relationship with a knowledge base is dangerous, making one susceptible to cults. Likewise, knowledge needs some personal expression or it becomes simply an academic exercise.

The four quadrants revealed by overlapping these two axes (as shown in figure 5) form a basis for helping us understand how children come to faith in Christ and grow in their relationship to him. In the midst of so many overwhelming individual differences, the diagram allows us to view spiritual formation from a larger perspective so we can understand what is taking place inside the heart and mind of the believer. The following discussion explores the four quadrants of spiritual development or formation, and the children's ministry approaches that reflect each one.

Quadrant 1: Contemplative-Reflective

This quadrant is characterized by periods of quiet reflection, introspective prayer, and storytelling. Its goal is twofold. The first goal is to empty the mind of self-absorbed thoughts to enable one to come before God as a clean vessel. Confession and honest self-assessment are essential to this process. The second goal is to find a place of solitude for quiet meditation. One can meditate on Scripture, reflect on a quiet song playing in the background, or gaze at a piece of artistic expression of spirituality (e.g., a sculpture, painting, etc.). Individuals in this quadrant can usually recall moments when God was "real" to them in a time of turmoil, doubt, or transition.

Figure 5. Spiritual Formation and Children's Ministry Models

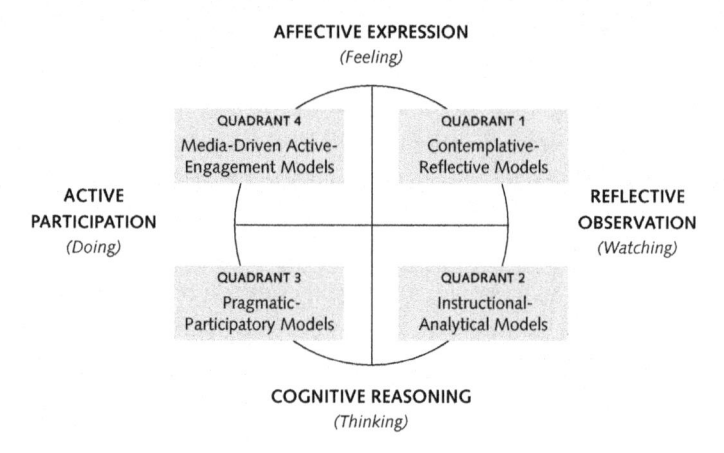

```
                    AFFECTIVE EXPRESSION
                         (Feeling)

            QUADRANT 4              QUADRANT 1
          Media-Driven Active-    Contemplative-
          Engagement Models       Reflective Models
ACTIVE                                                   REFLECTIVE
PARTICIPATION                                            OBSERVATION
(Doing)                                                  (Watching)
            QUADRANT 3              QUADRANT 2
          Pragmatic-              Instructional-
          Participatory Models    Analytical Models

                    COGNITIVE REASONING
                         (Thinking)
```

They value stories of the faith and often ponder the great insights brought about by the early church fathers in their historic writings. They tend to be verbal people when it comes to describing their own relationship with God and they are often engaged in dialogue with others about spiritual matters.

Prayer is the primary outcome of this expression of spirituality:

> This school is dominated by contemplative prayer. Centering prayers are typical. Their purpose is to occupy and free the mind so that one can dwell with God. [Reciting] prayers known by heart can achieve the same purpose. The oldest prayers in the church are centering prayers such as "Lord Jesus Christ, Son of God, have mercy on me a sinner" (Westerhoff, 1994, p. 57).

Thomas Merton, a Trappist Monk with the religious name of Father Louis, has become one of the most prominent names associated with spirituality in the twentieth century. Tyson (1999) cites Merton, speaking on the issue of contemplative prayer:

> Contemplation is the highest expression of man's intellectual and spiritual life. It is that life itself, fully awake, fully active, fully aware that it is alive. It is a spiritual wonder. It is spontaneous awe at the sacredness of life, of being. It is gratitude for life, for awareness, and for being. It is a vivid realization of the fact that life and being in us proceed from an invisible, transcendent, and infinitely abundant Source. . . . Hence it is more than a consideration of abstract truths about God, more even than affective meditation on things we believe. It is awakening, enlightenment, and the amazing intuitive grasp by which love gains certitude of God's creative and dynamic intervention on our daily life. (pp. 421–22)

Those in the contemplative-reflective quadrant believe that Christian spirituality must go beyond the simple transmission of biblical information. "Christians must move through the words of revelation into vital and personal contact with the risen Christ who desires to live now as the eternal God in our souls. Beyond mere religion, even beyond being saved, there should be the active pursuit of intimate relationship with God" (Callen, 2003, p. 94).

From a programmatic point of view, the contemplative-reflective approach is heralded by Jerome Berryman, Founder of the Center for the Theology of Childhood, and author of the popular book, *Godly Play: A Way of Religious Education* (1991; see also Berryman, 1995). Three other advocates of this position are Ivy Beckwith (2004), Scottie May, and Catherine Stonehouse (1980, 1998, 2001). The latter two have published an excellent book that describes their views on contemplation, the Godly Play model, and guided imagery in programming children's ministry (see May, Posterski, Stonehouse, & Cannell, 2005).

QUADRANT 2: INSTRUCTIONAL-ANALYTICAL

Those who promote instructional-analytical approaches have a high regard for cognitive thought processing. These individuals nurture their spirituality primarily through a consistent and systematic study of God's word. They take the time to explore Scripture in detail, looking for authoritative answers. They may punctuate their conversations with "My professor says . . ." or "My pastor claims . . . ," as they use this authoritative individual to defend their point. Children in this quadrant enjoy Bible memorization activities like quiz games and sword drills. They gravitate to memorization programs like Awana because they receive positive reinforcement for their efforts.

The instructional-analytical approach is characterized by a systematic presentation of biblical teaching, emphasis on Scripture memory with elaborate reward systems, and hierarchical design structures. Ministry models such as Awana, Boys Brigade, and Pioneer Girls are typical of this paradigm. Awana was founded by Pastor Lance "Doc" Latham and Art Rorheim of the North Side Gospel Center in Chicago in the 1940s. It was organized as a ministry in 1950 and quickly caught on with other churches. Children loved the positive reinforcements of stickers, badges, and patches that motivated young children to compete with others for these prizes. The acronym stands for "Approved Workmen Are Not Ashamed" based on 2 Timothy 2:15. Today, there are clubs in all fifty states; and more than 10,400 churches in the United States run Awana programs. Awana can also be found in 3,200 churches in 109 countries on 6 continents. Although many programs could fit into this particular quadrant, Awana best personifies its characteristics for our purposes here.

Quadrant 3: Pragmatic-Participatory

Ministry models that fit within this rubric include those with a propensity toward choreographed singing, dramatic presentations of Bible stories, numerous activities within a teaching hour, and a mild integration of instructional technology. "Learning in a context of activity and fun" might be the mantra that is advanced by those in this quadrant. Pragmatic participants are active learners and rarely enjoy sitting still for long periods of time. These students want to get involved; they are active learners and need assistance staying on task. They look for practical application to Bible stories and enjoy opportunities for "getting their feet wet" in the fundamentals of the faith. They ask pertinent questions during Bible studies because they need to know that Bible stories have relevance for today. Sometimes they appear to test authority, and some ministry leaders may see their questioning as threatening or argumentative—rather than as an important way for these students to learn. Also, these children typically like to make crafts and to explore. To them, sitting and listening is dry, dull, and boring. They would choose assisting at a homeless shelter on Saturday night over listening to a Bible story about helping those in need. In essence, they are the doers of our world.

Pragmatic-participatory children's ministry programs may offer a ninety-minute learning session on Sunday morning that is divided into five or more segments. Each segment has a purpose, and transitions between segments are carefully considered in order to facilitate a seamless progression. A typical morning program includes elements such as singing, skits, drama, a Bible story, puppets, games, and narratives. Technology is a critical component of the program, and various elements are presented via technology such as recorded music, PowerPoint presentations, creative video segments, and television or movie clips. At some point during the presentation, time is given for the students to break into smaller groups with an adult participating in the interaction. These small groups provide personal contact with the students who might otherwise remain anonymous.

Children's ministries across North America that characterize this approach would include Willow Creek's (South Barrington, Illinois) popular "Promiseland" curriculum, Saddleback Community Church's (Mission Viejo, California) "Empowering Kids" curriculum, or Northpoint Church's (Alpharetta, Georgia) "KidStuf" curriculum. Group Publishing is also a strong proponent of this paradigm through their action-oriented children's curriculum products (e.g., "Active Learning").

Quadrant 4: Media-Driven, Active-Engagement

This ministry model is characterized by high energy and is heavily vested in instructional technology, with children always in motion. These children love creative expression, guided imagery, music, drama, and activities, they are always moving and love the *process* of learning as much as the end result. For them, the joy of discovery may be more enjoyable than achieving the instructional objective of the lesson. For those who may not be familiar with guided imagery, it is a very passionate form of storytelling. Whereas storytelling is a preferred way of learning for those in the contemplative-reflective quadrant (quadrant #1), those in this quadrant need more engagement, and guided imagery provides this. In this form of expression, the storyteller moves from describing the events of the passage to getting the students to enter into the story itself. By describing the details of the event, acting out the story, changing voices to match the dialogue, using props to display actions, and perhaps even wearing costumes that depict various roles, this extreme version of storytelling goes beyond the cognitive transfer of information to the engagement of the mind, body, and heart of the learner.

Learners in the media-driven, active-engagement quadrant also enjoy using creative expression as they learn. Rather than listening to a story about a parable, they might prefer changing the story to make a contemporary adaptation in order to apply the lesson in today's context. These students tend to engage life issues enthusiastically and desire to participate actively in solving problems. They are generally optimistic about life, and look for what *could* be as opposed to what already *is*. They may view authority with suspicion and enjoy working with students like themselves. They generally do not prefer to read or sit for long periods of time without some creative expression or activity.

From a programmatic perspective, engaging these students requires the use of the dramatic arts, video, and impacting music. No program component should last for more than ten minutes, considering how these children value constant motion and activity. Although there are a number of excellent examples of this model around today, KIDMO is the poster child of this paradigm and is an extremely popular children's ministry program across North America. It is currently in two thousand churches and approximately forty churches per month start using the program. KIDMO is based on a philosophy of ministry that promotes the idea that reaching children should involve fun, active games, technology, and interactive music. Very few churches can operate at the level of quality that is required for learners in this media-driven, active-engagement quadrant, so KIDMO has developed a media-enhanced, self-contained program for elementary and preschool children that is available on DVD. The church starts the program by playing the DVD and stops at appropriate places along the way for personal interaction with the students. Small groups are essential as vital links for relationship development and long-term learning.

Conclusion

Though there are no agreed-upon definitions for spirituality, spiritual formation, or spiritual maturity, that should not preclude one from investigating it. For summary purposes, Christian spirituality may be defined as the interaction between one's theology and the living out of that theology in daily practice.

> A central feature is that spirituality derives its identity from the Christian belief that, as human beings, we are capable of entering into a relationship with God who is both transcendent and, at the same time, indwelling in the heart of all created things. (Sheldrake, 1995, p. 60)

Christian spirituality is to be lived out in community with other believers and also in the midst of the lost. The Holy Spirit enables spiritually minded-believers to be drawn into fellowship with God and the Spirit empowers believers in their Christian commitment.

Programs designed to help facilitate this spiritual maturing process for children must take into consideration children's learning process. Children perceive and process spiritual insights in a variety of ways; therefore, this chapter has explored approaches to children's ministry in light of various ways of thinking about children's spiritual formation.

As children's ministry leaders begin the process of choosing or changing their approach to their ministry, time pressures tend to drive decisions. Often programs are chosen on the basis of expediency. "This looked good at the conference," or "I just saw this great new curriculum in the catalogue," or perhaps, "Some friends of mine just tried this at their church and it worked great for them" are some of the reasons for selecting a particular ministry direction. But when something as important as a ministry program and subsequent curriculum are chosen based on such surface-level thinking, crisis waits in the wings.

A new approach or new curriculum should be considered in light of foundational theological beliefs as well as key philosophical and spiritual principles. What is called for is a "ministry time out" where the children's ministry team takes the time to ask themselves the hard questions in proper sequential order, for example:

- What are the theological traditions of our church?
- What doctrinal distinctives are non-negotiable?
- What biblical truths do we want taught, and at what stages of development?

Once the team establishes important theological foundations, they will need to ask the philosophical questions such as:

- What do we want our ministry DNA to look like here?
- Do we prefer to work through volunteers to accomplish our ministry goals or do we hire professionals to lead it?
- How does what we do integrate with the greater context of family ministries; are we self-supporting or an integrated part?
- Are we about evangelism, discipleship, or both?

And finally, the ministry team will need to consider important issues of children's spiritual formation such as:

- How can we balance the various learning styles of different children in order to meet children's spiritual needs?
- What role does worship play?
- When and how can we include a contemplative-reflective element in what we do?
- How can we utilize media to foster children's spiritual growth?
- How can our ministry make Christian truth relevant?
- How can we harness children's creativity for their spiritual growth?

This chapter's focus is providing ministry leaders with an overview of four models of ministry as a bridge between ministry theory and practice. Each model offers different spiritual emphases and meets children in different ways, and each has its own strengths and weaknesses. Selecting one model or approach may be a daunting task. Ministry leaders may choose a contemplative, reflective approach, or, on the other hand, a more didactic or instructional model. Or they may be drawn to a media-driven model, or to one that creatively engages the children. Perhaps a combination is called for: one approach can be followed for the Sunday morning children's learning time, and another approach for a Sunday evening or Wednesday evening gathering.

Since there is no "one size fits all" children's ministry program, ministry leaders should take care to ensure that the chosen methods and materials are consistent with the stated priorities of the church, for example, the church's tradition and theology. Most importantly, the model should be congruent with the church's spiritual goals for its children. Among the most important goals for any children's ministry program is to create excellent opportunities to foster children's spiritual formation. Considering the available options is a key responsibility for ministry leaders; this chapter offers timely resources for this formidable undertaking.

References

Beckwith, I. (2004). *Postmodern children's ministry: Ministry to children in the 21st century.* Grand Rapids: Zondervan.

Berryman, J. (1991). *Godly Play: A way of religious education.* San Francisco: HarperCollins.

Berryman, J. (1995). *Teaching Godly Play: The Sunday morning handbook.* Nashville: Abingdon.

Callen, B. L. (2003). *Authentic spirituality: Moving beyond mere religion.* Grand Rapids: Baker.

Holmes, U. T., III. (1980). *A history of spirituality.* New York: Seabury.

Kolb, D. A. (1981). Learning styles and disciplinary differences. In A. W. Chickering (Ed.), *The modern American college* (pp. 232–55). San Francisco: Jossey-Bass.

Kolb, D. A. (1984). *Experiential learning: Experience as the source of learning and development.* Englewood Cliffs, NJ: Prentice Hall.

Kolb, D. A., & Fry, R. (1975). Toward an applied theory of experiential learning. In C. L. Cooper (Ed.), *Theories of group process* (pp. 33–57). London: Wiley.

May, S., Posterski, B., Stonehouse, C., & Cannell, L. (2005). *Children matter: Celebrating their place in the church, family, and community.* Grand Rapids: Eerdmans.

Sheldrake, P. (1995). *Spirituality and history.* Maryknoll, NY: Orbis.

Stonehouse, C. (1980). *Patterns of moral development.* Waco, TX: Word.

Stonehouse, C. (1998). *Joining children on the spiritual journey: Nurturing a life of faith.* Grand Rapids: Baker.

Stonehouse, C. (2001). Knowing God in childhood: A study of Godly Play and the spirituality of children. *Christian Education Journal, 5*(2), 27–45.

Tyson, J. R. (Ed.). (1999). *An invitation to Christian spirituality: An ecumenical anthology.* New York: Oxford University Press.

Westerhoff, J. H., III. (1994). *Spiritual life: The foundation for preaching and teaching.* Louisville: John Knox.

12 Equipping Children for Ministry

Jane Carr

As a young girl my fondest memory of church was arriving early on Sunday mornings with a bag full of things my mom had prepared for her Sunday school class. All week my mom would gather supplies, and I would join her in punching out flannel graph figures, getting craft materials ready, and listening to her tell the story as if our front room were her classroom. On Sunday morning we would arrive early to set up, my mom would say a quick prayer for each child, and then she would punch "play" on her cassette recorder. Once kids started arriving, I was off to my own class—but on occasion she would let me stay and help.

Over the years I did not think much about that weekly routine or the impact that it had on my life. I left that small town to head to college, and soon after found myself in ministry as a children's pastor. A little over a year ago I returned to the church I grew up in to attend my mother's memorial service. After the service I took a moment to walk back in the classroom that she had taught in for almost twenty years. A flood of memories overwhelmed me. I could almost hear the sound of "I may never march in the infantry, ride in the cavalry, shoot in the artillery . . . but I'm in the Lord's army" coming from her small cassette recorder. It was the first time that I began to consider that my mother's example of faithful service and her encouragement to help her each week may have contributed to my desire to serve.

As children's pastors, teachers, and leaders in the church, we spend a great deal of time telling kids to sit still, be quiet, and listen. What would happen if we got kids excited about doing something with their faith at an earlier age? Perhaps the next generation would grow up with the understanding that serving was simply a way of life for a follower of Christ.

Biblical and Theological Integration

Scripture is clear that we are created for good works (Eph 2:10). Spiritual gifts have been bestowed upon believers for use in the body of Christ (1 Cor 12:1–10, 28–31; Rom 12:3–8). No place in Scripture do we see any indication that spiritual gifts are given only to adult believers, nor do we see any indication that a child who comes to Christ should wait until a certain age or time to use their gifts. It is clear that these gifts were given for the common good of the body, and that, in fact, the members of the body who might appear to be insignificant are, in actuality, quite necessary. Using the analogy of the body, Paul emphasizes the importance of each person in the church. The encouragement here is to use the gifts we have been given and encourage others to use theirs.

In Ephesians 4:11–12 Paul further encourages us as leaders of the church to take responsibility to equip the saints—fellow believers in Christ—for service, with the end result being that the church is built up to its fullest measure. Furthermore, in 1 Peter 4:10–11 Peter says that we should live in the expectation that we will each receive a special gift that should be employed in serving one another. In doing so, we will be good stewards and God will be glorified as others see Jesus in us.

Service and Spiritual Formation

Serving one another not only results in building up the church, but also in building up the individual believer. Our ultimate desire is to be formed spiritually into the image of Christ. When Jesus walked on this earth, he left us an amazing image of a man who, in humility, gave himself to others. In Matthew 20:28 Jesus tells us that he came "not to be served, but to serve and to give his life as a sacrifice for many." The picture of Jesus as a servant is nowhere more evident than in the account of John 13 where he washed the feet of his disciples. Taking the position of a servant, kneeling with a pitcher of water, a pan, and a towel to wash the dust-covered feet of his followers. In verse 15 Jesus says, "For I gave you an example that you also should do as I did to you." Chuck Swindoll (1981) in his insightful book, *Improving Your Serve*, points out that in this particular passage, Jesus is not saying, "I did something for you, now you do something for me." Rather, the emphasis in this passage is that we are never more like Jesus than when we are serving others.

In his excellent work, *The Spirit of the Disciplines*, Dallas Willard (1988) includes service in his list of what he describes as "disciplines of engagement." According to Willard, a discipline is "an activity undertaken to bring us into more effective cooperation with Christ and his Kingdom" (p. 158). In essence, a discipline is something that increases our ability to become more mature in Christ. Though service can be a simple act of love and kindness, it is also a discipline to "train [us] away from arrogance, possessiveness, envy, resentment, or covetousness" (p. 182). Therefore, serving others can play a vital role in forming us spiritually.

Richard Foster (1978), in his classic, *Celebration of Disciplines*, says it this way:

> Of all the classical spiritual disciplines, service is the most conducive to the growth of humility. When we set out on a consciously chosen course of action that accents the good of others and is, for the most part, a hidden work, a deep change occurs in our spirits. (p. 130)

Throughout Scripture we are encouraged to serve one another. Peter urges us to be hospitable to one another (1 Pet 4:9). Paul encourages us to be devoted to one another and give preference to one another in honor (Rom 12:10–13), encourage and build up one another (1 Thess 2:7–8; 5:11), be compassionate toward one another (Eph 4:32), care for one another (1 Cor 12:25), instruct one another (Rom 15:14), bear one another's burdens (Gal 6:2), comfort one another (2 Cor 1:4), and love one another (John 13:34). Deep change occurs in us when we embrace service.

In addition, as our ability to love others through acts of service increases, so does our ability to love God. Klaus Issler (2001), in his recent book *Wasting Time With God*, draws a direct connection between loving God and loving others. In Matthew 22, Jesus sums up the greatest commandment by quoting two Old Testament passages that refer to loving God and loving others. Issler points out an important link connecting these two commands when he states, "How we love God impacts how we love others. And how we love others impacts how we love God" (p. 39). As we learn to love others more deeply, we will experience a deeper relationship with Christ.

Scriptural Examples of Children Serving

The Bible gives us several examples of young people being set apart for service. In 1 Samuel 1:20–28 we find a young boy named Samuel. Samuel was probably about three years old, the customary age for weaning, when his mother Hannah brought him to the tabernacle to dedicate him to the Lord. Hannah was giving Samuel to God for a lifetime of service, a significant decision for a woman who had been barren many years prior to Samuel's birth. Unlike child dedications that we observe in our churches today, Samuel would remain with Eli the priest and grow up serving the Lord as Eli's helper or assistant.

In this role Samuel's responsibilities may have included opening the tabernacle door each morning (1 Sam 3:15), cleaning the furniture, and sweeping the floors. As he grew older, Samuel probably would have assisted Eli in offering sacrifices. The very fact that Samuel wore a linen ephod, a garment worn only by priests, shows that he was indeed a priest in training (1 Sam 2:18).

In 1 Samuel 16:5–13 we see another young man named David. In this passage we observe Samuel, now a grown man himself, seeking the next king of Israel. Perhaps he was looking for someone strong and of good stature, an impressive looking man. Seven sons of Jesse pass by Samuel and to each of them Samuel replies that the Lord has not chosen these. Interestingly enough, Samuel must ask Jesse if these are all his children, to which Jesse replies that the youngest remains (in a sense, the least likely to be used by God in such a significant way), and he is out doing his chores. David is brought in and the Lord lets Samuel know that this is the one to be anointed king. Samuel anoints David with oil to symbolize that he would be set apart for service to God.

Another amazing young person was an eight-year-old king named Josiah (2 Kgs 21:24–26; 22:1–2). Of all the kings mentioned throughout the Old Testament, it is rare to find one who obeyed God completely. Josiah was such a king. For eighteen years he reigned obediently and, at the age of twenty-six, he began instituting reforms based on God's laws (2 Kgs 23:19–24; 2 Chr 34:15–28, 33). It was Josiah's early years that laid the foundation for his later task of reforming Judah.

Scripture also notes the service of other children. In the Old Testament, a little servant girl in the story of Naaman was not afraid to tell Naaman's wife about the power of God (2 Kgs 5:2–4). As well, in the New Testament we see a young boy involved in the work of the Lord. In John 6:5–13, the disciples notice a young lad with five loaves and two fish. Knowing that this certainly could not feed the crowd at hand, the disciples gave little thought to what the boy had to offer. However, Jesus took what a young child offered and used it to accomplish one of the most spectacular miracles recorded in the Gospels.

These passages are a great reminder that age is no barrier when it comes to being used by God. The Lord has given spiritual gifts to believers to be used in the body of Christ so that the church might be effective. Throughout Scripture we see glimpses of young people who were able to do great things for the kingdom. We should expect no less of young people today; in fact, we should encourage it all the more.

Influence of Childhood Volunteer Experiences

Prior life experiences, especially those in childhood, influence how likely adults are to volunteer. In the spring of 2002 the Girl Scouts of America conducted a study of volunteer trends among eighteen- to twenty-nine-year-olds. Throughout the study volunteers spoke of a "tradition of volunteering" that was rooted in their childhood experiences. Over 60 percent had volunteered during childhood. Participants noted growing up around volunteering, the influence of family members who volunteered, and opportunities they had to volunteer. Some mentioned the positive effect of seeing a parent or grandparent involved in volunteering, while others mentioned the direct impact of being involved themselves in school-sponsored community service projects or service-oriented organizations such as Girl Scouts or 4-H. Some of these experiences began as early as elementary school (Schoenberg, Pryor, & Hart, 2003).

Wymers' (1999) study exploring motivations for church volunteering reveals that values learned in childhood serve as a stimulus for volunteering. Many participants in the study describe having parental role models and observing the joys of serving that they see in their parents. Others mentioned volunteering with a parent and the influence it had on their own desire to serve as an adult. In addition, being involved as a child in service organizations such as the Boy Scouts also had a strong impact on continued motivation for volunteering later in life.

MODELS OF KIDS DOING MINISTRY TODAY

Most children's ministries today focus their creative energies on the evangelization and discipleship of children. They offer excellent, well-planned events and programs that encourage children to form significant relationships, memorize Scripture, learn Bible stories in new and innovative ways, and experience deep and moving worship. However, many churches are overlooking the importance of creating opportunities for children to authentically serve. Some churches are addressing this gap by offering formal, ongoing opportunities for children to be involved in serving.

Several years ago I created CMPros, an online e-group that networks children's ministry professionals. Over two hundred children's ministry professionals, representing about 180 churches around the nation, participate in CMPros. Recently, I posted a series of questions about service opportunities for children in the churches these ministers serve. Some of the questions included,

- What age/grade of children are allowed to serve?
- Is there some type of formal application process and training program? Briefly describe.
- What opportunities are there for kids to serve in the church, in local outreach opportunities, or on missions trips?
- How have you seen their involvement in serving impact their faith?

Of the 180 churches represented on CMPros, 32 described some type of "kids in service" program, 46 responded that they do not offer opportunities for children to serve, and 102 did not respond to the posted questions. (For a complete list of the questions posted, see Appendix A.) The following descriptions of service programs for children draw on the data collected from this online survey.

"Kids in Service" Programs

Churches that offer formalized "kids in service" programs are typically churches that have paid staff and multiple weekend services. The program is usually designed for children in upper elementary, beginning in fourth or fifth grade. Parental involvement is key to the success of these types of programs. Parents are expected to understand the commitment of their child's involvement in a service program, to encourage their child in their ministry assignment, and to serve occasionally with their child.

Children who desire to participate in the program complete a formalized application/screening process very similar to the type of process an adult volunteer might complete. The children wear official name tags that designate them as volunteers and work alongside adult volunteers in an area of weekend ministry for a year. The programs often have catchy names such as "Super Servants," "Leaders in Training," and "Kids in Xtreme Service."

Participating children are involved in ongoing training opportunities designed to equip them with the skills and knowledge necessary for their area of service, while helping them understand what it means to serve and volunteer in the church. Children are given ongoing feedback and accountability throughout the program. They develop good patterns for service as they are expected to be on time, contact someone if they are going to be absent, attend their own class one hour as well as serve a second hour, be a good role model whether at church or at school, and seek to grow in their own Christian walk.

Program coordinators see the transformation that takes place in kids who are involved in ongoing service opportunities in the church. Short-term effects include children not wanting to miss church, children behaving better among their peers because of their role as leaders in the church, and children feeling a sense of community and ownership in the church. One program coordinator told a story of a fifth-grade girl who invited her friends from school to come to a special event at the church. The girl proudly showed her friends the room where she leads worship every Sunday for the first graders and was overheard saying, "This isn't just my church; it is like my second home." Long-term effects include the discipline of serving on a regular basis or a sense of calling to ministry or the mission field. One program coordinator related how children who began serving in fourth grade are now in high school and college and still serving today. Another coordinator mentioned that he has seen several children now in adulthood go on to become pastors, missionaries, or assume significant roles of leadership in the church.

Community Service or Missions Projects

Smaller churches tend to involve children in serving through the use of community service or missions projects. These types of projects are more sporadic and require less paid-staff oversight. Projects might include collecting certain items to be distributed through the church or given to a local organization; serving in the community with various organizations such as assisted living centers, the Special Olympics, unwed mothers' homes, public parks and recreation programs; or connecting with missionaries or mission agencies through letter-writing or offering projects. Many of these types of projects involve the entire family. One church conducts four community service projects throughout the year for elementary-age children. The project is an all-day event where parents and children attend a preservice training meeting, then participate in the actual service project, and return to the church for a debriefing experience. One project coordinator described the impact on the participants in the following way:

> Kids always come back with great stories of how God gave them an opportunity to talk to someone or put a smile on someone's face. Our projects give kids the opportunity to actually do something for someone else, not just talk about it in a classroom. I see ... those who participate [become] more active in other aspects of church—reaching out to new kids, offering to help in their classes, and setting a good example.

Other churches conduct church-wide community outreach opportunities. These intergenerational events provide reciprocal benefits for children and adults. Children have the opportunity to serve alongside parents, grandparents, and others in the church, allowing them to experience the greater faith community living out a lifestyle of service. Adults are equally impacted by the faith and boldness of a child. One project coordinator described an event where they were handing out water bottles in the park and inviting people to church. While adults were more hesitant, children displayed a greater degree of boldness and were uninhibited in sharing their faith or talking to people about church. This experience became a great faith challenge for the adults in the congregation.

Day Trips or Short-Term Missions Trips

Other churches have included children in day trips to the inner city, poverty stricken areas, or places impacted by disaster. Some churches have gone as far as inviting children on short-term international missions trips. For the most part these types of experiences are exclusive to upper elementary children and often include at least one parent.

In these instances children minister to other children who are less fortunate than themselves, and experience God at work in their lives. As one children's leader said, "You can sit in a classroom each Sunday and learn everything about God, but it's totally different when you get out there and see for yourself that God is really who He says He is." During much of childhood, ideas and beliefs about God remain untested, and, therefore, may not be integrated into a child's personal faith in a meaningful way. Events such as these allow children to take what they have learned about God, apply it to real-life situations, and debrief the experience with significant adults in their lives who can help them incorporate it into their faith in a meaningful way.

Another unique aspect of these types of trips is the inclusion of parents. Having parents travel with their children provides a shared experience that can be talked about for years to come. This is often the missing link in youth missions trips. Youth return home from a life-changing missions trip only to find that they feel a certain disconnect as they attempt to explain an experience that only they have had. As one children's leader explained, "When children and parents are taken away from the routines of life and do ministry together, they return home with memories, photographs, and shared experiences that will last a lifetime."

Involving children in ministry can take many different forms. Whether in the context of a formal ongoing "kids in service" program, a community service project, or a short-term missions trip, it is easy to see that these experiences have long-lasting effects on children, parents, and the faith community. Though very few churches have formal programs to involve children in service, churches are increasingly seeking ways for children to be involved in service opportunities, both inside and outside the church. These churches are discovering the value of a holistic ministry that includes evangelism, discipleship, fellowship, worship, *and* serving.

Yet, there still remain churches that do not see involving children in serving as a priority. These churches report not having enough time or resources, in particular, paid staff or volunteers who are willing to oversee service-oriented programs or events. Others see their church and their children's ministry as simply too small. The fact that they only have one weekend service often limits ongoing service opportunities. In some cases the number of children in elementary ministry alone is so small that involving kids in weekend serving would significantly impact class sizes. Other churches simply do not see it as important; parents, volunteers, and church leadership see little value in involving children in serving opportunities.

The Spiritual Value of Involving Children in Serving

What, then, is the value of involving children in serving? To address this question, children who had been serving in an ongoing "kids in service" ministry program for at least one year were interviewed. Two large churches in Southern California were identified and sixty-five children participated in the study. The study incorporated both qualitative and quantitative research methods. All participants were fourth through sixth graders. The children were asked a series of questions to discover what motivates them to serve, ways in which they have seen God use them in the lives of others, and how serving has impacted their lives. (For a full list of the interview questions, see Appendix B.)

Motivations for Serving

Interestingly, not one child mentioned that a parent or other adult encouraged them to sign up for the "kids in service" ministry program. The primary motivator for the children was a desire to serve God and the church. For example, one child said, "I felt like I needed to get involved in something at church"; another said, "I enjoy knowing that I'm helping God." Another child mentioned that even though she knows that what she is doing is for the church, it feels like she is giving back to God. Serving God is also seen as a way to become closer to God. One child put it best: "I wanted to serve because I knew it was a way to help God in His work in the church, and also a way to become closer to Him."

A secondary motivator was to help others. A significant number of children mentioned being drawn to younger children and loving being around kids. This may be influenced by the fact that the majority of volunteer opportunities for upper elementary are with preschoolers and primary-age children. One child said, "I really find myself wanting to have a relationship with kids so that I can help them learn about Jesus." For others, it is a way to turn their focus off themselves and onto others: "I wanted to do something for others, rather than just always doing things for myself."

Why Children *Should* Serve

Their responses indicate that children do not perceive themselves as having the limitations that adults might place on them. To a child, the real question is, "Why wouldn't you want a child to serve?" It is clear to children that God wants "us" to serve, and of course that "us" must include them. As one child proclaimed, "Well, I want everyone to know about God. Don't you?" The children's responses revealed their belief that what they do makes a profound difference in the lives of others. As one child articulated, "It's important for kids to serve at church so the church can grow." Still another child put it this way: "God can use you in different ways, even in ways you don't see."

The children in the research tended to see their stage in life as an asset, not a liability:

- "Kids respond better to kids closer to their age."
- "Kids aren't the future, they're right now."
- "Kids need someone to look up to and have support from."
- "Some kids need people in their lives to minister to them, and it's awesome to be that person."

Through serving, children often see things that they can do that adults are unable to do. "One day one of the kids I was working with wouldn't listen to the other teachers and would only listen to me. It really made a difference in my life." As children minister to other children, they begin to see themselves as people that God is using in the lives of others.

How Have You Seen God Use You?

Some children gave global answers to this question such as, "Every time I serve I feel like God is using me." Other children gave very specific answers:

- "When a newcomer came and didn't want to leave her mom, I gave her a sticker and told her she would be okay and she was fine the rest of the time."
- "Once I was leading worship in first grade and a little girl was really excited and was dancing and singing as loud as she could! When I walked offstage she came up and gave me a hug."
- "A girl in my preschool class was upset and wanted me to hold her. She stopped crying and I know God really used me that day."
- "A little girl had wandered away from her group and couldn't find her leader. It took awhile, but I helped her to find her group again."

One child's response offers insight into her deep trusting faith: "I don't really know, I can't remember a time like that. But I know God will use me in His plan somewhere even if I can't see it now."

Spiritual Growth in Children Who Serve

Children who are involved in serving are challenged spiritually. The discipline of serving provides opportunities for children to take on new responsibilities, learn the value of completing tasks, and work with people of all ages. The intergenerational experience of serving alongside adolescents, young adults, and older adults gives children the opportunity to see the faith of believers at different stages of life. It also teaches them respect for the church and for others. As one child said, "I've learned to treat the church like it's God's home and to respect those in leadership."

Many church leaders are hesitant to involve children in service because they fear that removing children from their own age-level classes will inhibit the learning process. However, children are always learning, and in the context of serving perhaps they are learning even more: "I've learned things in the preschool class that I serve in that I did not learn in my fourth grade class." Serving also inspires children to keep growing in their relationship with God: "Since I've been serving, I've rededicated my life to Christ." By helping other kids learn, children begin to actually see how much they know about God. This gives them confidence to share their faith with others and encourages them to want to know more:

- "Being involved in kids' ministry shows me how far I've come and how much more I want to grow."

- "When all the little kids really get into the Bible stories, it shows me that I should really get into the Bible."

- "When I see kids look up to me it reminds me to look up to God."

- "It challenges me when kids look up to me and ask me questions about God. I don't always know the answer, but it makes me want to find it that next week."

Serving also impacts a child's desire to attend church. Children shared stories of insisting that their parents return home early from vacation because they did not want to miss serving on Sunday. One child said, "Serving makes me look forward to coming to church." In recent years there has been a steady decline in church attendance among adolescents and college students. For decades, pastors and leaders in the church have sought solutions to the age-old question: "How do we keep young people interested in church?" A fifth-grade girl involved with a "kids in ministry" program put it best when she said, "I used to hate going to church because I heard the same old stories over and over again, but now I love it." Larry Fowler (2004) in his book *Rock Solid Kids* claims that involving children in serving at an early age is the most effective thing we can do to engage them. He lists permanence—their desire to remain engaged in their faith and not abandon it when they are older—as one of the key benefits of having children involved in serving.

Children who serve also sense a great confidence in God and his ability to work in their lives. Some of the children's responses are, "I've seen how much God can do through me"; "I've seen God at work in my life"; and "When I serve, it is like I know that God is real." Through serving, children learn to depend on God as they see him at work in their lives. One girl recalled that "there was a little girl who was mentally challenged and I think that God was using me to be the one to be patient with her. It was difficult, but I felt God help me do it." Another boy remembered the help God gave him as he told a story to a group of preschoolers: "I was nervous about teaching, but God helped me explain the story of Adam and Eve."

Serving also gives children a sense of purpose and meaning in life: "I know now that helping each other is a vital part of life"; "Serving has helped me understand why God put us here"; "I know that God wants to use my life for something greater." George Barna (2003) maintains that even in the midst of a complex society, children still have the same basic needs they have had for decades: "to be trusted, to be loved, to feel safe, and to identify a significant purpose in life" (p. 24). Serving allows children the opportunity to discover this greater purpose, a purpose that some people search for their entire lives.

Conclusion

Serving provides children an opportunity to turn their focus off themselves and on to others. As one child sums up, "I wanted to do something for others, rather than just always doing things for myself." Dallas Willard (1988) reminds us that service is more than a simple act of love and kindness; it is a way in which we train ourselves away from the worldly constraints of arrogance, possessiveness, envy, resentment, and covetousness. Doing things for others frees us from the sinful pull of the world that tells us that self, rather than God, is at the center. Serving also deepens children's love and knowledge of God. Children describe sensing a closeness with God when they serve. As Issler (2001) points out, when we learn to love others more deeply, we experience a deeper relationship with Christ.

As we involve children in service opportunities, we move beyond mere information-giving and move toward life transformation. Barna (2003) in his book *Transforming Children Into Spiritual Champions* stated, "Your spiritual condition by the age of thirteen is a strong predictor of your spiritual profile as an adult" (p. 41). Childhood is a crucial time for establishing foundational Christian values that will be carried into adulthood. Providing opportunities for children to live out their faith in the context of serving is an essential part of their spiritual formation.

References

Barna, G. (2003). *Transforming children into spiritual champions*. Ventura, CA: Regal.
Foster, R. J. (1978). *The celebration of discipline*. New York: HarperCollins.
Fowler, L. (2004). *Rock solid kids*. Ventura, CA: Gospel Light.
Issler, K. (2001). *Wasting time with God*. Downers Grove, IL: InterVarsity.
Schoenberg, J., Pryor, D., & Hart, D. (2003). *Voices of volunteers, 18–29*. New York: A Report from the Girl Scout Research Institute.
Swindoll, C. R. (1981). *Improving your serve*. Waco, TX: Word.
Willard, D. (1988). *The spirit of the disciplines*. New York: HarperCollins.
Wymer, W. W. (1999). A qualitative analysis of church volunteerism: Motives for service, motives for retention, and perceived benefits/rewards from volunteering. *Journal of Ministry Marketing and Management, 5*(1), 51–64.

Appendix A

Questions Posted on CMPros

I'm conducting a research study to discover what churches are doing to help kids identify their spiritual gifts and use them to serve others.

If your church provides opportunities for kids (elementary age) to serve either in the church, in local outreach opportunities, or through missions trips, please answer the following:

1. What age/grade of children are allowed to serve?
2. Is there some type of formal application process and training program? Briefly describe.
3. What opportunities are there for kids to serve in the church, in local outreach opportunities, or on missions trips?
4. How have you seen their involvement in serving impact their faith?

If your church does not provide opportunities for kids (elementary age) to serve, please answer the following:

1. Have you ever considered providing opportunities for kids to serve at your church, in local outreach, or through missions trips?
2. If not, what has prevented you from doing so?

CMPros@yahoogroups.com

Appendix B

Interview Questions

1. How long have you been involved in serving at your church?
2. What made you decide to start serving?
3. What area do you serve in?
4. What do you enjoy most about serving?
5. How has serving helped you grow spiritually?
6. Finish this sentence: When I am serving I feel . . .
7. If you were telling your friends why it is important that kids like you serve at church, what would you say?
8. Share a story about a time that you were serving and you felt like God was really using you to help others.

13 Documenting Children's Spiritual Development in a Preschool Program[1]

Judy Harris Helm, Stacy Berg & Pam Scranton

THE MISSION OF NORTHMINSTER LEARNING CENTER OF NORTHMINSTER Presbyterian Church in Peoria, Illinois, is to reach out to meet the needs of families by providing a nurturing, caring environment for approximately two hundred children from a variety of denominations. Programs provided by the learning center include:

- Discovery Preschool—a Reggio-inspired, faith-based preschool using the Project Approach, documentation and authentic assessment
- Curiosity Corner—a developmentally appropriate enrichment program for children twenty-four to thirty-six months
- After Care—a place where children ages five to eleven come after school to socialize and enjoy planned activities
- Summer Camp—weekly themes, outdoor games, sports, arts, crafts, and nature programs for ages six to eleven
- Kindergarten—a Reggio-inspired, faith-based full-day kindergarten program that implements Project Approach, documentation, authentic assessment, and engaged and active academic learning experiences

We believe that each age has distinct developmental characteristics. We naturally adjust our verbal interactions with children of different age lev-

---

1. A modified version of this chapter appeared in the Fall 2007 *Christian Education Journal* and is reprinted here with permission from *CEJ*.

els—simplifying vocabulary and adjusting the complexity of concepts. We approach faith education in the same way. We view each child as an individual *en route*, on a journey, to becoming a functioning adult.

As part of our program, we use "Godly Play" in the preschool, kindergarten, and after care programs. We also developed our own position statement, *Recommended Practices in Religious Education for Preschool Programs*, for staff and parent orientation. This document describes our beliefs and how we use religious education, prayer, and Bible stories in our program.

Documentation

A significant part of the Northminster Learning Center program is the documentation of children's work, both for assessment and to guide instruction. Documentation is defined as "the collection of evidence of learning" (Helm, Beneke, & Steinheimer, 1998). The staff use photographs, anecdotal notes, audio and video recordings, collections of work, and narratives to provide evidence of child learning and development. The staff of Northminster Learning Center is adept at documenting and using documentation. Their work has been featured in a number of books (Helm, Beneke & Steinheimer, 1998; Helm & Beneke, 2003; Helm & Katz, 2001) and exhibits (Chicago Children's Museum, 2004). Through documentation, the teacher makes it possible for others to "see" the learning that takes place when appropriate teaching occurs. Good-quality documentation can do the following:

- Provide evidence of children's learning in all areas of a child's development
- Offer insight into the complex learning experiences provided to children
- Provide a framework for organizing teachers' observations and recording each child's special interests and developmental progress
- Emphasize learning as an interactive process by documenting what children learn when they are engaged in active exploration and interaction with adults, other children, and materials
- Show the advantages of activities and materials that are concrete, real, and relevant to the lives of young children

- Enable the teacher to assess what children know or can and cannot do so the teacher can modify the difficulty, complexity, and challenge of an activity as children are involved with it and as they develop understanding and skills (Helm, Beneke, & Steinheimer, 1998, p. 24)

Programs at Northminster Learning Center are faith-based; therefore, spiritual development is also documented. Documentation includes photographing children involved in Godly Play and religious activities, recording what children say, and engaging children in conversation about spiritual issues. Though teachers already collect a portfolio item for spiritual development for each child's systematic portfolio, spiritual development samples are also added to the portfolios that document growth in language, literacy, math, science and other academic areas.

Documentation can capture for the teacher, the parent, the congregation, and the public, a vision of the child's growth in spiritual development. Viewers of documentation can also see the strengthening of a variety of intellectual and social dispositions, or habits of mind, which occurs while the children learn to work together in a faith community. An example of a disposition would be the ability to listen to another point of view or to be reflective. Documentation enables the teacher to monitor each child's development and, in this way, evaluate and adjust the experiences the child and group have at the learning center.

Documentation is regularly shared among staff members informally. In addition, formal discussions of documentation occur during "Super Tuesdays," which are professional learning group meetings. It was during one of these meetings while discussing a portfolio item for spiritual development that so many questions were generated that the group decided to initiate a year-long study of children's spirituality.

The Study Group

During the 2005–2006 school year, the staff decided to deepen their understanding of children's spiritual development by increasing the depth and quality of documentation of children's growth in spiritual development. A sub-group of staff members formed a Children's Spirituality Study Group that also read and discussed research and literature on children's spirituality.[2]

2. Members of the Children's Spirituality Study Group: Stacy Berg, Megan Boeker,

Documenting Children's Spiritual Development in a Preschool Program 217

The study group met monthly and began by creating questions about the development of spirituality in children. Some of the questions they identified were,

- Can we document children's spiritual development?
- Do spirituality and children's religious beliefs progress on a predictable developmental timeline?
- What do we know about the growth of children's ability to understand and profit from religious instruction?
- Can we use documentation to help others understand the importance of supporting children's spiritual development?

Experiencing God and Spiritual Growth with Your Child (Ratcliff, 2005) was selected as the core reading material to foster discussion in the group. The group also read from Robert Coles (1990) and Ratcliff (2004). The Venn diagram in figure 1, constructed from Ratcliff and May's ideas (2004, p. 11), explained and demonstrated the sometimes overlapping concept of spirituality and religion, and assisted the group in understanding the difference between encountering God and knowing about God.

This diagram also provided a clearer framework for guiding the documentation process.

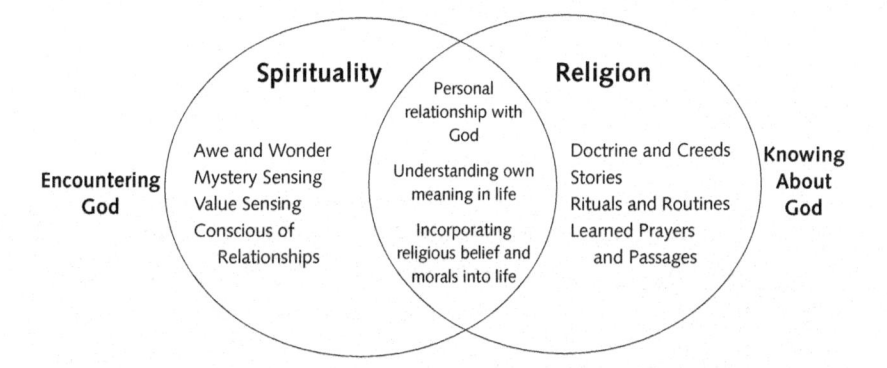

Figure 1: Spirituality/Religion Venn Diagram

Encountering God

Spirituality
- Awe and Wonder
- Mystery Sensing
- Value Sensing
- Conscious of Relationships

Personal relationship with God
Understanding own meaning in life
Incorporating religious belief and morals into life

Religion
- Doctrine and Creeds
- Stories
- Rituals and Routines
- Learned Prayers and Passages

Knowing About God

Although documentation of spirituality had been an ongoing component of the life of the center, during this school year the staff decided to deepen

---

Mary Ann Gottlieb, Lee Ann Glatz, Judy Harris Helm, Judy Hultgren, Nicki Igoes, Rachelle McConaghie, Pam Scranton, Lora Taylor, and Stacey Williams.

their understanding by increasing the depth, quality, and time spent reflecting on documentation of children's development in spirituality. Within the first couple of months the staff was able to answer their first questions.

The Panels

A documentation display was created which consisted of five panels approximately 20" x 30" each (see figures 2 through 6). The first two panels explained the documentation process and the study group's definition of spirituality and how it fits in the Northminster Learning Center's program. Each of the other panels presented a question for the viewer and then displayed documentation that enabled the viewer to answer the question. The panels were displayed at eye-level on easels in the following sequence:

1) How we documented and studied children's spiritual development (see figure 2)

2) What is spirituality? How is it fostered in our program? (see figure 3)

3) Documentation of Awe and Reverence (see figure 4)

4) Documentation of Prayer (see figure 5)

5) Documentation of Understanding of Bible Stories (see figure 6)

Each panel followed the design principles outlined in *Building Support for Your School: Using Children's Work to Show Learning* (Helm & Helm, 2006). The principles included using a question to encourage the viewer to draw his own conclusions, keeping the focus on one or two main points, using large photos or children's work to capture and keep attention, and capitalizing on the power of narrative.

A complete documentation panel is shown in figure 4, "How old do children have to be to experience awe and reverence?" By viewing and interacting with this panel, viewers realized that children sense the power of God and the mystery of God's world in many different ways. The caption under the photo of the little boy washing his hands reads:

> During learning center time, Mason (2.7 years) showed an interest in the Bible. While he was holding it, Mrs. McConaghie told him God wrote the book and God's words were on the pages. Mason carefully set the Bible down and went to the sink and washed his hands. He then got the Bible again, sat in the big rocking chair and respectfully turned the pages of the book.

Figure 2: Documentation of Children's Spirituality
How we documented and studied children's spiritual development.

During the 2005-2006 school year, the staff decided to deepen their understanding of children's spiritual development by increasing the depth, quality, and reflection on documentation of children's growth in spiritual development. A "Children's Spirituality Study Group" also read and discussed research and literature on children's spirituality.

Documentation includes photographing children involved in Godly Play and religious activities, recording what children say, and engaging them in conversation.

Teachers collect a systematic portfolio of children's work samples to document growth in language, literacy, math, science and other academic areas. A portfolio item for spiritual development was added.

Members of the Children's Spirituality Study Group:

Stacy Berg
Megan Boeker
Mary Ann Gottlieb
Lee Ann Glatz
Judy Harris Helm
Judy Hultgren
Nicki Igoe
Rachelle McConaghie
Pam Scranton
Lora Taylor
Stacey Valentin

Figure 3: What is spirituality?
How is it fostered in our program?
Children's spirituality is the development of a relationship with God.

Our first task was to define children's spirituality. We began with a diagram from Ratcliff and May (2004) showing the relationship between religion and spirituality.

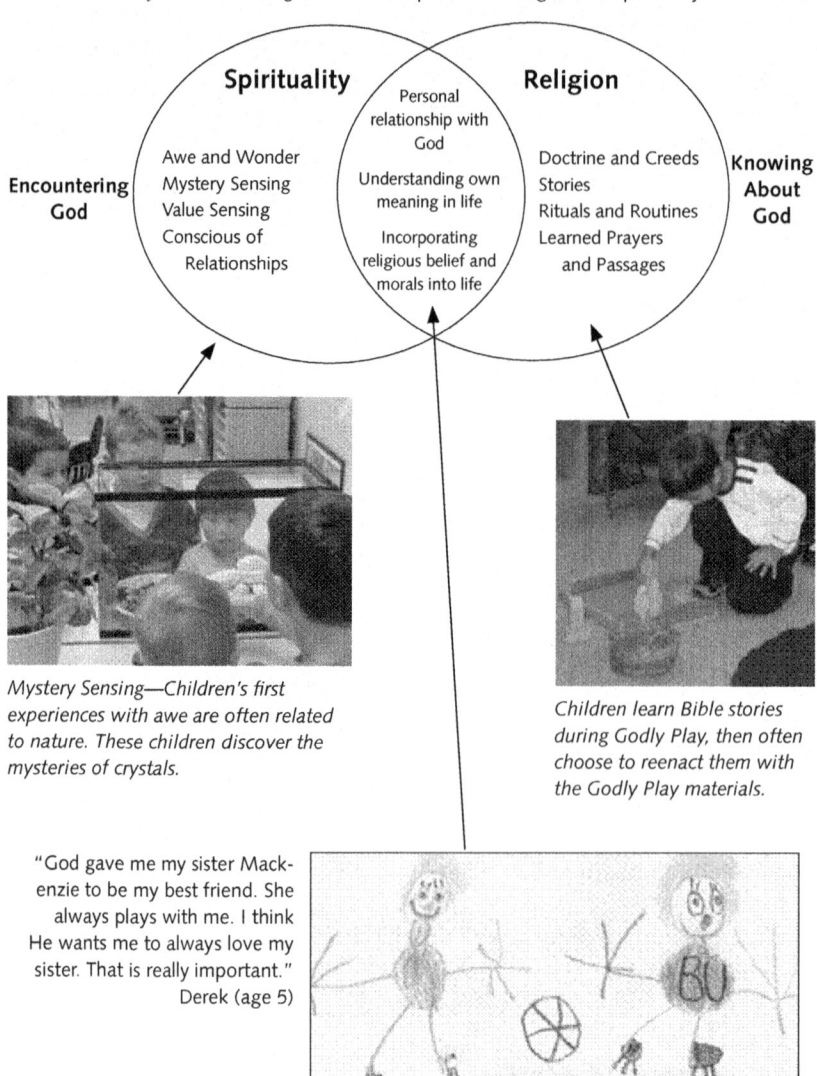

Encountering God

Spirituality
- Awe and Wonder
- Mystery Sensing
- Value Sensing
- Conscious of Relationships

- Personal relationship with God
- Understanding own meaning in life
- Incorporating religious belief and morals into life

Religion
- Doctrine and Creeds
- Stories
- Rituals and Routines
- Learned Prayers and Passages

Knowing About God

Mystery Sensing—Children's first experiences with awe are often related to nature. These children discover the mysteries of crystals.

Children learn Bible stories during Godly Play, then often choose to reenact them with the Godly Play materials.

"God gave me my sister Mackenzie to be my best friend. She always plays with me. I think He wants me to always love my sister. That is really important."
Derek (age 5)

Figure 4: How old do children have to be to experience awe and reverence?

Children sense the power of God and the mystery of God's world in many different ways.

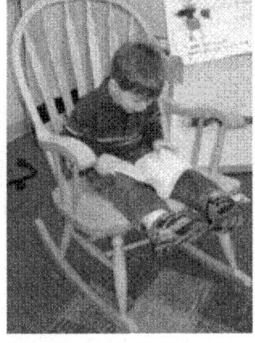

During learning center time, Mason (2.7 years) showed an interest in the Bible. While he was holding it, Mrs. McConaghie told him God wrote the book and God's words were on the pages. Mason carefully set the Bible down and went to the sink and washed his hands. He then got the Bible again, sat in the big rocking chair and respectfully turned the pages of the book.

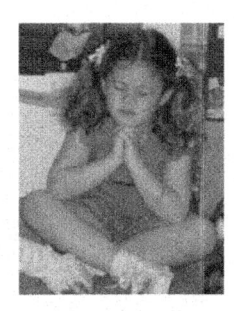

Lexie (age 4) prays during the Lenten Godly Play session. Children often show intense concentration and separation from others during prayer time.

Older children express their fascination with the powers of God as shown in these drawings of God.

1. Jonathan (age 8): "He floats around because a person like that shouldn't have to walk."

2. Megan (age 7): "I drew muscles because he is more powerful than anybody."

3. Tyson (age 8): "He is a spiritual gleam of light."

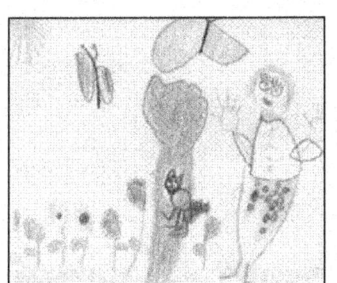

"I drew creation. God made us things so we could live. God made the world beautiful and that makes my heart happy. I love God for that." Kay (age 5)

Figure 5: When young children pray do they think they are talking to God?

A child's understanding and use of prayer is affected by the child's age and experience.

Addison (2.2 years) spontaneously prays before eating her pretend dinner in the dramatic play area just as the class does at snack time.

Peyton (age 4) was praying because her teacher's child was ill. Other children began their playtime. Peyton continued praying for Mrs. Taylor and Nicholas until she had finished talking to God even though other children were actively involved in play all around her.

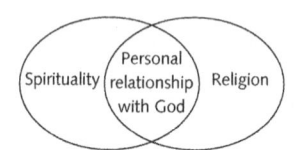

MacKenzie (age 9): "Little kids should pray cause they're God's children. Grownups and bigger kids should teach the littler ones to get quiet and pray every day, because praying is how you get Jesus in your heart."

Spirituality (Personal relationship with God) Religion

Which documentation on this board reveals a relationship with God?

Figure 6: Are Bible stories meaningful to young children?

Children learn parables, sacred stories, and liturgical routines through Godly Play.

Megan (age 3) arranges the materials to retell the story of the Good Shepherd (Psalm 23) in her own words using her own language. She places the cool water, the dark scary places and the Good Shepherd who leads the sheep to safety in the proper places as she tells the story.

"Jesus was very important to Zacchaeus, 'cause he was the Savior. And I know Jesus loves everybody, even when you sometimes make a bad choice. That happens to me." Brennan (age 5)

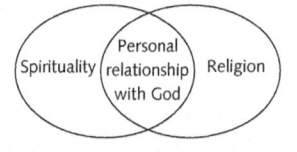

MacKenzie (age 9): "I'm telling Jena a Godly Play story. It's the one where Jesus goes into the wilderness. Jena was a good listener. I think kids like Jena should know about Jesus and his miracles. They should learn that even when they do something bad, God and Jesus will forgive them."

Another panel, shown in figure 5, addresses the question, "When young children pray, do they think they are talking to God?" One caption from that panel reads,

> Peyton (age 4) was praying because her teacher's child was ill. Other children began their playtime. Peyton continued praying for Mrs. Taylor and Nicholas until she had finished talking to God even though other children were actively involved in play all around her.

After the displays were mounted, they were viewed by congregation members before and after church, and by teachers and other professionals who had come to the center for Open Door, a professional development day at the center. Participants were invited to complete surveys before and after viewing the exhibit. Sixty-seven exhibit viewers completed both surveys.

Survey Results and Discussion

After the data from the surveys was collected and analyzed, change was revealed most significantly in two areas: (1) understanding of the importance of spirituality in the early years, and (2) motivation to participate in the development of children's spirituality.

Religion versus Spirituality

The first items on the survey were about the distinction between spirituality and religious knowledge (encountering God in a relationship and knowing about God). The majority of the participants agreed on the pre-viewing survey with the concept that there is a difference between knowing about God and actually having an encounter with God. Viewing the documentation panels resulted in no significant change on these items because of high initial agreement on the pre-viewing survey. For example, 90 percent of the participants disagreed with the statement, "Religion and spirituality are the same thing," in the pre-viewing survey.

Spirituality in the Early Years

Many viewers underestimated the importance of the early years in spiritual development. There was significant change in their estimates about the age level that spiritual development begins, due to the experience of viewing the documentation. Participants were asked to select the age from a series of age groups (2 years old, 3–5 years old, 6–9 years old, 9–12 years old and 13–18 years old) that children need to be before they could complete a series of spiritual development tasks (such as experience awe and reverence or apply religious teachings). Our documentation showed these to occur as early as age two and definitely in the preschool-kindergarten age range.

Figure 7 displays the changes that the post-viewing surveys revealed. For example, before viewing the documentation displays, many of the viewers felt that children had to be six or older (school age) before they exhibited spiritual experiences that Ratcliff and May (2004) defined as appearing in the sphere of "Encountering God." The post-viewing survey showed that this perception changed significantly after viewing the documentation panels. Other changes were similarly dramatic.

Table 1

How old do you think children need to be before they can . . .	% pre-view selecting age 6 or older	% post-view selecting age 6 or older
experience awe and reverence regarding God's *world*	12%	2%
experience awe and reverence regarding God's *Word*	35%	14%
establish a meaningful relationship with God	45%	17%
feel like they are actually communicating with God in prayer	38%	8%
apply lessons from religious teachings to their lives	31%	9%

Adult Understanding of Concepts and Commitment to Support

In addition, even though our viewing group consisted of those already acquainted with religious education, this information about children's early spiritual development was new to them. Post-viewing data showed that 53 percent disagreed with the statement, "I already knew most of the information in this exhibit about children's spirituality before viewing this exhibit." Almost half (45 percent) agreed or strongly agreed with the statement: "I was surprised how spiritual young children could be."

Most important to our study group was the response to the statement, "I feel more motivated to participate in the spiritual development of young children," with 79 percent either agreeing or strongly agreeing and only 3 percent disagreeing with this statement. That statement alone made our documentation of children's spiritual development and sharing the documentation worthwhile.

Revisiting Our Questions

The process of gathering, documenting, and evaluating the spiritual experiences the children encountered led to a variety of conclusions regarding the initial questions of our study group.

Can we document children's spiritual development?

Faith development was no more difficult for our teachers to document than were other areas of young children's growth and development. Recording children's comments about their drawings was one of the best ways to document their spiritual insights and understandings. See for example, the drawings in figure 4. Kay, age 5, says about her picture: "I drew creation. God made us things so we could live. God made the world beautiful and that makes my heart happy. I love God for that." Jonathan, Megan, and Tyson express their fascination with the power of God with the following quotes about their pictures:

1. Jonathan (age 8): "He floats around because a person like that shouldn't have to walk."

2. Megan (age 7): "I drew muscles because he is more powerful than anybody."

3. Tyson (age 8): "He is a spiritual gleam of light."

The use of the Venn diagram, which we encountered in our study process, provided a context to discuss and share what we were seeing and collecting because it provided definitions of spirituality, religion, and how these overlap and become integrated.

Do spirituality and children's religious beliefs progress on a predictable developmental timeline?

Evidence of incorporation of religious stories increased with age and experience. Brennan, age 5, said: "Jesus was very important to Zacchaeus, 'cause he was the Savior. And I know Jesus loves everybody, even when you sometimes make a bad choice. That happens to me" (figure 6). And MacKenzie, age 9, said:

> I'm telling Jena a Godly Play story. It's the one where Jesus goes into the wilderness. Jena was a good listener. I think kids like Jena should know about Jesus and his miracles. They should learn that even when they do something bad, God and Jesus will forgive them. (Figure 6)

Though we did observe differences in the children that appeared to be related to their ages, and that coincided with the descriptions we were reading in the literature, we also saw surprising evidence of encountering God in very young children, younger than many of us predicted. Several of the comments displayed on the panels reveal early spiritual insights, for example, the comment about Mason's handling of the Bible mentioned previously (figure 4). One photograph shows a two-year-old praying. The caption reads: "Addison (2.2 years) spontaneously prays before eating her pretend dinner in the dramatic play area just as the class does at snack time" (figure 5). Another photograph shows Megan and says,

> Megan (age 3) arranges the materials to retell the story of the Good Shepherd (Psalm 23) in her own words using her own language. She places the cool water, the dark scary places and the Good Shepherd who leads the sheep to safety in the proper places as she tells the story. (Figure 6)

What do we know about the growth of children's ability to understand and profit from religious instruction?

The children's ability to understand and profit from Godly Play, a form of religious instruction, was greater than we had anticipated. We documented spontaneous prayer, rituals and routines, and applications of lessons from stories and passages. One photograph in figure 4 shows a preschooler praying with eyes tightly closed. The caption under the photo reads: "Lexie (age 4) prays during the Lenten Godly Play session. Children often show intense concentration and separation from others during prayer time." In figure 3, Derek (age 5) says: "God gave me my sister Mackenzie to be my best friend. She always plays with me. I think He wants me to always love my sister. That is really important." Also, four-year-old Peyton's prayer that was mentioned earlier, was a spontaneous response to the news of the illness of her teachers' child (figure 5).

Can we use documentation to help others understand the importance of supporting children's spiritual development?

The sharing of the documentation was very successful in building support for our program. Congregation members do not always understand the importance of preschool education and the need to support the learning center. We believe that documentation provided not only a way to educate parents but also to build support for the continuation and expansion of our program.

Implications

Seldom do churches do a good job of telling the story of successful faith building or outreach programs. Yet, our experience demonstrates that evidence is easy to collect and easy to share as well as being enormously powerful. At Northminster Learning Center, the majority of the children in our care are preschoolers and as such do not have full competence of verbal expression. They are also non-representational in their art work, and less likely to spontaneously express their thoughts about their own growth and development.

As we work with our smaller number of older, after-school-care children, we often note how much easier the task of documentation is with children who can draw, write, reflect, and do their own documentation. Indeed, primary-age children, young teens, and teens should be encouraged to reflect upon their own faith journeys and participate in documenting that journey.

Evidence of helping individuals on these journeys should be a regular and ongoing process in churches—yet, we tell that story so little. The documentation, and especially the sharing of that documentation, can be a powerful tool to communicate how churches are fostering and nurturing spiritual development in children.

References

Berryman, J. (1995). *Godly play: An imaginative approach to religious education.* Nashville: Abingdon.

Chicago Children's Museum. (2004). *The power of documentation: Children's learning revealed.* (Exhibit)

Coles, R. (1990). *The spiritual life of children.* Boston: Houghton Mifflin.

Helm, J. H., Beneke, S., & Steinheimer, K. (1998). *Windows on learning: Documenting children's work.* New York: Teachers College Press.

Helm, J., & Beneke, S. (Eds.). (2003). *The power of projects: Meeting contemporary challenges in early childhood classrooms—strategies and solutions.* New York: Teachers College Press.

Helm, J., & Helm, A. (2006). *Building support for your school: Using children's work to show learning.* New York: Teachers College Press.

Helm, J., & Katz, L. G. (2001). *Young investigators: The project approach in the early years.* New York: Teachers College Press.

Ratcliff, D. (Ed). (1995). *Handbook of religious preschool education.* Birmingham, AL: Religious Education.

Ratcliff, D. (Ed.). (2004). *Children's spirituality: Christian perspectives, research, and applications.* Eugene, OR: Cascade.

Ratcliff, D. (2005). *Experiencing God and spiritual growth with your child.* Unpublished manuscript. Retrieved May 10, 2006, from www.childspirituality.org.

Ratcliff, D., & May, S. (2004). Identifying children's spirituality, Walter Wangerin's perspectives, and an overview of this book. In D. Ratcliff (Ed.), (2004), *Children's spirituality: Christian perspectives, research, and applications* (pp. 7–21). Eugene, OR: Cascade.

For

Families

14 Parenting Styles and Children's Spiritual Development

Sungwon Kim

Parenting advice often alternates its focus between love and control. For example, Gordon (1970) opposed forceful discipline in his book, *Parent Effectiveness Training*: "Each and every time they [parents] force a child to do something by using their power or authority, they deny that child a chance to learn self-discipline and self-responsibility" (p. 158). Dobson (1992) expressed a contrary opinion in the book, *The New Dare to Discipline*: "Children thrive best in an atmosphere of genuine love, undergirded by reasonable, consistent discipline.... Permissiveness has not simply failed as an approach to child rearing. It's been a disaster for those who have tried it" (p. 7). Each successive generation adheres to the advice from favorite authorities in the area of parenting (Larzelere, 2001, p. 81; Whelchel, 2000, p. 19). In the midst of advice with different—and sometimes contrary—foci, each successive generation adheres to the advice from favorite authorities on parenting.

Several studies stress the importance of parenting styles by ascertaining the influence on children's psychological attributes, academic achievement, social competence, problem behaviors, and spiritual development. This chapter examines parenting style models and their characteristics, the influences on parenting styles, and outcomes of parenting styles. The chapter focuses on the relationship between parenting styles and parents' religiosity, as well as their children's spiritual development, and then concludes with a discussion of biblical principles of parenting.

Parenting Style Models and Theories

Baumrind (1966, 1967) first described three prototypical parenting styles—authoritative, authoritarian, and permissive. She established these styles by categorizing children's levels of social competence and function as well as observing and interviewing parental interaction with the children. Levels of parental warmth and control were the measuring standards used to define the various styles (Morrison & Cooney, 2002, p. 144; Sclafani, 2004, p. 44). In 1983, Maccoby and Martin revised Baumrind's original rubric by proposing four parenting styles: authoritative, authoritarian, indulgent, and uninvolved or neglectful (Morrison & Cooney, p.144). Heath (2005) notes, "two dimensions that distinguish among those parenting patterns: accepting versus rejecting and demanding versus undemanding" (p. 25).

The chart in figure 1 charts the four parenting styles. The degrees of control/demand/expectation and love/support/responsiveness help create a grid that explains these four styles (Ratcliff, 1995, p. 66; Sclafani, 2004, p. 45).

Figure 1: Parenting Styles
Love/Support

Control/Demand	High	Low
High	AUTHORITATIVE *loving, supportive* *demanding, controlling*	AUTHORITARIAN *unsupportive* *demanding, controlling*
Low	PERMISSIVE/INDULGENT *loving, supportive* *indulgent, non-demanding*	INDIFFERENT/NEGLECTFUL *uninvolved* *little discipline*

Authoritative Parenting Style

Authoritative parents are described as controlling and demanding, yet caring and sharing their ideas and feelings with their children (Ballantine, 2001, p. 46; Heath, 2005, p. 25). Parents such as these are characterized as having high standards, showing interest and engaging in the child's life, granting autonomy, offering acceptance and trust to the child, and finally, giving emotional support. This support consists of well-developed communication skills, reasoning, affection, and flexibility (Ballantine, 2001, p. 46; Lim & Lim, 2003, p. 23).

Generally, across the literature, more positive outcomes are found in the children of authoritative parents than in the children of parents with any other style. These positive outcomes include higher achievement, more emotional maturity, a more disciplined lifestyle, and healthier social interactions (Heath, 2005, p. 26; see also Jaffe, 1997, p. 160). Domitrovich and Bierman (2001) report that perceived warm and non-hostile parenting styles can predict a child's perception of warm, non-hostile peer relations; this perception can also lower the possibility of a child's lonely and victimized self-perception (p. 252). Hickman, Bartholomae, and McKenry (2000) find that the authoritative parenting style, the mother's high level of education, and the high level of self-esteem are significant predictors of the satisfactory academic adjustment of college freshmen (p. 47).

Authoritarian Parenting Style

Authoritarian parents are characterized as demanding but not responsive; they control and discipline, but rarely support. They engage with their children mainly from their perspective and seldom trust their children (Ballantine, 2001, p. 46; Balswick et al., 2003, p. 21; Gunnoe, Hetherington, & Reiss, 1999, p. 201).

The authoritarian parenting goal is unconditional obedience (Lim & Lim, 2003, p. 23; Ratcliff, 1995, p. 66), emphasizing parental authority and physical punishment for misbehaving (Lerner, Noh, & Wilson, 2001, p. 102). Authoritarian parenting seems to have biblical supports of disciplinary principles such as using corporal punishment and emphasizing obedience (Hood, Spilka, Hunsberger, & Gorsuch, 1996, p. 66).

Children of authoritarian parents tend to be more passive and dependent as well as less self-confident and socially skillful than children of other style parents (Heath, 2005, p. 27). Jaffe (1997) states that children of authoritarian parents are more emotionally unhealthy and unstable than children in the other three parenting style groups (p. 160).

Permissive and Indulgent Parenting Styles

Permissive parents provide a stark contrast to authoritarian parents; they do not control or demand (Heath, 2005, p. 28); they are affectionate and child-centered, but non-demanding. Permissive parents allow children to control their own will and activities (Ballantine, 2001, p. 46; Balswick et al., 2003, p. 22; Lim & Lim, 2003, p. 23), and they tend to inconsistently apply parenting rules. Often, they give their child anything he or she requests (Lerner, Noh, & Wilson, 2001, p. 102).

Taken to its extremity, the permissive style does not exercise control, and it manifests itself as indulgent (Ratcliff, 1995, pp. 66–67). Overindulgent parents find their children's unhappiness intolerable and will continually seek to prevent it. The child's desires and needs come first, and parents take on the tasks that a child could or should do (Gross, 1989, p. 7).

Children of permissive parents tend to be less mature, happy, independent, and socially adaptable than children of authoritative parents (Heath, 2005, p. 28). They usually do not make an effort to help others, and they seldom exhibit moral values held by their parents (Strommen & Hardel, 2000, p. 60).

Neglectful and Indifferent Parenting Styles

Neglectful parents make few demands of their children, and they do not properly respond to them (Ballantine, 2001, p. 46; Balswick et al., 2003, p. 23). This indifference and lack of involvement are observed in neglectful parents along with random expressions of love and discipline (Heath, 2005, p. 30).

The main difference between indifferent and neglectful parents is found in the parents' degree of control and responsiveness. Indifferent parents indicate medium to low levels of control and responsiveness, while neglectful parents exhibit few signs of control and love (Ratcliff, 1995, p. 66). When parents practice continuous indifference, their children demonstrate intellectual, social, and disciplinary problems such as poor academic achievement, peer rejection, or delinquency (Heath, 2005, p. 30; Jaffe, 1997, p. 160).

INFLUENCES ON PARENTING STYLES

Parenting styles are influenced by a variety of factors: the children's and parents' personal characteristics, demographic factors, and cultural norms.

Children's Influences

The parent-child relationship is reciprocal; both parents and children affect each other (Roberts, 1994, p. 285). The following characteristics of a child influence the quality of the parent-child relationship: age, gender, birth order, whether the child is from a first marriage or a remarriage, and physical, intellectual, mental, and social competencies (Ambert, 2001, pp. 32–33; see also Brooks, 2004, pp. 6–7).

Parental Influences

The following parental characteristics can be affected by children and also cause an effect on the children: age, socioeconomic status, ethnicity and culture, religion, educational level, personality, health, marital status, family life stage, life stress, marital satisfaction, marital conflict strategies, and original families (Ambert, pp. 37–38; see also Bigner, 2002, pp. 124–25; Jaffe, 1997, p. 163; Brooks, 2004, pp. 6–8; Peterson, Steinmetz, & Wilson, 2003, p. 1; Quah, 2003, pp. 64–67; Roberts, 1994, p. 285).

A study by Aunola, Nurmi, Onatsu-Arvilommi, and Pulkkinen (1999) suggests that the authoritative parenting style and low parental stress were predicted by parents' high level of self-esteem and their use of mastery-orientation strategy.[1] The authoritarian parenting style was associated with a low socio-economic background (pp. 313–14). Querido, Warner, and Eyberg (2002), however, found that lower income was associated with the permissive parenting style, while higher income was associated with the authoritative parenting style. The mother's lower education was related to both the authoritarian and the permissive parenting styles (p. 274).

Cultural Influences

Parenting styles are also related to cultural beliefs and values. For example, in some Eastern countries, mothers tend to be warm and nurturing with children, while fathers are expected to play the role of the disciplinarian (Balswick et al., 2003, p. 21).

Authoritative parenting is found to be the most adaptive style in Western societies, where individualism is valued; authoritarian parenting is rooted in the collective cultural values common in patriarchal, agrarian societies. Consequently, authoritarian parenting is the preferred parenting model in Asia, Africa, and South America (Aunola et al., 1999, p. 314; Greenfield & Suzuki, 2001, p. 25; Gunnoe, Hetherington, & Reiss, 1999, p.

---

1. Master orientation strategy is the confident ability to accomplish tasks by setting goals and planning necessary processes (Aunola et al., 1999, p. 308).

201; Peterson, Steinmetz, & Wilson, 2003, pp. 1–2; Rudy & Grusec, 2001, p. 203).

To a certain extent, some cultural differences can be explained by the parents' level of education. Parents with a low level of education value obedience and conformity. An example of this phenomenon is that there has been a change from authoritarian parenting to more permissive parenting in recent decades—parents with a higher level of education are more likely to accept these trends, whereas less educated parents are more reluctant to change their parenting styles (Aunola et al., 1999, pp. 314–15).

In summary, children's needs, competences, and characteristics—as well as parents' characteristics and demographics—influence parenting styles. In addition, cultural values are decisive in one's parenting style.

Parenting Styles and Child Outcomes

Different parenting styles tend to produce different outcomes in children. The common outcomes that researchers have investigated include psychological attributes, academic achievement, and troubled behaviors.

Psychological Attributes

A secure attachment to parents can be predicted by the levels of parental responsiveness and sensitivity (Sclafani, 2004, p. 52). Neal and Frick-Horbury (2001) demonstrated differences among three parenting styles on college students' attachment: 70 percent of participants with authoritative parents were securely attached, 12.5 percent of those with authoritarian parents were securely attached, and zero percent of those with permissive parents were securely attached (p. 181).

Milevsky, Schlechter, Netter, and Keehn (2007) examined perceived parenting styles and adolescent children's self-esteem, depression, and life-satisfaction. The researchers found that adolescents whose mothers were authoritative scored higher on self-esteem and life-satisfaction and lower on depression than did counterparts whose mothers used the other three styles; adolescents with permissive mothers showed a higher score on self-esteem than did adolescents whose mothers practiced the authoritarian and the neglectful styles. Children with authoritative fathers scored higher on self-esteem and life-satisfaction than did children with the authoritarian and neglectful fathers. The children whose fathers used the authoritative style scored lower on depression than did children of permissive and neglectful fathers (p. 44).

Academic Achievement

As for children's academic achievement, many recent studies have concentrated on the relationship between academic success and parenting styles (Aunola, Stattin, & Nurmi, 2000; Gonzalez, 2001; Hickman, Bartholomae, & McKenry, 2000; Huang & Prochner, 2004; Joshi, Ferris, & Wilson, 2003; Pong, Hao, & Gardner, 2005; Spera, 2005). Pong, Hao, and Gardner examined family decision-making styles, parents' responsiveness, and the school performance of immigrant adolescents; there are four types of family decision making styles:

- Joint decisions (typical of authoritative parenting styles)
- Unilateral parent decisions (associated with authoritarian parenting styles)
- Unilateral adolescent decisions (typical of permissive parenting styles)
- Ambiguous decisions (common with neglectful parenting styles). (p. 935)

Pong et al. found that, when compared to joint decisions, the other three decision-making styles were associated with lower grade point averages (GPA), with the lowest GPA found among those who exhibit an ambiguous decision-making style (p. 942).

Leung, Lau, and Lam (1998) investigated the relationship between parenting styles and academic achievement of school-aged children in Hong Kong, the United States, and Australia. The participants were rated on their general parenting style (authoritative, authoritarian, permissive, neglectful) as well as their academic parenting style (academic authoritative, academic authoritarian, etc.). The researchers found that Chinese parents were higher in general authoritarianism, and lower in general and academic authoritativeness compared to the other two groups. Chinese and American parents scored significantly higher in academic authoritarianism than did their Australian counterparts. Children's academic achievement was negatively associated with academic authoritarianism in all populations and was positively related to general authoritarianism only in Hong

Kong. In addition, academic achievement was positively related to general authoritativeness in American and Australian groups (pp. 165–67).

Troubled Behaviors

The third attribute considered, children's behavioral problems, are also highly influenced, and predicted, by parenting styles. Aunola and Nurmi (2005) examined whether certain combinations of mothers' and fathers' parenting styles—affection, behavioral control, and psychological control—predict the internal and external problem behaviors of five- and six-year-old children. The results showed that a mothers' high level of affection combined with a high level of psychological control predicted the increases of the children's internal and external problem behaviors. Mothers' behavioral control, when only combined with a low level of psychological control, decreased children's external problem behaviors (p. 1152).

Querido, Warner, and Eyberg (2002) found that caregivers who reported a higher level of child behavior problems were more likely to report a lower level of education and income, and they were more likely to endorse either the authoritarian or the permissive parenting styles. The counterparts who reported a lower level of child behavior problems endorsed the authoritative parenting style (p. 274).

Parents' Religiosity and Their Parenting Styles

Parents' degree of religiosity and denominational affiliation influence their parenting styles and their relationships with their children. Gunnoe, Hetherington, and Reiss (1999) demonstrated that parental religiosity is positively related to authoritative parenting for both parents, and that the mothers' religiosity is negatively associated with the authoritarian parenting (p. 199). Wheeler's findings (1991) are different than those by Gunnoe, Hetherington, and Reiss; he found that non-Christian parents tended to score higher on the authoritative scale, and Christian parents tended to be more authoritarian than their non-Christian counterparts. The more involved parents were in church activities, and the more they tended to use authoritarian parenting and the less they tended to practice authoritative parenting (Wheeler, p. 57).

Shin (2002) also investigated the relationship between parents' religiosity and parenting styles. She adopted Allport's explanation that religiosity is divided into intrinsic and extrinsic religiosity. Intrinsic religiosity means a person "has interiorized the total creed of his [or her] faith without reservation," whereas extrinsic religiosity is defined as "a self-serving utilitarian, self-protective form of religious outlook which provides the believer with comfort and salvation" (pp. 6–7). Furthermore, extrinsic religiosity consists of both personally-oriented and socially-oriented religiosity. One with extrinsic-social religiosity is religious for social reasons (p. 7). Shin found a positive relationship between parents' intrinsic religiosity and parents' authoritative style, and also between parents' intrinsic religiosity and parental warmth. Fathers' intrinsic religiosity showed a negative relationship with their authoritarian style. There was a positive relationship between parents' extrinsic-social religiosity and their authoritarian style, and a negative relationship between mothers' extrinsic-social religiosity and their warmth (p. 148).

A positive relationship between the fathers' religiosity and the high quality relationship with their children was reported in studies by Wilcox (2002, pp. 788–89) and King, Furrow, and Roth (2003, p. 388) respectively. Bartkowski and Xu (2000) found that a father's church attendance was positively related to paternal supervision, effective parenting, and father-child interaction (pp. 472, 475). Mahoney, Pargament, Tarakeshwar, and Swank (2001) suggest that parents' religion influences their appraisals of their children and facilitates family functioning. Parents devoted to their religion often value a warm and interactive relationship with their children (p. 589); Smith and Kim's (2003) research found similar results. Youths whose parents attended worship services at least once a week, compared to those whose parents did not attend, were more likely to have: (1) mothers who both praised them and demanded much from them, (2) fathers whom they highly respected and whom they wanted to resemble, (3) fathers who supported them and tried to keep promises to their children, and (4) a low incidence of leaving home due to family problems (p. 6).

Several studies compared parenting styles within different denominations. Wilcox (1998) found that conservative Protestant parents exhibited authoritative and authoritarian characteristics. Their parenting style stressed obedience and corporal punishment, which are common in authoritarian parenting, along with warmth and expressive interaction that characterize authoritative parents. After comparing conservative Protestant parents with less conservative parents, Wilcox found that conservative parents praised and hugged their children more often than less conservative parents (p. 806).

Bartkowski and Xu (2000) indicated findings similar to Wilcox that conservative Protestant fathers were more likely to supervise their children than Catholic and moderate Protestant fathers (p. 472). They were also more likely to show emotional warmth toward their children than their Catholic or unaffiliated counterparts (p. 475). King (2003) found that conservative Protestant fathers reported more negative experiences with children than did Catholic fathers or other Protestant fathers (p. 391) that was contrary to Wilcox, and Bartkowski and Xu's findings. Quah (2003) found that non-Buddhist/Taoist parents emphasized character formation in their parenting practice. Buddhist/Taoist parents would more frequently discourage their children's opinions, emphasize obedience and respect for authority, and would less frequently give children family responsibilities than other counterparts in the study. The children of Buddhist/Taoist parents were less likely to ask questions and talk about their problems (p. 75).

As indicated, there are conflicting findings among the studies on parenting styles among the religious. For example, though Wheeler (1991) found a tendency for Christian parents to be more authoritarian than their non-Christian counterparts, Gunnoe, Hetherington, and Reiss (1999) reported a negative relationship between mother's religiosity and authoritarian parenting. Christian parents tend to practice a disciplinary role that is a common denominator in both authoritative and authoritarian parenting styles. A main difference between the two styles is the degree of love and support. As several studies have indicated, religiously devoted parents often employ the authoritative parenting style, that is, they show characteristics such as showing affection, spending time, and interacting with children as well as disciplining and supervising children.

Parenting Styles and Children's Spiritual Development

Parents also profoundly influence their children's spiritual development. This influence is due, in part, to the fact that children cannot see the invisible God, but they can see their parents who they may understand to live in God's presence. Children learn the reality of God through their parents' practice of the presence of God (Downs, 1994, p. 147). Myers (1996) suggests that variables such as parental religiosity, the quality of the family relationship, and traditional family structure aid religious transmission (p. 858). Regarding the parent-child relationship, parental support and moderate levels of control fostered religious transmission (p. 865).

Dudley and Wisbey (2000) studied the relationship between parenting styles and children's commitment to the church. They found that warm and caring relationship with both parents best predicted the children's commitment to the church as well as worship attendance (p. 49). Dudley and Wisbey describe four parenting styles (similar to Maccoby & Martin's [1983]) that combine the level of parental love and control: affectionless control, affectionate constraint, weak/absent bonding, and optimal bonding. The children of mothers who exercised affectionless control (comparable to authoritarian) showed the highest church dropout rate and the lowest level of enthusiastic membership. Children whose parents exercised affectionate constraint (comparable to authoritative) reported the highest level of enthusiastic membership and the lowest dropout rate (pp. 47–48).

Parents also deeply influence their children's concept of God, that is, their understanding of God, feelings toward God, and belief in God. Hertel and Donahue (1995) examined parental God-concepts and child-rearing attitudes as predictors of God-concepts among youth. They found that parents' images of God were reflected in the youths' impressions of parenting styles, which in turn predicted youths' God-images (p. 196). Buri and Mueller (1993) indicated that parental nurturance and authoritativeness were positively related to the children's concept of God as loving, while parental authoritarianism was negatively correlated with the children's concept of God as loving (p. 21).

Several studies demonstrate that a positive, close relationship between parents and children is associated with children's perception of a loving, close, and forgiving God, and that children of controlling and punitive parents have a punishing God image (Hyde, 1990, p. 96; McIntosh & Spilka, 1995, p. 51; Potvin, Hoge, & Nelsen, 1976, p. 18; Tamminen, 1991, p. 192; and Vianello, Tamminen, & Ratcliff, 1992, p. 63). The parents' use of corporal punishment or anger, however, did not show a significant relationship with stern, punishing, and frightening God-images (Tamminen, p. 192).

Hood et al. (1996) reported that parents' discipline styles influence children's God-concept development (p. 67). Dickie et al. (1997) found that children trained with power-oriented discipline perceived God as less nurturing than did children who received less power-oriented discipline. Children who reported high levels of love-oriented discipline perceived

God to be more powerful than did children who reported low levels of love-oriented discipline (pp. 36–37). In a later study, Dickie et al. (2006) conducted similar research to find whether the parents' levels of punishing/judging discipline style affect young adult children's concepts of the closeness, nurturance, power, and punishment/judgment of God. The results indicated that the mothers' punishing/judging discipline style, not that of the fathers, affected young adults' God concepts. For example, the highest scores on closeness to God were from young men who reported a high level of maternal punishing/judging discipline and young women who reported a low level of maternal punishing/judging discipline. Overall, children's perception of God as a nurturing and punishing being was related to the mothers' punishing/judging discipline (Dickie et al., 2006, p. 62).

Nunn investigated the parental use of the threat that "God will punish you if you misbehave" as an attempt to control their children's behavior. Nelson and Kroliczak (1984) replicated and extended Nunn's findings. They found that the children whose parents tended to use the threat also tended to view God as malevolent, to have higher self-blame scores, and to feel a greater need to be obedient (pp. 267, 273–75).

Bao, Whitbeck, Hoyt, and Conger (1999) examined the influence of parental acceptance on the transmission of religious beliefs and practices to their adolescent children. Mothers' God-concept affected their daughters' concept when they felt their mothers' acceptance. On the contrary, fathers' religious importance, fathers' church attendance, and fathers' God concept had a greater impact on daughters' God concept for the groups with low parental acceptance than for groups with moderate or high parental acceptance (pp. 368–69). The researchers explain the unexpected result by suggesting that fathers' acceptance of daughters, unlike that of mothers, seems to have a compensatory role in transmitting the fathers' God-concept to daughters (p. 369).

To conclude, a variety of parental factors—religiosity, God-concept, the parent-child relationship, parenting styles, and discipline styles—influence children's spirituality, religiosity, and God-concept. Concerning the parent-child relationship, parental love, support, care, and acceptance are always required for children's healthy spiritual growth. Several studies, however, showed varying results regarding parental discipline. Two key factors the research identifies are the motivation and manner of discipline. Love-oriented discipline (versus power- or punishment-oriented discipline) appears to be most helpful for the children's spiritual development. In conclusion, as Dudley and Wisbey's (2000) study indicated, the affectionate constraint style, also known as the authoritative style, resulted in the most positive spiritual outcomes in children.

BIBLICAL PRINCIPLES OF PARENTING

God's unconditional love and grace, including disciplinary action for his children, is the model for parenting that God provides (Balswick et al., 2003, p. 115). The relationship between God and his loved ones models the relationship parents should have with their children. Love motivates discipline, which leads to righteousness and peace. God's role as a parent is similar to the authoritative parenting style in that he exhibits a high degree of both love/support and discipline/control (pp. 114–15).

God describes himself as a loving parent, for example, in Deuteronomy 1:31, God is pictured as a father who carried his son: "There you saw how the Lord your God carried you, as a father carries his son, all the way you went until you reached this place" (NIV). In Isaiah, God is portrayed as a nursing and nurturing mother: "Can a mother forget the baby at her breast and have no compassion on the child she has borne? Though she may forget, I will not forget you! See, I have engraved you on the palms of my hands" (49:15–16a, NIV); and "As a mother comforts her child, so will I comfort you" (66:13, NIV). To express God's unfailing love for Israel, Hosea uses a metaphor of a parent's longing for a wayward child:

> When Israel was a child, I loved him, and out of Egypt I called my son. But the more I called Israel, the further they went from me. They sacrificed to the Baal and they burned incense to images. It was I who taught Ephraim to walk, taking them by the arms . . . I led them with cords of human kindness, with ties of love; I lifted the yoke from their neck and bent down to feed them . . . How can I give up, Ephraim? How can I hand you over, Israel? . . . My heart is changed within me; all my compassion is aroused. (Hos 11:1–4, 8, NIV)

God is pictured not only as loving, supporting, and nurturing, but he is also depicted as disciplining those he loves. The author of Hebrews describes that discipline as a symbol of God, the loving Father:

> My son, do not make light of the Lord's discipline, and do not lose heart when he rebukes you, because the Lord disciplines those he loves, and he punishes everyone he accepts as a son. Endure hard-

> ship as discipline; God is treating you as sons. For what son is not disciplined by his father? If you are not disciplined (and everyone undergoes discipline), then you are illegitimate children and not true sons. Moreover, we have all had human fathers who disciplined us and we respected them for it . . . No discipline seems pleasant at the time, but painful. Later on, however, it produces a harvest of righteousness and peace for those who have been trained by it. (Heb 12:5–9, 11, NIV)

God's grace brings both salvation and discipline to his people (Bridges, 1994, p. 79; Titus 2:11–12). For instance, the Lord who led and protected Israel for forty years in the desert also disciplined them as a loving father disciplines his son (Deut 8:5).

As Scripture indicates in God's role as parent, discipline is an integral part of parenting. Christian parents would do well to emulate his example. Dobson (1992) says that discipline makes healthy lifestyles possible, and also characteristics such as self-control, respect, kindness, and peacefulness (p. 250). Many verses in Proverbs mention correcting children: 13:24; 22:15; 23:13–14; 29:15; 29:17. And Ephesians 6:4b says, "Bring them [children] up in the training and instruction of the Lord" (NIV).

One caution should accompany the teaching regarding discipline. Ephesians 6:4 reads, "Fathers, do not exasperate your children" (NIV). In the ancient world, fathers had absolute authority and were sometimes harsh; this is the reason that Paul includes the warning against provoking children to anger (Snodgrass, 1996, p. 322). In this passage, a father's attitudes, words, or actions that provoke his children to anger are prohibited. Examples of a parent's exasperating behaviors could include severe discipline, unreasonable demands, unfairness, and condemnation (Lincoln, 1990, p. 406).

Conclusion

The scriptural parenting goal is to draw a biblical picture of God in the hearts of children and to teach them how to accompany him in daily life (Whelchel, 2000, pp. 19–20). The best way to accomplish this goal is to examine how God parents his own children with love and discipline. God's parenting principles are congruent with parenting experts who recommend a balance of love and control. For example: "Healthy parenthood can be boiled down to those two essential ingredients, love and control, operating in a system of checks and balances" (Dobson, 1978, p. 52). This dual focus is also confirmed by Sclafani's (2004) list of the following foundational parenting skills: "consistent discipline, meeting the child's needs for love and nurturance, and the control and guidance functions of parenting" (p. 1).

The parenting style that exhibits most nearly this balance between love and control is the authoritative style. Authoritative parents communicate to their children in a respectful and rational manner; the children are accepted and respected by parents. The parents value both "autonomous self-will and disciplined conformity"; they affirm the child's present qualities, but also set standards for future conduct (Baumrind, 1966, p. 891). In sum, authoritative parents are loving and supportive, while offering and enforcing appropriate boundaries and guidelines. As this paper shows, recent research suggests that the principles undergirding authoritative parenting, in particular, promote children's spiritual growth and development.

References

Ambert, A. M. (2001). *The effect of children on parents* (2nd ed.). New York: Haworth.

Aunola, K., & Nurmi, J. E. (2005). The role of parenting styles in children's problem behavior. *Child Development, 76*, 1144–59.

Aunola, K., Nurmi, J. E., Onatsu-Arvilommi, T., & Pulkkinen, L. (1999). The role of parents' self-esteem, mastery-orientation, and social background in their parenting styles. *Scandinavian Journal of Psychology, 40*, 307–17.

Aunola, K., Stattin, H., & Numri, J. E. (2000). Parenting styles and adolescents' achievement strategies. *Journal of Adolescence, 23*, 205–22.

Ballantine, J. (2001). Raising competent kids: The authoritative parenting style. *Childhood Education, 78*, 46–47.

Bao, W. N., Whitbeck, L. B., Hoyt, D. R., & Conger, R. D. (1999). Perceived parental acceptance as a moderator of religious transmission among adolescent boys and girls. *Journal of Marriage and the Family, 61*, 362–74.

Balswick, J., Balswick, J., Piper, B., & Piper, D. (2003). *Relationship empowerment parenting: Building formative and fulfilling relationships with your children.* Grand Rapids: Baker.

Bartkowski, J. D., & Xu, X. (2000). Distant patriarchs or expressive dads?: The discourse and practice of fathering in conservative Protestant families. *The Sociological Quarterly, 41*, 465–85.

Baumrind, D. (1966). Effects of authoritative parental control on child behavior, *Child Development, 37*, 887–907.

Baumrind, D. (1967). Child care practices anteceding three patterns of preschool behavior. *Genetic Psychology Monographs, 75,* 43–88.

Bigner, J. J. (2002). *Parent-child relations: An introduction to parenting* (6th ed.). Upper Saddle River, NJ: Merrill Prentice Hall.

Bridges, J. (1994). *The discipline of grace: God's role and our role in the pursuit of holiness.* Colorado Springs: NavPress.

Brooks, J. B. (2004). *The process of parenting* (6th ed.). New York: McGraw-Hill.

Buri, J. R., & Mueller, R. A. (1993). Psychoanalytic theory and loving God concepts: Parent referencing versus self-referencing. *The Journal of Psychology, 27,* 17–27.

Dickie, J. R., Ajega, L. V., Kobylak, R. R., & Nixon, K. M. (2006). Mother, father, and self: Sources of young adults' God concepts. *Journal for the Scientific Study of Religion, 45,* 57–71.

Dickie, J. R., Eshleman, A. K., Merasco, D. M., Shepard, A., Wilt, M. V., & Jonson, M. (1997). Parent-child relationship and children's images of God. *Journal for the Scientific Study of Religion, 36,* 25–43.

Dobson, J. (1978). *The strong-willed child: Birth through adolescence.* Wheaton, IL: Tyndale.

Dobson, J. (1992). *The new dare to discipline.* Wheaton, IL: Tyndale.

Domitrovich, C. E., & Bierman, K. L. (2001). Parenting practices and child social adjustment: Multiple pathways of influence. *Merrill-Palmer Quarterly, 47,* 235–63.

Downs, P. G. (1994). *Teaching for spiritual growth: An introduction to Christian education.* Grand Rapids: Zondervan.

Dudley, R. L., & Wisbey, R. L. (2000). The relationship of parenting styles to commitment to the church among young adults. *Religious Education, 95,* 39–50.

Gordon, T. (1970). *P.E.T. Parent effectiveness training: The tested new way to raise responsible children.* New York: Peter H. Wyden.

Gonzalez, A. (2001). Undergraduate students' goal orientations and their relationship to perceived parenting styles. *College Student Journal, 5,* 182–92.

Greenfield, P. M., & Suzuki, L. K. (2001). Culture and parenthood. In J. C. Westman (Ed.), *Parenthood in America: Undervalued, underpaid, under siege* (pp. 20–33). Madison: The University of Wisconsin Press.

Gross, J. (1989). *Psychology and parenthood.* Milton Keynes, UK: Open University Press.

Gunnoe, M. L., Hetherington, E. M., & Reiss, D. (1999). Parental religiosity, parenting style, and adolescence social responsibility. *Journal of Early Adolescence, 19,* 199–225.

Heath, P. (2005). *Parent-child relations: History, theory, research, and context*. Upper Saddle River, NJ: Pearson.

Hertel, B. R., & Donahue, M. J. (1995). Parental influences of God images among children: Testing Durkheim's metaphoric parallelism. *Journal for the Scientific Study of Religion, 34*, 186–99.

Hickman, G. P., Bartholomae, S., & McKenry, P. C. (2000). Influence of parenting styles on the adjustment and academic achievement of traditional college freshmen. *Journal of College Student Development, 41*, 41–54.

Hood, R. W., Jr., Spilka, B., Hunsberger, B., & Gorsuch, R. (1996). *The psychology of religion: An empirical approach* (2nd ed.). New York: Guilford.

Huang, J., & Prochner, L. (2004). Chinese parenting styles and children's self-regulated learning. *Journal of Research in Childhood Education, 18*, 227–36.

Hyde, K. E. (1990). *Religion in childhood and adolescence: A comprehensive review of the research*. Birmingham, AL: Religious Education.

Jaffe, M. L. (1997). *Understanding parenting* (2nd ed.). Boston: Allyn and Bacon.

Joshi, A., Ferris, J. C., & Wilson, S. (2003). Parenting styles and academic achievement in college students. *Psychological Reports, 93*, 823–28.

King, P. E., Furrow, J. L., & Roth, N. (2003). The influence of families and peers on adolescent religiousness. *Journal of Psychology and Christianity, 21*, 109–20.

King, V. (2003). The influence of religion on fathers' relationships with their children. *Journal of Marriage and Family, 65*, 382–95.

Larzelere, R. E. (2001). Combining love and limits in authoritative parenting. In J. C. Westman (Ed.), *Parenthood in America: Undervalued, underpaid, under siege* (pp. 81–89). Madison: The University of Wisconsin Press.

Lerner, R. M., Noh, E. R., & Wilson, C. M. (2001). Parenting adolescents and adolescents as parents: A developmental contextual perspective. In J. C. Westman (Ed.), *Parenthood in America: Undervalued, underpaid, under siege* (pp. 99–116). Madison: The University of Wisconsin Press.

Leung, K., Lau, S., & Lam, W. L. (1998). Parenting styles and academic achievement: A cross-cultural study. *Merrill-Palmer Quarterly, 44*, 157–72.

Lim, S. L., & Lim, B. K. (2003). Parenting styles and child outcomes in Chinese and immigrant Chinese families: Current findings and cross-cultural considerations in conceptualization and research. *Marriage and Family Review, 3*, 21–43.

Lincoln, A. T. (1990). *Word biblical commentary* (Vol. 42). Dallas: Word.

Maccoby, E. E., & Martin, J. A. (1983). Socialization in the context of the family: Parent-child interaction. In P. H. Mussen (Ed.) & E. M. Hetherington (Vol.

Ed.), *Handbook of child psychology: Vol 4. Socialization, personality, and social development* (4th ed., pp. 1–101). New York: Wiley.

Mahoney, A., Pargament, K. I., Tarakeshwar, N., & Swank, A. B. (2001). Religion in the home in the 1980s and 1990s: A meta-analytic review and conceptual analysis of links between religion, marriage, and parenting. *Journal of Family Psychology, 15*, 559–96.

McIntosh, D. N., & Spilka, B. (1995). Religion and the family. In B. J. Neff & D. Ratcliff (Eds.), *Handbook of family religious education* (pp. 36–60). Birmingham, AL: Religious Education.

Milevsky, A., Schlechter, M., Netter, S., & Keehn, D. (2007). Maternal and paternal parenting styles in adolescents: Associations with self-esteem, depression, and life-satisfaction. *Journal of Child & Family Studies, 16*, 39–47.

Morrison, F. J. & Cooney, R. R. (2002). Parenting and academic achievement: Multiple paths to early literacy. In J. G. Borkowski, S. L. Ramey, & M. Bristol-Power (Eds.), *Parenting and the child's world: Influences on academic, intellectual, and social-emotional development* (pp. 141–60). Mahwah, NJ: Lawrence Erlbaum.

Myers, S. (1996). An interactive model of religiosity inheritance: The importance of family context. *American Sociological Review, 61*, 858–66.

Neal, J., & Frick-Horbury, D. (2001). The effect of parenting styles and childhood attachment patterns on intimate relationships. *Journal of Instructional Psychology, 28*, 178–83.

Nelsen, H. M., & Kroliczak, A. (1984). Parental use of the threat "God will punish": Replication and extension. *Journal for the Scientific Study of Religion, 23*, 267–77.

Peterson, G. W., Steinmetz, S. L., & Wilson, S. M. (2003). Introduction: Parenting styles in diverse perspectives. *Marriage and Family Review, 35*, 1–4.

Pong, S.-L., Hao, L., & Gardner, E. (2005). The roles of parenting styles and social capital in the school performance of immigrant Asian and Hispanic adolescents. *Social Science Quarterly, 86*, 928–50.

Potvin, R. H., Hoge, D. R., & Nelsen, H. M. (1976). *Religion and American youth: With emphasis on Catholic adolescents and young adults.* Washington DC: United States Catholic Conference.

Quah, S. R. (2003). Ethnicity and parenting styles among Singapore families. *Marriage and Family Review, 35*, 63–83.

Querido, J. G., Warner, T. D., & Eyberg, S. M. (2002). Parenting styles and child behavior in African American families of preschool children. *Journal of Clinical Child Psychology, 31*, 272–77.

Ratcliff, D. (1995). Parenting and religious education. In B. J. Neff & D. Ratcliff (Eds.), *Handbook of family religious education* (pp. 61-86). Birmingham, AL: Religious Education.

Roberts, T. W. (1994). *A systems perspective of parenting: The individual, the family, and the social network*. Pacific Grove, CA: Brooks/Cole.

Rudy, D., & Grusec, J. E. (2001). Correlates of authoritarian parenting in individualist and collectivist cultures and implications for understanding the transmission of values. *Journal of Cross-Cultural Psychology, 32*, 202-12.

Sclafani, J. D. (2004). *The educated parent: Recent trends in raising children*. Westport, CT: Praeger.

Shin, E. H. P. (2002). The nature of the relationship of parental religiosity and parenting styles with the religiosity of Korean Christian college students. Doctoral dissertation, Biola University, La Mirada, CA.

Smith, C., & Kim, P. (2003). *Family religious involvement and the quality of family relationships for early adolescents*. Chapel Hill: The University of North Carolina Press.

Spera, C. (2005). A review of the relationship among parenting practices, parenting styles, and adolescent school achievement. *Educational Psychology Review, 17*, 125-46.

Strommen, M. P., & Hardel, R. A. (2000). *Passing on the faith: A radical new model for youth and family ministry*. Winona, MN: Saint Mary's.

Snodgrass, K. (1996). *The NIV application commentary*. Grand Rapids: Zondervan.

Tamminen, K. (1991). *Religious development in childhood and youth: An empirical study*. Helsinki: Suomalainen Tiedeakatemia.

Vianello, R., Tamminen, K., & Ratcliff, D. (1992). The religious concepts of children. In D. Ratcliff (Ed.), *Handbook of children's religious education* (pp. 56-81). Birmingham, AL: Religious Education.

Wheeler, M. S. (1991). The relationship between parenting style and the spiritual well-being and religiosity of college students. *Christian Education Journal, 11*, 51-62.

Whelchel, L. (2000). *Creative correction: Extraordinary discipline ideas for everyday*. Wheaton, IL: Tyndale.

Wilcox, W. B. (1998). Conservative protestant childrearing: Authoritarian or authoritative? *American Sociological Review, 63*, 796-809.

Wilcox, W. B. (2002). Religion, convention, and paternal involvement. *Journal of Marriage and Family, 64*, 780-92.

15 A Qualitative Understanding and Application of the Deuteronomy 6 Commandment for Parents

Marcia McQuitty

> Hear O Israel: The Lord our God, the Lord is one. Love the Lord your God with all your heart, with all your soul, and with all your strength. These commandments that I give you today are to be in your hearts. Impress them on your children. Talk about them when you sit at home and when you walk along the road, when you lie down and when you get up. Tie them as symbols on your hands and bind them on your foreheads. Write them on the doorframes of your houses and on your gates. (Deut 6:4–9, TNIV)

Biblical Narrative

Before there was time, God created the heavens and the earth. He created human beings in his image and gave them dominion over all his other creations. These created beings were to live in harmony and fellowship with God, and when children came, they were to teach their children the ways and wonders of their Heavenly Father. Unfortunately, sin entered the world through Satan's enticement, and the first family no longer lived as God had intended.

As the biblical narrative unfolds, we see God calling people to a faith relationship with himself, and the family becoming the nucleus for a world that constantly changes. God made a covenant with Abraham and said, "For I have chosen him, so that *he will direct his children and his household after him* to keep the way of the Lord by doing what is right and just, so that the

Lord will bring about for Abraham what he has promised him" (Gen 18:19, TNIV, emphasis added). Education in the home became paramount.

The defining event in the life of the Old Testament Israelites was their deliverance as a people from slavery in Egypt. So amazing were the miracles performed on behalf of God's chosen people, they were instructed to never forget, but *to tell their children from generation to generation*. But once again many of the Israelites, and even their priests and religious leaders, failed to tell their children and chose to follow foreign gods and foreign ways. Prophets came to warn them but they did not listen. The magnitude of their sins against God led to years of slavery and exile.

The fulfillment of God's plan and provision for humankind came with the birth of his son, Jesus Christ. When Jesus began his early ministry, he saw the results of religious leaders who had forgotten God's commands and had failed to walk in the ways of their Lord. In his disappointment and frustration, Jesus said, "Are you not in error because you do not know the Scriptures or the power of God?" (Mark 12:24, TNIV). One of the religious leaders pressed Jesus and asked him, "Of all the commandments, which is the most important?" And Jesus replied by quoting from Deuteronomy 6, "Hear O Israel: The Lord our God, the Lord is one. Love the Lord your God with all your heart and with all your soul and with all your mind and with all your strength" (Mark 12:29–30, TNIV). The Shema was central to the life of the Israelite people, and in this Old Testament passage specific instructions were given to parents to teach their children about the wonders and provisions of their Heavenly Father; the parents were to teach in such a way that the word of God would be a part of the very fabric of their lives. Yet, Jesus knew that the religious leaders who were responsible for instructing the people were not obeying God's commands in their own lives and in their families.

Parents Today

Down through the ages many parents have failed to follow God's commands, live by his Word, and teach their children spiritual truths. This is true today. Many attend church on a regular basis but know very little about the Bible. Parents have turned over biblical instruction to teachers in the church. If parents do not know the Scriptures, how can they cultivate a relationship with God and know, firsthand, his power in salvation through Christ?

Eugene Peterson (2006), pastor, theologian, and author, is convinced that we must read the Bible for the purpose of allowing God's Word to transform us into his image. He says,

> It is clear that we live in an age in which the authority of Scripture in our lives has been replaced by the authority of the self: we are encouraged on all sides to take charge of our lives and use our own experience as the authoritative text by which to live. (p. 59)

It is no wonder that parents are concerned about the influence of culture, divorce, busy lifestyles, lack of discipline, financial pressures, negative media, and materialistic influences on their children.

The Apostle Paul, writing to the Ephesians, says,

> When I think of the wisdom and scope of God's plan, I fall to my knees and pray to the Father, the Creator of everything in heaven and on earth. I pray that from his glorious, unlimited resources He will give you mighty inner strength through his Holy Spirit. And I pray that Christ will be more and more at home in your hearts as you trust in him. May your roots go down deep into the soil of God's marvelous love. And may you have the power to understand, as all God's people should, how wide, how long, how high, and how deep his love really is. May you experience the love of Christ, though it is so great you will never fully understand it. Then you will be filled with the fullness of life and power that comes from God. (Eph 3:14–19, NLT)

As followers of Jesus Christ, parents should be students of his Word, experience his power in their everyday lives, and teach these spiritual truths to their children. By not knowing the Scriptures and the power of God in their lives, parents miss the blessings that only God can give.

Through personal experiences in leading parenting conferences in local churches, I have heard many parents say that they know they *should* be imparting spiritual truths to their children but they do not know *how*. One minister invited a well-known author of children's resource materials to come to his church and lead a parenting seminar. He invited churches in his town to join with his congregation. Planning for at least two hundred, he was quite surprised when only forty parents attended. After the conference, he asked parents in his church why they did not attend. Repeatedly, they said, "we do not want to feel guilty when we hear things we know we are not able to do." Would these parents be willing to teach spiritual truths to their children if they knew *how* to do it? George Barna (2003) in his book *Transforming Children Into Spiritual Champions* says that "four out of five parents (85%) believe they have the primary responsibility for the moral and spiritual development of their children but more than two-thirds of them abdicate that responsibility to the church" (pp. 77–78). Would these parents accept their responsibility to convey spiritual truths to their children if they knew *how*?

Qualitative Study

Students in a doctoral seminar were given an assignment to interview the faculty members at Southwestern Baptist Theological Seminary in an attempt to find out *how* their parents had imparted spiritual truths to them. These participants were chosen because they were strong, practicing Christians from a variety of academic backgrounds, cultures, and family situations. It was believed that many of these participants would recall specific ways their parents had influenced them in their Christian journeys. Also, the students knew the professors and would be able to interview them during the semester.

At the first class meeting, each faculty member's name was placed on a separate index card and placed on the conference table. The students selected ten faculty members they wanted to interview. The students worked together and developed a series of questions to use in the interview (see Appendix A). After looking at the Deuteronomy 6 passage, the students discussed a variety of ways that parents today could pass on spiritual truths to their children; ultimately, four general foci formed the heart of the interview questions:

1. It was decided that a knowledge of Scripture would be necessary for children to know the ways and commandments of the Lord.

2. In order for the children to enter into a heart-connected relationship with the Lord, they must be taught how to pray.

3. Because Scripture contains over eight hundred references on giving, the students decided to include questions about tithing and giving.

4. A fourth set of questions related to obedience to the Lord in following His plan for their lives through the study of missions and outreach in the community.

The dean of the School of Education Ministries was asked to send to each professor a set of questions including a note of introduction explaining the nature of the study. Professors were encouraged to read the questions in advance and to think about specific stories from their childhood that they could share in the interview. The students set up their interviews at various times during the semester, and ultimately fifty-eight professors (of a possible one hundred) were able to participate.

The study's goal was to surface anecdotes that illustrate ways the professors' parents had used to pass on to their children the key spiritual disciplines of Bible study, prayer, giving, and missions education/reaching out to others. When the interviews were completed, coded, and analyzed, several themes emerged from the data. Some parents did little or no actual teaching of spiritual truths in the home; they left spiritual training to persons in the church. Other parents explicitly taught their children to read Scripture and to pray. Many parents *modeled* their faith rather than intentionally teaching their children how to live out their faith. Sometimes extended family members were involved in the specific teaching of spiritual truths to the children. And in most of the families, church attendance was central; missing a service was never an option.

As these themes ran throughout the interviews, there were also specific stories shared with the interviewers. The stories and anecdotes that surfaced in this research represent an initial collection of ways to help parents today know *how* to communicate spiritual truths to their children.

The Role of Scripture

> You have been taught the holy Scriptures from childhood, and they have given you the wisdom to receive the salvation that comes by trusting in Christ Jesus. All Scripture is inspired by God and is useful to teach us what is true and to make us realize what is wrong in our lives. It straightens us out and teaches us to do what is right. It is God's way of preparing us in every way, fully equipped for every good thing God wants us to do. (2 Tim 3:15–17, NLT)

James Emery White (2006), president of Gordon Conwell Theological Seminary, writes, "we are always one generation away from being biblically illiterate" (p. 57). According to him, the starting point for an education should be biblical literacy. White reminds us that Augustine became interested in reading the Bible when he came under the influence of Ambrose, a Christian pastor in Milan, and that Augustine experienced God's grace and forgiveness of sin when he read Scriptures and encountered truth. Today, parents need to help their children develop a love for God's Word so that they will encounter truth at an early age.

Twenty-six professors mentioned specific ways their parents communicated the importance of reading and studying the Bible. Some families read the Bible together each morning and evening, while some observed their parents reading the Bible, taking notes, or preparing to teach Sunday school or preach a sermon. Some parents would read the Bible to the children and then encourage each child to ask questions regarding certain passages and verses. One mother taught her children the importance of memorizing Scripture and encouraged them to select a "life verse" and live by the spiritual truth expressed in the verse.

In one family, the father taught the Sunday school lesson to the whole family on Saturday evening. In another home, the mother prepared a "theme table" where she placed objects that related to the Sunday school lesson for that week. Another mother printed the books of the Bible on index cards and actually taped them to the wall in the dining room. She intentionally taught the children the books of the Bible by reading the names on the cards before and after each meal. When the children left for college, she wrote letters to them and always included Bible verses.

One mother focused on biblical promises. When her children left for college, she gave each one a new Bible and marked in red the promises God had given her for her children. This mother put Scripture verses in lunch boxes, on bathroom mirrors, and in other places in the home so that her children would be "surrounded by God's Word." Another parent always reminded her children to read their Bible before going to bed at night. It was the practice in one home to have the children quote from memory Psalms 23, 91, or 121 whenever they left for school. One professor remembered that when he became a Christian at eight years old, his desire to read the Bible was so strong that he often used a flashlight under the bed covers to read his Bible.

Dr. Marion (Bud) Fray (2001), former missionary to Zimbabwe and missons professor at Southwestern Seminary, tells the story of a professor at Oklahoma Baptist University who made a commitment to read a gospel a week. The first week of the month he read Matthew; the second week he read Mark; the third week he read Luke; and the fourth week he read John.

He continued this practice for twenty-five years. The son of this professor watched this daily Bible reading and later wrote:

> Not only did Dad become the person who knew the most about the physical life of Jesus on earth, but he became like Him. He spoke like Him. He loved like Him. The things that angered Jesus angered him. He did only what he heard his Father say to him. (p. 16)

John Stott (1972) concurs that "a major purpose of Scripture is to show God's people how to lead a life that is worthy of Him. And pleasing to Him" (p. 39).

The Role of Prayer

> Don't worry about anything; instead, pray about everything. Tell God what you need, and thank Him for all he has done. If you do this, you will experience God's peace, which is far more wonderful than the human mind can understand. His peace will guard your hearts and minds as you live in Christ Jesus. (Phil 4:6–7, NLT)

Edward McKendree Bounds (1997), Methodist pastor and editor of the *Christian Advocate,* the weekly newspaper for the Methodist Episcopal denomination of the South in the late nineteenth century, left us with a rich collection of research and personal accounts of men and women who knew how to pray. With confidence, he tells his readers that the most important lesson we can learn is how to pray (p. 11). In his writings he tells of the late Charles Spurgeon, a man who lived in constant fellowship with his Father in Heaven. He was ever in touch with God, and thus it was as natural for him to pray as it was for him to breathe (p. 26).

Twenty-seven professors mentioned ways their parents demonstrated the importance of prayer. Several professors mentioned specifically being taught that prayer was important, that prayer brought results, and that prayer was a spiritual discipline. Several professors referred to their mothers as "prayer warriors." One family prayed together every morning after reading the Bible. They kept a prayer list and prayed for people in the church, specific friends in need, family health issues, and provisions they could not afford to purchase due to the lack of finances. As a family they saw God answer their prayers and provide in miraculous ways.

One mother prayed for missionaries on their birthdays. She taught her children that "God always answers prayers in His time and in His way. God's answers to our prayers involve His Kingdom plan and purpose." In one family, prayer became an important part of birthday celebrations. Before eating the birthday cake, family and friends gathered around the table and prayed for the person having the birthday.

Several faculty members grew up in Communist countries, and their families prayed daily for safety and survival. They learned to depend on God for "everything." They prayed for their family and neighbors and for non-believers. They were taught specifically that when they read their Bible, this was God speaking to them, and when they prayed, this was the way they spoke to God.

One professor remembered experiencing overwhelming fear as a child when having to play the piano in front of people. His mother took him aside and told him that they were going to pray and ask God to take away this fear. They knelt together and prayed, and from that time on, he was able to play the piano in public arenas without crippling fear.

Another professor remembered going with his father on pastoral visits. As a young child, he would watch his father counsel people in their homes and pray with them for their specific needs. When he grew up, he found himself well prepared to make home visits and pray for others because of his father's example. Several faculty members reported seeing their parents kneeling by their bed and praying. Mothers and grandmothers were remembered as persons who prayed for family members' salvation.

One faculty member who was raised in a very poor economic environment remembers needing a pair of shoes. His mother gave him some money to go to the nearby store to purchase food for the day. He asked her if he could also have money to buy shoes. She told him there was no money for shoes but they could pray. They knelt together and asked God to provide the shoes. When he got to the store, the man who helped him asked him why he was not wearing any shoes. When he told the man in the store about the lack of money, the man went away and returned with a note for his mother and money for shoes. From then on when anyone asked him about his new shoes, he proudly told them, "God gave me my shoes!"

E. M. Bounds (1997) retells the biblical story of the prophet Samuel who was born to Hannah, a mother who prayed for a child. Samuel spent his first months in the presence of a praying mother. Samuel knew God in boyhood and in manhood. Samuel obeyed God and asked for guidance in times of need. "If more children were born of praying parents, brought up in direct contact with the house of prayer, and reared in prayer environments, more children would hear the voice of God's Spirit speaking to them" (Bounds, p. 419).

The Role of Giving

> Do not store up for yourselves treasures on earth, where moth and rust destroy, and where thieves break in and steal. But store up for yourselves treasures in heaven, where moth and rust do not destroy, and where thieves do not break in and steal. For where your treasure is, there your heart will be also. (Matt 6:19–21, NIV)

> Cast but a glance at riches, and they are gone, for they will surely sprout wings and fly off to the sky like an eagle. (Prov 23:5, NIV)

Randy Alcorn (2003), pastor and author, notes that Jesus had more to say about how we view and handle our possessions than any other subject recorded in the four gospels. It is Alcorn's belief that

> nothing will interfere more with our children's relationship with God—or even prevent them from having such a relationship—than a life centered on things. Our greatest legacy to our children is to help them develop their inner lives, their spiritual selves, their hearts for God. We must intertwine these lessons with the building of strong character, moral fiber, and rugged biblical values that can endure the beatings of a godless materialistic society. (p. 405)

Twenty faculty members mentioned specific ways their parents taught them about tithing or giving financially to the Lord and his work on earth. Several remembered their parents putting money in an envelope and talking to them about giving to their church a portion of the money they had earned. Some parents gave a dollar to each child as an allowance, and then taught them to put one dime per week in the offering envelope to be taken to church on Sunday. Several parents had specific containers in the kitchen where they kept their money to be given to the church.

When some professors reached the age when they began making money for themselves, their parents intentionally showed them how to divide their wages into three areas: one for giving, one for saving, and one for spending. Some parents talked to their children about the blessings that came from tithing to the Lord and the joy of being able to give more than the tithe.

One professor told the story of spending time in the home of her great uncle. This uncle owned a large oyster factory and had many employees to whom he also rented homes. As he made personal visits to collect the rent, he would tell the employees about the joy they would receive if they chose to follow God's command and give part of their wages to him. He also told them that if they gave a tithe of their wages to the Lord and at the end of the year they had not received God's blessings, he would return to them all the money that they had given to the Lord's work. Not one who had chosen to tithe had asked for the money to be returned. As she listened to these stories, she decided to begin tithing when she received money from her next baby-sitting job.

Dr. Scott Rodin (2000), former president of Eastern Baptist Theological Seminary, writes, "that from our earliest days we need to be taught…to become stewards of all that God has given to us. Learning to be stewards in God's Kingdom must be done in the home [with] parents who teach and model the life of the steward" (p. 174).

The Role of Outreach

> Go and make disciples of all the nations, baptizing them in the name of the Father and the Son and the Holy Spirit. Teach these disciples to obey all the commands I have given you. And be sure of this, I am with you always, even to the end of the age. (Matt 28:19–20, NLT)

Andrew Murray (1980), minister of the Dutch Reformed Church in South Africa in the late nineteenth century, believed that Christ's commands were meant to be obeyed. "If this is not done, the accumulation of Scripture knowledge only darkens and hardens our hearts" (p. 34). Paul of the New Testament set an example for us by reaching out to people needing to hear the message of Christ's love and salvation. Down through the ages great men and women have obeyed God with their very lives. William Carey left England to go to the people of India with the gospel message. David Brainerd left his family in New England to minister among the Susquehanna, Delaware, and Stockbridge Indians of America. Lottie Moon left a comfortable home in Virginia to live and share God's love among the people of China.

Only nine professors mentioned specific ways their parents shared with them the importance of missions education. One professor remembered his parents buying clothing and food for needy families. One professor remembered his parents making a decision to sell their home and land in the country in order to move to town so they could witness and minister to the people in a poorer neighborhood. Some parents kept mission magazines, books, and pictures in the home and shared them with their children.

Some of the younger faculty members went on mission trips with their parents during summer vacation. Mission meetings were held in some homes to educate and pray for missionaries. Furloughing missionaries were invited into homes for dinner and to spend the night. Faculty members reported learning about mission activities by listening to adult conversations.

Wes Stafford (2005), president and CEO of Compassion International, grew up on the mission field and witnessed countless children living in poverty. He asks, "What if every North American family sponsored a child in poverty? What a huge impact this would have on the child—and on the sponsoring family" (p. 238). Stafford asks sponsoring families why they choose to sponsor children and he frequently receives answers such as:

> Well, we really care about the little guy in Kenya, but we also do it for our own children. More than anything we want our sons and daughters to grow up compassionate, caring, and warm hearted. We know that won't be learned by our lectures. They won't pick it up at the mall or on television. They'll learn it by how we use our money, what we pray about, and the relationships we build through the letters back and forth. So, to be honest, we are using your program to disciple our own children. (p. 238)

Conclusion

Children who come from strong Christian homes and are intentionally taught the importance of reading the Bible as a form of listening to a living God; praying to God as a means of sharing their deepest concerns and joys; giving of their means to the Lord as an awareness of his constant and abundant provisions and love for his children; and learning about and participating in missions in obedience to the Lord's command are truly blessed.

Evangelist Billy Graham grew up in a strong Christian home with loving parents who modeled and taught him the words and ways of the

Lord. His parents prayed for his salvation. At the age of sixteen in a revival service held by Mordecai Ham, Billy Graham made a public decision to accept Jesus Christ as Lord and Savior. His parents provided a spiritual foundation or "fertile soil," but Billy Graham made his own decision at the Holy Spirit's prompting. In his autobiography, Dr. Graham (1991) said, "I could not depend on my parents' faith, nor could I depend on my church membership and saying 'I believe in the Apostles Creed' every Sunday, or taking the bread and wine at communion" (p. 28). Billy Graham was blessed by having a strong Christian family; their influence contributed to his personal response to the Holy Spirit's prompting to follow Jesus Christ as Lord and Savior.

Knowing *how* to teach spiritual truths to children is important for parents to understand, but very difficult to accomplish. In a press release from LifeWay Christian Resources (www.lifeway.com), the president and CEO Dr. Jimmy Draper (now retired) shared his insights on what he called the second-generation syndrome. Dr. Draper was blessed with strong Christian parents and grandparents. In an attempt to shed insight on this matter, he provided a list of observations to show *how* this happened in his family:

1. The Bible was honored and revered in each generation as being the completely reliable and inerrant Word of God.

2. Never have any of us ever heard our parents fighting, shouting at each other, or in any way mistreating one another. Love, kindness, and grace were lived out before us and are present in each of these generations. Such things are "caught" more than "taught."

3. Regular involvement at all church services (and usually all activities) was a given in our lives. We never knew we had a choice; yet we never felt we were made to attend!

4. We were taught compassion, kindness, and generosity. Each of our homes has been havens for friends and others to whom we ministered. Tithing and much more was a practice in our homes. It truly is more blessed to give than to receive.

5. Integrity, consistency, and obedience to God have been the characteristics of each family. We all learned early on to stand for what was right and to oppose what was wrong. And we learned to do it in a strong and firm, yet kind, way. Convictions don't have to brutalize others!

6. Christian morality and biblical ethics were and are practiced and lived out in our homes. Consistency has always been a strong character trait in our families. "Do as I say and not as I do" has never worked! "What you see is what you get" is a good descriptive phrase for our families. We have never been good at putting on airs or pretending to be something we are not.

7. Daily fellowship with the Lord and drawing strength from His Word continues to be a strong pattern in our lives. We can't make it one day without Him! He said, "You can do nothing without me" (John 15:5).

8. Forgiveness and grace have always been the pattern. All of us understand that we are frail and sinful and in need of forgiveness and grace, so we learned to forgive others as we ourselves need forgiveness. By keeping this at the forefront of our lives, we have avoided family squabbles, disputes, and divisions that are so often seen. Our family really enjoys being together.

9. All of these things are wrapped up in our unswerving conviction that the Lord Jesus Christ has a plan for our lives and we have found our fulfillment in Him. (Draper, 2005)

As Dr. Draper implies, children's spiritual growth and development are heavily dependent on God's truths being both modeled and intentionally taught by parents. The psalmist agrees:

> My people, hear my teaching; listen to the words of my mouth. I will open my mouth with a parable; I will teach you lessons from the past—things we have heard and known, things our ancestors have told us. We will not hide them from their descendants; we will tell the next generation the praiseworthy deeds of the Lord, His power, and the wonders He has done. (Ps 78:1–4, NIV)

One of the interviewees said that whenever he left his house each morning, his mother would encourage him to remember "whose you are and who you represent." His spiritual identity was reinforced each day by this loving, spiritual woman. With a knowledge of the Scriptures lived out in the very fabric of our lives and through the power of Jesus Christ and the guidance of the Holy Spirit, we can pass on life-giving spiritual truth to our children.

REFERENCES

Alcorn, R. (2003). *Money, possessions and eternity*. Wheaton, IL: Tyndale.

Barna, G. (2003). *Transforming children into spiritual champions*. Ventura, CA: Gospel Light.

Bounds, E. M. (1997). *E.M. Bounds on prayer*. New Kensington, PA: Whitaker.

Draper, J. T. (2005, October 19). Second generation syndrome. Retrieved May 6, 2006, from www.lifeway.com/lwc/article_main_page/0%2C1703%2CA%25253D161132%252 526M%25253D200916%2C00.html?

Fray, M. (2001). *It is enough*. Columbus, GA: Brentwood.

Graham, B. (1997). *Just as I am: The autobiography of Billy Graham*. San Francisco: Zondervan.

Murray, A. (1980). *The inner life of Andrew Murray*. Grand Rapids: Zondervan.

Peterson, E. H. (2006). *Eat this book*. Grand Rapids: Eerdmans.

Rodin, S. (2000). *Stewards of the Kingdom*. Downers Grove, IL: InterVarsity.

Stott, J. R. W. (1972). *Your mind matters*. Downers Grove, IL: InterVarsity.

Stafford, W. (2005). *Too small to ignore*. Colorado Springs, CS: Waterbrook.

White, J. E. (2006). *A mind for God*. Downers Grove, IL: InterVarsity Press.

Appendix A

Interview Questions

What can you remember about your childhood and the influence your parents had on your spiritual growth in the home?

Bible reading

> Do you remember seeing your parents read the Bible?
>
> Did your family read the Bible together? When?
>
> Were you ever told why reading the Bible was important?
>
> Did your parents ever teach you from the Bible?
>
> Did your family ever have a time of worship in the home?

Prayer

> Do you remember seeing your parents pray in the home?
>
> Do you remember having times when the family gathered to pray?
>
> What did your parents teach you about prayer?
>
> Did you ever pray for specific items and know that God answered?

Tithing

> Did your parents teach you about tithing?
>
> Do you ever remember seeing/knowing that your parents gave money to the Lord's work?

Missions

> Did your parents teach you about missions? How?
>
> Did you ever go on a mission trip with your parents?

16 God Across the Generations: The Spiritual Influence of Grandparents

Holly Catterton Allen with Heidi Schultz Oschwald

BEFORE 1990, THE LIMITED AMOUNT OF RESEARCH FOCUSING ON GRANDparenting explored general topics such as styles of grandparenting (e.g., Neugarten & Weinstein, 1964) or the meaning of grandparenthood (e.g., Kivnick, 1982; Miller & Cavanaugh, 1990). For the last two decades, scholarly interest has mushroomed due to several demographic factors: the general aging of the American population, the enormous baby boomer generation entering the grandparenting phase in the life cycle, and the dramatic rise in custodial grandparenting (first revealed in the 1990 U. S. Census). Though the issues and challenges of custodial grandparenting (grandparents raising their grandchildren) have predominated in the literature (see e.g., Cox, 2000; Edwards & Daire, 2006; Fuller-Thomson, Minkler, & Driver, 1997; Hayslip & Goldberg-Glen, 2000; Hayslip & Patrick, 2006; Robinson & Wilks, 2006), a thick, rich database of research concerning grandparenthood in general has also emerged; and as the boomer generation embraces the role of grandparenting, recent literature is addressing the grandparent-grandchild relationship in particular (see e.g., Anderson, 2005; Kemp, 2004; King & Elder, 1997; Mueller & Elder, 2003; Weber and Absher, 2003). Numerous concerns are explored in this literature, for example, communication issues (Anderson, 2005), gender differences and frequency of contact (Reitzes & Mutran, 2004a), and sociodemographic variables (Silverstein & Marenco, 2001). Grandparent identity and satisfaction are current topics that intersect with the focus of this chapter on grandparents' spiritual influence on grandchildren.

The Role and Meaning of Grandparenthood

Relatively few studies of grandparenthood have investigated grandparent role meanings (Reitzes & Mutran, 2004a, 2004b). Neugarten and Weinstein (1964) explicated several styles of grandparenting: formal, fun-seeker, surrogate parent, reservoir of family wisdom, and distant figure. Kivnick (1982) described five aspects of the meaning of grandparenthood: centrality, valued elder, immortality through clan, reinvolvement with personal past, and indulgence. Kornhaber and Woodward (1981) identified several roles for grandparents including mentor, role model, wizard, and nurturer. Thomas (as cited in Reitzes & Mutran, 2004b) constructed a measure of grandparent identity with three dimensions: symbolic meanings, authority, and satisfaction dimensions including the idea of nurturance.

Reitzes and Mutran (2004a) state, "past studies have found that the grandparent role [is] among the more central roles held by middle-aged and older men and women" (p. 11). Part of that "central role" is the influence that grandparents desire to have on their grandchildren; Neugarten and Weinstein's (1964) "reservoir of family wisdom," Kivnick's (1982) term "valued elder," and Thomas's and Kornhaber and Woodward's (1981) "nurturer" indicate this desire. Weber and Absher (2003) note that "grandparents are very interested in sharing the wisdom of their years with grandchildren" (p. 76). And part of that wisdom, for some grandparents, is passing on their faith.

Grandparenting and Religious Influence

The religious/spiritual facet of the grandparent-grandchild relationship has been neglected in the literature. King, Burgess, Akinyela, Counts-Spriggs, and Parker (2006) note this oversight: "Few empirical studies of grandparenting address religion" (p. 79). The Fuller-Thomson, Minkler, and Driver (1997) profile of 3,477 grandparents does not address religious issues; the Hayslip and Goldberg-Glen (2000) edited volume does not; nor does the Miller and Cavanaugh (1990) study. The edited volume by Hayslip and Patrick (2006) offers one chapter that explores religion as a coping mechanism for custodial African-American grandparents (Crowther, Swanson, Rodriguez, Snarski, & Higgerson). Kornhaber and Woodward's (1981) study of grandparents and grandchildren mentions religion only very briefly. Even the classic work on grandparenting by Neugarten and

Weinstein (1964) only includes denominational affiliations of grandparents as part of the demographic information.

Recently a few articles have emerged that explore grandparents and their religious/spiritual influence on their grandchildren. King and Elder (1999) interviewed 585 grandparents to examine "how various aspects of a grandparent's religousness are related to involvement with their grandchildren" (p. 317). In Weber and Absher's study (2003), one hundred grandparents were interviewed to explore the types of memories they would like to leave with their grandchildren:

> A constant theme throughout the interviews was that of shared religious and spiritual values. Many families spoke of their religious faith and how it had impacted their families' lives for generations. Grandparents shared about their belief in God through their histories, items of value (e.g., family Bible), role (spiritual guide or sage), stories, and advice. (p. 84)

Taylor and Wise (2004) asked ninety undergraduate students with at least one living grandparent to complete a questionnaire assessing their understanding of their grandparents' influence on the formation of their values. The students gave a similar questionnaire to their grandparent(s) (n = 148) assessing the grandparents' perception of their influence on their grandchildren's value formation. Taylor and Wise found that "both grandchildren and grandparents perceive grandparents to exert greater influence in the formation of grandchildren's family, *religious,* and educational values than in their political values and moral beliefs" (p. 86, emphasis added).

King et al. (2006) sought to "delineate the ways African American grandparents transmit their religious values to younger family members" (p. 75). These researchers interviewed fifty-seven members of multigenerational households; the participants in this study indicated that the grandparents expressed their religious beliefs "through religious instruction, religious modeling, and intercessory prayer and by promoting the religious value of family relationships" (p. 83).

There also exists a growing base of popular literature within the Christian community that offers practical advice and spiritual insight to grandparents including Boucher's *Spiritual Grandparenting: Bringing our Grandchildren to God* (1991) and Endicott's *Grandparenting by Grace: A Guide Through the Joys and Struggles* (1994). Simmons (1997) lists about a dozen such books published in the 1990s. More recent books of this genre include *Parents and Grandparents as Spiritual Guides* (Cloyd, 2000) and *The Power of a Godly Grandparent* (Bly & Bly, 2003). Though generally not empirical, the anecdotal material in these books is helpful and supportive to grandparents desiring to spiritually influence their grandchildren.

A second gap in the literature is that most researchers studying grandparenting issues (even grandparent-grandchild relationships) most frequently interview only the grandparents, not the grandchildren (see e.g., Fuller-Thomson et al., 1997; King & Elder, 1999, 1997; Kivnick, 1982; Miller & Cavanaugh, 1990; Mueller & Elder, 2003; Robinson & Wilks, 2006; Weber & Absher, 2003). Though there are exceptions in the literature (e.g., Kahana & Kahana, 1970; Kemp, 2004; Kornhaber & Woodward, 1981; Lussier, Deater-Deckard, Dunn, & Davies, 2002 [none of which focus on spiritual or religious issues]), most researchers interview or survey only grandparents. Of the four articles cited earlier that address religious/spiritual themes among grandparent-grandchild relationships (S. King et al., 2006; V. King & Elder, 1999; Taylor & Wise, 2004; Weber & Absher, 2003), only S. King and her colleagues, and Taylor and Wise interviewed the grandchildren (as well as the grandparents).

This chapter seeks to supplement existing literature by sharing grandchildren's perspectives on their grandparents' spiritual behaviors and attitudes. Weber and Absher (2003) indicate that grandparents want to influence their grandchildren spiritually. Christian grandparents particularly are aware of the injunction in Scripture: "Only be careful, and watch yourselves closely so that you do not forget the things your eyes have seen or let them slip from your heart as long as you live. Teach them to your children *and their children after them*" (Deut 4:9, NIV, emphasis added). Questions that emerge here are, "Do grandparents influence their grandchildren spiritually? If so, how? How do grandchildren perceive their grandparents spiritually?"

Methodology

For my doctoral field research on children's spirituality (Allen, 2002), I interviewed forty children in Christian families, seeking understanding of their spiritual development. Though the focus of the dissertation research was not grandparent-grandchild relationships, the children in the study mentioned their grandparents in response to a variety of questions, and their responses yielded several pages of data.[1] I did not analyze or process this particular data for the dissertation; however, for a course I was teaching on children's spiritual development, one of my students, Heidi Schultz (now Oschwald), worked with the 250 pages of raw data, sorting, analyzing, and coding the references the children made to their grandparents. This chapter, drawing on this raw data that testifies to the spiritual influence grandparents have on their grandchildren, is the collaborative result of that work.

The entire interview protocol for the field research consisted of around twenty questions (see Appendix A). Among the first questions asked was, *"Of all the people you know, who do you think knows God the best?"* The children had opportunity to name three or four different people who they thought knew God well. Altogether the children named 135 people. Of the forty children, twenty-seven named their mothers, and twenty-nine mentioned their fathers or stepfathers. Besides mentioning friends (nine), friends' parents (seventeen), pastors (three), Sunday school teachers (three), and other relatives (nine), ten of the children said that their grandmothers knew God, and four children named their grandfathers.

In the interview protocol, when children named someone they thought knew God, the next question was, *"What is it about that person that makes you think he (or she) knows God?"* In regard to grandparents knowing God, the children said things such as:

- The grandparent mentions God in birthday cards
- The grandparent practices a daily quiet time with God
- The grandparent is loving like God is
- The grandparent shows faith in God in times of stress such as natural disasters
- The grandparent brings gifts.

1. Altogether, forty nine-, ten-, and eleven-year-old children were interviewed from six churches in Tennessee and California in 2001–2002. All of the children attended church regularly with their parents. The children represented a cross-section of evangelical churches—two Vineyard churches (one large, one small), a Baptist church, a Bible church, a renewal Presbyterian church, and a progressive Church of Christ. In three churches, the children worshiped with their parents, attended Sunday school, and participated in an intergenerational small group. In the other three churches, the children attended Sunday school and participated in children's church on Sundays while their parents worshiped. The purpose of the dissertation was to explore the connection between intergenerational Christian experiences and spiritual development in children.

Some children mentioned a spiritual experience while in the presence of a grandparent. The children's responses were colorful, insightful, and very observant. For example, Abigail, age ten, said of her grandmother:[2]

> She goes to church in Georgia [where she lives] and she talks about God like every single time she comes [to visit]. She reads her Bible and writes in her journal every single morning and she's nice and she's patient and she just has a lot of self-control. (Allen, 2001)

Grandmothers, grandfathers, or great-grandparents were mentioned in connection with God a total of twenty-six times by thirteen different children. The basic focus of this chapter is to document grandparents' spiritual behaviors, insights, and attitudes from the perspective of the grandchildren.

Findings and Discussion

The research cited earlier regarding the role and meaning of grandparenthood indicates that many grandparents want to have a lasting influence on their grandchildren. Grandparents expressed this influence in terms of work ethic or family identity; some also added a dimension of spiritual influence (Weber & Absher, 2003). The responses of the children in the field research, as well as anecdotal data from recent literature (both empirical and non-empirical), offer support for the idea that grandparents influence children's spirituality through their frequent prayers, their wonderful stories, their clear example, their quiet witness, their availability to share experiences of wonder, and their ability to lavish love, grace, and mercy over grandchildren in deep need of such gifts.

Prayer

King et al. (2006) report that "grandparents believed that intercessory prayer was an important part of their religious role in the family" (p. 88). It was a primary way they influenced their grandchildren. The children in the dissertation research support this idea.

As stated earlier, in response to the question, *"Who do you know who knows God?"* the forty children in the study named 135 friends, relatives,

---

2. The children in the field research chose a pseudonym from a list of biblical characters to be used in the published reports of the study.

and acquaintances. The next question asked was, *"What is it about [that person] that makes you think he (or she) knows God?"* This question yielded a wide range of responses; each child could describe each of the persons they mentioned with an array of descriptors. Altogether, 380 descriptions were offered (with several duplicates). One of the most common responses to this question was that the person who knows God "goes to church" (thirty-two); "reads the Bible" was another common response, with twenty-five accompanying comments; and "praises" or "worships God" was mentioned seventeen times. The children gave other answers that were less tied to religious activities such as "they just act like it" or "I can just tell" (twenty) or "they are 'sweet' or 'happy' or 'nice'" (twenty). However, the most frequent response to the question was *prayer*. Thirty-five children said that the way they knew their mom, dad, grandma, sister, pastor, friend, or teacher knew God was that they pray.

In describing why they thought their grandmother or grandfather knew God, the most common answer was the grandparent's prayer life. Eve, age ten, responded, "She [my grandmother] prays for everybody a lot." When asked how she knew her grandmother prayed for everybody, Eve said, "Sometimes she tells me and sometimes you just know." Nathaniel, age ten, also mentioned his grandmother as someone who knew God: "She's the best prayer warrior I know. She's been faithful all my life to prayer. . . . She spends a very long time every day in prayer" (Allen, 2001).

Benjamin, eleven, mentioned one of his grandfathers, saying, "He helps me go to the Lord. He and my dad help me go to the Lord, as does my mom. He was praying for me a lot" (Allen, 2001). Benjamin also added about his grandmother: "She's very strong in prayer; . . . when she was sick we would pray for her, she would pray for us, . . . and she would pray for herself after she had prayed for everybody else that she knew of" (Allen, 2001).

The grandchildren in the King et al. (2006) study also testified to the influence of their grandparent on their prayer lives. Allison said, "I have watched my grandmother bring the family together. I have learned to pray from her. She and my great-grandmother, they are prayer warriors" (p. 86).

Interestingly, the children also prayed *for* their grandparents. Bartholomew, age eleven, said, "My grandmother is having surgery and I asked Him to watch over her during the surgery, and my great-grandpa just had his ninety-second birthday and I pray that God will watch over him." Benjamin said, "Well, my grandmother that had cancer, she recently had a small stroke, and that was really scary, and when I thought of that, I thought of God and I was really praying for her." The children in the King et al. study (2006) also prayed for their grandparents. Eleven-year-old Keisha said, "I was really worried about Pop-Pop, so I just got on my knees and asked, 'Can God put His right hand on Pop-Pop's leg and make him feel better?'" (p. 87).

Stories

Weber and Absher (2003) note that grandparents "take the role of providing continuity and passing down family stories and traditions very seriously" (p. 76). The grandparents in the Weber and Absher study told stories about "how their faith in God ha[d] been so important to their family history" (p. 82).

The children interviewed for the dissertation research interspersed their responses to questions with stories about their grandparents. In response to the question, "And what about someone who knows God, what does that look like?" Hannah, age eleven, shared this powerful story:

> Like my grandmother, they were in a tornado . . . when they lived in Texas, and they [had] just become Christians and they went in the hallway and said, "Oh, we need some blankets and things." But they didn't have a chance to get anything, and when the tornado was over, everything was gone but the hallway. And grandmother said, "You can do this and I have faith in You."(Allen, 2001)

Benjamin, age eleven, gave short vignettes that he had heard from both his grandfather and grandmother. He explained that his grandfather really knew the Lord, and that he had been raised in China: "He was born there and stayed there for eleven years. He explains to me stuff about when he was there. He helps me go to the Lord" (Allen, 2001). His grandmother, someone else he named as an adult who knows God, also had shared experiences from her life with him, especially of the years she had taught children in the Middle East and how she led some of those children to faith.

Through the stories the grandparents had told them over the years the children were able to see that their grandparents knew God. The Weber and Absher (2003) study highlights, in particular, the importance of stories. Bly and Bly (2003) advocate telling grandchildren stories of the past and stories that tell about the grandparents' faith journeys. Stories act as mechanisms through which grandparents can teach succeeding generations how to live lives consistent with family and religious values (Robbins, Scherman, Holeman, & Wilson, 2005). Personal stories add meaning and coherence to their grandchildren's lives and offer structures with which to frame their experiences. Grandparents carry in their very being a sense of history that even their own children, their grandchildren's parents, may not yet have grasped (Weber & Absher).

Grandparents as Models

Weber and Absher (2003) note that grandparents "view themselves as . . . role models sharing with grandchildren the importance of spiritual values, family heritage, education, and work ethic" (p. 76). Banks (1997) says that "the most important contribution a grandparent can make is in terms of imparting and modeling faith" (p. 466). Children learn how to act and live through the examples of the adults in their lives. Cloyd (2000), in her book entitled, *Parents and Grandparents as Spiritual Guides,* points out how faith and actions are combined. "By the lives we lead, grandparents can model for their grandchildren lives that exemplify faith in God, strong values, respect for all human beings, and a sense of self-worth" (p. 92).

King et al. (2006) note that "grandparents modeled religious behavior as a way of expressing their religiosity to their family members" (p. 86). Mia, age fifteen, said, "My grandfather's example has made all of us. He was a Christian, and his example has shown us that it is possible for us to lead a close-to-perfect life. It is really big to us" (p. 86).

Boaz, age eleven, in describing why he thinks his grandfather knows God, said,

> Well, he usually talks about the Bible or stuff he has heard on the radio about God, and if one of us says something [that leads to] something he can say about God, he says it. He has a bunch of versions of the Bible. He's a really nice guy. You can kind of just tell. You know how in classes and stuff when you were young, people would say, "You're with God" and people could see the light in you; that's pretty much it. (Allen, 2001)

Eve, age ten, said she knew her grandmother knows God "because . . . everything she does is with God, and every time she . . . sends me a birthday card, it is always about God. She reads the Bible every day" (Allen, 2001). Zipporah, age eleven, talked about the kindness and character her grandmother displays before her:

> Every morning she wakes up at [about] 5:00 and she does . . . a devotional until 11:00 or so, and sometimes it's earlier or later, and she'll just do that and spend the whole day . . . praying and making sure she has her time with God. . . . She's really kind. She's not easily angry at you. She tries to act like God would act. (Allen, 2001)

This young girl is aware of her grandmother's character, that is, the goodness and grace that her grandmother demonstrates, and these attributes have a positive impact on Zipporah's idea of God.

Cloyd (2000) offers the following story of a man who lived a long distance from his grandson. On a recent visit,

> the little boy was waiting at the window for him, as always. After they greeted each other, the little boy noticed that his grandfather had on a baseball cap. The little boy ran quickly to his room and got his own cap and put it on. Then they sat down together in a rocking chair with the grandfather holding his grandson. The grandfather's feet were tired after his long trip, so he reached down and untied his shoes and took them off. Then he set them neatly, side by side, beside the chair. The little boy observed this, and then he too untied his shoes, took them off, and set them neatly beside his grandfather's. The grandfather said that he realized at that moment how important his presence was to his grandchild and how his life must always reflect the life that he wanted his grandson to emulate. (pp. 105–6)

Of course, grandparents sometimes have a negative influence on their grandchildren. Banks (1997) says, "Some grandparents embrace life, deal constructively with their losses, and maintain a sense of optimism and hope. Others become negative, are critical of the oncoming generation, and cover life, family, and community with a blanket of darkness" (p. 465). And children notice; they pick up on these attitudes. One of the questions asked in the field research interview was, "*What is the difference between someone who knows God and someone who knows about God?*" Esther, age nine, answered, "My grandma and grandpa on my dad's side don't know God; but my grandma and grandpa on my mom's side do know God, and have a strong relationship with God." When asked, "*So what is the difference?*" she continued:

> Those grandparents [dad's parents] don't have the friendly relationship with God that my mom's parents have. They know about

God, [but] they don't go to church. I don't think they have a Bible at their house.... [I] think they have Jesus in their head, but they don't have him in their heart. (Allen, 2001)

Nathaniel, age ten, said of his Dad's dad: "He was an angry man. He divorced with my grandma.... He's an angry man" (Allen, 2001). These vignettes clearly show that children do not automatically think grandparents are simply wonderful; they discern hypocrisy and unkind behavior, and recognize them as being ungodly.

The task of grandparenting calls for a reexamination of our own spiritual lives. Cloyd (2000) discusses the importance of being aware that we are observed and looked up to by children: "If we are serious about this task, we must be intentional about caring for our own spiritual lives, even as we are in the process of guiding our children (and grandchildren) along the way" (p. 39). Endicott, author of *Grandparenting by Grace* (1994) says, "Children imitate those they love the most. Everything we do and say around a grandchild risks mimicking" (p. 53).

Sharing Unhurried Time

Children crave attention and love. When grandparents are able to take time to sit, play, or just enjoy their grandchildren, it helps children to understand that they are loved, cared for, and appreciated. When grandparents allow for this unhurried time to happen, a special bond develops between the child and grandparent. Grandparents can be people who allow children to reveal themselves emotionally and feel reassured that they are loved. Robbins et al. (2005) say that "grandparents are frequently mentioned as providers of emotional and tangible support for their grandchildren" (p. 62). Hansen (1996) remembers the special bond that took place between her and her grandfather:

> I recall the feel of holding his hand as we walked down the street, watching his intense mischievous eyes, and his walking me home from the restaurant at nights when my parents were still hard at work. There is a special trust and comfort that I had with him and a sense that he was old, yet not really. He was a part of my young life that became memorable, and perhaps that is in some measure why I have been so committed to intergenerational activity ... to assure that continuity of caring and value from one generation to the next. (p. 75)

White (1988) tells how those special moments with grandparents can affect a child's experiences: "Those powerful personal moments (often quiet moments and in solitude) are shaped in great part by caring others, younger and older, who surround and encourage the occasion of those mystical peak experiences" (p. 57). Feeling and knowing that grandparents care for them as individuals helps children develop as whole people.

Atchley (1996) talks about the daily time her grandmother spent with her reading Bible stories:

> For my fifth birthday (in 1944), Granny gave me *The Golden Book of Bible Stories*, a large, thick book with deep blue binding, big print, and beautiful color prints depicting biblical scenes. We were living in a small city in the North Carolina mountains then, and the weather was chilly and dreary a lot that fall. We had a wide cast-iron grate in the living-room fireplace, where we burned huge chunks of coal to warm the small brick house. Granny and I got in the habit of sitting close together on the overstuffed horsehair couch, and in the flickering light she would read aloud those exciting and inspiring stories. We did this just about every day, and by my sixth birthday I could read them to her. (p. 71)

Her grandmother not only gave her a gift, but also spent dedicated time with her grandchild almost every day, reading and teaching her about the different characters and events in the Bible. Children need others to spend time with them. After children are able to trust a person, they will be more open, honest, and vulnerable with that person because they know that he or she is reliable and really cares about them.

Benjamin, age eleven, said of his grandfather, "He has set me straight when my mom couldn't really. He's a doctor or really he is a surgeon. He helps me . . . he explains to me things that my mom can't and stuff like that" (Allen, 2001).

Nathaniel, age ten, said about his grandmother:

> She is very sweet and generous. She's willing to do a lot of things. She's poor, well she's not that poor, but she's pretty poor, but if I ask her to, if it's like a special day and I want to go out to eat or something, then I ask her and she will probably say 'yes.' She's willing to do it for me. (Allen, 2001)

Nathaniel is appreciative of his grandmother's time and willingness to be caring and loving toward him; he also knows that she wants him to be happy and that she loves him.

Children need love and attention, and grandparents are supportive figures who can provide a place for children to relax, feel loved, and be deeply cared for. Many of the comments in the research reveal that children appreciate the time their grandparents spend with them just talking, reading the Bible or stories together, or praying together. The childhood memories that Hansen (1996), Atchley (1996), and others share, as well as the accounts of the research participants, support the idea that those special, unplanned, and quality times grandparents spend with their offspring can and do impact their grandchildren's spiritual lives.

Spoiling and Blessing

Common themes that appeared in the interviews with grandparents were the concepts of spoiling and blessing. Bly and Bly (2003) offer a new perspective on spoiling; they actually *advocate* spoiling one's grandchildren. They say, "To spoil implies giving someone better than he or she deserves. Every kid needs a bit of that. The Bible is crammed with accounts of how God spoils us, that is, gives us better than we deserve. It's called grace" (p. 30). Grandparents can spoil because they understand what they missed out on when they were children; and, when they were parents, they knew they should not spoil their children. Bly and Bly (2003) also highlight the concept of blessing in Genesis 48:9–28. Blessing grandchildren can have a powerful, positive impact on them by demonstrating grace and love that is not just the result of good behavior, but is bestowed simply because the grandchildren are loved.

Though the children in the dissertation research and the other empirical data did not use the words "spoil" or "bless," these concepts were embedded in many of their comments. Phoebe, age eleven, said of her grandmother: "When we are somewhere out, she will try her hardest to be down here for me whenever I need her" (Allen, 2001). As mentioned earlier, Nathaniel, age ten, said that though his grandmother was poor, if he wanted to go out to eat for a special occasion, "then I ask her and she will probably say yes. She's willing to do it for me" (Allen, 2001). And Myra, age twelve, said,

> [My grandparents] are so proud and enthusiastic about us. Not more than my parents, of course, but I guess they show it more. I'll tell you, I don't know what I did to have them love me and make such a fuss about me. It's almost embarrassing sometimes. I mean, when I'm around my friends, but I really love it. (Kornhaber & Woodward, 1981, p. 12)

Conclusions

Grandparents long to hold a place of honor and importance in the hearts of their grandchildren. They hope to influence the new generation, to pass on their values, their understanding, their wisdom, and their faith. The children in this study attest to the fact that they see, they notice, and they are witnesses to the ways their grandparents live lives of faith before them. They are beneficiaries of the love that is bestowed on them—of the grace and the blessing that grandparents pour over them. They receive and carry into their futures the experiences and memories of grandparents who knew God.

Cloyd (2000) writes tenderly about the impact her grandfather had on her and the other children in her family when her grandfather would take time to nurture the children's spiritual lives with his kind words and heartfelt actions:

> My grandfather, a devout man who lived his faith daily, greatly influenced my life. Often my grandfather would gather his grandchildren around him for a time of prayer of for reading the scripture. He would take us in his arms and say to us, "Remember, now, you belong to God and God loves you very much." His words and actions always touched me deeply. There are several ways to describe our life together with God. My grandfather alluded to one of these ways. What he was saying, although he never used these words, was that we are in a covenant relationship with God. (p. 25)

The mere act of taking time to read to and pray with grandchildren strongly impacts them. They realize that they are not only loved and cared for by their grandparents, but also by God.

In the preface to *Holy Listening* by Margaret Guenther, Alan Jones (1992) reflects on Guenther's metaphor of spiritual direction as midwifery, and her emphasis on the importance of "older people (the elders) in bringing souls to term" (p. xii). Jones says that Guenther

> conjures up the image of the Appalachian granny woman who is wise, resourceful, and experienced. Her role is to assist in the birth of babies who are born in the remote and hard-to-reach areas of the mountains. We need spiritual grannies and grandpas who have the time and the wisdom to wait patiently in out-of-the-way places of the spirit and quietly bring new things to birth in others. (p. xii)

REFERENCES

Allen, H. C. (2002). *A qualitative study exploring the similarities and differences of the spirituality of children in intergenerational and non-intergenerational Christian contexts.* (Doctoral dissertation, Talbot School of Theology, Biola University, La Mirada, CA).

Allen, H. C. (2001). [Children's interviews.] Unpublished raw data.

Anderson, K. (2005). The grandparent-grandchild relationship: Implications for models of intergenerational communication. *Human Communication Research, 31,* 268–94.

Atchley, R. C. (1996). Grandparents remembered. *Generations, 20*(1), 71–72.

Banks, R. (1997). Grandparenting. In R. Banks & R. P. Stevens (Eds.), *The complete book of everyday Christianity* (pp. 465–67). Downers Grove, IL: InterVarsity.

Bly, S. A., & Bly, J. C. (2003). *The power of a godly grandparent.* Kansas City, MO: Beacon Hill.

Boucher, T. M. (1991). *Spiritual grandparenting: Bringing our grandchildren to God.* New York: Crossroads.

Cloyd, B. S. (2000). *Parents and grandparents as spiritual guides.* Nashville: Upper Room.

Cox, C. B. (Ed.). (2000). *To grandmother's house we go and stay: Perspectives on custodial grandparents.* New York: Springer.

Crowther, M. R., Swanson, L. M., Rodriguez, R. L., Snarski, M., & Higgerson, H. K. (2006). Religious beliefs and practices among African American custodial grandparents. In B. Hayslip & J. H. Patrick (Eds.), *Custodial grandparenting: Individual, cultural, and ethnic diversity* (pp. 271–86). New York: Springer.

Edwards, O. W., & Daire, A. P. (2006). School-age children raised by their grandparents: Problems and solutions. *Journal of Instructional Psychology, 33,* 113–19.

Endicott, I. M. (1994). *Grandparenting by grace.* Nashville, TN: Broadman & Holman.

Fuller-Thomson, E., Minkler, M., & Driver, D. (1997). A profile of grandparents raising grandchildren in the United States. *The Gerontologist, 37,* 406–11.

Hansen, J. C. (1996). Grandparents remembered. *Generations,* 20(1), 75–76.

Hayslip, B., Jr., & Goldberg-Glen, R. S. (Eds.). (2000). *Grandparents raising grandchildren: Theoretical, empirical, and clinical perspectives.* New York: Springer.

Hayslip, B., & Patrick, J. H. (Eds.). (2006). *Custodial grandparenting: Individual, cultural, and ethnic diversity.* New York: Springer.

Jones, A. (1992). Preface. In M. Guenther, *Holy listening* (pp. ix–xiii). Cambridge, MA: Cowley.

Kahana, B., & Kahana, E. (1970). Grandparenthood from the perspective of the developing grandchild. *Developmental Psychology,* 3(1), 98–105.

Kemp, C. (2004). Grandparent-grandchild relationships over time: An examination of continuity and change across three generations. *The Gerontologist (Program Abstracts: 57th Annual Scientific Meeting),* 44(1), 279.

King, S., Burgess, E. O., Akinyela, M., Counts-Spriggs, M., & Parker, N. (2006). The religious dimension of the grandparent role in three-generation African American households. *Journal of Religion, Spirituality & Aging,* 19(1), 75–96.

King, V., & Elder, G. H. (1999). Are religious grandparents more involved grandparents? *Journal of Gerontology: Social Sciences,* 54B, S317–28.

King, V., & Elder, G. H. (1997). The legacy of grandparenting: Childhood experience with grandparents and current involvement with grandchildren. *Journal of Marriage and the Family, 59,* 848–59.

Kivnick, H. Q. (1982). Grandparenthood: An overview of meaning and mental health. *The Gerontologist, 22,* 59–66.

Kornhaber, A., & Woodward, K. L. (1981). *Grandparents/grandchildren: The vital connection.* Garden City, NY: Doubleday.

Lussier, G., Deater-Deckard, K., Dunn, J., & Davies, L. (2002). Support across two generations: Children's closeness to grandparents following parental divorce and remarriage. *Journal of Family Psychology, 16,* 363–76.

Miller, S. S., & Cavanaugh, J. C. (1990). The meaning of grandparenthood and its relationship to demographic, relationship, and social participation variables. *Journal of Gerontology, 45,* P244–46.

Mueller, M. M., & Elder, G. H. (2003). Family contingencies across the generations: Grandparent-grandchild relationships in holistic perspective. *Journal of Marriage and Family, 65,* 404–17.

Neugarten, B. L., & Weinstein, K. K. (1964). The changing American grandparent. *Journal of Marriage and Family, 26,* 199–204.

Reitzes, D. C., & Mutran, E. J. (2004a). Grandparenthood: Factors influencing frequency of grandparent-grandchildren contact and grandparent role satisfaction. *The Journals of Gerontology: Psychological and Social Sciences*, *59B*, S9–16.

Reitzes, D. C., & Mutran, E. J. (2004b). Grandparent identity, intergenerational family identity, and well-being. *The Journals of Gerontology: Psychological Sciences and Social Sciences*, *59B*, S213–19.

Robbins, R., Scherman, A., Holeman, H., & Wilson, J. (2005). Roles of American Indian grandparents in times of cultural crisis. *Journal of Cultural Diversity*, *12*(2), 62–68.

Robinson, M. M., & Wilks, S. E. (2006). "Older but not wiser": What custodial grandparents want to tell social workers about raising grandchildren. *Social Work & Christianity*, *33*, 164–77.

Simmons, H. C. (1997). Grandparenting: A bibliographic review. *Journal of Religious Gerontology*, *10*(3), 73–79.

Silverstein, M., & Marenco, A. (2001). How Americans enact the grandparent role across the family life course. *Journal of Family Issues*, *22*, 493–522.

Taylor, A., & Wise, R. (2004). The influence of grandparents on grandchildren's value formation: Assessing the perspectives of grandparents and grandchildren. *The Gerontologist (Program Abstracts: 57th Annual Scientific Meeting)*, *44*(1), 86.

Weber, J. A., & Absher, A. G. (2003). Grandparents and grandchildren: A "memory box" course assignment. *Gerontology & Geriatrics Education*, *24*(1), 75–86.

White, J. W. (1988). *Intergenerational religious education: Models, theory, and prescription for interage life and learning in the faith community*. Birmingham, AL: Religious Education.

Appendix A

Interview Protocol

People who know God:

    Of all the people you know, who do you think knows God the best?

    Why do you think that person knows God?

    Are there other reasons why you think knows God?

    Is there someone else you know who knows God really well? Why do you think so?

    Do you have any questions you want to ask me?

Feelings about God:

    When you think about God, how do you feel?

    Can you tell me about a time when YOU felt surprised or amazed about God?

    Sorry or guilty toward God? Can you tell me about that time?

    Happy about God? Can you tell me about that time?

    Sad about God? Can you tell me about that time?

    Scared about God? Can you tell me about that time?

    Angry at God? Can you tell me about that time?

    Love for God? Any time in particular?

Knowing God:

    What is the difference between someone who *knows* about God and someone who knows God?

    How do you think someone gets to know God?

    Do you think you know God?

    What are some things that you do that help you know that you know God?

Prayer:

Do you talk to God (prayer)? In your mind, in your imagination, out loud?

What sort of things do you talk to God about?

In what ways does God talk to us?

Have you ever thought God talked to you?

Other possible questions:

Have you ever felt God close to you? Would you tell me about that?

Were you ever afraid or alone, and you think God helped you?

Has your family ever needed special help and you think God helped?

Have you ever been at the mountains, or in a park, or at the ocean, and thought God was nearby? Would you tell me about that? (Allen, 2002, pp. 371–73)

For

Specific

Populations

17 The Place of Forgiveness in the Reintegration of Former Child Soldiers in Sierra Leone

Stephanie Goins

My doctoral research examined the reintegration of former child soldiers in Sierra Leone, West Africa. This research considered issues related to children's participation in war and how their reintegration into family and community might have been affected post-war. Specifically, I explored the role of forgiveness in their reintegration and rehabilitation process—forgiveness that would contribute to their recovery from war and its effects.

I begin this chapter with a brief overview of the child soldier phenomenon, followed by a synopsis of the war in Sierra Leone, and children's participation in the war. The social construction of childhood is considered, as this pertains to how former child soldiers might be perceived by others. The fact of children's participation raises the question of how they can be supported in their post-war recovery. In order to address this question, constructs of forgiveness drawn from the fieldwork are examined. These constructs, along with literature research on childhood and forgiveness, form the basis for ways to think about working with former child soldiers, referred to as "best practices."

The Child Soldier Phenomenon

Children participating in armed conflict is not a new phenomenon. Historical research reveals that children have been included in war in various contexts for centuries. However, since World War II, the nature of conflict has changed, to the extent that Brett and McCallin (1998) label this period of history "the era of the child soldier" (p. 20). The Coalition to Stop the Use of Child Soldiers (CSUCS) reports that between 2001 and 2004, armed groups in over twenty countries recruited children (those under eighteen years old) to participate in civil and state wars. International standards require that children be protected from recruitment; nevertheless, it is estimated that 280,000 children are currently participating in armed groups worldwide (CSUCS, 2004).

Children are used in conflicts by government armed forces, paramilitary and other government-backed groups, and by armed opposition groups. The Optional Protocol to the Convention on the Rights of the Child, already signed by more than one hundred governments, was a major step in preventing government and armed forces from recruiting children, and as a result, such recruitment has been reduced in a number of countries. However, the majority of children fighting today are not part of government armed forces; rather, they belong to non-state armed groups, serving various roles within the groups (CSUCS, 2004). It is not unusual for these groups to force children to commit acts that deliberately and strategically separate them from their families and communities. This has significant implications for their reintegration and recovery.

The Sierra Leonean Context

Civil war began in Sierra Leone in 1991 with a small group of men and youth known as the Revolutionary United Front (RUF). These men were led by Sierra Leonean Corporal Foday Sankoh who purportedly believed that through this initiative, corruption in the government would be eliminated, the country's resources properly and justly used, and the needs of the civilian population met. Corruption, economic mismanagement, and instability caused Sierra Leone to plummet to the ranking of least developed nation in the countries listed by United Nations Development Program (UNDP) in the 1990s. The RUF's method of fighting injustice devastated Sierra Leone and its citizens, undermining time-honored traditions and values that served as their cultural glue. Tens of thousands of people were killed, mutilated, and raped; over half of the population was displaced; and much of the country's infrastructure was destroyed.

Over the ten-year period of the civil war, several armed groups were operating either against the RUF or in alignment with them. As with most contemporary conflicts, the civilian population was often threatened. Some fled for their lives, others were forced to support the armed groups, and still others joined an armed group or were abducted into it. By the end of the war in 2002, the estimates of child recruitment, both voluntary and forced, varied from five thousand to fourteen thousand; and some said the latter was far too conservative (Mawson, Dodd, & Hilary, 2000; Mazurana & Carlson, 2004; Shepler, 2005). Children were forced to kill family members, kill or humiliate village chiefs and elders, amputate hands, feet, ears, noses, or buttocks, and burn down villages. Females of all ages were raped, some by boys, and at times boys were forced to rape women older than their mothers, adding more humiliation to the rape for the elderly women.

The Place of Forgiveness

When the conflict ended, one significant question for the country was how to help former child soldiers to reintegrate, rehabilitate, and recover. It would not be enough for children to disarm and demobilize, though certainly this is a first step. Would they be able to, or be given permission to, simply reintegrate? What did they think and need? What did civil society think and need? According to Willmer (2003),

> The practical issue which people in and after war have to deal with is how a war with all its consequences may be forgiven and how those who have made war can make a new and better community together. (pp. 9–10)

Though ideas concerning forgiveness are applied most often to personal or individual relationships, the principles of forgiveness apply within communities as well. It is suggested that "forgiveness is the hallmark of all social relationships" (Wright, 1996, p. 290). Tavuchis (1991) says that forgiveness is crucial in dealing with particularly difficult situations. Communities recovering from civil war are surely among the most difficult of situations.

Communal forgiveness is likened to bearing one another's burdens, particularly the burdens of wrongs done to one another (Jones, 1995). The community should be a place of belonging and mutual support (Long, 2000; Biggar, 1997); however, communities recovering from civil war cannot be mutually supportive until the process of forgiveness has at least begun. Forgiveness promotes well-being through variables such as positive emotions (e.g., feelings of love) and social support (Toussaint & Webb, 1995).

According to Shults and Sandage's (2003) research, forgiveness, trauma, resilience, and restoration are interrelated.

Biblical passages describe forgiveness as mutually beneficial, for offenders and offended alike. These include covering over an offense (Rom 4:7; Ps 32:1), sweeping it away (Isa 44:22) or blotting it out, and even removing it from memory (Isa 43:25).[1] The most frequently translated word for forgiveness is "aphiemi," which means to send off or away, or to release (McCullough, Thoresen, & Pargament, 2001), but actually speaks more of liberation. According to Watts (2004), forgiveness is a liberation at "the deepest personal level; it is not simply about exoneration from moral shortcomings" (p. 55). In this case, forgiveness has potential to free both offender and offended from the effects and moral shortcomings of the offense.

Conversely, unforgiveness does not liberate, but binds. It may bind us to poorer mental health, as has been shown when negative emotions (e.g., bitterness and hatred) associated with unforgiveness are not acknowledged or dealt with (Worthington, Berry, & Partott, 2001). Without forgiveness, individual flourishing, as well as group cohesion and support, is limited at best. In addition, numerous biblical passages suggest that unforgiveness has grave consequences (Matt 6:14; 18:35; Mark 11:25). Obviously, unforgiveness contributes to relational negativity and an inability to reconcile, and can lead to vengeful actions. Without forgiveness, the vision for a different future is limited (Willmer, 2003). Therefore, forgiveness may be the best option for the community and its members to recover and be remade.

I began this project with these biblical and psychosocial premises, and through the fieldwork, examined how forgiveness was understood and how it worked within the three processes mentioned earlier: reintegration, rehabilitation, and recovery. Forgiveness was shown to be an enacted language that could be observed best in particular contexts and situations.[2] Forgiveness was shown to support resilience in children, which has implications for their recovery. Constructs and processes of forgiveness contribute towards nurturing the spiritual development of former child soldiers and should, therefore, be considered as best practices to incorporate on their behalf.

---

1. See Volf (2005), particularly p. 142, for an elaboration of these and other passages.

2. This process will be explored later in this chapter.

Best Practices

In light of the discussion above, I will now discuss the "best practices" identified and gleaned from the research. These practices may help those who work with former child soldiers fashion their understandings, efforts, and/or programs to nurture this population's spiritual development and well-being.

Best Practice 1: The construction of childhood is cultural and should be considered when working with former child soldiers.

Childhood is a social construction. Internationally, at least as is specified in documents like the Convention on the Rights of the Child (CRC), the definition of a child is anyone under the age of eighteen years old. Sierra Leone is a signatory to the CRC, as well as to the African Charter on the Rights and Welfare of the Child—which likewise defines a child as under eighteen. However, there is also the local construction of childhood that is relevant to everyday life for civil society and is not necessarily age-dependent. This is where notable differences appear in the way childhood is understood.

In Sierra Leone, the nature of children is perceived as innocent, "not responsible," needing to be "under instruction" and protected.[3] Children are expected to contribute to the family as laborers (Krech, 2003; Shepler, 2005; Zack-Williams, 2001). Both young and older children participate in family chores, before and after school; that is, if they are able to go to school. This is particularly the case for girls, who are often needed to care for younger siblings. Children sell goods on the streets, work the farm, do laundry in the nearby stream or river, or help with other family needs. As well, children do not question the expectations to contribute their labor and any wages to the family.

The status of a Sierra Leonean child is not necessarily established by a fixed age, but is dependent on several factors. In rural areas, status changes for the child upon initiation into a secret society, which can happen as young as eight. This involves life training, in which a child learns respect for elders, secret songs, and different skills such as hunting for boys and cooking for girls. The time period for transitioning from childhood to adulthood varies from society to society, and according to gender. The

---

3. These terms/phrases emerged from my fieldwork.

period is longer for boys because of what they need in terms of acquiring possessions and status (Shepler, 2005). For a girl, as soon as she has a child, she is considered an adult. On the other hand, childhood for city dwellers might be construed differently. Children generally attend school longer and, therefore, have an extended childhood. They are less likely to join secret societies and to marry early; however, they are still expected to participate in family responsibilities.

The construction of childhood is challenged by children's participation in war. While not all children committed heinous offenses, many of them did and this has complicated the question of their culpability (regardless of whether they were abducted or volunteered). Additionally, because the construction of childhood is not solely dependent on chronological age, and the understanding of childhood cannot be confined to particular characteristics, it becomes even more difficult to answer this question: Is the child who participates in an armed group a victim, a perpetrator, or both? Most would assume that she or he is a victim. Yet, at least in part, the social construction of childhood determines how a former child soldier is viewed in terms of culpability.

For instance, if a child is "under instruction," then the expectation is that a child soldier would not deviate from that expectation. Or, if the child is "not responsible" while the adult is "responsible," then it stands to reason that the child soldier would not be held accountable. In both cases, the child could be seen as a victim. On the other hand, if a child committed reprehensible acts, even under the instructions of an adult, is that child not in a different category—that of perpetrator? Or if the child of fifteen is commander over individuals older than he (a common circumstance), is not that child a "responsible perpetrator"?

Perhaps it would be more accurate to call the child both victim and perpetrator. Both categories have implications. It will obviously depend, in part, on the social construction of childhood (as well as the cultural meaning given to specific offenses). More importantly, how might the label *victim* or *perpetrator* affect the spiritual development and nurturing of a former child soldier? How does forgiveness for this child victim/perpetrator figure into the child's reintegration into family and community and ultimately facilitate recovery?

In this context, what does forgiveness look like? Forgiveness has different meanings in different disciplines and cultures, just as childhood does. Discourse from Sierra Leonean children in this study reveal their understandings of forgiveness, and their insights illuminate that children comprehend spiritual truths—more than one might presume.

Best Practice 2: In nurturing children's spiritual development, work from the premise that children are able to comprehend spiritual truths more realistically and helpfully than one might presume.

Children in the study gave profound descriptions of forgiveness; in one group discussion, children offered the following descriptions:

- Accept them as brothers and forget about the past (like if they cut your arms off)
- Love the person more, be glad together, and share things in common
- Do not point out those who have wronged you
- Be like the father in the story of the prodigal son
- Embrace them after forgiveness; this shows a heart change.

One of the common themes in the above descriptions is that children see forgiving as an action (or a purposeful non-action, such as not pointing out the wrongdoer). Therefore, forgiving is not solely an intrapersonal event—an internal process where one thinks forgiving-type thoughts or has forgiving-type feelings.

In the excerpt below, this twelve-year-old boy identifies how he understands forgiveness, how forgiveness is helped and hindered, why he should forgive, and how the nature of a transgression might affect forgiving, all in a short paragraph:

> Forgiveness means to have mercy on what someone has done to you. At school . . . my friend hurt me. I sometimes forgive and forget. Sometimes I forgive but do not forget, like when one of my friends drops a burning (piece of) plastic [on me] . . . and sometimes I do not even forgive but forget when it [has] taken a long time. I forgive because God said we must [forgive] our enemy when they have done wrong to us, and you would not [know] what would happen in the time to come when you [may] hurt your companion or someone and you want [him] to forgive; that [is] why I forgive people. There are some things that someone does wrong and it will be very difficult to forgive, like for

instance killing someone, it will be very difficult to forgive; and there are also some incidents that are very easy to forgive, like hitting someone.

This excerpt demonstrates that children comprehend concepts and processes in practical, realistic, and even profound ways. They sometimes communicate their understandings in ways that enable others to comprehend concepts and processes more clearly. Thus, while adults may attempt to nurture children's spiritual development, children may do exactly that for adults.

Thankfulness and Hope

Forgiveness is helped by thankfulness. According to the data, persons who were thankful tended to be more forgiving. Children in this research were thankful that war was finished, that one still had family left, that the home had not burnt down, that one had a uniform to wear to school or a school-book bag. However, if losses seemed too much to bear, forgiveness was hindered. The key link seemed to be hope. If one has hope, one is encouraged to be thankful and forgiving. On the other hand, without a thankful and/or hopeful attitude, some children talked about not being happy, feeling despair, and wanting to revenge wrongs. In these cases, unforgiveness characterized their responses to wrongs. As pointed out earlier, unforgiveness affects our spiritual development. Conversely, then, nurturing a thankful and hopeful attitude within children could be helpful to their spiritual development.

Talking and Listening

Children need to talk. One day, before a visit to an interim care center (ICC), I spoke with the ex-patriot psychologist in charge. He said to me, "Don't go dredging up the things that these children did. It doesn't help them." The same message was communicated from the center's program manager, a Sierra Leonean. As a foreigner who did not know these children, I could respect and appreciate their perspective. Nevertheless, it seemed important that children have caring people with whom to talk.

Opportunities for the children to tell their stories and be heard did exist in several ICCs where children were being rehabilitated and awaiting either reunification with family or foster placement. Father Chema

Caballero, whose story is told in the book he co-authored *Yo No Quiera Hacerlo (I Did Not Want to Do It)* (Sangro & Caceres, 2002), spent countless hours with former child soldiers, listening to their stories and seeing their transformations as they came to terms with their actions. He said they talked of their offenses, but also their sufferings, their hunger, and how they missed their parents and going to school. Ultimately, they would pray, "Papa God, please forgive me. I did not want to do it. They made me do it." Father Chema's story shows the important role confession plays in their receiving forgiveness.

Best Practice 3: Any work with former child soldiers should provide them the opportunity to confess what they have done, and to ask for and receive forgiveness, to be right with God, with others, and with themselves.

Children who participate in war long for and seek forgiveness (Boyden, 2003; Jareg, 2005). In their narratives, former child soldiers write about committing an offense and wanting forgiveness from God and others. For instance, one boy writes of being forced to break a woman's leg, "but not with my heart," indicating his need, and desire, for forgiveness. Another boy talks about being forced to rape a young girl and his need for forgiveness from God, from the girl, and from her family. His story is not unusual; armed groups forced many children to commit offenses against their own families and communities—consequently severing those relationships and securing the children's loyalty to the armed group. The resulting shame and guilt can create "powerful barriers" between the child and community (Keen, 2005), as well as a devastating blow to the child's conscience (Herman, 1992).

Forgiveness is a way to deal with former child soldiers' multiple losses—and their families' and communities' losses as well. These losses are both practical and emotional, having consequences for both victims and perpetrators. Staff with non-governmental organizations (NGOs) spoke about their work with former child soldiers, and the way that forgiveness worked in relation to children's reintegration with family and community, and their recovery. They found constructs of forgiveness significant in improving children's lives after war. At two different ICCs, staff spoke of former child soldiers seeking forgiveness from God and others. Another NGO staff member orchestrated ways for former child soldiers to physically serve their communities and thus demonstrate repentance through this form of restitution.[4] What these stories illustrate is that children knew what they had done, though they may not have understood the long-term consequences of their actions.

However, a very real situation for female former child soldiers is related not to what they did, but what was done to them. A significant number of girls and women I spoke with had been raped—some having the rapists' children—and were consequently stigmatized. Their forgiving involves their personal violation, and sometimes their subsequent violation of others. It is a complex process, victims ultimately becoming perpetrators. Nevertheless, these female victims/offenders (as well as the others noted in this section) desire acceptance, love, and care—which in practical terms translates into forgiving and welcoming, enabling their restoration and recovery.

Former child soldiers also face another forgiveness issue—forgiving themselves. Forgiving the self has received very little attention by social science researchers (Tangney, Boone, & Dearing, 2005). Focus may more often be placed on resolving feelings of shame and guilt over offenses and violations of the conscience; however, these issues are integrally related to self-forgiveness. Individuals from shame-based cultures, as in Sierra Leone, would be more inclined to hide their offenses due to feelings of unworthiness (Augsburger, 1986; Shults & Sandage, 2003). Yet, self-forgiveness is a key part of recovery for these victims/perpetrators. Tangney et al. (2005) write,

> Reconciliation with the self is a necessary component of self forgiveness; . . . the consequences of not forgiving the self may even be more severe than the consequences of not forgiving another. One can avoid an unforgiven perpetrator, but one cannot avoid an unforgiven self. (p. 144)

Forgiveness processes, and particularly self-forgiveness, are uniquely related to cultural construction and practice; thus, what is meaningful and helpful varies from culture to culture.

---

4. This Sierra Leonean man and his wife founded the Nehemiah Rehabilitation Project, a community-type organization that works with former child soldiers.

Best Practice 4: Cultures operate differently; therefore, what might work or have meaning for children in individualist cultures may not work or have meaning for children in collective cultures.

When working with children from individualist cultures, we might place more emphasis on the child's uniqueness and personal achievement. In terms of a positive self-identity for the child, these qualities are more highly valued. However, in collective cultures, the identity of the child is bound up in the group to which he or she belongs. If membership in a group is lost, self-identity is lost (McCullough, Sandage, & Worthington, 1997, p. 164). Children flourish in the context of the group, for again, the child's person is affirmed by relationship and belonging within a group. Thus, how the child is taught and nurtured is integrally affected by the involvement of significant others.

Culture, likewise, shapes one's experience of forgiveness: "forgiveness is understood and practiced in ways that are culturally shaped" (Sandage & Williamson, 2005, p. 50). In collective cultures, like Sierra Leone, forgiveness is a communal practice. Both social systems and group solidarity influence forgiveness more in collective cultures than do personality or religious affiliation in individualist cultures (Bandura, 1995; Hong, Watkins, & Esadaoin, 2004). That is not to say that individuals do not forgive, but that forgiveness is understood as an interpersonal process and is influenced by the group.

Forgiveness involves *the other*—it involves the victim and perpetrator, as well as the family and community of both victim and perpetrator. Likewise, forgiveness with regard to former child soldiers involves the victims and perpetrator, that is, the child, the caregivers and/or family members, and the community (which can include quite a list of positions within that community) in a proactive, social process.

Thus, if teaching and practicing forgiveness is considered part of the child's spiritual development, it must be conveyed in a language that is understood; in this case, in the communal language of forgiveness. Children in collective cultures would best understand, grasp, and practice forgiving as a communal process. Children's talk of forgiveness, as noted previously, illustrates this.

This idea of a communal process has implications for forgiving the self. In collective cultures, forgiving self is integrally tied to experiencing forgiveness from others, including deity. One former child soldier writes that he was able to forgive himself because he knew that both God and his family had forgiven him. Their forgiveness put him in right relationship; therefore, he could forgive himself.

Best Practice 5: Work from the premise that children are resilient and have agency.

Though the damage child soldiers sustain is undeniably severe, children are capable, adaptable, and active agents of change (Boyden, 2000; Boyden & Mann, 2005; Coles, 1986; Protacio-De Castro et al., 2002). My fieldwork certainly verifies this. Children who suffered immense losses, and who themselves might have been perpetrators of those losses, were able to adapt to extremely challenging and difficult circumstances. Their resilient natures and their hopes for a better future seem to support their ability to adapt.

One particularly inspiring story illustrates this point. A former child soldier, who had reintegrated into his village without difficulty, saw others (especially those who had been part of the RUF rebel group) for whom integration was difficult. He and some peers formed a theater group and used skits to portray the difficult issues of reintegration to the villagers, hoping to inspire them (the villagers) to accept the ex-rebels. He said, "War is terrible, terrible, terrible. But some good has come out of it." Some of that "good" was his shared accomplishment of bringing about forgiveness and reintegration for former child soldiers in various villages.

Clearly, work with former child soldiers is not a lost cause; these children are not beyond recovery, regardless of what they may have been involved in. There is hope. In fact, their resilient natures give them hope *and* make us hopeful for them. Therefore, one goal in working with former child soldiers is to find ways to encourage their resilient natures, as well as their power and ability to make their lives, and others' lives, different and better. And one such way we can encourage and support their resilient natures is through established, loving relationships.

Best Practice 6: Children need and rely on love and relationship with significant others, both adults and peers, in order to overcome difficulties and challenges.

Children need continuity of care by their caregiver(s) (Yule, 1999). As well, children need to sense the trustworthiness of their caregivers, and that their significant others are in control. When children feel secure and loved, positive emotional development is enabled (Erikson, 1950; Yule, 1999). Boyden and Mann (2005, pp. 17–18) write that personal and familial dynamics, as well as environmental factors and cultural processes, mediate a child's response to adversity.

The role of these mediating factors cannot be overstated. Studies on children in war illustrate the role adults play in children's lives. They reveal that adult behaviors and responses are crucial determinants in the way children adjust psychologically (Garmezy, 1993; Janoff-Bulman, 1992; Gleser, Green, & Winget, 1981). It is not only the conflict that can damage the child; it is also, and even more so, the degree of support and protection children are given during and after the conflict that influences their well-being (Boyden & Mann, 2005, p. 14).

It was very evident from the data that children suffered most and found life most challenging when they felt alone and/or unloved. A few children write about wanting to kill themselves for lack of this kind of loving, relational support. Thus, one of the most obvious ways to support children in their recovery is to remember their need for love, and then to provide that love.

Conclusion

Several inferences can be drawn from the "best practice" statements and discussions. Former child soldiers who have a relationship with God understand that restoration with God is important to their well-being and spiritual growth. Even when former child soldiers make no mention of a supreme being in their discourse, they often display a sense of right and wrong, acknowledging that they have violated important values. Therefore, it is important to provide them with opportunity to confess and repent, as this is a restorative practice for them.

In nurturing a child's understanding of constructs and processes such as forgiveness, it is important to consider the child's culture and worldview, and to fashion the nurturing process in a culturally relevant way. Thus, the implications are that forgiveness, most appropriate in a communal, interpersonal context, are best taught and encouraged within that context.

Children can teach us too, and as adults, we must not underestimate or patronize them, despite their pasts. Adults who work with former child soldiers may be perplexed about who these "children" are, feeling that former child soldiers do not fit into their concept of childhood. Yet, despite their pasts, former child soldiers need acceptance, love, and care. If they are ostracized, the chances for a hopeful recovery and different future are lessened.

In situations of protracted war or mass violations, is forgiveness limited? There is obviously nothing beyond God's ability to do. Some children said that with God, nothing is impossible. Nevertheless, in working with communities and families of former child soldiers, we should carefully consider the depth of their pain and loss as we attempt to come alongside them in the recovery process.

References

Augsburger, D. W. (1986). *Pastoral counseling across cultures.* Philadelphia: Westminster.

Bandura, A. (1995). *Self-efficacy in changing societies.* New York: Cambridge University Press.

Biggar, N. (1997). *Good life.* London: Society for Promoting Christian Knowledge.

Boyden, J. (2000). *Children and social healing.* (Working paper # 00–05). London: London School of Economic and Political Science.

Boyden, J. (2003). The moral development of child soldiers: What do adults have to fear? *Peace and Conflict: Journal of Peace Psychology, 9*(4), 343–62.

Boyden, J., & Mann, G. (2005). Children's risk, resilience, and coping in extreme situations. In M. Ungar (Ed.), *Handbook for working with children and youth: Pathways to resilience across cultures and contexts* (pp. 3–25). Thousand Oaks, CA: Sage.

Brett, R., & McCallin, M. (1998). *Children: The invisible soldiers.* Vaxjo, Sweden: Radda Barnen Save the Children Sweden.

Coalition to Stop the Use of Child Soldiers (CSUCS). (2004). *Child soldiers global report 2004.* Retrieved January 10, 2005, from http://www.child-soldiers.org/library/global-reports

Coles, R. (1986). *The political life of children.* Boston: Atlantic Monthly Press.

Erikson, Erik H. (1950). *Childhood and society.* New York: Norton.

Garmezy, N. Z. (1993). Vulnerability and resilience. In D. C. Funder, R. D. Parke, C. Tomlinson-Keasey, & K. Widaman (Eds.), *Studying lives through time* (pp. 377–97). Washington, DC: American Psychological Association.

Gleser, G., Green, B., & Winget, C. (1981). *Prolonged psychosocial effects of disaster: A study of Buffalo Creek.* New York: Academic.

Herman, J. (1992). *Trauma and recovery.* New York: Basic.

Hong, F., Watkins, D., & Esadaoin, K. P. (2004). Personality correlates of the disposition towards interpersonal forgiveness: A Chinese perspective. *International Journal of Psychology*, 39(4), 305–16.

Janoff-Bulman, R. (1992). *Shattered assumptions: Towards a new psychology of trauma.* New York: Free.

Jareg, E. (2005). Crossing bridges and negotiating rivers: Rehabilitation and reintegration of children associated with armed groups. Retrieved December 17, 2007 from, http://www.child-soldiers.org/psycho-social/english

Jones, G. (1995). *Embodying forgiveness.* Grand Rapids: Eerdmans.

Long, W. M. (2000). *Health, healing, and God's Kingdom: New pathways to Christian health ministry in Africa.* Oxford: Regnum.

Keen, D. (2005). *The best of enemies: Conflict and collusion in Sierra Leone.* Oxford: James Currey.

Krech, R. (2003). *The reintegration of former child combatants: A case study of NGO programming in Sierra Leone.* Toronto, Ontario: University of Toronto Press.

Mawson, A., Dodd, R., & Hilary, J. (2000). *War brought us here.* London: Save the Children.

Mazurana, D. & Carlson, K. (2004). *From combat to community: Women and girls of Sierra Leone.* Hunt Alternatives Fund.

McCullough, M. E., Sandage, S., & Worthington, E., Jr. (1997). *To forgive is human: How to put your past in the past.* Downers Grove, IL: InterVarsity.

McCullough, M. E., Thoresen, C. E., & Pargament, K. I. (2000). *Forgiveness: Theory, research and practice.* New York: The Guilford.

Protacio-De Castro, E., Balanon, F. A., Camacho, A. A., Ong, M. G., Verba, A. G., & Yacat, J. A. (2002). *Integrating child-centered approaches in children's work.* Philippines: Save the Children (UK) Philippines and Program on Psychosocial Trauma and Human Rights.

Sandage, S. J., & Williamson, I. (2005). Forgiveness in cultural context. In E. L. Worthington Jr. (Ed.), *Handbook of forgiveness* (pp. 41–55). New York: Routledge.

Sangro, F. M., & Caceres, J. C. Caballero. (2002). *Yo No Queria Hacerlo (I Did Not Want to Do It).* Madrid: Publicaciones de la Universidad Pontificia Comillas Madrid.

Shepler, S. A. (2005). Conflicted childhoods: Fighting over child soldiers in Sierra Leone. Dissertation. University of California at Berkeley.

Shults, F. L., & Sandage, S. J. (2003). *The faces of forgiveness: Searching for wholeness and salvation.* Grand Rapids: Baker.

Tangney, J. P., Boone, A. L., & Dearing, R. (2005). Forgiving the self: Conceptual issues and empirical findings. In E. L. Worthington Jr. (Ed.), *Handbook of forgiveness* (pp. 143–58). New York: Routledge.

Toussaint, L., & Webb, J. R. (2005). Theoretical and empirical connections between forgiveness, mental health, and well-being. In E. L. Worthington Jr. (Ed.), *Handbook of forgiveness* (pp. 349–62). New York: Rutledge.

Tavuchis, N. (1991). *Mea culpa: A sociology of apology and reconciliation.* Stanford: Stanford University Press.

United Nations. (1989). *Convention on the Rights of the Child.* General Assembly Resolution 44/25. Retrieved October 11, 2003, from http://www.unhchr.ch/html/menu3/b/k2crc.htm

United Nations. (2000). *Optional protocol to the Convention on the Rights of the Child on the involvement of children in armed conflict.* General Assembly Resolution A/RES/54/263. Retrieved October 11, 2003, from http://www.unhchr.ch/html/menu2/6/protocolchild.htm

Volf, M. (2005). *Free of charge: Giving and forgiving in a culture stripped of grace.* Grand Rapids: Zondervan.

Watts, F. (2004). Christian theology. In F. Watts & L. Gulliford (Eds.), *Forgiveness in context: Theology and psychology in creative dialogue* (pp. 50–68). London: T. & T. Clark.

Willmer, H. (2003). Forgiveness and politics. From *The forgiveness papers* series of the Embodying Forgiveness Project. Belfast: Centre for Contemporary Christianity in Ireland (CCCI). Retrieved December 14, 2007, from http://www.econi.org/Resources/ resources_forgiveness.htm

Worthington, E. L., Jr., Berry, J. W., & Partott, L., III. (2001). Unforgiveness, forgiveness, religion, and health. In T. G. Plante & A. C. Sherman (Eds.), *Faith and health: Psychological perspectives* (pp. 107–38). New York: Guilford.

Wright, N. T. (1996). *Jesus and the victory of God* (Vol. 2). Minneapolis: Fortress.

Yule, W. (1999, June 30). *From pogroms to "ethnic cleansing": Meeting the needs of war affected children.* Paper presented at the Emanuel Miller Lecture, London.

Zack-Williams, A. B. (2001). Child soldiers in the civil war in Sierra Leone. *Review of African Political Economy, 87,* 73–82.

18 Voices Unheard: Exploring the Spiritual Needs of Families of Children with Disabilities[1]

MaLesa Breeding & Dana Kennamer Hood

UNTIL RECENTLY, THE DISCUSSION CONCERNING DISABILITIES AND SPIRItuality was virtually non-existent, and even now, the literature is quite limited. In the last decade, however, a number of articles have emerged on the value of religion and spiritual development for children with disabilities and their families (Bennett, Deluca, & Allen, 1995; Poston & Turnbull, 2004; Webster, 2004). This more recent literature addresses quality of life for families of children with disabilities, and they offer coping strategies for parents and siblings (Tarakeshwar & Pargament, 2001). The literature, however, offers few models for how a ministry can go about meeting the needs of the entire family once a child with a disability is born.

According to *Christianity Today*[2] there are an estimated fifty million people with disabilities of all kinds in the United States, and six hundred million worldwide. Each one, to borrow a phrase from the late Mother Teresa, is "Jesus in distressing disguise." Families of children with disabilities live in all communities, yet many are not a part of a church. Churches have not been especially welcoming to these families.

Collins, Epstein, Reiss, and Lowe (2001) say that families who have religious ties tend to have better coping skills in dealing with the added stress of caring for their children with disabilities. These religious ties provide (1) a framework to make meaning, (2) practical resources, and (3) hope that

---

1. This chapter in an earlier version appeared in the Fall 2007 *Christian Education Journal* and is reprinted here with permission from CEJ.
2. "Fear Not," 2005.

can lead to positive acceptance (Poston & Turnbull, 2004). Unfortunately, parents of disabled children are not likely to visit a church without an invitation or knowledge that a program exists for their children (Fuller & Jones, 1997), and currently, few of these programs exist. Many families have endured great disappointments and embarrassments when they have assumed that anyone, even the church, will accept their children.

Though most active Christians believe that churches are places of support and acceptance to all families, they would be surprised to find that religion may not necessarily be supportive and may even be a source of stress for others (Bennett et al., 1995). In fact, Tarakeshwar and Pargement (2001) report that 30 percent of families with autistic children have been abandoned by their church. This abandonment can take many forms, from apathy to direct rejection of their child.

As indicated, churches and faith communities struggle in their response to persons with disabilities and the ministry needs of their families. We address the following interrelated questions: How does a child with a disability impact the faith journey of the child's family? And how, from the family's perspective, can faith communities provide support? The findings and ideas promoted in this chapter are based primarily upon a qualitative study conducted in 2006 with members of King David's Kids, a support group for families of children with disabilities. Our purpose is not to generalize findings from this study, but to raise questions for churches by presenting the voices of those walking this often difficult, and little understood, journey.

King David's Kids:
A Ministry Model as Context

Ministry and support to families of children with disabilities often begins with a core of individuals who have family members with disabilities. In February 2000, a group of parents with developmentally disabled children, along with interested professionals, founded King David's Kids (KDK). The group consists of interdenominational Christians, and the goals of the organization include (1) providing support and encouragement through bi-monthly meetings, (2) teaching the message of Jesus to children with disabilities in ways that they can "hear," while families attend support meetings and have respite time, (3) providing education and training to parents and caregivers, (4) supporting siblings by providing special events, education, and group activities uniquely structured for them, and (5) providing a Vacation Bible School for developmentally delayed children and their siblings.

The vision of KDK came from a mother of an autistic child while she was traveling from a conference. She shared that this vision came out of an overwhelming burden:

> God made it heavy on my heart. I got out a piece of paper and started writing out a brochure and a mission statement and kind of a general outline for it and it kind of just all flowed out of my heart onto a piece of paper . . .

The regular meetings of KDK occur twice a month on Tuesday nights. The evenings are comprised of three separate sessions. While special needs children participate in modified Bible classes and play time, the siblings meet with counselors for support. The parents conduct their own biblically-based, faith-oriented support group that begins each evening with prayer and a bountiful potluck dinner.

Volunteers are essential to the success of KDK; without them to work with children with special needs, the parent group cannot meet. Two very important criteria are required of volunteers: (1) they must have a working knowledge of the needs of children with disabilities and the families' needs, and (2) they must have a strong willingness to work consistently with children who are difficult to teach and often difficult to manage.

METHODOLOGY

King David's Kids consists of approximately sixteen to twenty families. Our study participants included seven parents and two siblings who regularly participate in KDK. We conducted primarily semi-structured interviews using a phenomenological lens. The interviews were held during the support group meeting times, and the interviews were tape-recorded and transcribed. The data were then analyzed utilizing the constant comparative method for coding emerging themes. All investigators examined the data, and study participants were debriefed and allowed to review data and give input.

Results and Discussion

Following are the research participants' responses; first, the voices of two fourteen-year-old siblings representing two different families talk about the challenges inherent in family life. Their responses are followed by seven parents representing five families. For some of these families, the diagnosis of the disability was recent, while others had lived with the child's disability for several years. The parents include those new to KDK, those who had been coming for many years, and the founding parents of the program. Not only do the voices of the parents echo those of the two teenage participants, but they also provide insight into their own faith journey and what they need from faith communities.

Responses of Siblings

Kassie and Mindy are fourteen-year-old middle-school students who have been attending KDK for several years, Kassie since she was ten and Mindy since she was eleven. Kassie's parents live together; and Mindy's parents are divorced. Both of the girls attend church together where Kassie's father is the minister. Kassie's mother began a Bible class at their church several years ago for children with disabilities. While my immediate purpose is to describe the spiritual development of these girls, it is helpful to examine the circumstances of their lives and the lens through which they view their personal experiences.

Family Life

When asked about family life, the girls compare themselves with their friends' lives, their friends who do not have siblings with disabilities. "I can't even imagine not having [Tiffany] as my sister because I wouldn't know how to . . . I wouldn't know how to . . . " Mindy turns to Kassie and asks, "Could you imagine having a regular sister?" Kassie smiles and responds, "No, I go to my friend's house and it's so different, like they're always fighting and everything. And that's so different at our house . . . I mean [Jana] gets on my nerves sometimes but we don't fight."

Both participants are concerned for their parents raising their younger sibling with a disability. Mindy reported concerns for her mother's ability to sleep:

> Tiffany has to sleep with my mom now because one time she went to sleep by herself and we found her in the morning and she was just lying on the ground [due to a seizure]. I've seen her go into [a seizure] because I was waking her up from a nap and she just went into one and it was just scary. Now we're just afraid. Well, I'm afraid for my mom because whenever I saw it I thought, "Oh my gosh, that's really bad!"

Mindy's sister suffers from approximately two seizures a week, usually during the sleeping hours. Kassie is also concerned for her parents when her sister becomes ill:

> It's just so hard for [my parents] when she gets sick. She doesn't have any words at all so she can't tell us. You can tell that my parents feel bad because they don't know how to help their kid. They just get this look on their face like "we don't know what to do," and they don't know how to help her. And then sometimes they kind of get in a bad mood and kind of snappy at each other and me and everybody. Then everybody just gets all mad and then my sister is running around and she's screaming because she doesn't feel good, but we don't know how to help her.

Coping strategies for the girls vary. Each attempts to cope using different approaches; the need to cope with such difficulty is apparent in their voices. I asked the girls to explain what happens in these difficult situations. Kassie continues:

> Well, I mean, at first I try to get my sister to go to a different room and just try to keep her occupied so that [my parents] can calm down. But that doesn't usually work because she really wants my mom.... After I try, I just usually go to my room and turn on the music or turn on my TV or something so that I can't hear.

Both also report that their attempts to help their parents are often unsuccessful. Consequently, they either isolate themselves in their rooms or attempt to drown out the noise with music or the television. Mindy also escapes to her room where she paces in silence. "I'm a worrier. I know I worry too much."

Because both girls are in a youth group at church, they have many opportunities to be away from the home and with friends who share common interests. But they are concerned for their parents when they are away from home, saying things such as, "My parents can't really get away from the house like I can." So, while being with friends is a coping mechanism for the girls, their concern for family remains. "I can get my mind off the problem for a while if I go out with my friends [from church], but I still feel bad that I left my mom back there." Kassie adds, "I just feel bad for my parents for having to go through this. I mean, I can leave, but they just can't leave their kid."

Clearly, these teenagers feel a sense of responsibility for their siblings and to their families:

> I guess I'm a little bit responsible. I get her ready in the mornings. I feed her and I like to take her on walks. I don't think about it being a responsibility though. It's just what you do. So if my mom isn't doing it and it needs to be done, then I just go and do it.

The sense of personal responsibility extends into the future. Thoughts of their own future are presented with an overwhelming sense of responsibility. Very early on, these girls grapple with the moral and ethical issues unique to families of children with disabilities (Gottlieb, 2002).

> I'm really dreading... after my parents are gone. I have to decide where she goes. Because I can't just keep her, I don't think. I want to... but I'm going to have a life. And I'd rather not put her somewhere where she's not going to like it. I'd just rather not put her anywhere else whether she likes it or not. I have this feeling that people just don't understand her like I do.... And so I just think about it all the time—what I'm going to have to do whenever I get older, you know? I try not to think about it because I really don't want it to come, but I know it's going to come.

Few fully grasp the biblical concept of sacrificial love in the way these young women do. They struggle with what it means to lay their lives down for another.

Social Life

The girls' social life is not unlike the social life of many teenagers. They are concerned with what others think. Of course, their concerns go beyond those of teenagers who do not have siblings with disabilities. Mindy and Kassie have much to say about others' perceptions, as seen in this description of a simple trip to the store:

> Tiffany has a big wheelchair. And I mean it's really big because she's bigger now. It's this huge purple chair. It's really big and just trying to get through the store—there's like a thousand people all over, and people don't think, "Oh, you have a wheelchair and you need to get through." You have to say, "Excuse me. Sorry."

Concern for what others think was a major theme:

> I guess other kids don't have to worry about being embarrassed if their siblings come to their games or go to their school or if you're in public and your friends see you there. They don't really have to worry about that.

> A lot of people at my school thought I was an only child because my sister was never around. Then when they find out I have a sister, they ask me where she goes to school, and when I tell them they say, "Really?" and I say "Yeah," and you just have to explain the whole story.

> I get embarrassed when we go places; [Tiffany] will start throwing a fit and just start screaming and we can't make her stop. There's nothing we can do. I just get embarrassed for her. Well, it's not so much that I'm embarrassed for her—it's just watching other people look at her. It's really annoying. And my parents get upset by it and that makes me really sad too. Surely their parents taught them not to stare at people, I mean, come on! And adults stare too. I think it's even worse for adults because they just stare; they ought to know better.

When asked about having friends in their home, they both confess that this is not something they do often:

> I think [my friends] are just kind of confused. They don't really know how to act or they don't really know what to say or what to do. Sometimes my friends will ask me "What's wrong with her?" And when you say autism, no one really understands it. So it's really hard to explain to them why she's being like this. Like, if she does something weird while we're in the house. Okay, my sister loves shoes. There's this one pair of boots—my dad's old boots—that we always have to wear. And [my sister] will just go up to someone and make them wear those shoes. And they ask, "What's she doing?" And you can't really explain why she's doing it. It's just what she does. So I think to myself, "Shut up and wear the shoes. It really doesn't matter; just do it."

> When people come over to our house to spend the night, it's just kind of hard because sometimes I have to get Tiffany dressed or something like that and that's kind of weird for them because they don't do that and she's 13 [years old]. That makes it a little awkward.

Social development is intertwined with spiritual development. For these girls, spiritual immaturity is not an option because of the unique family and social context. At younger ages than most, they already deal with the Christian virtues of humility, forgiveness, and unconditional acceptance of others at a depth that many of us never confront.

Spiritual Development

Evidence of spiritual development is reflected in a deep and abiding faith in God and a commitment to remain connected to him for peace and strength. Mindy began by talking about prayer. "Prayer helps me to be more calm. I know God has a plan and that all this will be okay." Kassie adds, "Yeah, He's in control. He knows what He's doing and this is happening for a reason. The hard things we are going through are going to make us stronger." As the conversation continued, the girls reflected further on their relationships with God:

> God gives us good days like a day when my sister is really happy or something like that. When that happens I know that God is showing me that it's not always going to be bad. There are going to be fun times.

> Yeah, and sometimes when I'm doing my devotional or reading my Bible, God will lead me to a verse that goes with what I'm going through. Then every time things start getting hard with [my sister] I can just remember it.

> Having a sibling with a disability is not always bad. It's good. It teaches you a lot of lessons. I just wish people would take the time to actually get to know [someone with a disability] before they just automatically think, "Oh, I don't want to have anything to do with them." I just want others to know the good things about my sister. I don't want people to feel sorry for us or for her. I think God picks special people to have siblings or kids like that.

> I think that more churches should have a special needs ministry because that would really reach out to a lot of families, and I'm

sure a lot of families can't go to church because there's no place for their kid.

Experiences with Churches

Both girls attend church where they are surrounded by people who love and accept their siblings with disabilities. This unique church is comprised largely of families who have a child with a disability. Church communities, however, have not always been accepting. Both recall events where their families felt rejection from someone at church:

> If I hadn't met [Kassie's family] at KDK, we wouldn't be going to church. I probably wouldn't even have a relationship with God. We've been turned away by churches because they didn't have a place for Tiffany.

> You can't just put [our sisters] in the nursery. There'll be a nursery and usually the nursery has just got toddlers, then you start taking little five- and six-year-olds in and you can't put them in the nursery. Pretty soon, they come to you and say, "We can't keep them in the nursery." Then they tell you that you can't take them into church because they're screaming, and they just say, "Sorry, you're going to have to go somewhere else."

> And you think that a church ... would make a place for them. But they don't. It's not their responsibility to have to find a place for them. It's just one kid. Maybe if there were more, they would find a place for them, but not just one.

These girls clearly recognize what most forget—that we serve a Savior who teaches the parable of forsaking the ninety-nine sheep for the one who is lost. Christians are called to care for "the one."

Responses of Parents

These parents, like the teenage girls, can feel isolated, and they describe life as unpredictable and often fragmented. A common frustration that the parents voiced is misinformed judgment from those who do not understand the implications of disability. One mother said of her autistic son:

> They just think it is a discipline problem or he meant that rudely. Not, oh he has autism or he has whatever, and I think that's the hardest thing. You know it's easier for people to have to deal with

> people in wheelchairs, but when you get into the more developmental problems with them, they don't know what to do; they don't understand.

Another parent said:

> We heard things like, "If you would spank her, she wouldn't be this way. My child used to do that, but I spanked [him] and now [he doesn't] act that way."

Even when others were aware of the diagnosis, sometimes there was little support:

> When we got the diagnosis of autism . . . there was the initial, "Oh, I'm sorry," and then that was about it. I think . . . people didn't understand the long-term implications of autism or what that meant to us, but we felt extremely isolated.

In the midst of their own feelings of helplessness and frustration, they were hearing the message that they were just not doing things right.

Spiritual Support

King David's Kids provides a faith context where these parents feel welcome and understood. While their voices are often excluded from conversations in which parents of children without disabilities share stories about T-ball and ballet lessons, at KDK their voices are heard and validated:

> I come because they can understand. Even if her behavior is extreme, the other parents can relate. We celebrate little stuff, the small things our kids do. . . . They are big for us. Other parents wouldn't understand that, but here we all do.

One couple shares that the first night they attended KDK they were overwhelmed by the opportunity to talk about their child, "We talked more that night about Trey than [we] ever [had]. It was unreal." When asked why they attend KDK, often the first thing mentioned is the opportunity to talk about their child to others who understand.

Their stories of personal and spiritual growth affirm the power of religious experience to provide a "framework to make meaning" of the disability, and to give them "hope that can lead to positive acceptance" (Poston & Turnbull, 2004). One father described how their participation provided for his family the path to salvation. Prior to their involvement with this ministry, faith had not been a significant aspect of life for his family:

> Before we came to KDK we were just trying to figure out what to do. We had a special needs child that was four years old. We were struggling with just not knowing anything. And then we went to KDK. We met on a Thursday night and it was just a bunch of families. It didn't seem like church. It didn't seem like anything to do with church. We would say a prayer, but it was just people sharing things and they all had kind of similar things that we could all kind of relate to. . . . Basically they were giving testimonies and I didn't know what they were doing. I didn't know what a testimony was.

As time went on, this father not only learned what a testimony is, but also God has given a voice to his own personal testimony:

> I give credit to God; Tiffany's favorite verse is in John 9 where the apostles are asking Jesus why this guy was blind and he says it is nobody's fault. It was basically that it just proved that God can be glorified. Jonathan's special because God can be glorified through him. Because Jonathan is the way he is, our family has been saved. You know we have been brought to Christ through the struggles. It is all part of God's plan.

King David's Kids' support meetings for parents include Bible study; and these studies have helped parents make sense of their experiences:

> It started off as a place where we could at least come and be with other parents. It has become in recent years a place . . . well, it has really shown me that the Bible has applications for parents with special needs kids that I didn't see.

Insights About Churches

The parents also describe rejection by churches. One parent had been told that it would be best to find another church where they would "probably feel better." In the interview, she responds, "I don't think Jesus would have ever said that." Several parents recount the frustration of trying to go to church:

> We went through at least three years of not really being able to attend church because there wasn't a place for her (the child with

autism) and it was always very difficult to get her into the building. Then she would get in there and have a hard time and they would immediately call us to come get her and take her home because they couldn't deal with her behavior. I understand that, but it just got to the point of, "Why am I wrestling her into the building if I am just going to turn around and take her home?"

These parents know that their children exhibit behaviors that can be very difficult to manage in the church setting:

It is not easy to teach these children. They sometimes act out and they are aggressive and parents know that. I think they are terrified to bring their child to a new place and have him act out and kick and scream the whole time.

You know, just be open and honest with them (the parents) and say, "You know, we're not sure how to handle this but we would like to try." They will give you some suggestions. Parents would be happy to do that and we know that our child is different.

In the spirit of 1 Corinthians 13, one parent reminds us that while strategies and programs are important, the heart is central to working with these children:

Someone can teach you how to do modifications. Someone can teach you how to structure the class. Someone can teach you all of those things. [But] if you don't have the attitude of Jesus and the heart of Jesus toward those kids, then it doesn't matter. If you do, then the rest can come.

We then asked what message they would give churches seeking to minister to families of children with disabilities, they say that churches must move beyond merely "finding a place" for them. What these children need is to be truly welcomed, and the parents' deepest desire is that their children be wanted, not just tolerated:

Welcome them, number one. The parents need to know above all else that you love their children and not just that you love their children but that you *want* their children.

Convey to those parents every time you see them that you are happy when their child is there and you are sad when their child is not there. And unless there is blood, don't go get those parents during worship service. Let them know you are perfectly comfortable dealing with the child. If there is a behavior problem or a meltdown, that you love them anyway. It is not a burden for you to deal with if they have a meltdown. Reassure them of that over and over and over.

One parent describes the overwhelming feeling when one church welcomed his child in this way:

> It was different with the church that John pastors. He (his son with autism) was never overlooked. He was looked for, you know? It was like, "We want this kid. We want him." They wanted him. It wasn't, "We can find a spot for him." It was, "We want him. If ya'll want to come too that's great, but we want him." That was different. That was really everything to us.

For these parents, welcoming their children includes recognizing their spiritual capacity. "We want people to believe she can learn about Jesus." When the focus is on the child's cognitive capacity, the risk is that we will ignore the intuitive aspects of relationship with God (Webster, 2004):

> Show those kids the love of Jesus and . . . that God has promised that we will know His voice and that in some way, some how, in a way that we don't understand, God has promised that these kids can know Him and will know Him.

In addition to recognizing that these children can experience authentic relationships with God, they can also serve as a witness to God's love and acceptance of all people:

> You want to meet everybody's needs, but in a way God might use some of the special needs children to show others that people might love them too. If the people at this church can love somebody who doesn't fit into society, maybe they can love me too. Seeing that God loves them (children with special needs) and has a place for them might help reach others. God works that way.

Christianity Today (2005) has described families of children with disabilities as one of the greatest unreached groups of our time. The families in this study have found a place to belong, to be encouraged, and to grow spiritually. However, they recognize that this is not the experience of all families.

Conclusion

Families of children with disabilities face many struggles—financial, health, emotional, social—as well as the simple activities of daily life. As such, many turn to their faith and spirituality to find meaning and purpose in their lives. Many of these families are in search of religious communities for their needed support. Without that support, however, parents are either reluctant to attend or are unable to benefit from attending because they spend their time providing direct support to their children with disabilities. In other cases, church members actually reject families with these children.

The families' comments in this study show that they need at least three things: (1) acceptance of their child with disabilities, (2) spiritual and emotional support, and (3) a program for their special-needs child so that the other family members can have a meaningful experience in religious practice.

Although this is important, serving families of children with special needs does not simply begin in the Sunday school teacher's classroom. Serving these families ultimately depends upon the entire church; it means making a commitment to the special-needs child through his or her adulthood. What vision do we have for including people with disabilities in our churches? Should we discuss with the leaders of our churches a mission statement regarding individuals with disabilities?

A well-grounded philosophy among the leaders of any organization is fundamental to the success of such a program. Are all members in the church treated fairly? Does everyone have an opportunity to contribute? Are individuals with disabilities really included in the worship service or are they relegated to a small section in the auditorium? Are they greeted when they enter the sanctuary or must they keep to themselves? Do we have enough accessible parking? Are the aisles wide enough to accommodate wheelchairs?

Faith provides a framework through which families—all families—can bring meaning to their lives. Given this premise, are there opportunities to explore how the biblical text brings relevance and meaning to these families' unique journeys? How can we, the church, connect those families who are farther along in the journey with those who have heard "the bad news" for the first time? How can we provide them with a safe space to grieve the loss and lament freely, and ultimately empower them to move forward to claim joy despite the struggle? Should we send teachers to seminars and workshops so that they can receive the proper training? Because divorce rates among parents of children with disabilities are higher than average, what are we doing to minister to these families?

If our churches provide a place of community, then we must not draw the proverbial lines around those who are included and those who are excluded. All of us—not just some of us—comprise the body of Christ.

An "inclusive" church is grounded in an attitude of acceptance. Once the church adopts this attitude, it will drive the church's decisions and actions (Breeding, Hood & Whitworth, 2006). The lives of these children and their families have not been lived in vain, and we have learned a great deal about hope from them. As one parent says, "I think as time goes on, most churches will find a way to reach our kids, especially if they understand it is critical."

REFERENCES

Bennett, T., Deluca, D., & Allen, R. (1995). Religion and children with disabilities. *Journal of Religion and Health*, 34(4), 301–12.

Collins, B. C., Epstein, A., Reiss, T., & Lowe, V. (2001). Including children with mental retardation in the religious community. *Teaching Exceptional Children*, 33(5), 52–58.

Fear not the disabled. (2005). *Christianity Today*, 49(11), 28–29.

Fuller, C., & Jones, L. (1997). *Extraordinary kids*. Colorado Springs, CO: Focus on the Family.

Gottlieb, R. (2002). The tasks of embodied love: Moral problems in caring for children with disabilities. *Hypatia*, 17(3), 225–35.

Poston, D., & Turnbull, A. (2004). Role of spirituality and religion in family quality of life for families of children with disabilities. *Education and Training in Developmental Disabilities*, 39(2), 95–108.

Tarakeshwar, N., & Pargament, K. (2001). Religious coping in families of children with autism. *Focus on Autism and Other Developmental Disabilities*, 16(4), 247–60.

Webster, J. (2004). Religious education for children with severe learning difficulties: Constructing a framework, finding a medium, exploring a story. *Support for Learning*, 19(3), 119–24.

19 The African American Church and Its Role in Nurturing the Spiritual Development of Children

La Verne Tolbert & Marilyn Brownlee

ONE OF MY FIRST SUMMER JOBS AS A TEENAGER DURING THE 1960S WAS working for a community development program in New York. I was given the task of surveying an area in Harlem, an urban center predominantly populated by African Americans. My assignment was to conduct a census of businesses by walking approximately a mile, and recording the number of restaurants, convenience stores, churches, and other businesses in that twenty-block radius. It was an educational assignment, one that sparked for me an inquisitive journey into the role of the church in the black community.

There was at least one church on every corner. On most blocks, there were two or perhaps three small "storefront" churches—churches that emerged primarily as a response to the rural migrants from the South who simulated their rural church experience in an urban environment by worshiping in smaller, intimate settings (Baer, 1984). There were also megachurches in Harlem; these large congregations with memberships of two thousand to five thousand existed long before the term was coined in the 1980s.

One of the two megachurches I remember was a Pentecostal church called Refuge Temple on 125th Street. I recall this church's pioneering radio broadcast as well as its rigorous ordination process in which my dad participated. Refuge Temple, with Bishop Robert C. Lawson as its founder-pastor, spawned dozens of smaller ministries including my father's storefront church when he became a pastor. The other megachurch was Canaan

Baptist Church on 116th Street where Dr. Wyatt Tee Walker was pastor. My aunt, Lorraine Springsteen, was Executive Assistant to Dr. Walker, so our families were close. This made for much excitement since Dr. Walker walked alongside Dr. Martin Luther King Jr. at the height of the Civil Rights Movement.

As I conducted this mini-census, I counted more churches than restaurants, more churches than schools, more churches than shoe stores, more churches than beauty and barber shops, and more churches than clothing stores. In fact, there were more church buildings than any other entity. As a community, Harlem could have been defined as "church row."

Recent data support the idea that African Americans are consistent church-goers. According to Barna (2003), religion plays a greater role in the lives of African Americans than in the lives of white Americans, and the overwhelming majority belong to churches and attends them regularly. A survey by the National Urban League indicates that over three-fourths (79 percent) of all African Americans belong to churches and two-thirds (67 pecent) attend church at least once a month (Hill, 1987). Seventy-one percent of African American parents send their children to Sunday school regularly (Hill).

This is good news.

Role of the Church

Church attendance is key to the African American family because of its significant role in the spiritual, social, and political life of the African American community. During the 1960s and 1970s, the church became the catalyst for the Civil Rights Movement, birthed in the heart of Birmingham, Alabama. Like many others who were championed by their pastors as they marched on Washington DC, my parents, aunts, and uncles voted with their feet to become one with the chorus at the foot of the Washington Monument to herald the end of a bad beginning in America. Encouraged by powerful preachers to be both strong and non-violent, young people sat at lunch counters throughout the South and refused to leave. Personal courage and absolute reliance upon God were qualities that were forged Sunday to Sunday in compelling sermons and inspirational choruses; these messages and songs reflected the core of a people whose faith that Almighty God could accomplish the impossible was profoundly unshakable. Perhaps at no other time has the African American church demonstrated the power of its leadership to uniformly rally as it did then (Warren, 2001).

Today, the church continues to be the hub of spiritual, political, and social awareness in the black community. Here, children are ushered into relationship with this same God who intervened in their history, just as he did for the Israelites when Pharaoh's army drowned in the Red Sea. The children hear the famous legacies of Sojourner Truth, Frederick Douglass, Booker T. Washington, W. E. B. DuBois, Dr. George Washington Carver, Langston Hughes, Ida B. Wells, Rosa Parks, Andrew Young, and Maynard Jackson—and the not-so-famous such as my aunt, Sylvia Henderson:

> And what more shall I say? For time will fail me if I tell of Gideon, Barak, Samson, Jephtha, of David and Samuel and the prophets, who by faith conquered kingdoms, performed acts of righteousness, obtained promises, shut the mouths of lions, quenched the power of fire, escaped the edge of the sword, from weakness were made strong. (Hebrews 11:32–34a)

These heroes and "sheroes," who stood firmly under God's banner, left an imprint on my generation and influenced me in other profound ways. For example, during the time that my own nuclear family was disintegrating due to my birth mother's mental illness, "church mothers" (those saints, as they were respectfully called, who wore white dresses, hats, and gloves every Sunday) took me and my siblings to their homes often for weeks at a time. They fed us, comforted us, encouraged us, and prayed with us. As a result of these significant role models—as well as my father, Roy Powlis, who served God with the tenacity of Job, my grandmothers whose singing and praying are vivid memories, Gladys, the youth choir director, and Philip and Stephen, our youth leaders who developed creative ministries that made going to church seem like a holiday—I serve the Lord Jesus Christ today by similarly ministering to children, teens, and young adults. As a child, going to church was integral in instilling a sense of hope and optimism that God would positively impact my life despite my immediate circumstances. This hope was reinforced through the church's human resources—the "church folk" who helped me cope.

Connection to Spiritual Development

Attending church services should make a difference in people's lives. According to Roehlkepartain and Patel (2005), youths who are more engaged in church

> are least likely to participate in a range of risky behaviors, and they are more likely to have a sense that they are cared for by others, that their lives have meaning and purpose, and that they have more positive relationships with family and nonparent adults. (p. 326)

Wagener et al. (2003) claim that religious involvement enables youth to thrive by fostering positive developmental outcomes and pro-social behavior. Nowhere is this engagement or involvement more crucial than in single-parent families who rely upon their extended church family to form the nucleus, without which it is impossible successfully to rear children.

> Often, the question is raised of how Black women who are single can manage so well in raising their children alone. The answer is they are not alone. The church provides a kind of extended family fellowship that provides significant adults to relate to the children, and it also provides material and human resources to the family. (Hale-Benson, 1982, p. 53)

Acknowledging that the African American church is a powerful entity in the community, the question addressed here relates to the church's role in the spiritual realm. How well does the African American church nurture the spiritual development of children and youth?

To address this question, a working definition of spirituality is essential. Mattis, Ahluwalia, Cowie, and Kirkland-Harris (2005) believe that spirituality is intrinsically tied to ethnicity and culture because spiritual development is connected to role models—parents, siblings, and religious leaders. The authors also include in their description of spirituality within the black community spiritual practices that are sometimes associated with people of African descent—mysticism, superstition, or rituals such as voodoo.

This definition is too limiting. Spirituality must include *personal* faith, which is at the heart of biblical Christianity. Because children can and do know God personally in ways that often transcend any cultural convention, faith must be inclusive in the definition for this discussion. For my purposes here, I offer the following definition:

> a conscious relationship with God in Jesus Christ through the Holy Spirit within the context of a community of believers that fosters that relationship as well as the child's understanding of and response to that relationship (the operational definition stated on the Children's Spirituality Conference website, www.childspirituality.org).

Nurturing this relationship is the passion of every sincere children's pastor, teacher, and volunteer—how is this accomplished?

Children's ministries are often criticized for being too busy and having too many activities. But according to Dallas Willard (1998), there are many "activities that have had a wide and profitable use among the disciplines of Christ" (p. 158). Activities through which spiritual disciplines are realized are important contributors to spiritual growth. Willard categorizes these disciplines into the disciplines of abstinence (solitude, silence, fasting, frugality, chastity, secrecy, sacrifice), and the disciplines of engagement (study, worship, celebration, service, prayer, fellowship, confession, submission).

Activity has a purpose. Churches where little children can sing in choirs, for example, offer them the opportunity to worship by praising their Heavenly Father. Camps and retreats provide the venue for solitude and quiet time to commune with God through nature (Westerhoff, 2006). Sunday school and children's church provide opportunities for individual and corporate prayer, worship, and Bible study. Such activities foster spiritual growth in the lives and minds of the very young.

Scriptural Basis: The Luke 2:52 Triad

Scriptural support for nurturing spiritual development in children is found in Luke 2:52: "And Jesus increased in wisdom and stature, and in favor with God and man" (see figure 1). In this example, three areas of growth are evident: Nurturing Development Toward God (wisdom) as shown in figure 2, Nurturing Development Toward Self (stature) as shown in figure 3, and Nurturing Development Toward Others (favor) as shown in figure 4.

Figure 1

"And Jesus increased in wisdom, and stature, and in favor with God and man" (Luke 2:52).

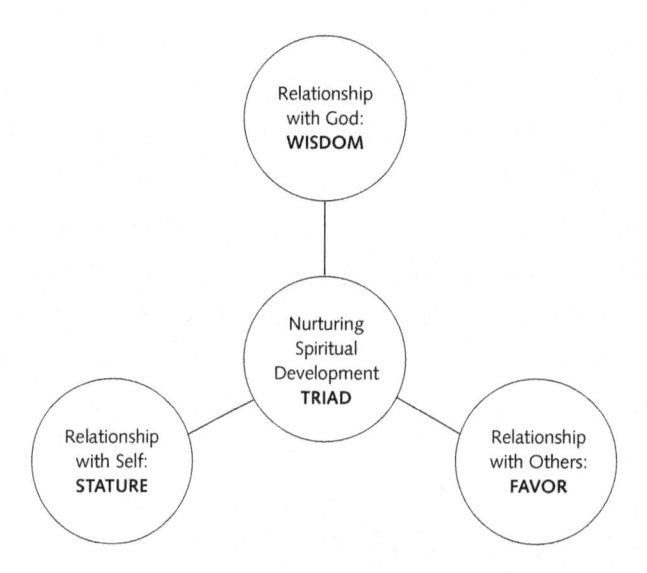

- Relationship with God: **WISDOM**
- Nurturing Spiritual Development **TRIAD**
- Relationship with Self: **STATURE**
- Relationship with Others: **FAVOR**

Wisdom results through a relationship with God, since knowledge is rightly applied to every aspect of life. Wisdom is nurtured through the disciplines of engagement—worship, celebration, prayer, confession, and study.

Figure 2: Nurturing Development Toward God

Wisdom—Spiritual Disciplines of Engagement

- Worship, Celebration
- Prayer, Confession
- Study

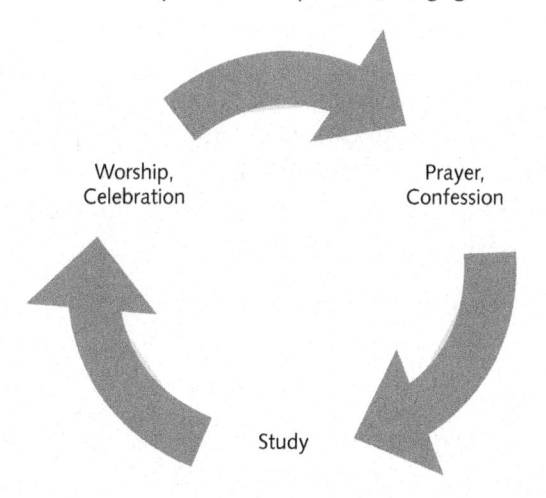

As Jesus grew in stature, more than physical growth is implied. The emotional self develops and a healthy sense of personal worth produces the ability to make right decisions because a right relationship with God fosters right relationships with self and others. According to therapist and author, Minnie Claiborne, "When our spirit is regenerated through a relationship with Jesus Christ, it impacts our soul (mind, will, and emotions), which affects our decisions. Our decisions, in turn, influence our behavior which ultimately affects how we live" (personal communication, July 23, 2007). The disciplines of abstinence—chastity, frugality, solitude, silence, secrecy, fasting, and sacrifice—are expressions of self-esteem or better yet, God-esteem.

Figure 3: Nurturing Development Toward Self
Stature—Spiritual Disciplines of Abstinence

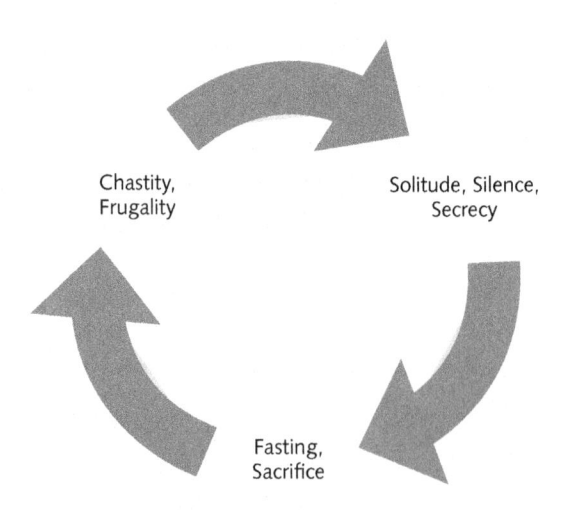

- Chastity, Frugality
- Solitude, Silence, Secrecy
- Fasting, Sacrifice

Increasing in favor with God and man indicates that from a sincere relationship with God, Jesus developed into a compassionate human being who properly related to others. Willard's disciplines of engagement are operative here—service, fellowship, submission.

Figure 4: Nurturing Development Toward Others
Favor—Spiritual Disciplines of Engagement

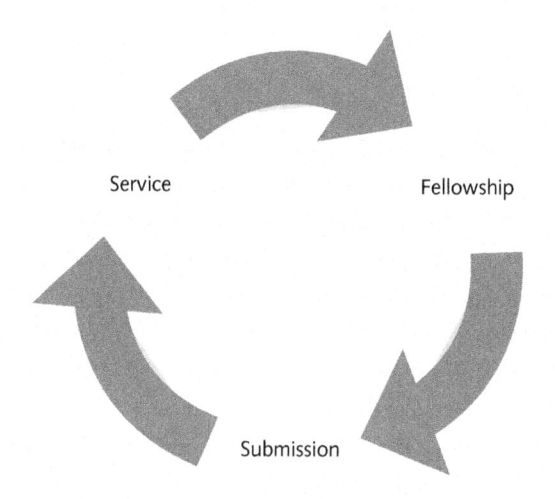

Service

Fellowship

Submission

Here I examine children's ministry activities as a means of fostering and nurturing spiritual development through age-appropriate application of the disciplines of abstinence and engagement in consideration of the Luke 2:52 Triad—a model that may assist in the development and/or evaluation of ministries whose goal is the spiritual nurture of children.

Examining Four Ministries

The nurturing environment of four ministries with a firm commitment to developing children spiritually (Newman, 1995) will be profiled with Willard's disciplines of abstinence and engagement in mind, as well as the Luke 2:52 Triad. These four ministries include Project SPIRIT in Atlanta, Georgia; Christian Stronghold Baptist Church in Philadelphia, Pennsylvania, Friendship Baptist Church in Yorba Linda, California, and Crenshaw Christian Center in Los Angeles, California. In addition to surveying the programs of these selected churches, an interview with a teenager about his memory of children's church provides a snapshot of the impact that Christian education has had on nurturing his spiritual formation.

Project SPIRIT in Atlanta is a nationally implemented program of the Congress of National Black Churches (CNBC). Its goal is to meet the needs of families by providing:

- After-school tutorial programs
- Saturday school
- Living skills enhancement program for children
- Parenting education program
- Pastoral counseling training program

Project SPIRIT, a Carnegie Corporation sponsored program, focuses on economic and social development within black communities. The after-school tutorial programs for children six to twelve years old lasts thirty-six weeks and aims to strengthen skills in reading, writing, and arithmetic. There is also a weekly six-hour parents' program adapted for black parents from Systematic Training for Effective Parenting, as well as a pastoral counseling program enabling participating ministers to become more helpful in dealing with a range of family problems. Project sites include Oakland (California), Indianapolis (Indiana), and Atlanta (Georgia). Limited evaluation of Project SPIRIT suggests the beginnings of positive effects on self-image and school performance, which are two aspects of the Luke 2:52 Triad (stature and favor).

Christian Stronghold Baptist Church (CSBC) in Philadelphia has as its goal to reclaim the urban family through the following strategies:

- Start when people are single
- Disciple both men and women
- Equip couples for marriage
- Increase crisis intervention and counseling
- Minister to children and youth

By inviting church members to be spiritual "uncles" and "aunts" to better serve children before they approach adolescence, each child is provided with extended family or role models who are invited each year to the child's home for special events such as birthdays and graduations. It is during these times that the child is encouraged to think about the next steps in his or her life, a process that encourages integration of biblical principles for development of self (stature). Ministry to children and youth assists in development toward God (wisdom), and discipleship/counseling nurtures development toward others (favor).

Friendship Baptist Church in Yorba Linda is under the leadership of Bishop James D. Carrington. Reverend Kenneth C. Curry Jr. is Minister of Children and Youth. Friendship has developed a dynamic spirit-filled program entitled Kingdom Kids Children's Ministry whose goal is to involve children in the ministry. Children are encouraged to

- Carry the Word of God in their hearts
- Be witnesses of God's good news
- Become true worshipers of God
- Read their Bibles daily
- Talk to God daily through prayer

Friendship provides typical children's ministry offerings such as children's church, Vacation Bible School, children's choir, and summer camp, as well as an annual Harvest Festival, Easter Celebration Weekend, and Christmas program. Beyond these activities, Friendship also offers

- Family Night (Wednesday evening; includes KIDZ Time Bible study)
- Bible Time (a Tuesday Bible study)
- Children's Scholarship Ministry (college preparatory program)
- Children's Prayer Breakfast
- Baptism Class
- Movie Night (Thursday evenings)
- Tutoring
- Dance Ministry
- Children's Usher Ministry
- Brownies/Daisies and Girl Scouts
- Cub Scouts/Boy Scouts

Friendship is an example of a nurturing environment that fosters spiritual growth according to the Luke 2:52 Triad. Worship, Bible study, and prayer nurture development toward God; tutoring, Brownies/Daisies, Girl Scouts, Cub Scouts, and Boy Scouts nurture development toward self. Children develop socially and educationally through the scholarship ministry and tutoring program. The opportunity for children to participate as ushers and in the dance ministries nurtures development toward others.

At Crenshaw Christian Center (CCC) in Los Angeles, California, Frederick K. C. Price, founder-pastor, has a children's ministry called Crenshaw Kidz that Minister Harges Pittman coordinates. At CCC, children and teenagers are the church's priority, and full-time staff is employed for the children, teens, and young adults. Teenagers have their own building—the Youth Activity Center—a $5 million state-of-the-art gymnasium fashioned after the Staples Center. A similar undertaking is envisioned for the children.

In addition to annual celebrations for children and teens (Christmas, Resurrection Sunday, Hallelujah Night), there are myriad activities designed to nurture spiritual development by embracing the spiritual disciplines of abstinence and engagement. The following chart categorizes these activities according to the Luke 2:52 Triad:

Children's Church (Sunday Morning)	Wisdom
Kidz UnLocked Bible Study (Tuesday Evening)	Wisdom
Children's Choir	Wisdom/Stature/Favor
Helps Ministry (volunteer ushers, hostesses, media assistants)	Favor
Fearless Sex ('tweens/teens abstinence education)	Stature
Dance Ministry	Stature/Favor
Drama Ministry	Stature/Favor
Big Brothers/Big Sisters	Stature
Camp	Wisdom/Stature/Favor
Puppet Ministry	Stature/Favor

To further evaluate CCC's children's ministry, I was inspired by Roehlkepartain and Patel's (2005) chapter, "Congregations: Unexamined Crucibles for Spiritual Development." The authors interviewed a Muslim teen about his experience as a member of his particular congregation. Using this model, I decided to interview one of the teenagers at CCC where

I serve as Director of Christian Education Ministries overseeing ministry to children, teens, and young adults. My purpose was to view the children's ministry through the lens of a teen who grew up in the children's ministry.

Reflections of a Teenager

Ryan[1] is fifteen years old, and he has been a part of CCC since birth. Ryan is representative of many of the teenagers, both male and female in the inner city of Los Angeles, who are being raised in single-parent homes. He has had disciplinary problems at school and at church.

After Teen Bible Study one night last year, Ryan threatened to fight another teen. He was not permitted to attend Teen Bible Study for a period of time. Instead, our pastoral staff counseled him. After three months, Ryan and his mother pleaded with me to allow him to return, and I consented. Although he still remains a challenge at times, there has been a marked difference in his attitude and behavior.

With his mother's permission, I conducted a telephone interview with Ryan. My assistant, Monique Cowan, recorded the conversation. Following is the interview and my commentary. Ryan's responses are in italics.

How did Children's Church help you grow as a Christian?

Children's Church helped and hurt. I wasn't always paying attention, so I wasn't listening to what I should have been listening to.

Were there times when you doubted God or his Word? If so, why?

Sometimes I wonder why I do the things that I do. Why am I defiant? How can I stop myself from doing the wrong things and do the right thing?

I'm wondering if your defiance has anything to do with your dad.

Yeah. I never lived with him. I lived with my mom all of my life. He used to come around up until I was four. I don't really think about it anymore. Forget it.

When Ryan mentioned the fact that his dad used to come around, he stopped talking abruptly. Not having his father around has had a great impact on Ryan, and we could hear his pain.

With the acknowledgment that "the family is the locus of spiritual development" (Boyatzis, Dollahite, & Marks, 2005, p. 297), the absence

---

1. Ryan's name has been changed to protect privacy.

of the dad is a significant loss for any family. "Since the lack of parental involvement in the lives of children is one of the primary characteristics of at-risk children, changing the parents is one of the greatest challenges" (Newton, 2004, p. 389). Extending Christian education to include a family ministry that supports and strengthens families could be of great assistance to the spiritual development of children.

What helps you now?

I see how [the other teens at church] act and I try to act the same way as they do instead of the opposite. When I'm in school, I stick to myself to stay out of trouble.

How other teens act influences Ryan to correct or alter his behavior. The value of positive peer-influence during adolescence is important in the developmental process of spiritual maturity. "During adolescence, personal integration is facilitated not only by abstract ideology but by having it lived out in the flesh. Religions often provide opportunities for adolescents to interact with peers and build intergenerational relationships as well" (King, 2003, p. 199).

What has hurt you? For example, did the time when I didn't allow you to attend Teen Bible Study hurt you?

Staying away helped me because I know that now I don't have to run with the crowd and run with everyone else and get caught up in the mix.

What do you wish you had learned?

I'm paying attention to what's going on now; I'm learning about God now.

Did you ever sing in the Children's Choir?

No.

Did you attend Children's Church most Sundays?

Every Sunday.

Did you go to Children's Bible Study?

No.

Although Ryan attended church faithfully on Sundays, he did not attend Tuesday Children's Bible Study that offers rich opportunity for relationship building among the students who attend. Not only did Ryan miss out on the time in the Word, but also he would have benefited from the positive peer interaction.

Did you go to camp during the time you were in Children's Church?

No.

Here, the spiritual discipline of solitude was absent. Children who live in our nation's inner cities need to escape the city streets occasionally. Often, poor children are not afforded the chance to experience the great outdoors by going to camp.

Were there any other ministries, for example, ushering, that you were a part of?

No.

Again, this was a missed opportunity for Ryan's spiritual development. "When congregations . . . exercise intentionality in their practices with children, they create 'webs of meaning' and action that form a comprehensive matrix to nurture children that . . . increases the opportunity for children to be shaped by those practices" (Mercer, Matthews, & Walz, 2004, p. 252).[2]

If you were to describe someone who you think is spiritual, how would you describe him or her?

Faithful to God . . . always happy to go to church . . . happy to give . . . always in church every Sunday.

"Faithful to God." Faith is a constant theme that is religiously taught in our worship setting. It is significant that Ryan defines a spiritual person as a person of faith, a person who is faithful to God. In her interviews with forty children from intergenerational and non-intergenerational Christian contexts, Holly Allen found that, according to these children, knowing God is a faith issue, [and] believing in God is part of this complex definition (Allen, 2003).

Ryan's description of spirituality is additionally defined by external behaviors, for example, "always in church every Sunday." In Allen's study (2003), the children "seemed to comprehend that knowing God entails relationality, but they also placed a strong emphasis on the outward signs of

---

2. "Webs of meaning" are children's concrete, personal experiences that connect spiritual concepts so that the abstract is now understood practically in the life of the learner.

that inward relationship, for example, obedience, church attendance, and godly behaviors" (p. 8).

Ryan's mother brings him to the church campus seemingly at every opportunity, and they attend most services and events. "Worshiping together in a close and intimate setting reveals our inner spiritual lives to our children and theirs to us" (Allen, 2003, p. 3).

According to Ryan, spiritual people are "people who are happy to give." At CCC, obeying God by adhering to the tithing principle is a foundational message. Offering time is a joyful time on Sunday mornings. Apparently, this portion of the service communicates to Ryan something about being spiritual, about having a relationship with God and loving his Word enough to be obedient.

If Ryan's primary worship experience occurred in a separate, non-intergenerational environment, would he have this same evaluation of people who are spiritual? This portion of the interview has profoundly impacted how I view Allen's (2003) warning that "learning how to be God's people has become less a joining in with community, and more a gathering of age-segregated groups to study about being God's people" (p. 5). We are at a point in our ministry where we are increasingly concerned about passing the faith to the next generation, about reaching the children and teens in our community. Is this better accomplished with a separate church for our children and for our teenagers so that we may address their developmental needs more specifically, with more upbeat music, video presentations, drama and the like on Sunday mornings? Perhaps age-appropriate Bible study classes, rather than a separate "church" for children and teens, may be a net that catches those who crave lessons that more directly speak to their developmental needs. In this way, intergenerational worship will still be encouraged, with everyone benefiting from each other in mutuality.

Marilyn Brownlee (a student who contributed portions of this chapter as part of the requirements for an independent study on Dynamics of Christian Formation at Haggard School of Theology/Azusa Pacific University) uses an interesting phrase to describe her childhood church attendance—"drug addiction":

> I can remember countless times as a child when I was at the church because of *drugs*. "I was *drug* to worship service"; "I was *drug* to Sunday school"; "I was *drug* to Bible study"; "I was *drug* to prayer meeting"; "I was *drug* to revival, pastor's anniversary, men's

day, women's day, whatever was happening at the church, you can best believe that our family was *drugged*. My grandmother, Lizzie Stembridge, lived and served at my childhood church. She made sure that her family, especially her children and grandchildren, developed an intimate relationship with Christ at church and at home.

Marilyn's grandmother did not play the waiting game as Harry Jackson describes, where parents delay the spiritual growth of their children—"waiting until they are older, waiting until they can think more deeply, waiting until their behavior suggests they need a more sophisticated ministry" (Barna & Jackson, 2004, p. 133). When we wait, the greatest opportunity for developing spiritual growth in children is missed. The importance of bringing children to church, of immersing them in a culture where they can learn about God and where they are free to respond to that relationship is foundational to spiritual growth.

Do you consider yourself spiritual?

Sometimes.

What has been most important in shaping you spiritually?

My grandmother; she lives in Riverside.

What are your plans for the future?

I will attend Clark College in Atlanta when I graduate.

Once you are an adult, how likely are you to continue to go to church?

Asked about his intentions to attend church once he becomes an adult, Ryan states his commitment in the affirmative that, on a scale from "very likely" to "not at all likely," he is very likely to continue going to church. Fowler and Dell (2005) report that "substantive content of faith traditions, with their scriptures, liturgies, ethical teachings, and visions of the Holy, do provide strong, distinctive, and unique elements for religious formation" (p. 43). Despite his disciplinary challenges, I am confident that Ryan will continue to attend church.

Conclusion

The African American church nurtures children's spiritual development by offering activities that enable expression of the spiritual disciplines of abstinence and engagement. These spiritual disciplines or activities promote spiritual growth according to Luke 2:52 so that children grow in their relationship with God (wisdom), their understanding of themselves (stature), and their relationship with others (favor).

The Luke 2:52 Triad encourages us to think about the spiritual development of the whole child with greater emphasis on creative ways to foster and nurture that development. The reminder that intimate, personal, and immediate spirituality serves as a protective factor for African American youth (Haight, 2002) is a promise that spiritual development has social rewards. In abstinence education, for example, studies indicate that church attendance is a significant factor in teenagers' decisions to avoid premarital sexual activity (Tolbert, 2007).

Our families, neighborhoods, schools, and extended communities should be reflections of children who know and love God, who intimately experience his love for them and, therefore, love themselves with the capacity to love others also. It is only then that the church on every corner will make a difference in the streets on which we live.

References

Allen, H. C. (2003, June). Nurturing children's spirituality in intergenerational Christian settings. Paper presented at the Children's Spirituality Conference, Concordia University, River Forest, IL.

Barna, G. (2003). *Transforming children into spiritual champions*. Ventura, CA: Regal.

Barna, G., & Jackson, R. H. (2004). *High impact African-American churches*. Ventura, CA: Regal.

Baer, H. A. (1984). *The black spiritual movement: A religious response to racism*. Knoxville: The University Press.

Boyatzis, C. J., Dollahite, D. C., & Marks, L. D. (2005). The family as a context for religious and spiritual development in children and youth. In E. C. Roehlkepartain, P. E. King, L. Wagener, & P. L. Benson (Eds.), *The handbook of spiritual development in childhood and adolescence* (pp. 297–309). Thousand Oaks, CA: Sage.

Fowler, J., & Dell, M. L. (2005). Stages of faith from infancy through adolescence: Reflections on three decades of faith development theory. In E. C. Roehlkepartain, P. E. King, L. Wagener, & P. L. Benson (Eds.), *The handbook of spiritual development in childhood and adolescence* (pp. 34–45). Thousand Oaks, CA: Sage.

Haight, W. L. (2002). *African-American children at church: A sociocultural perspective.* New York: Cambridge University Press.

Hale-Benson, J. E. (1982). *Black children: Their roots, culture, and learning styles.* Baltimore: Johns Hopkins University Press.

Hill, R. (1987). The black family: Building on strengths. In R. Woodson (Ed.), *On the road to economic freedom* (pp. 71–92). Washington, DC: Regency Gateway.

King, P. E. (2003). Religion and identity: The role of ideological, social, and spiritual contexts. *Applied Developmental Science, 7*(3), 197–204.

Mattis, J. S., Ahluwalia, M. K., Cowie, S. E., & Kirkland-Harris, A. M. (2005). Ethnicity, culture, and spiritual development. In E. C. Roehlkepartain, P. E. King, L. Wagener, & P. L. Benson (Eds.), *The handbook of spiritual development in childhood and adolescence* (pp. 283–296). Thousand Oaks, CA: Sage.

Mercer, J. A., Matthews, D. L., & Walz, S. (2004). Children in congregations: Congregations as contexts for spiritual growth. In D. Ratcliff (Ed.), *Children's spirituality: Christian perspectives, research, and application* (pp. 249–65). Eugene, OR: Cascade.

Newman, D. S. (1995). *With heart and hand: The black church working to save black children.* Valley Forge, PA: Judson.

Newton, G. (2004). Ministering to unchurched, urban, at-risk children. In D. Ratcliff (Ed.), *Children's spirituality: Christian perspectives, research, and application* (pp. 383–96). Eugene, OR: Cascade.

Roehlkepartain, E. C., & Patel, E. (2005). Congregations: Unexamined crucibles for spiritual development. In E. C. Roehlkepartain, P. E. King, L. Wagener, & P. L. Benson (Eds.), *The handbook of spiritual development in childhood and adolescence* (pp. 324–36). Thousand Oaks, CA: Sage.

Tolbert, L. (2007). *Keeping your kids sexually pure: A how-to guide for parents, pastors, youth workers, and teachers.* Philadelpia: Xlibris.

Wagener, L. M., Furrow, J. L., King, P. E., Leffert, N., & Benson, P. L. (2003). Religious involvement and developmental resources in youth. *Review of Religious Research, 44,* 271–84.

Warren, M. A. (2001). *King came preaching: The pulpit power of Dr. Martin Luther King Jr.* Downers Grove, IL: InterVarsity.

Westerhoff, J., III. (2006, June). The church's contemporary challenge: To help adults to grow up spiritually with their children. Keynote address at Children's Spirituality Conference, Concordia University, River Forest, IL.

Willard, D. (1988). *The spirit of the disciplines*. New York: Harper Collins.

PART III

Facing the Challenges for the Future

20 Reimagining the Spirit of Children: A Christian Pedagogical Vision

Karen Crozier

THE BIBLICAL WITNESS CONTAINS SEVERAL ACCOUNTS OF CHILDREN REflecting, embodying, and modeling aspects of the divine, transcendent world. Hannah, the mother of Samuel, dedicated her newborn to the Lord, and the Bible says he grew in stature and favor with the Lord and the people (see 1 Sam 2:26 specifically, or 1 Sam 1:1—4:1 for the narrative on the birth and spiritual development of Samuel). Likewise, Luke's account of the birth narrative of Jesus indicates that Jesus, too, grew in wisdom and stature, and experienced the favor of God (see Luke 2:40). Then, in Jesus' public ministry, he not only embraces and blesses children, but he also uses children as the model for adults on how one gains access into the kingdom of heaven (Mark 10:13–16; Matt 18:1–5). In valuing and affirming children's worth, Jesus positions children as both teachers and students, and not merely as empty vessels waiting to be filled. Furthermore, the spiritual development examples of Samuel and Jesus, as well as Jesus' response to children, indicate that children are to be seen as spiritual beings.

However, another strand of Scripture tempers such a positive rendering of children's natural spiritual development. In Psalm 51:5, King David asserts, "Indeed, I was born guilty, a sinner when my mother conceived me" (New Oxford Annotated Bible). In his adult reflection on childhood, David indicates that the root, or source, of his guilt can be traced back to the womb. He claims to have been oriented toward inherent unlawfulness and transgression from the very beginning of his life.

Rather than grappling with the paradox or tension within the biblical witness concerning children's spiritual status, some Christian communities focus almost exclusively on this second strand. Children are viewed as sinful and alienated from both God and the faith community until they are converted to Christ. Prior to the conversion experience, they may rarely be affirmed or nurtured on spiritual matters but, rather, socialized into a religious community that views them as spiritually dead. The clear implication of this view is that spiritual life begins the moment one accepts Jesus as Savior (even though one may be eight, ten, or twelve years old).

As an ordained minister, practical theologian (Christian educator), and former early childhood educator, I do not want to dismiss children's spiritual reality and experience until they repent of their sin and accept Jesus as Savior. Hence, the challenge before me is how to model for others, and nurture within an explicit Christian educational context, the spirituality of *all* children.

Some may argue that this approach to children's spirituality is impossible or could lead to religious relativism and a weakening of the Gospel in its presentation. They may question my inclusivity or my hesitation to repeatedly induce children to confess Christ as Savior. Others may want to deny my Christianity altogether because I am not beginning with a theology of children as sinners who are bereft of spiritual life and meaning. I hope to allay these charges with the analysis and reflection in this chapter. I hope my commitment to Christianity and to God will be evident as well as my understanding of the significance of the Christian faith in nurturing children's spirituality.

There is one major question that I address in this paper: How can Christian theology in general (and evangelical theology in particular) become more effective in nurturing children's spirituality? In addressing this question, first I present research on nurturing children's spirituality by scholars who examine children's spiritual experiences beyond the parameters of Christianity or any other religious or faith community. In essence, these scholars explore children's spirituality regardless of their self-identified religious or areligious affiliation. Next, I turn to the Christian tradition to unveil its wisdom and depth on childhood in general and children's spirituality in particular. Finally, I provide a vision for how Christians in our respective educational settings can nurture children's spirituality regardless of the child's religious or nonreligious background or experience through what I call a critical, multicultural pedagogy. This pedagogy incorporates the research contributions on children from non-Christian as well as Christian perspectives. Furthermore, it provides a working framework for how both evangelical theology and Christian theology in general can be broadened in order to nurture children's spirituality. The implications of social science, theological, and biblical research on children's spirituality inform this Christian pedagogical vision.

Children's Spirituality Beyond Christianity

Daniel Scott (2005), a child and youth care specialist, contends that the nature and scope of children's spiritual experiences are often independent of a religious affiliation or experience, and that children can have similar spiritual encounters as adults. This distinction between spiritual and religious experience implies that prior to the entrance of any institutionalized, formal religion, children, as well as adults, have a spiritual orientation that is an inherent part of being human. Furthermore, the claim that children's spiritual experiences can be equal to an adult's spiritual experience challenges traditional theoretical paradigms of developmental psychology that position the later years as the more mature and sophisticated expressions of human experience.

In demonstrating and validating the spiritual lives of children, Scott (2005) draws on a number of persuasive sources including United Nations' documents on the rights of children and extensive empirical research conducted by Robert Coles, a child psychiatrist, and David Hay and Rebecca Nye, who are respected experts on children's spirituality in the United Kingdom. According to articles from the United Nations Convention on the Rights of the Child, children's spiritual development is different from children's religious identity and freedom. In short, Scott understands the difference between the two as follows: spiritual development is integral to all human development whereas religion is not (p. 169). For Scott, the Convention views religion as a particular cultural expression belonging to issues of minority rights and human equality, and not human development.

This distinction between spirituality and religion is the foundation of Scott's argument, and it positions spirituality as a biological process for all humans regardless of one's religious affiliation. He carefully uses the research of Coles, as well as Hay and Nye, to demonstrate the spiritual capacity of children across cultural, religious, and secular lines. Coles conducted his research in the United States and in other parts of the world while Hay and Nye specifically focused on children in the United Kingdom. Two points are of significance from these bodies of research, as noted by Scott. First, for Coles, in caring for a Roman Catholic female during her psychiatric treatment, Scott (2005) explains how Coles had to begin to take seriously the religious life of the child and then how this dialogue led Coles to conclude that the girl's spiritual life was not synonymous or equal to her religious life, but it was believed to be something more (p. 175). Second, in building on this possible distinction between spirituality and religion, Scott notes how Hay and Nye claim that one can be spiritual without necessarily referring to God, by affirming and arguing the reverse of what Karl Rahner, the prominent Catholic theologian, believes—that one can talk about God without being spiritual (p. 175). In both cases, spirituality is related to religion, but it is also perceived to be something more innate and personal than religion.

To date, there does not exist a general interpretative heuristic that accounts for the spiritual development of the child, although, as will be discussed in more detail below, Hay and Nye's (2006) work takes aggressive steps in this direction. Nevertheless, Scott (2005) leaves his readers with something substantial even though it is not a sound theoretical paradigm. He asserts that adults need to view children as pilgrims and visionaries in light of their spiritual development (p. 178). If done accordingly, adults will remain open to the divine and transcendent world as experienced and named by the child, and will be able to learn from and support children on their spiritual journeys. Hopefully, in the process, the adult will be able to reclaim her or his childhood of spiritual knowing that may have been overlooked, ignored, or marginalized by a culture that has tended to view children as spiritually invisible and insignificant.

Like Scott, Barbara Kimes Myers (1997, p. xi), professor of child development, also engages the idea that spiritual experience and development are a part of all children's lives whether or not they are affiliated with a particular religion. Myers unabashedly argues that children's spirituality is evident "when it is not squelched, nullified, neglected, or in other ways repudiated or overlooked" (p. 3). Myers reminds us that the spiritual life of children needs to be nurtured, affirmed, and celebrated, and when it is not, adults and the world that adults have created are largely to blame.

Trained in child development research and theory, Myers (1997) exhorts her readers to be cautious of psychological, cognitive theories because they can become blinders rather than lenses (p. 5). She asserts, "Our use of theory may result in missing the 'something new' that could be bubbling on the edge of the subject (not the object) of all such effort; that is, we often miss the child" (p. 5). Placing the child at the center as subject, rather than as the object to be studied, challenges both researchers and those adults who draw upon developmental theory to be open to both its strengths and limitations when describing the child. Quite often, children transcend theoretical paradigms that go undetected and unacknowledged because the adult can only see what the theorist has deemed as important and actual.

Although Myers (1997) is critical of developmental theory and research, she nevertheless draws on Erik Erikson's notion of relational developmental dialogue to highlight the complex, dynamic interaction that occurs between child and adult in the development of both (see p. 8). According to Myers, Erikson is one developmental psychologist who always challenged himself, critics, and readers to look beyond his theoretical framework for other rationales that could explain what occurs in human psychosocial development (see p. 8). This "looking beyond" implies a sensitivity and openness towards transcendence, a place that challenges both the child and adult to move beyond apparent obstacles or constraints.

Myers (1997) employs Bernard Lonergan's theology of transcendence to integrate human development and spirituality in a way that may (or may not) include religion (see p. 11). Lonergan contends that humanity has an innate dissatisfaction with self and world, and is therefore looking to move beyond, climb over, or transcend this dissatisfaction. Convinced that human beings, and specifically children, are always in a process of transcending, Myers identifies this as the spirit of the child as the child lives at the limits of her or his experience (see pp. 12–13).

Both Myers (1997) and Scott (2005) envision a world where spiritual identity and development are positioned alongside cognitive, behavioral, physical, and emotional human development. In addition, they both question adult perspectives of children's spiritual development; this challenges researchers to carefully tend to the experiences and linguistic expressions of children so that what is reported will more accurately reflect the *children's* viewpoint and perception rather than what the adults want or expect to hear.

Two such researchers who modeled what Myers and Scott propose are Hay and Nye (2006) in their research of children's spirituality in the United

Kingdom. In a cultural context where Christianity is not the dominant religion, where secular or nonreligious systems and worldviews prevail, Hay and Nye sought to understand children's spiritual identity and development in order to provide assistance to Britain's school system in its mandate to integrate spirituality into the curriculum. In essence, Hay and Nye's research project generated essential data for teachers and administrators describing the spiritual-talk of children (see p. 9). By attentively listening to children of varying religious and nonreligious backgrounds discuss their experiences and thoughts on the divine, Hay and Nye were able to describe "the notion of 'relational consciousness' as the most fundamental feature of their spirituality" (p. 131).

According to Hay and Nye (2006), relational consciousness refers to an unusual perception or conscious awareness that is expressed in relation to self, other people, world, and God (see p. 109). The researchers note that the degree of awareness or consciousness the children exhibited was of a metacognitive type—the children were able to offer an objective insight on their subjective experience. In addition, their relational connection and depth of knowing did not remain confined to their immediate surroundings. The children expressed an understanding of self and the cosmos in a communal, oftentimes unified way.

The concept of relational consciousness emerged as the unifying framework of children's spiritual experiences for Hay and Nye, and integrated their other three aspects of children's spirituality: awareness-sensing, mystery-sensing, and value-sensing. These three concepts became viewed as more dynamic and complex through the interpretative lens of relational consciousness. That is, these three "sensings"—the child's ability to be aware of a particular experience in the here-and-now, the mystery of an experience and the child's inability to elucidate it even though the child remains intrigued by what has occurred, and the child's insight to discern the moment and respond accordingly—become more than linear, isolated experiences due to relational consciousness.

Theoretically, Hay and Nye (2006) argue that relational consciousness is "an entirely natural and human disposition . . . separate from and prior to the discursive intellect, though it is certainly a matter with which the intellect becomes preoccupied in the context of a greatly enlarged awareness of one's environment" (pp. 134, 137). With this term, the researchers assert three fundamental points concerning spirituality. First, every human possesses access to the metaphysical world from birth, and this reality should not be seen as something extraordinary. Second, although cognitive development can assist one's relational consciousness, relational consciousness precedes the emergence of intelligible speech. Hence, relational consciousness is something more than one's cognitive, rational development, and this suggests that the mentally and linguistically disabled can be included in this broader understanding. Finally, Hay and Nye point out that this innate human propensity to be aware of, and connected to, the physical and metaphysical worlds is contrary to the current individualistic, independent, selfish, and disconnected approach to human existence. This disconnect suggests that in some way our Western world tends to quench the spiritual nature of adults as well as children.

Scott (2005), Myers (1997), and Hay and Nye (2006) present a vision of children's spirituality that challenges many adult-oriented notions of the child in both social science and the church. First, they present the child as completely human and whole at birth, not an immature or inadequate adult. Second, they argue that spirituality is related to (but not solely contained within) the domain of religion. Third, by affirming the spiritual life of the child, they likewise explicitly affirm the spiritual, transcendent world based not on logical, propositional statements that are often void of experience, but on their belief in the validity of the spiritual experiences of the child. Because Scott, Myers, and Hay and Nye take children seriously, children's experiences and worldviews are epistemologically legitimate and provide insights and critiques to the world adults have constructed.

If Scott (2005), Myers (1997), and Hay and Nye (2006) are correct in their assertion that spirituality is an integral part of children's human development, then does this suggest that many Christian traditions, including my evangelical community, hinder children's spiritual development either by overlooking or altogether rejecting children's and youth's spiritual experiences *until their conversion*? Are the scholars who speak of spirituality outside of a religious community articulating a different vision of spirituality that many within Christianity would find problematic because it could be called "secular spirituality"? Might it be possible to find common ground?

Children's Spirituality within Christianity

In general, Christian systematic theologians, practical theologians, Christian educators, and biblical scholars are beginning to generate more provocative research and scholarship on children and childhood (Bunge, 2001, 2006; Berryman, 1991; Ratcliff, 2004; Stonehouse, 1998; May, Posterski, Stonehouse, & Cannell, 2005; Yust, 2004; Yust, Johnson, Sasso, & Roehlkepartain, 2006; Gundry-Volf, 2001). For example, Marcia Bunge's seminal volume, *The Child in Christian Thought* (2001), provides a historical theology of major Christian figures and their understanding of children in the Christian community. What one learns from this extensive (yet initial) study of theology and childhood is the plethora of theological orientations within Christianity concerning perspectives of, and responses to, children. In a more recent publication on children and adolescent spirituality, Bunge (2006) argues that Christianity has not produced well-developed, robust theologies in spite of its care and concern for children. According to Bunge, these developing deliberative theologies need to include the needs and vulnerabilities of children as well as the gifts and strengths children bring to both families and faith communities.

In her exegesis of Christian historical theology, Bunge (2006) explores six foci that constitute a working paradigm for how Christianity understands the child and childhood. Children are (1) gifts of God and sources of joy, (2) sinful creatures and moral agents, (3) developing beings who need instruction and guidance, (4) fully human and made in the image of God, (5) models of faith and sources of revelation, and (6) orphans, neighbors, and strangers in need of justice and compassion (pp. 58–62).

These foci provoke numerous, diverse images and perceptions of children that are both contradictory and complex. Two examples follow. First, a child is God's gift and a source of joy—yet sinful. This (seeming) incongruity suggests that what God gives to a family and particular faith community somehow, someway becomes influenced by a condition that is not affiliated with the source of the gift. Thus, maintaining consistency with the predominant Augustinian and Calvinist theological tradition of the fallen nature of humanity, children are included as those who must be redeemed—while they are simultaneously seen as a blessing from above. Second, a child is fully human and made in the image of God yet can be counted among the earth's marginalized. This marginalization suggests that though the Christian tradition views the child as a human in her own right, given by God, and a reflection of God, somehow in the process of being parented and welcomed by church and society, the child becomes perceived as something other than the reflection of the divine or possibly something less than fully human. How else can we account for the mistreatment, abuse, and sometimes blatant disregard of children's needs that has characterized some of Christian history?

Because of the conflicting, yet insightful, nature of Bunge's (2006) six varying views, one cannot be appropriated in isolation from the other when nurturing children in the Christian tradition. Bunge contends that if Christian theologians, churches, and disciples critically retrieve and hold these views in tension, doing so could lead to a broadening of Christian understanding of, and commitment to, children (see p. 255).

New Testament scholar Judith Gundry-Volf offers a biblical theological framework on children and childhood that can inform Christianity's response to nurturing and welcoming children. Gundry-Volf (2001) argues that Jesus' teaching regarding children and the reign of God and discipleship, as well as his healing and exorcisms involving children, offers the Christian tradition more provocative, profound insight than the apostolic vision and reflections on the family and children. Unfortunately, according to Gundry-Volf, what has occurred in many Christian traditions and theologies is the appropriation of the more limiting tradition of the epistles and apostles at the expense of the radical vision of Jesus (see p. 58).

As in Bunge's theological exposition, Gundry-Volf (2001) articulates that children were perceived as gifts of God, a sign of God's blessing, loved and received within the Hellenistic and Judaic cultures (see p. 34). However, Jesus elevates children to a status not common in either of these cultures. First and foremost, Jesus asserts in Mark 10:13–16 that children, too, were recipients of the reign of God even though they were considered powerless and lowly within their social standing (see p. 38). Second, in this same pericope, Jesus asserts that children are not only participants of the reign of God but they are also models of entering God's reign. To underscore Jesus' progressive response to children, Gundry-Volf says, "nowhere in [prior] Jewish literature are children put forward as a model for adults" (p. 39). Third, in Mark 9:33–37, Jesus informs his disciples that welcoming or serving children (who possessed the least amount of power and voice in society) elevated the adult's status from the least to the greatest in the reign of God (see pp. 43–44). Finally, what might possibly be considered to be the ultimate role of children in Jesus' ministry is articulated when he asserts that to welcome children is to welcome both Jesus and the one who sent Jesus (see p. 44).

Both Markan pericopes suggest that those doing Christian theology and ministry should have children at the center if they want to be counted as noble in the things of God. Or, to put it another way, they also suggest that those of us doing Christian theology and ministry who overlook and marginalize children are acting inconsistently with the life and teachings of Jesus. However, when one turns to the epistles, there is little information on the role of children in general, and when children are discussed, it is usually metaphorically or in relation to parents (Gundry-Volf, 2001, p. 48). Unlike the broader Greco-Roman culture, first century Christians believed that children had access to their parents' God (p. 56). Moreover, if the parents were not treating children as described by the Lord Jesus Christ, then children were not obligated to obey their parents within this Christian household (pp. 55–56).

Although there are other passages that refer to children in the ministry of Jesus and in the epistles, space does not permit an extended discussion. Nevertheless, this brief yet helpful discussion about nurturing children in the Christian tradition provides a healthy lens for understanding children and their spirituality that is, in many ways, similar to the research conducted on children's spirituality outside of Christianity. For example, Myers' (1997) understanding of children suggests that they should be seen as subjects in their own right instead of as merely objects to be studied. Within the Christian tradition, Bunge (2006) indicates that children are seen as moral agents or subjects as well, and Gundry-Volf (2001) painstakingly reveals how children are models for adults in the ministry of Jesus and not merely imitators of them. Moreover, in the scholarship on children in Christianity and beyond the Christian tradition, there is an affirmation of children where they are in their stage of life as recipients and participants in the particular human community as spiritual beings. Children do not have to become adults or merely comply with adult standards to be connected to the spiritual, transcendent world.

More research is needed to compare and contrast insights into and constraints on children's spirituality within faith communities and beyond. In my discussion, I do not intend to reduce or simplify the similarities, but merely highlight the more pronounced commonalities in an attempt to broaden the scope of how Christianity in general, and evangelical Christianity in particular, can become more sensitive and redemptive in nurturing children's spirituality. Furthermore, it is hoped that researchers outside of Christianity will reconsider the contribution of the Christian faith tradition as well as other faith traditions in celebrating and embracing the child. Conscious of this biased research agenda and reality, Yust, Johnson, Sasso, and Roehlkepartain (2006) assert:

> The wisdom of a specific religious community is generally relegated to perpetuating that tradition among the children of the faithful; it is not often explored by scholars for its interpretative usefulness as we talk about the shape of human societies, the challenges of creating just and caring relationships, and solving the global . . . crises and the world's future. (p. 4)

A Christian Pedagogical Vision

The rich depth and complexity of Christianity concerning children's spiritual development requires a pedagogy that is flexible and inclusive of the children who are taught. Christian educators must be sensitive to the diverse backgrounds and experiences of children and families who enter churches in the United States. Religious, spiritual, racial, ethnic, gender, and class differences are realities that can neither be dismissed nor ignored when nurturing God's children. Even in predominantly homogenous religious contexts, children need to be sensitive to the world that exists beyond the boundaries of their church and school, and understand their identity and role in participating in the well-being of humanity and God's redemption in the world. Hence, a critical, multicultural pedagogy is one such response to the demands of teaching and affirming children from different backgrounds in the Christian tradition while simultaneously acknowledging their insight and connection to the divine, spiritual world.[1]

---

1. My understanding of a critical, multicultural pedagogy is greatly influenced by Paulo Freire, a Latin American scholar, activist, and pedagogue. For three decades, Freire expounded on his critical pedagogy in the context of adult literacy development and political empowerment for the poor and oppressed in developing countries. Many of the concepts that I use in this paper are Freire's. However, in this paper, three major differences exist between Freire and me. First, I appropriate Freire in a Christian religious context, and he employed his pedagogy in non-religious contexts even though he offers a vision for how the Church can become more empowering in its educational ministry (see Freire, *The Politics of Education*, 1985). Second, I add the word "multicultural" because in Freire's Latin American context, he dealt primarily with class issues. However, in the United States, race, ethnicity, gender and *age* are issues that need to be included as well as class. Third, I am using the pedagogy in the context of children's spirituality instead of adult literacy. Thus, I attempt to make the pedagogy relevant for my context instead of merely transposing the pedagogy from one context to another.

In general, a critical, multicultural pedagogy takes into consideration the diversity of social experience and location while simultaneously encouraging children to question and name their worlds. In the past, children's Christian education curriculum has generally marginalized or even excluded children's spiritual realities and experiences. What would happen if Jesus' teachings on children were taken seriously in the Christian education curriculum? What would happen if children were at the center of Christian education, worship, ministry, theology, and experience? What kind of values and ideologies would emerge that would radically change the form and substance of Christianity? Christian scholar Kristin Herzog (2005) argues that "putting a child at the center of theology will mean . . . acknowledging that our relationship with God finds expression in our relationship with children" (p. 11). In essence, children must be given priority as subjects, as persons, and as participants while both adults and children construct, define, and redefine the world in light of a God who is present in the adults' service to children.

Another aspect of a multicultural pedagogy is that it does not assume that the child is a blank slate or passive object. Rather, children are perceived to be teachers as well as students, and the teacher also positions herself or himself as student as well. Thus, a community of learners and teachers is created in an attempt to affirm the diverse experiences and voices of the participants in the teaching and learning process. Of course, some might wonder if anything and everything is accepted as normative in this pedagogical process and experience. In short, the answer is no. In giving up one's exclusive power, the teacher does not become powerless or invisible in the process. However, in incorporating what is known about children's spirituality, the Christian educator must become comfortable with engaging difference while simultaneously challenging students to do the same in light of the educator's understanding of the Christian tradition. In this vein, the adult's understanding of faith and spiritual matters is also brought under scrutiny as the children's experiences and voices may broaden, challenge, or in other ways alter an adult's perception. The mutual, dialogical nature of this pedagogy nurtures both teachers and students as they remain open to discerning the God of Christianity in community, creation, and the sacred text.

The goal is to embody and pass on the tradition, but it should be done in a way that hears the experiences of children. Consequently, this pedagogy could foster and affirm a relational connectedness in children's experiences of the *numinous* as documented by Hay and Nye because "entering God's realm means constantly growing and changing like a child, not struggling for independence, success, and heaven's reward for virtue, but realizing absolute interdependence and vulnerability" (Herzog, 2005, p. 42).

The problem-posing component of this pedagogy invites Christian educators to generate open-ended questions about the Christian tradition, instead of yes/no or right/wrong responses. If done appropriately, this could affirm children's curiosity and insatiable desire for questioning and searching (Herzog, 2005, p. 17). If children do not have the opportunity to explore and examine their world, their imaginations are stifled and their ability to deal with complexity is compromised. For example, in the discussion of a difficult text that adults view as an ultimate model of faith, such as Abraham's sacrificial offering of his son Isaac, children often experience it differently and should be given the opportunity to explore their fears, hopes, thoughts, and concerns about such a text.

According to Herzog (2005), although there are times when children should be told definitive answers, for the most part, children do not have to learn dualistic notions of understanding the world, but should be encouraged to remain open to the good and bad in nations, people, and institutions (p. 131). With a problem-posing pedagogy, both children and adults are challenged to see and understand the world as complex, ambiguous, and filled with dialectical tensions that offer insight into this world and beyond.

The deepening epistemologies that emerge from a critical, multicultural pedagogy are not generated merely in order to gain more knowledge; rather they work at a much more complex level to inform both the child's and the adult's ethical responses in the world. Hence, as children and adults explore and examine the Christian tradition and the sacred in the world, actions that are consistent with the spiritual and religious values of Christianity will be generated from these explorations. Those children who are just beginning to seek faith or are questioning the relevance of Christianity can also find a space to respond in dialogue with the Christian tradition. All children regardless of their religious (or areligious) situation can be nurtured to think about how to live in the world in a way that nurtures, fosters, enhances, and cultivates their spirituality.

References

Berryman, J. W. (1991). *Godly play: An imaginative approach to religious education.* Minneapolis, MN: Augsburg.

Bunge, M. J. (2001). *The child in Christian thought.* Grand Rapids: Eerdmans.

Bunge, M. J. (2006). The dignity and complexity of children: Constructing Christian theologies of childhood. In K. M. Yust, A. N. Johnson, S. E. Sasso, & E. C. Roehlkepartain (Eds.), *Nurturing child and adolescent spirituality: Perspectives from the world's religious traditions* (pp. 53–68). Lanham, MD: Rowman & Littlefield.

Freire, P. (1985). *The politics of education: Culture, power and liberation* (D. Macedo, Trans.). South Hadley, MA: Bergin & Garvey.

Gundry-Volf, J. (2001). The least and the greatest: Children in the New Testament. In M. Bunge (Ed.), *The child in Christian thought* (pp. 29–60). Grand Rapids: Eerdmans.

Hay, D., & Nye, R. (2006). *The spirit of the child* (Rev. ed.). London: Jessica Kingsley.

Herzog, K. (2005). *Children and our global future: Theological and social challenges.* Cleveland: Pilgrim.

May, S., Posterski, B., Stonehouse, C., & Cannell, L. (2005). *Children matter: Celebrating their place in the church, family, and community.* Grand Rapids: Eerdmanns.

Myers, B. K. (1997). *Young children and spirituality.* New York: Routledge.

Ratcliff, D. (Ed.). (2004). *Children's spirituality: Christian perspectives, research, and applications.* Eugene, OR: Cascade.

Scott, D. (2005). *Spirituality and children: Paying attention to experience.* In H. Goelman, S. K. Marshall, & S. Ross (Eds.), *Multiple lenses, multiple images: Perspectives on the child across time, space, and disciplines* (pp. 168–96). Toronto: University of Toronto Press.

Stonehouse, C. (1998). *Joining children on the spiritual journey: Nurturing a life of faith.* Grand Rapids: Baker.

Yust, K. M., Johnson, A. N., Sasso, S. E., & Roehlkepartain, E. C. (Eds.) (2006). *Nurturing child and adolescent spirituality: Perspectives from the world's religious traditions.* Lanham, MD: Rowman & Littlefield.

Yust, K. M. (2004) *Real kids, real faith: Practices for nurturing children's spiritual lives.* San Francisco: Jossey-Bass.

21   The Church's Contemporary Challenge: Assisting Adults to Mature Spiritually *with* Their Children

John H. Westerhoff III

IN 1900, ELLEN KEY AND OTHER EDUCATORS PROCLAIMED THE TWENTIeth century to be the century of the child. Interestingly, theologians proclaimed it to be the Christian century. It is clear now that neither of these proclamations held true. Perhaps that is the reason we are here.

In a sense, children were not discovered until the eighteenth century. Before then there was no such thing as children. There were miniature adults—and adults. The discovery of children was a mixed blessing. Now they were only children, and adults had to do things to them so that they would become adults.

In 1904 G. Stanley Hall wrote a book called *Adolescence: Its Psychology and Its Relations to Physiology, Anthropology, Sociology, Sex, Crime, Religion, and Education*. Since then we have actually believed that adolescence exists. We forget that childhood and adolescence are social constructions of reality; they are not necessarily real. We make them real in our minds, and sometimes because we do, the terms work against us, and against those the terms are describing. Perhaps it would be better if we stopped using the words *children* or *adolescents*, and talked about *people* and the different characteristics they share at different times in their lives. In any case, the terms childhood and adolescence are the social constructions of reality that have caused us to think in certain ways, some of which have affected children negatively.

Doing Things *To* Children

We have construed the relationship between children and adults in three ways. The first way involves the idea that we do things *to* children.

For decades we assessed, considered, and appraised persons primarily in terms of chronological age. We did this for so long that we created a metaphor for our relationship with children; that metaphor is a production line. In this production line metaphor, the child (or youth) is a valuable piece of raw material; the teacher, the adult, is a skilled technician; and the process is molding each valuable piece of raw material into the teacher/adult's predetermined design. We do things *to* children. The philosophy behind this way of thinking emerges from John Locke's ideas: the child is born into and characterized as an empty slate and everything has to be put in. Skinner's behaviorism has the same roots.

This philosophy or worldview is still embraced by many parents and teachers who pattern their relationships with children, as well as their educational efforts, accordingly. I suggest that while there is some truth in this line of thinking, it is highly limited truth. This mindset produces a learning environment that focuses almost exclusively on instruction and training, mostly in a schooling context. For example, we would teach children all about the Bible and its content but not how to live as a people formed by their *engagement* with its content. As a consequence we might only create a *magna cum laude* atheist who knows all about the Christian life of faith, but has no desire to become Christian.

Doing Things *For* Children

For a long time we isolated people by age, but when we ultimately realized that chronological age expectations were too rigid and problematic, we came up with a second image or way of thinking about people, that is, developmental stage. And the metaphor changed. The metaphor for this developmental perspective is a greenhouse. In the greenhouse metaphor, the child is a valuable seed; the adult teacher is a gardener; and the process is then caring for each individual seed until it grows up to its own. We do not do things *to* children; we do things *for* children. Of course there is always a book written on how much sun they need, how much light they need, and how much fertilizer they need to guide you as you do this, but now you are doing it *for* them.

This perspective derives from the psychology of Jean Piaget as well as the philosophy of Jean-Jacques Rousseau who saw a child as a flower, a plant that comes naturally into being. This image of doing things *for*—bringing it out of them rather than putting it into them—has become a significant image and in some ways, it also offers some interesting concepts. However, I suggest that it too, is highly limited.

An Imminent Transition

What makes conceptualizing our lives and life such a complex task is that we must do so from within a particular historical, social, and cultural setting. And for us, this setting has been modernity, or the age of reason.

There are certain transitional centuries in history in which there is massive change followed by a long period of living into that change. The first century was an obvious one; the fourth century was also (Christendom was birthed). The tenth and eleventh centuries were crucial—with the division of the Church East and West, and flourishing of the age of faith in the West. The sixteenth century brought the dramatic reformation and counter-reformation that led to the age of reason. I now suggest that in the twenty-first century we have entered a new transitional time in human history. What we accomplished in the last five centuries needs to be affirmed but also seriously questioned. Since the seventeenth century, we have been living in the age of Enlightenment, or *modernity*.

If you want one story (really a parable) that captures how it happened, Johann Sebastian Bach had been hired to teach Bible in school. (Even in those days musicians had to do something else to learn a living.) The only way Bach could conceive of teaching Bible was to have a choir school. When a new rector came to the school, he said the children must study more and sing less. Bach argued that they must sing more and study less. Bach lost, and that was the birth of modernity and the end of the age of faith.

The Age of Reason

Modernity has been characterized as the age of reason. I am suggesting that the age of reason has run its moral limits, and something new will emerge. We do not know what that is going to be; we cannot make it happen. We experience dis-ease, but we do not know why or what is going to emerge.

This age of reason has profoundly influenced how we perceive faith. Because of the emphasis on reason, faith was redefined. Faith had always been understood as perception: our images of God, our images of self, our images of life. We seemed to forget that the word "creed," which comes from the Latin *credo*, literally means "I believe in"; however, an equivalent, but more dynamic translation would be: "I give my love to, I give my loyalty to" [this particular image of God]. It is a love song, not propositional truth or doctrine to be intellectually acknowledged as true.

Our understanding of ethics also changed. Ethics once was about character—our sense of identity and therefore, how we are disposed to behave. In modernity, ethics became moral decision-making. Doctrine and moral decision-making can be taught in a classroom by instruction; faith and character, however, cannot be taught in a classroom by instruction. The schooling-instructional model of learning is inadequate for moral learning. Human beings are not deciders who only need information on right and wrong to live a Christian life. They are perceivers who, having been formed by participating in a community's way of life, see life and their lives in ways that make living as a believer in Jesus Christ and a member of his church possible.

Modernity, the age of reason, also attempted to eliminate dualisms, for example, our material and spiritual lives. Because our focus was on reason, we could not conceive of a world that is fundamentally spiritual—with both material and non-material dimensions. And since we could not isolate and study objectively and rationally the spiritual or non-material, we were left with only the material dimension that could be observed, studied, quantified. As a result, we eliminated the spiritual from our conversations.

We turned the world into an object for our investigation. The field of psychology emerged as a social science to study people. People became objects for our investigation (by the way, for their good, but they were still objects). We stopped praying Scripture; we stopped meditating on Scripture. Instead, we studied, scrutinized, and analyzed Scripture. We turned Scripture into an object for our investigation, rather than the subject that engages us. Among other reasons, we did this so we could have a world that we could understand, control, and manage. We believe we can, and therefore should, control or manage nature and history, our political and economic systems, and even our own lives. That is original sin—to believe that we can manage and control anything in this world. We cannot control things around us; every time we try, we simply mess up the world differently.

This understanding is alive and well. People want to know how they can make everything better and be successful, how they can make a difference. I would suggest that these are the wrong questions, at least for Christians. For Christians the question is not how we can make a difference, but how we can live in the difference God has made. And not how we can be successful and make everything better, but how we can be faithful.

We also need to reconsider how we think about children, and how we think about the spiritual life, because our thinking has been heavily influenced by the very world that I suggest is coming to an end.

Doing Things *With* our Children

I suggest that if we are to counter the negative aspects of modernity and prepare to enter a postmodern era, we need to change our understanding of children and our adult relationships with them. Rather than chronological age and doing things *to* children or developmental stages and doing things *for* children, we should think of childhood as a characteristic of life; we should be doing things *with* children, creating a relational model of equals—a model in which all of us have something to offer each other. Adults need children, children need adults. We all need each other.

The image or metaphor we will use for this way of thinking is pilgrimage. The child is a pilgrim; the adult is a co-pilgrim; and the process is a shared journey together through life. This metaphor calls for us to do things *with* the child—not *to*, not *for*, but *with*. It is the philosophy of Aristotle; it is the psychology of the cultural anthropologist Clifford Geertz. Applying this metaphor, we use the language of formation, rather than instruction, training, or education (the latter concept being understood as *critical reflection* on experience in the light of the gospel).

Formation, as I define it, is the *participation in* and the *practice of* a particular way of life. It is a natural process; it occurs whether or not we plan for it. In cultural anthropology it is called enculturalization. It is not a question of "Are we forming people in the church, home, school, or neighborhood?" It is "How are we forming them? And are we being intentional?"

So how does formation occur? The answer in Greek is *catechesis*—which in English is christening. Now regretfully, christening for many people became baptism. And while it is possible to use the word that way, it is not very helpful, because there is a difference between adjectives and nouns. If I ask you, "Are you a Christian?" the answer is relatively simple; if you have been baptized, the answer is yes. But if I ask you, "Are you Christian?" now you have a problem on your hands; you may think about it and at noon say, "I'm not sure"; by four o'clock "it's iffy"; and by six, "not at all." To be Christlike is about a way of life.

Our problem is that the church is filled with people who are Christians, but do not intend to *be* Christian. We have to live into the reality of our baptism. Baptism tells us the truth about ourselves; we spend the rest of our lives becoming who we already are. Who we are is established in our baptism, and formation is the process of christening or catechesis that takes place by our participating in and practicing the Christian life of faith in a community that understands itself as being the body of Christ.

The early church did not convert people in the world and then bring them to church. They attracted people because of the life that they lived, and when people came to them and asked why they lived as they did they said, "Come live with us. Model your life after ours. Imitate us. Be formed by living with us. We are not going to do something *to* or *for* you but *with* you." That process of nurturing was also converting. It *transformed* lives as well as *formed* lives; the process is the same.

Basically this process is to teach as Jesus taught. During Jesus' day, the traditional rabbi was in the synagogue lecturing, and students would come and sit down at the teacher's feet and take notes. We all know this tradition—the schooling, instructing tradition. But Jesus in essence said, "Come. Identify with me, observe me, and imitate me." We're called to teach as Jesus taught. We must remind ourselves that the book is the *Acts of the Apostles* and not the *Talk of the Apostles*. James, the brother of Jesus, warned us that not many of us should become teachers. Why? Because we will be judged with greater strictness (Jas 3:1). And then James goes on to say that the tongue is ultimately evil (3:2–12). So perhaps we should not *say* anything—we should just *live* it. That is hard to do; it is easier to say "do what I *say*" than to say "do what I *do*." Jesus' way is the way of being *with*.

There is a story about a man going through the land of fools and everyone is running out of the land of fools, screaming, "There's a monster in the field! There's a monster in the field!" He looks at the "monster" and sees that it is a watermelon. He says to himself, "Those stupid people!" He picks up a watermelon, cuts it, and takes a big bite of it to show them that it is not a monster. However, they say, "He's killed the monster; he will kill us, too!" So they kill him. Another man comes to the land of fools and they are all running away from the monster; he runs with them. Eventually he says, "I think we can stop running now." He lives with them near the edge of the field. And one day they realize on their own that the monster was just a watermelon. Now, who was the true teacher? The one who let their lives be a resource for their learning.

Children and Adults

Let us return to our discussion about characteristics of life. Adults are considered to be intellectual; they are rational, productive, and independent. Children, on the other hand, are dependent, pre-rational, and non-productive. So in the past, we considered it our duty to do things *to* or *for* our children to make them into adults. In our new way of thinking, we could say that maybe those very characteristics of a child are what adults need as well. St. Paul reminds us to no longer be child*ish*, but Jesus reminds us to be child*like*. The best way for us as adults to learn to be childlike is to be with children so they can influence us as we influence them.

We are interdependent creatures. One Christian is no Christian; you cannot be Christian alone, only in a community. And we are all dependent on God, absolutely. Dependence is part of what it is to be a spiritual being. Children know that because that is who they already are; that's their characteristic. If we do things with them, and let them influence us, we will regain that sense of absolute dependence.

Children are non-productive; that is really what spirituality is all about, being non-productive. Aristotle's wisdom about leisure includes the idea that our work will never have meaning or purpose unless we have meaningful leisure. What is leisure? Leisure is its own end. Work always has another end. For example, if I am jogging to stay healthy, jogging becomes work; it has another end. That does not mean it is not good; it is just not leisure time, it is not Sabbath time. Leisure is time when you are doing nothing for any purpose. You are just *being*—very hard to pull off. Only in the United States do we use a particular word: vacation. We vacate; we escape. That is why we are just as tired when we return as we were when we left. The rest of the world takes what is called a holiday, a much nicer idea. A holiday is Sabbath time; it is *being*—being with God, being with yourself. It is the non-productive side of life. It is essential. Children, naturally, are non-productive—until we teach them to work all the time. In fact, I have heard educators say, "Play is children's work"—a terrible idea. What is wrong with just play? Why does it have to be for some other purpose—like work?

Our last characteristic of children is that they are pre-rational. Not irrational—pre-rational. They live in the intuitive way of thinking and knowing. That is natural for them, but necessary for all of us. There is both an intuitive way as well as an intellectual way of thinking and knowing. We need both reason and revelation; revelation is based upon the intuitive way of thinking and knowing. It has always been true that the great scientists have kept these two ways of thinking and knowing together. They know that reason alone has never given us a new idea. New, fresh, novel, unique ideas come about in dreams, in visions, and in all kinds of intuitive ways. And then, of course, one must use reason to make some sense of the idea. But the idea itself did not come through reason. It has always amazed me that almost everyone I have known in theoretical math or theoretical physics was also a musician—very interesting. It was not the engineers—the practical people—who were the musicians, but the theoretical scientists, the ones who dream of theories. Theory comes out of the intuitive, pre-rational world of the imagination—that is, the world of the arts.

Young children are born artistic, amazingly creative until they are taught not to be. There is a time to teach technique, I am told by art teachers and dance teachers. That point comes when children want precision; at that point you may teach them specific aspects of drawing, or dancing or singing, but then you must set them free again to go back to what they already possessed; that is how they become great artists, great dancers, great musicians. There will be times for them to concentrate on that other way of knowing and thinking, but they must always return to where they began to be truly creative.

Children can teach us adults how to be pre-rational again; they have as much to offer us as we have to offer them. The world of the imagination is a very real place. I have been trying to teach theology this way for a number of years; it is very difficult. What I usually do is give all the students some clay; but first they contemplate, they empty their minds, they free themselves of all the stuff they brought with them. Then they take their clay, and they become a friend to their clay. I suggest that they might want to eat it, smell it, listen to it, play with it, become its friend. Then they are blindfolded and I say to them, "Let your clay tell you what it wants to become; let it shape itself in your hands. And when you get to a point where you are pretty sure you know what it wants to become—it is virtually there—take off your blindfold, finish it, and then give it away." That is the intuitive way of thinking; that is the creative process: contemplation, freeing the mind from preconceived ideas, engaging the medium, discovering the subject of the clay. There is an often-told story of Michelangelo hammering on a boulder outside his home. A curious neighbor asked. "What are you doing, hammering on that boulder?" Michelangelo is said to have replied, "There's an angel inside, and I'm trying to let it out." It is already there; the task is to bring it out, to discover it, engage it, uncover it. You embody it, bring it into being, and then you release it, because you cannot be creative if you hang onto it. You have to give it away. That way you cannot fall in love with it or try to create more just like it—and cease to be creative.

Sir Alister Hardy, a renowned biologist in England, in 1963 gave the Gifford lectures in which he challenged the scientific community to take seriously the role of spiritual experience as a central feature in human life. In 1969, he founded the Center for the Study of Spirituality at Oxford, and in 1979, he wrote *The Spiritual Nature of Man*, a classic. When Hardy retired, Edward Robinson became the second director for the Center for Spirituality. (Edward Robinson, by the way, is a sculptor.) Robinson produced a book called *The Original Vision: A Study of the Religious Experience of Childhood* (1983), one of the great books of the twentieth century, the result of twenty-five years of study on the spirituality of children. It is a fascinating book.

What Robinson (1983) discovered was that children, even children younger than five years old, had significant religious (or spiritual) experiences, but because they could not name them, could not explain them, could not understand them, could not quite talk about them, we said they did not have them. In interviewing the hundreds of participants in his study, Robinson found that their spiritual experiences tended to occur in three venues or settings: nature, art, and ritual. We should have guessed that.

In the history of religion, religion always begins with nature. Nature is always at the core of it. People sometimes say that they experience God when they are hiking through the woods. I would say that it is a limited experience of God, but it is a real experience. Being in the woods, wandering through nature, entering the natural world is what kids so love to do. It is one place to experience the divine.

The second venue Robinson (1983) found was the arts; always remember that religion was danced before it was ever believed. One cannot separate the arts—drama, music, dance, and visual art—from human life or the spiritual life. They are absolutely essential. However, it is hard to maintain this theo-poetic truth; it is a very different and deeper truth than discourse. To illustrate, I will share a story about my curious-minded little daughter who, when she was in preschool, came home one Sunday with a problem. In our house, we had made our living room into an art center with a space to paint, a record player the children could turn on, and places to sit and listen to music. Our daughter, Jill, came home this Sunday and said, "Daddy, draw me a table." I said, "Well, you know how to draw a table." And she burst into tears. I said to myself, "This is obviously a larger issue than it appears to be." So I asked, "What's the problem?" She said, "The teacher showed us how to draw a table, and I can't do it." Here is a child who for five years had played with creative material, and in one disastrous moment, some well-meaning adult destroyed her creative confidence. It is that fragile.

So what did we do? Well, I said, "You blindfold me and I'll blindfold you." And we crawled up onto the table, and I said, "Now kiss it, and smell it, play with it. What color are you feeling?" Jill told me, and then I said, "Fine, good, now take off your blindfold and you paint your table; use that color. I'll do one too." Jill quickly began; we compared her imaginative table with numerous famous paintings of tables in very different artistic styles. And her artistic, creative talent had been reborn. Through our participation in the arts one can experience God even as a young child.

The last setting Robinson (1983) discussed was ritual; children are the most ritualistic people in the world. We all know that as parents. You may be bored with the story that you have read over and over, and so you try to be original; children do not like that. Also they want to hear the same story all the time, and it is very important to them to hear the whole story, just as it is written. You want to speed it up and go to a party on Friday night; it is not going to work. You might as well pace it out and let it go its own natural way, because ritual is important to children and children are naturally ritualistic.

Rituals are repetitive, symbolic actions, in both words and deeds, that manifest and express a community's sacred story. These rituals, these symbolic actions, are the basis of the spiritual life. For this reason we must not eliminate our children from participating in our rituals of worship. If our rituals are not meaningful to our children, change the liturgy—do not send the children out.

Conclusion

Our challenge is to end our thinking that children have nothing to teach adults, that children are only the objects of adult teachers who need to do things *to* and *for* them until they become adults. Our contention is that children have much to teach adults especially in terms of the spiritual life. We adults need to do more with our children, sharing experiences in nature, the arts, and communal rituals, nurturing the pre-rational, dependent, non-productive (playful) dimensions of human life.

Adults, having wisely given up their childishness as St. Paul recommends, need to become childlike as Jesus taught. When that occurs it is as T.S. Eliot (1942/1971) wrote, "We shall not cease from exploration, and the end of all our exploring will be to arrive where we started and know the place for the first time" (p. 145). Children are God's gift to aid us to mature spiritually.

Modernity has provided us with many blessings, but it has also been detrimental to our spiritual lives. In this age of transition into a postmodern era with its new perceptions about human nature and life, it would be well for us to rethink our understandings of children so that we might nurture and nourish our spiritual lives by doing more with them and becoming more like them.

References

Eliot, T. S. (1942/1971). Little Gidding. In *The complete poems and plays: 1909–1950* (pp. 138–45). New York: Harcourt.

Hall, G. S. (1904). *Adolescence: Its psychology and its relations to physiology, anthropology, sociology, sex, crime, religion, and education.* New York: Appleton.

Hardy, A. (1979). *The spiritual nature of man.* London: Oxford University Press.

Robinson, E. (1983). *The original vision: A study of the religious experience of childhood.* New York: Seabury.

22 THE Story and the Spiritual Formation of Children in the Church and in the Home

Catherine Stonehouse & Scottie May

IT WAS OUR PRIVILEGE TO PRESENT THE CLOSING ADDRESS AT THE 2006 Children's Spirituality Conference. We wanted to turn our attention toward the future and anticipate where those of us who work with children in Christian settings should go from here. We chose to focus on three avenues for fostering the development of children's spirituality in the future:

1. Emphasizing the power of THE Story, that is, the biblical metanarrative.
2. Helping our children be bicultural.
3. Promoting research related to children's spiritual development.

THE POWER OF *THE* STORY

Let's begin with another look at the importance of THE Story. A few months ago a colleague introduced me (Stonehouse) to a new book, *The Drama of Scripture: Finding Our Place in the Biblical Story* (Baker, 2004) by Craig Bartholomew and Michael Goheen. I have always valued the Scripture's role in the spiritual nurture of children, but as I read *The Drama of Scripture* I was gripped in a new way by how profoundly important the story of Scripture is to the child's spiritual formation.

Needed: A Story to Give Meaning

Human beings seem to be created with the need to figure things out, to understand how things work, and to make meaning out of their experiences. We see this in toddlers who are full of questions, "What's that? Why? Who makes the clouds move?" They love stories about what things are and how things work, as well as stories about themselves and their parents' lives. These stories help children discover meaning.

Bartholomew and Goheen (2004), however, point out that we need not only the stories of our own lives and the things around us, but also we need a

> large background story if we are to understand ourselves and the world in which we find ourselves. Individual experiences make sense and acquire meaning only when seen within the context or frame of some story we believe to be the true story of the world. (p. 18)

These authors believe that everyone lives out of some story, whether or not they are conscious of it. This story is sometimes referred to as a metanarrative—the big story that makes sense of the pieces of our lives.

Most Christians believe that we find the true story of the world in the Bible. That should mean, then, that Christians would embrace the biblical story as their metanarrative. It is not just a source for theological concepts, or a collection of interesting ancient stories. It is THE Story that should guide our living as Christians and help us make sense of life and find meaning for our lives.

I think we would all agree that we want our children to know that metanarrative. However, we and our children live in a culture permeated by a very different story, and our society unrelentingly teaches us its metanarrative. Our cultural metanarrative is a captivating story—so captivating that families are totally immersed in it. On May 24, 2006, CBS News reported that one-third of families in the United States have the television on all the time and that 20 percent of toddlers have a television in their own bedrooms.

The cultural story continually calls out to all of us, children and adults alike, not only from the television, but also from the Internet, from the merchandise that fills our stores, and from our neighbors and friends. Everywhere we turn we hear the story that permeates our culture. Our children will learn that story, whether we want them to or not.

In the light of these realities we face a critical question: Which story—the biblical story or the culture's story—will be the primary one our children use to make sense of their lives? That question raises other questions. When will our children learn the biblical story? From their earliest awareness? During the elementary school years? Or will they not learn the story until high school, as young adults?

And most importantly, will they make the biblical story their own, their primary meaning-making story? Will this happen early in life so that they can try to understand the cultural story *from within the biblical story*? Or, will our children learn the *cultural story first* and use *it* as the lens through which they understand Scripture? Which story is primary will make a profound difference in how we and our children understand each of these stories. Whether or not the biblical story becomes primary in the lives of our children will be powerfully influenced by what we as leaders in the faith community and parents believe about the biblical story and how we tell that story.

The Forming Power of Scripture

So what do we believe about Scripture? What do we believe about how best to tell THE Story? What was God's intention in giving us this story? Three points from Bartholomew and Goheen (2004) address these questions and are keenly relevant to our ministry with children: (1) God intends that the biblical story be formative, (2) God intends that children meet God in THE Story, and (3) God intends that we make the biblical story our story.

God Intends that the Biblical Story be Formative

Bartholomew and Goheen say:

> It is the divine author's intention to shape our lives through [the Bible's] story. To be shaped by the story of Scripture we need to understand two things well: the biblical story is a compelling unity on which we may depend, and each of us has a place within that story. (p. 12)

The Bible is not just a collection of ancient stories, or a book of facts and life lessons to be learned.

This past year my (May) church began a series of messages on the kingdom of God. To introduce that series, we interviewed young children, asking them what the kingdom of God is like. We made a video of these responses. Here are some of their answers to the question: What is the kingdom of God?

"A magical place up in the clouds."

"A big castle."

"Texas?"

"The kingdom of God is . . . I forgot."

After the video clip was shown to our church, the congregation smiled, chuckled, and even laughed aloud. The reaction included comments such as, "Aren't they cute; when they are older they will be able to understand," and "I'm not sure how I would answer that question."

The interviews were conducted utilizing a rather traditional format—ask a question, then see how the children answer. I wonder how different their responses might have been (but not nearly so entertaining) if the children had heard that Jesus said the kingdom of God is "like a man who buys and sells. He is looking for good pearls. When he finds one good pearl worth much money, he goes and sells all that he has and buys it" (Matt 13:45-46, NLV). And if, at the close of the parable, the children had wondered what could be so great that the merchant would exchange everything he had for the Great Pearl, what would they have discovered about the kingdom? (Stewart & Berryman, p. 163). How would they have responded in the interview?

The kingdom of God is a key theme in the teaching of Jesus, and a growing number of biblical theologians see the kingdom as a major organizing theme for understanding the biblical drama. Children should begin to learn about such an important concept. But is the best way to tell children about the kingdom of God teaching or lecturing *about* it? It is important to note that Jesus used parables and stories to help his hearers understand the kingdom. Perhaps the best way for children to learn about the kingdom is by letting them hear the *story of the King*—the story that follows the actions of the king from creation through the drama of Scripture to God's plan for the full restoration of the kingdom of God. As Christians, we have hope—we know the last act of the story; we know that our God is still at work in history and that the final act of the drama will be full redemption.

To be formed by God's story, children need to hear the unified, exciting, unfolding story of God's acts in history. Specific events need to be connected to the flow of God's plan and actions. For children to really know and make that story their own, they need to experience the whole story, not just once, but repeatedly throughout their childhood.

This telling of the story begins in the family. A memory that weaves its way through my childhood (Stonehouse) is of Mom reading to us from the Elsie Egermeier's *Bible Story Book* (1947) every night. Today we have a wide variety of Bible story books for children of all ages that introduce them to an appropriate level of detail in the story. I (May) know a single mom who read a section of the Bible every night at bedtime to her daughters. She did not even skip over the hard, "messy" parts. It was a special time for the three of them. It made a safe place for her girls to learn THE Story and to ask their questions.

Our churches also need to provide a place in the children's curriculum where they hear and experience the "whole story" as an unfolding, unified story. In the church where I (Stonehouse) attend, each year our four-, five-, and six-year-olds make the journey from creation to the promised return of Christ. They meet our God who makes and keeps covenant and they learn about God's kingdom. There is no time line or memorizing of sequence for these young children. However, the story forms for them as they repeatedly experience it. Elementary, middle school, and high school youth would also profit from a semester-long walk through the biblical story.

I teach at Wheaton College (May) and students entering there—most from solid Bible-teaching, evangelical churches—do not know the biblical narrative, THE Story. They know pericopes, persons in the Bible, and biblical propositions—but many do not grasp the presence of the living God within this living story.

Young parents and those who work with our children in the church need the opportunity to learn the whole story. Children and adults alike need the big story that gives them meaning and can form and transform them across a lifetime. The evidence is clear. Our task is crucial. We must communicate God's story including its grandeur and glory (John 2:11).

God Intends that Children Meet God in THE Story

Bartholomew and Goheen (2004) say that "as we enter deeply into the story of the Bible, God will be revealed to us. We will also find ourselves called to share in the mission of God and his purposes with the creation" (p. 22). We do want children to know basic biblical facts. But our ultimate purpose is that they will get to know God—not just know *about* God, but know God.

A recent study (Renz, 1998) hypothesizes that giving children experiences with God before teaching about him enables them to ask "their" questions when they are ready. One way they experience God is to enter the stories of Scripture and see God in action, discover God's character event by event, and hear God speak to them in the story. They get to know God when we, children and adults together, celebrate the wonder and mystery of God's plans and God's ways. It happens when we present the biblical narrative as God's story with God as the main character. When we introduce the human characters in God's story, we want to tell their stories in a way that allows children to see God at work in their lives, to see God's plans for them and responses to them, to discover God's grace, mercy, and justice, in that order.

God Intends that We Make the Biblical Story Our Story

Bartholomew and Goheen (2004) encourage us to "invite readers [in our case, children] to make [the biblical story] their story, to find their place in it, and to dwell in it as the true story of the world" (p. 12). How do we invite children to make the story their own? Perhaps rather than *telling* children what the story means, we should lead them to engage the story reflectively, wondering about its meaning. One way this can be done is to *enter into* the biblical story, to walk around in it.

There are several approaches that can help children enter the biblical story. I (May) have been involved with one such approach for over fifteen years. I like to call it a hands-on, Bible-time museum. There are three components to this approach: story time, project time, and small group time. Envision a series that focuses on God's work in the life of the Apostle Paul. During story time, the story is told in any number of ways through first-person drama about some portion of Paul's life. The project time allows children to choose one of a variety of tasks that help them understand what life was like in Paul's day—something about travel, food, language, tent-making, and so forth. This segment is key to allowing the children to realize that Paul was a real person, in a real place, at a certain point in time. The small group time allows the children to ask questions, to apply the aim of the session in their own lives, and also to pray for each other. A series that has become a highlight is one where the children create the

Old Testament tabernacle and all its furnishings at a scale large enough for all 150 of them to enter the courtyard. Learning THE Story happens in an organic, living way.

Another way children can enter the story is through the "Godly Play" approach described by Sonja Stewart and Jerome Berryman in *Young Children and Worship* (1989). Berryman (2002) has now published extensive guidelines for using Godly Play. His Godly Play concepts flow directly from Catechesis of the Good Shepherd, an approach to the religious formation of children rooted in the Bible, the liturgy of the church, and the educational principles of Maria Montessori (1935/1965; see also Cavalletti, 1983; Lillig, 1998). Essentially, these are reflective approaches that intend to help children encounter God with a sense of awe and wonder—to help them consider the things of God with continued attention. A prepared environment makes it possible for children to find the quiet place within themselves—a place that all children have—where they can sense the presence and voice of God. Another important feature of Godly Play and Catechesis of the Good Shepherd is that they lead the children into the whole story; the children live in the story and reflect on that story, making it their own.

How we lead children into the biblical story is profoundly important. But we must not forget that, no matter how we understand the formative power of Scripture, or how well we tell the story, our children will be living in a world that lives by a very different story.

Helping our Children be Bicultural

Karen Marie Yust (2004) in her book, *Real Kids, Real Faith*, challenges us to help our children live in two cultures. We must help them to be *bicultural*, that is, they must live as Christians in the world's culture—they will be in the world, but not of the world. Thus they must become two-culture kids—Yust's phrase—identifying with the *Christian* culture, but living in the *world's* culture.

The *American Heritage Dictionary* (2000) defines culture as the "totality of socially transmitted behavior patterns, arts, beliefs, institutions, and all other products of human work and thought." Clifford Geertz, renowned Princeton cultural anthropologist, emphasized in his famous book, *The Interpretation of Cultures* (1973), the importance of *symbols* historically transmitted. How does this transmission happen? How are these values and norms learned?

A couple of generations ago, the American culture was more harmonious with Christian values. Neither of us (Stonehouse and May) needed to be bicultural in the same ways as today. In fact, we grew up singing the hymn "This Is My Father's World." But we also sang "This World Is Not My Home." There was not as much tension between these two worlds as there is today.

North American culture today is quite different. Postmodernity has cast a long shadow over our children and youth with its media-shaped reality and shifting view of truth. Unintentionally we may be forming *monocultural kids*—children so comfortable with the world's culture that a Christian culture is foreign to them. We assume that we can "teach" the Christian culture to the young and it will "take." Sometimes it might, but more often our teaching does not form them to be lifelong, faithful, obedient followers of Christ. Truth for our children needs to include a *lived* reality, that is, truth must be authentically experienced to be heard—not given in propositional truth statements only. In order for children to be bicultural—at home in the Christian culture yet able to function in the world's culture—they need to be living in a faith community, the shaping agent of the Christian culture. This faith community must be their primary culture.

Faith Communities Nurturing Bicultural Children

Rodney Clapp's (1993) challenging and controversial book *Families at the Crossroads* argues that the *faith family* (that is, the church) should be the child's primary family, and that the nuclear family is secondary to the faith family. He is not saying that biological families should relinquish their roles to the church, but rather, the church should regain its organic function as the body of Christ, in particular, being there for one another as we heed the many "one another" passages of the Epistles. Clapp's premise for the family and the church is radical. Is this possible in our society? Maybe.

If Clapp is right, and I (May) think he is, then our task is to invite and instruct adult leaders to use the biblical story to help shape families, to nurture them to see that the way to interpret the world's story is through the metanarrative of God, rather than unintentionally interpreting the biblical story through the world's story. This would also mean that the church must do things *with* children, not only *to* them and *for* them (as John Westerhoff challenges us to do in chapter 21 of this volume, pp. 355-65).

In many churches today, children's ministry seeks to be relevant—culturally relevant to the twenty-first century because that is what the kids know. This creates a problem. As we examine the teachings of Jesus, cultural relevancy was never his message. He used cultural metaphors and images, but his *message* was radically counter cultural (e.g., the Sermon on the Mount). Yet, he was always spiritually relevant. That makes all the difference. In many ways we have reversed what Jesus modeled for us: sometimes the goal has become cultural relevancy, especially in our methodology, resulting—perhaps—in spiritual irrelevancy.

A recent, very influential report sponsored by the Commission on Children at Risk (2003) is entitled "Hardwired to Connect: A New Scientific Case for Authoritative Communities." A group of scholars and professionals from a wide range of disciplines is calling for a major change in our society. These leaders believe our children need to be growing up in what they call an "authoritative community," and their report describes the characteristics of this authoritative community. The community needs to be intergenerational, warm, and enfolding; it needs to promote values that are lived, values to which the young are held accountable—and, very importantly, this community must give attention to the spiritual (p. 34). Where in our society do we have a better chance than *in the church* to provide this kind of community? The ultimate test of a Christian culture is the kind of community it creates for its children. How well are we doing?

Helping children live in the Christian story while they are part of today's culture is our task as faith communities—helping them live biblically, as holy, set apart people of God, serving the world. In community, children develop the vocabulary of faith. Surrounded by authentic worshipers who talk about and live out their faith with integrity, the Christian culture becomes familiar and comfortable for children.

Children need to be in a community where they see the biblical story lived—a community where the actions of those around them give meaning to the words and stories of Scripture. At two and a half years of age, my (Stonehouse) grand niece Catherine was fascinated by the Christmas story. She is a little preacher's kid. So she had heard the story at home and at the church where her parents served. She had also experienced the gift-giving of a supportive congregation. One Sunday morning during the Christmas season, while her parents were engaged in visiting after church, Catherine carried off one of the pretty gifts that a church member had given to her family. Later, her mother found the gift in the manger, at the front of the sanctuary. Catherine *knew the story* of wise men bringing gifts to the baby Jesus, and *she experienced a faith community* that lived out a giving spirit. These two influences led this little girl to become part of the story, bringing her gift to the baby Jesus. Children are blessed when they are nurtured in a faith community that winsomely lives the biblical story.

Families Nurturing Bicultural Children

Which culture is nurturing our children? The world's culture or the principles of the biblical Christian culture? Children are nurtured in the faith community and in the home. Our families must also be environments that reflect Christian culture; we must be living biblically. We must integrate God's story with all of daily life and use it to evaluate how we live. The family must live out and enjoy THE Story together.

Families need to provide a regular time and space when the deep, vital needs of the child are able to be satisfied, as Sofia Cavalletti (1983) describes throughout her book *The Religious Potential of the Child*. There must be space and time made for encounters with God through family rituals and symbols.

Four-year-old Kegan lives with her grandmother. A copy of Rembrandt's famous painting "Return of Prodigal Son" hangs on the dining room wall in her grandmother's home. After asking what the painting was about and hearing her grandmother's explanation, Kegan sat quietly looking out the window. Her grandmother asked her, "What are you thinking?" Kegan replied, "Nothing. I'm not thinking about anything. I'm just knowing."

Though we cannot be sure about what Kegan was "knowing," children are able to give themselves totally to God's love. This is a process that people such as Cavalletti (1983) have been watching for decades. It is as if the birth of a religious person occurs through the enjoyment of God's love—an enjoyment of God's love in the story and in worship. (See the first chapter of *The Religious Potential of the Child* for a full description of that process from Cavalletti's perspective.)

How can we help families enjoy God's story and worship together? One way is to guide parents to nurture and form children spiritually by providing experiences—not classes alone—where the parents can see

Christian nurturing lived out. Many young parents did not experience as children the kind of nurturing we are discussing. Experiencing faith-nurturing practices with other young families will release them to weave those formative practices into their home life. For many young couples, one of the most valuable things we as a faith community can do is to lead them into the biblical story to make it their own—to learn to love it and live it.

Research, Research, Research

Children's ministry leaders are very aware of the major changes in our culture, and many are trying to address the challenges created by those changes. But which of the methods and resources created in response to the societal shifts provide children with the nurture for which they hunger? Are there principles, values, and methods from the past that, if abandoned, will leave children spiritually undernourished? What can we do with these questions? Wait ten or fifteen years and see how the children now in our churches turn out? The stakes are too high to risk providing a generation of children with spiritual food that is low in nutrition or even toxic. Research is needed to assess the effectiveness of current ministries and to keep ourselves spiritually fit for service and leadership. We will mention just a few ideas to stimulate our thinking.

Researching Children's Spirituality

The past decade has seen a significant increase of research into the spirituality of children. We call for a continuation of such research that will help us understand children more fully as well as our role in helping children recognize God in their lives and in their world. Such insights call for us to *watch* and *listen*, *watch* and *listen*. Then we must analyze what we have seen and heard for patterns that can help us develop principles and hypotheses.

The Children's Spirituality Conferences have brought scholars and children's ministry leaders together to share their research and learn from one another. Our dream is that we will continue to work across denominational lines and theological perspectives for the emergence of increased common ground in how Christians view the nurture of children's spirituality.

Researching Ministry Models and Methods

We need to engage in research to discern the effect of ministry models. This begins with observing children in different ministry settings and asking astute questions. When visiting several large churches with my students, I (Stonehouse) was impressed by the comment one of the children's pastors made to the students. "Look at the children," she instructed. "How engaged are they?" Observing the level of engagement provides significant insight into the effectiveness of a ministry. Those who are up-front ministry leaders will do well to assign others systematically to observe the engagement of the children and report their findings to the ministry team.

The following questions raised by Shannon Daley and Kathleen Guy (1994) in their book, *Welcome the Child: A Child Advocacy Guide for Churches,* may help us evaluate the effectiveness of our faith communities:

> *Worship experiences:* How are concerns of children and families presented? How are children's abilities evident?
>
> *Education ministries:* Are children's issues addressed in adult education? What resources are available?
>
> *Service/Outreach:* What events help children learn giving and cooperation? What services are provided for early childhood?
>
> *Advocacy:* Who speaks for the children? What moves your congregation to action? [How can you] use that energy for the spiritual nurture of your children? (p. 44)

We also need longitudinal work that would help us identify long-term influences of current methods. We need to know if our ministries are really doing what we want them to do. For too long we have relied on attendance to be our main criterion of "success."

Personal Research

As leaders, professors, pastors, and publishers, how long has it been since we revisited our own understanding of the biblical story? Are we continuing to meet God in THE Story? Do we know God's story as the "compelling unity on which we can depend"? (Bartholomew & Goheen, 2004, p. 12) Are we still being formed spiritually more and more into the image of Christ?

Let us invite you to take a personal research journey to discover anew the biblical unifying themes that are most significant for children. This is research we need to do from time to time. One resource to launch that study could be Bartholomew and Goheen's *The Drama of Scripture* (2004). Before we lead others into a fresh understanding and love of the biblical story, we need to be renewed. You might also want to use *The Drama of Scripture* with parents and those who work with children in the church. Another resource that expands on some of the ideas we have tried to share is *Postmodern Children's Ministry* by Ivy Beckwith (2004).

In closing, we echo these words from the last paragraph of *Offering the Gospel to Children* by Gretchen Wolff Pritchard (1992):

> When the lessons and worship and art activities plumb the heights and depths of Scripture [and] when the church . . . makes it clear that what it has to offer is faith, hope, and love—then children know they are being fed, and they want to come back for more. We have them, often, for so little time. We can only pray that some of the taste of that Bread of Life, that Cup of Salvation, will stay in their mouths, and, by God's grace, when they are bigger and can make their own choices, they know where to find it, and come home. (p. 175)

May this be so in the faith communities we serve.

References

Boyer, M., & DeVinne, P. B., et al. (Eds.). (2000). *American Heritage dictionary of the English language* (4th ed.). Boston: Houghton Mifflin.

Bartholomew, C. G., & Goheen, M. W. (2004). *The drama of Scripture: Finding our place in the biblical story*. Grand Rapids: Baker.

Beckwith, I. (2004). *Postmodern children's ministry*. Grand Rapids: Zondervan.

Berryman, J. (2002). *The complete guide to Godly Play* (Series). Harrisburg, PA: Living the Good News.

Cavalletti, S. (1983). *The religious potential of the child* (P. M. Coulter & J. M. Coulter, Trans.). Ramsey, NJ: Paulist.

Clapp, R. (1993). *Families at the crossroads*. Downers Grove, IL: InterVarstiy.

Commission on Children at Risk. (2003). *Hardwired to connect: A new scientific case for authoritative communities*. New York: Institute for American Values.

Daley, S. P., & Guy, K. A. (1994). *Welcome the child: A child advocacy guide for churches*. New York: Friendship Press and Children's Defense Fund.

Egermeier, E. (1947). *Bible story book: A complete narration from Genesis to Revelation for young and old*. Anderson, IN: Warner.

Geertz, C. (1973). *The interpretation of cultures*. New York: Basic.

Lillig, T. (1998). *Catechesis of the Good Shepherd in a parish setting.* Chicago: Liturgy Training.

Montessori, M. (1965). *The child in the church.* St. Paul, MN: Catechetical Guild.

Pritchard, G. W. (1992). *Offering the Gospel to children.* Cambridge, MA: Cowley.

Renz, C. (1998). Christian education and the confirmation debate: Towards a theology of catechesis. *Journal of Christian Education, 41*(1), 53–65.

Stewart, S., & Berryman, J. (1989). *Young children and worship.* Louisville: Westminster John Knox.

Westerhoff, J. H., III. (2000). *Will our children have faith?* (Rev. ed.). Toronto: Morehouse.

Yust, K. M. (2004). *Real kids, real faith: Practices for nurturing children's spiritual lives.* San Francisco: Jossey-Bass.

23 "The Spirit of Children Future"

Donald Ratcliff

EARLIER IN THIS BOOK, THE HISTORY OF RESEARCH REGARDING CHILdren's religion, faith, and spirituality was explored by surveying more than a century of work in this area. From the perspective of one who has looked long and deep at the historical background of children's spirituality, it is tempting to extrapolate to the future. It may be foolhardy to predict anything very specific. Some latent issues, however, may provide clues to emerging issues likely to be of relevance in the years ahead.

A JOURNAL DEVOTED TO CHILDREN'S SPIRITUALITY FROM CHRISTIAN PERSPECTIVES?

This book reflects the growing interest in children's spirituality issues in Christian contexts. Will this explicitly Christian interest in children's spirituality expand sufficiently to support an American journal on the subject? At this time, existing scholarly journals that offer venues to accommodate this research include *International Journal of Children's Spirituality*, *Religious Education*, *Christian Education Journal*, *The Journal of Psychology and Theology*, *The Journal of Psychology and Christianity*, *Review of Religious Research*, and *Journal for the Scientific Study of Religion*. Outside the North American context, research is likely to be published in the *British Journal of Religious Education*, *Journal of Christian Education* (Australian), *Journal of Beliefs and Values*, and again, *The International Journal of Children's Spirituality*.

There is also a growing trend among secular journals to accept research on children's spirituality. Chris Boyatzis (2003) of Bucknell University has been particularly instrumental in fostering this approach by guest editing a special issue of *Applied Developmental Science* and hosting pre-conference sessions on children's spirituality at meetings of related professional organizations. The trend towards publication in secular journals could increase if the concept of children's spirituality as a general human phenomenon comes to be accepted among educators and social scientists in the United States, a view that was prevalent a century ago when this area of research first emerged.

With the potential for publication elsewhere, a journal devoted to Christian perspectives on children's spirituality may be unnecessary; an online periodical describing new books and articles, however, might be a welcome addition. One such effort (Ratcliff & Orona, 2007) is in its embryonic phase, only describing research-related books and not yet summarizing journal articles. It may eventually become an online periodical as funds and personnel become available.

How Broad a View of Children's Spirituality is "Christian"?[1]

Will the parameters of children's spirituality contract or expand? Will spirituality of the non-Western world come to even greater prominence in the years ahead, or will there be a parting of the ways between those who hold to a historic Christian (or Judeo-Christian) view of the world, and those who do not? I am not certain which way things will go; in fact, both could occur. If non-Western spirituality becomes more prevalent, a division could be precipitated.

I am stimulated by the presence of alternative theologies that, at least to some degree, have a convergence with the Bible. In addition, voices outside the Christian faith offer insights that are helpful. For example, my wife and I studied the Jewish feasts, perspectives, and other practices for many years, and included much of that richness into our family life. A second example surfaced in a research class I taught at a state university in the "Bible belt"; when I mentioned a possible relationship between faith and research, only one person in the class stayed afterward to engage in fruitful dialogue on this subject—a Muslim student. Judeo-Christian perspectives share some common aims and interests with Muslims who hold theologically

---

1. The perspective expressed here is that of the chapter author, and does not necessarily represent the views of other conference planning team members.

conservative views about divinity and are willing to engage in dialogue. A third example is a delightful and intelligent member of my extended family who includes Buddhist practices in his life; as I affirmed the quiet reflection in his practices, he described his appreciation for similar practices by early Christians. One need not convert to learn with people of other faiths.

For the purposes of this book and the conference to which it is related, the Christian faith has been chosen as the primary reference point, and indeed, some tasks can be accomplished more fully when there is sustained attention to children's spirituality within the context of a single faith tradition. Even within the Christian faith, there is uneasiness between those who affirm historic beliefs, as reflected in the ancient creeds and traditional theology, and those who question important doctrines such as the incarnation, atonement, resurrection, and authority of Scripture. While much can be learned from a variety of faith traditions, the departure from the historic common ground brings the very definitional aspects of Christianity into question. While those within the Christian faith have much to learn from one another's traditions, and even from those who do not affirm all of the basic doctrines, are there non-negotiable components that define Christian faith in a distinct manner from other faiths? If not, why use the designation "Christian perspectives" with "children's spirituality"?

I must admit to being torn at this point. I personally have benefited a great deal by dialogue with those who do not share all of the basic beliefs of Christian faith. There can be benefit in including in the dialogue those who question some traditional doctrines.

What is more important than position on some theological spectrum is the willingness to engage in dialogue with openness and receptivity. My hope is that the current conversation will continue with the rich mix of participants from mainline denominations, evangelical groups, and postmodern "emergents," as well as fundamentalist and New Age Christians. The central concern here is that those who enter the discussion, regardless of where they are on the spectrum of Christian beliefs, need genuinely to want to interact on the central topic—*Christian* perspectives of children's spirituality.

It is exciting to have the full breadth of historic Christians in dialogue, including some who have been underrepresented, overlooked, or even marginalized. To hear dialogue about children's spirituality between Roman Catholics, Pentecostals, Methodists, Orthodox Christians, Presbyterians, Baptists, Episcopalians, Lutherans, and those from Bible Churches and other denominations can produce much insight. May the interaction continue, and may it bear good fruit for all of the children in our churches!

Enhancing the Dialogue Between Researchers and Practitioners

Christian educators have much to learn from current research, and from those who conduct the research. Likewise, researchers need to hear from practitioners regarding the kinds of research that can best inform practice. Bringing a research perspective into practice may result in a greater emphasis upon evaluation, as well as encourage some experimentation with innovative approaches. It may also prompt rediscovery of the best traditional approaches and the "ancient-future" aspects of the faith, where early church practices are adapted to current church and parachurch contexts. Dialogue between researchers, denominational and megachurch administrators, and practitioners can be fruitful in many ways. To the degree possible, parents also need to be included in the dialogue; their voices need to be heard, considering the strong evidence that parents are the most powerful influences on their children's spirituality.

Researchers Working With Children

Dialogue between those who do research on children's spirituality and those who work with children first-hand can be facilitated in two ways: (1) researchers being involved in ministry with children; and (2) practitioners engaging in simple, research-oriented activities to better understand children in their care. In this manner, both researchers and practitioners are more likely to engage one another in dialogue that involves respect and better understanding for the other person's task.

Researchers need occasionally to be involved in teaching and nurturing children in the faith. Otherwise, it is easy to forget what the typical practitioner experiences with children. Ideally, researchers work with their own children and/or periodically help with church and parachurch activities. I personally have benefited by involvement with an inner-city mission when living in the Los Angeles area, as well as helping in public and private schools as a volunteer. I also help with church programs such as Vacation Bible School. As a university educator and researcher, I find that involvement with children keeps my outlook realistic, avoiding an idealistic, romanticized, or excessively theoretical image of children. As a result, my perception of research proposals and plans for personal research tend to be more focused on the actual world of children, ultimately yielding research that is driven by practical concerns as well as theory.

It also may be productive for researchers to spend time with children in contexts with which they are less familiar. The inner city, the juvenile facility, church-sponsored facilities for disabled children, and overseas experiences may all be valuable in this regard. Childhood varies considerably between cultures, as well as from one subculture to another. The increased sensitivity of researchers to this fact may not only increase their understanding of children in general, but also remind them of the amazing degree of variability from one child to the next, and from one cultural context to the next. While there has been some cross-cultural research in children's spirituality, comparisons across cultures and subcultures are seldom the object of research.

Parents and Teachers[2] Using the Methods of Research to Better Understand Children

Researchers who also work with children can help bridge the gap that practitioners perceive between themselves and researchers. Similarly, dialogue can be more effective for practitioners—teachers, parents, and others who work directly with children—if they develop some of the more germane skills of the researcher.

To invite parents and teachers into the world of the researcher, it may be wise to circumvent methodological technicalities and concentrate, rather, on how children speak about their spiritual lives to adults. Children have several voices, most of which are not heard by many teachers and parents in their lives. By using somewhat simplified variations of selected research procedures, these voices can be heard more clearly, and a better understanding of children's spirituality results. As a parent, I think of these activities as being like the photograph album that reflects the history of the family. By engaging in some of these activities, the logic involved in research is more likely to emerge, as parents and children's workers obtain more and better information about their own children's spirituality. The first rule of St. Benedict is carefully to listen by being attentive, watching,

---

2. "Teacher" is used here and throughout this chapter to refer either to a Christian educator affiliated with a church or parachurch group, or to a school teacher. Examples have been chosen that may fit either of these contexts.

and listening carefully (Derske, 2003). There are at least four different ways in which children are likely to "speak" their spirituality, and wise adults have "ears" for each of these.

Spirituality Speaks Through Observable Activities in Everyday Life

Recording detailed descriptions of activities is an important part of many research studies. An excellent investigative habit to develop is keeping an activity journal (daily if at all possible) that documents, in writing, key events and comments by children that reflect their spirituality. Parents and teachers can become adept at making good observations of their children by pushing themselves to see as much as possible. What appear to be minutiae at one point may end up being very significant later; therefore, seemingly inconsequential details should be recorded. A good description is vivid, so that one can quickly visualize later on exactly what happened. It can also be helpful to record details about body posture, eye contact, and other "nonverbal" language the child may manifest. Is this body language consistent with what the child says with words, or do these two communication modalities contradict? In most cases, though not all, the body language is more trustworthy than the words used.

Observations can be made more complete by taking photographs or making videos of what is happening. With today's digital cameras, photographs and videos cost little and can be a relatively permanent record of the child's spiritual interests.

Observation, both written and visual, of the words, actions, situations, and interactions of children can reveal much about their interior lives. Ultimately, the "data" of observations should be used in the service of a stronger relationship with and better understanding of the child.

Spirituality Speaks Through Artifacts and Art

Author and child development specialist Robert Coles (1990) is well known for having children draw pictures, and using the interpretation of the pictures to gain insight into the children's spirituality. Before he offers his interpretation, Coles usually asks children to give their interpretations. Children may be able to express in their drawings some of the deeper aspects of their lives that cannot be expressed in words. Drawings and other artwork can help teachers and parents understand their children better, although there is always the danger of seeing what one wants to see in the drawings. Observers should avoid drawing premature conclusions and expressing their ideas to children too soon. An observer's interpretation may preempt the child's own perception; after hearing an adult's analysis, the child may merely agree or repeat what the observer has said, even if the child has doubts about it.

Pictures taken by parents and teachers were mentioned under "observable activities," but it can also be helpful to have children take pictures to express or portray their thoughts. A Christian school in Hawaii tried this, handing out one-use cameras to all the children and asking them to take photographs that represented God to them. The children brought in amazingly insightful pictures, which were made into a book, *God's Photo Album* (Mecum, 2001). Parents and teachers may want to try this as well; insight into children's faith may be obtained that is impossible to gain in any other way.

The toys and other objects a child prefers may also say much about the child's spirituality. Discussing prized possessions can reveal the inner worlds of children. What possessions do they honor in a reverent manner? Do they treat religious objects in a different manner from other things?

Special activities and objects with unusual, unique, or extraordinary meanings and uses may be introduced to the child. When the children were younger, my family celebrated Passover with special garments, foods, and objects that are traditionally incorporated by those of the Jewish faith. This tradition initiated many conversations about how the Christian faith was rooted in the Old Testament faith. Similarly, the "Godly Play" approach to spiritual nurture is used by many churches; following the story, the children are permitted to play with special manipulatives to reenact the story. Teachers can make careful notes about children's actions and comments related to such activities and objects, complementing that record with photographs or videos.

Spirituality Speaks Through Hearing Words and Sounds

Often researchers make use of interviews to understand those they study. Interviews can also be conducted by parents and teachers. When my oldest son was ten, I interviewed him using a video recorder about what he would like in a wife some day, and then asked what he would like to tell her if he met her today. He stated, with a grin, "I wish I could marry you today." The day he was married—many years later, I must add—we played that video for the congregation!

Interviews related to spirituality should usually be open-ended and casual. Instead of questions that require only a "yes" or "no" (or some other short answer), open-ended questions will encourage children to describe their feelings and experiences of a spiritual nature. When an adult takes spiritual issues seriously, children are more likely to open themselves to that adult. In contrast, the teacher or parent who is didactic or critical about spiritual topics may generate distrust, and children may be less likely to share their thoughts and heart as a result. Scripture states that one should not judge quickly (John 7:24). If the child asks questions, a teacher or parent may choose not to give an easy, quick answer—even if one fits—as the child may gain more by pondering the question, wondering about possible answers, and reflecting carefully about their lives and ideas. If an adult gives quick answers, kids may see this is the ultimate goal—that is, to give a correct answer, rather than share how they actually feel about a matter.

While words are important, the child's tone is also a key to the inner person. Which spiritual topics excite the child, and which seem to be less interesting? The tone of voice, pitch, body posture, and eye contact that go with the words may be more important than the words themselves. Video recording may help track the child's body language with greater detail, while a good voice recorder may be quickly turned on when the child unexpectedly wants to talk about spiritual concerns. A rule of thumb for some researchers is that the best interviews are often not seen as interviews; they are spontaneous interactions usually initiated by the child. Parents and teachers should be aware of this, and have a pad of paper handy at all times to take notes as the child is talking; doing so will communicate your keen interest in what the child is saying. On the other hand, if writing notes or using the voice recorder is distracting or disconcerting to the child, the information, as well as insights, can be recorded later.

When observing a child's actions or speech, one may want to consider possible cause-and-effect relationships. Discerning cause is difficult since human behavior—including children's activities and words—is complex; usually there are multiple possible reasons for a given statement or action (Peck, 1995). But it is natural to consider the reasons why children act as they do and why particular statements are made. Again, the danger is to read an easy, "obvious" reason into what is said and done, when the full explanation is likely to be multifaceted. Listening carefully to the words of a child, and making repeated observations, may help the parent or teacher get at deeper, more complex reasons for statements and activities.

Spirituality Speaks Through Innovative Approaches

While observing a child and having discussions may produce insights into a child's spirituality, "experiments" of a sort may produce additional understanding. Usually, there is more trial and error in research than what is commonly thought, and the same can be said for good teaching. It is possible to conceive the whole area of experimentation as a sophisticated form of trial and error. Teachers may try new methods in their classrooms, and parents may want to experiment with different approaches to encouraging a child's spirituality.

Scores of ideas for parents and teachers are available that can encourage children's spiritual growth and experiences (see Ratcliff, 2007a, for example, as well as other chapters in this book). Some may work well for some teachers, some parents, and some children, while others may not resonate with a particular teacher, parent, or child. Spiritual leaders should find what makes a good fit between guide and child, as effectiveness may increase if methods are varied. Variation may forestall boredom. On the other hand, children may prefer ritualistic repetitiveness more than parents or teachers. Repetition may encourage quiet reflection that can be invaluable for a child. Reading a particular Bible story a fifth or even tenth time may be a means to better understanding for a young child, even though doing so may be tedious for the adult.

Experimenting with spiritual activities with children is sometimes avoided by teachers and parents because of the vulnerability involved. Some may feel there is one right way to guide children spiritually. Methods that work well in one setting may prove unsuccessful in other settings. But what will work in a given situation is often difficult to predict. No trustworthy book will state exactly how to encourage spirituality; if someone suggests one approach that is always best, suspicion is warranted. Teachers and parents need to be creative in this area, trying out new things if they sound appealing. If they seem not to work, discuss it with the child. He or she may not outwardly reflect what is going on deeply within. Yet if a method is ineffective, an alternative strategy is probably needed. In general, children are more likely to be forthcoming about their spiritual lives if they have significant adults who are accepting and honest, yet also willing to give new ideas a try. When it comes to children's spirituality, do not hesitate to experiment. (For a description of four relatively innovative approaches to spiritual nurture, see Ratcliff, 2007c.)

Leaders need to keep track of what works and what does not. The details of children's reactions should be journaled, as notations about prior successes can be encouraging when one has met failure in trying something new. Failures and successes may also be helpful to share with other teachers and parents informally, as well as with the public at conferences, blogs, and the like (with appropriate permission and/or confidentiality).

As adults observe, listen, and experiment, it is likely that they will grow as much or more than the children because of the reciprocal interactions between them. While in one sense, children are under adult care, they can also be spiritual siblings in the faith community. Thus they can be the adults' teachers, providing reminders of what was taught, often when adults need to hear it the most, but also when parents and teachers may want to hear it the least! Christ encouraged adult believers to learn from the children with whom they interacted (Luke 18:17), and that is no less true today than in the first century.

College and Seminary Classes and Programs Related to Children's Spirituality

It is possible that seminaries and other graduate programs will emphasize children's spirituality, and perhaps add entire programs in this area in the coming years, if interest continues to grow. Children's spirituality could be combined with children's ministry specializations; and certificate programs—with or without formal educational credit—are likely to emerge. Programs that significantly influence this field of study are likely to value both the use of existing research as well as provide instruction in methodology for the production of important research on children's spirituality. There are still many issues in need of research in this area (Ratcliff & Nye, 2006).

A new, yet also ancient, movement has arisen called "child theology." In some respects, this movement is conceptually related to children's spirituality, yet its advocates have not been centrally involved in children's spirituality publications and research. Children are described theologically in both the Old and New Testaments of the Bible, and many theologians throughout history have commented on children. Yet, for at least a century, children have been ignored by theologians; they simply have not been on the radar screen. Evidence of this can be obtained by examining virtually any textbook that surveys the discipline. Beginning in the early twenty-first century, a few scholars began to comment on theological topics related to children, sometimes considering what difference it might make to place "a child in the midst" of any theological topic (Willmer, 2002; White, 2001). Yet, most professional theologians continue to overlook the possibility that children might have an important place in their work. The textbooks simply have not added that chapter.

Will child theology merge with children's spirituality, providing a theological counterpoint to the predominantly social science perspectives of children's spirituality? Or will it continue to be a parallel movement that some children's spirituality people find interesting to examine? Will it fade with time, and return to the relative obscurity of the history of theology? It is too soon for a definitive response to these questions; but considering that the most noteworthy study to date is a superb historical review of theologians' comments on children (Bunge, 2001), and a follow-up volume is reportedly being developed, it is possible that other contemporary theologians will recognize the value of this relatively untouched field of study. Two major web pages (Child Theology Movement, n.d.; and Child Theology Web Page, 2006) document the most recent developments in this area, yet the initial spurt of activity appears to have slowed considerably.

Ideally, children's spirituality, as well as historic and current views of child theology, will be incorporated in seminary and non-seminary ministerial preparation programs in the future. The importance of both church- and parent-based nurture and instruction needs to be impressed upon future pastors, so they in turn will recognize and encourage such efforts from the pulpit.

There is great need for dialogue between those interested in spiritual formation and advocates of children's spiritual development. Theology and children's spiritual experience should be natural partners; advocates of spiritual formation could be a natural link between these. This partnership seems particularly likely if child development is conceptualized in a more holistic manner, with spirituality not merely being added to other areas of cognitive and social development, but rather seen as inseparable from these and other aspects of development. Religion and spirituality should relate to every area of the child's life.

Conclusion

Perhaps the greatest need is parental guidance. Many research studies have documented the far greater influence of parents than peers, school, and church on a child's spirituality (see Hyde, 1990). Yet, many parents feel at a loss as to how this can be accomplished. Parental instruction should involve not only simulated and perhaps even real demonstrations of spiritual guidance and instruction, but also include hands-on experiences between parents and their children (Ratcliff, 2007c). Workshops and retreats may be of great value in this regard, complemented by regular pastoral affirmations from the pulpit of the value of such learning experiences, and consequent activities of a spiritual nature at home between parents and children (Ratcliff, 2007a). The church must move beyond mere cognitive acquisition of biblical content—as crucially important as that is—to the encouragement of spiritual experience and perspectives at home, school, and church. Probably the greatest challenge for the children's spirituality movement is to offer concrete, usable, creative, promising ideas to parents for fostering and nurturing spiritual development in their children.

Not only should families be key actors in the spotlight, but also children should be affirmed in all their capacity to be involved with others spiritually (Ratcliff, 2007b). Indeed, relational consciousness is considered by some to be the defining attribute of children's spirituality (Hay & Nye, 2006). Children may have spiritual abilities that are rarely, if ever, tapped by those around them. They can share a faith story with friends. They can pray for each other, their parents, and other adults. They can share soup and a smile with the homeless. They can minister, comfort, encourage, and bless. And they can experience God. If children are in some respects spiritually exemplary, as Jesus affirmed, they have much to teach adults. Will we listen? Will we learn? He beckons to us, "Be a child."

Children can hug an aging saint and revive a lonely soul. They can watch a cloud and see an angel. They can touch a raindrop and feel the waves of Galilee. They can dance like Miriam and preach like Paul. They listen, and sometimes they can even hear the voice of God. He must smile at the child who really sees, really touches, really listens. He confides to us, "I am that child. To welcome a child is to welcome me" (Matt 18:5; Luke 9:48). When people have Jesus' view of welcoming children and children's spirituality, incredible changes for the better can be expected, things that cannot even be imagined. "Amen" (may that be so).

References

Boyatzis, C. (Guest ed.). (2003). Religious and spiritual development: An introduction. *Review of Religious Research, 44,* 213–19.

Bunge, M. J. (2001). *The child in Christian thought.* Grand Rapids: Eerdmans.

Child Theology Movement (n.d.). Retrieved March 13, 2007, from http://childtheology.org/.

Child Theology Web Page (2006, March 26). Retrieved March 13, 2007, from http://www.childspirituality.org/theology/.

Coles, R. (1990). *The spiritual life of children.* Boston: Houghton Mifflin.

Derske, W. (2003). *The rule of Benedict for beginners: Spirituality for daily life.* Collegeville, MN: Liturgical.

Hay, D., & Nye, R. (2006). *The spirit of the child* (Rev. Ed.). London: Jessica Kingsley.

Hyde, K. E. (1990). *Religion in childhood and adolescence: A comprehensive review of the research.* Birmingham, AL: Religious Education.

Mecum, K. (2001). *God's photo album.* San Francisco: Harper.

Peck, M. S. (1995). *In search of stones.* New York: Hyperion.

Ratcliff, D., & Orona, J. (2007). The children's spirituality database: Major research-based books. Retrieved June 15, 2007, from http://childspirituality.org/don/books.htm.

Ratcliff, D., & Nye, R. (2006). Childhood spirituality: Strengthening the research foundation. In E. Roehlkepartain, P. E. King, L. M. Wagener, & P. L. Benson (Eds.), *Handbook of spiritual development in childhood and adolescence* (pp. 473–483). Thousand Oaks, CA: Sage.

Ratcliff, D. (2007a). The family and the family of God as central aspects of faith formation. Retrieved July 13, 2007, from http://childspirituality.org/experience/family.htm.

Ratcliff, D. (2007b). Experiencing God and spiritual growth with your children. Retrieved July 14, 2007, from http://childspirituality.org/experience/

Ratcliff, D. (2007c). Four alternative approaches to encouraging children's spirituality. Presented at Nazarene Theological Seminary, April 10, 2007. Retrieved July 15, 2007, from http://childspirituality.org/don/approaches.htm.

White, K. (2001). "A little child will lead them": Rediscovering children at the heart of mission. Plenary session at the 2001 "Cutting Edge" conference. Retrieved March 27, 2007, from http://viva.org/?page_id=296.

Willmer, H. (2003). Child theology. Paper presented at the 2003 "Cutting Edge" conference. Retrieved March 27, 2007, from http://www.viva.org/?page_id=148.

Contributor Biographies

Holly Catterton Allen, PhD, is Associate Professor of Christian Ministries and Director of Children and Family Ministries in the Biblical Studies Division at John Brown University. She was Co-Director of the 2006 Children's Spirituality Conference, "Christian Perspectives" and was the guest editor for the Fall 2007 *Christian Education Journal* theme issue on children's spirituality, and she has written articles for *CEJ* and other journals. Dr. Allen was also a chapter contributor for *Children's Spirituality: Christian Perspective, Research, and Applications*; her scholarly interests are children's spirituality and intergenerational issues.

Michael J. Anthony, PhD, is Professor of Christian Education at Talbot School of Theology/Biola University. He has been a consultant to, and served on, numerous institutional boards. Dr. Anthony has authored/edited numerous articles and twelve books. His academic preparation includes doctoral degrees in Educational Administration from Southwestern Seminary and Developmental Psychology from The Claremont Graduate School. He travels throughout the world speaking at Christian Education conferences for churches, camps, and parachurch organizations. He is the chaplain for the Irvine Police Department, which brought him to Ground Zero soon after the September 11 attack. He also serves as a deputy sheriff in the reserve division of the Orange County Sheriff Department.

Stacy Berg, MEd, is an early childhood educator and Director of Northminster Learning Center in Peoria, Illinois. In her current position, she develops faith-based, developmentally appropriate programming for toddlers, preschoolers, and grade school children. Professionally, she enjoys consulting with teachers and programs, and presenting at conferences on supporting project work and faith-based education. Ms. Berg is co-author of *Teaching Your Child to Love Learning* and *Teaching Parents to Do Projects at Home*. She is an adjunct professor at Bradley University.

Chris J. Boyatzis, PhD, is a developmental psychologist whose primary interest is religious and spiritual development. He is an associate professor of psychology at Bucknell University in Lewisburg, Pennsylvania, and coordinator of Bucknell's Children's Studies minor. Dr. Boyatzis has edited special issues on child/adolescent spirituality in *Applied Developmental Science* (with P. E. King, 2004), *The International Journal for the Psychology of Religion* (2006), and *Review of Religious Research* (2003). He has authored many handbook chapters on religious and spiritual development, has organized since 2001 a preconference on the topic at the biennial meetings of the Society for Research in Child Development, and teaches and consults on religious education and family ministry models at a local and national level.

MaLesa Breeding, EdD, is Dean of College of Education and Human Services and she is Associate Professor of Communication Disorders at Abilene Christian University. Her interests are in the area of families of children with severe communication disorders. For the last seven years, Dr. Breeding has worked with a ministry support group called King David's Kids, which is a family ministry designed to provide support to families of children with disabilities. Dr. Breeding is co-author of *Let All the Children Come to Me: A Practical Guide to Including Children with Disabilities in Your Church's Ministry*.

Marilyn Brownlee, MACE, recently completed her graduate work at Haggard School of Theology/Azusa Pacific University. She is the youth ministry coordinator for Friendship Baptist Church in Yorba Linda, California where is the responsible for developing, implementing, and evaluating programs for youth ministry and training potential teachers. She has written adult, college, and youth Bible curriculum for church ministries. She is on staff at Teaching Like Jesus Ministries in Los Angeles; she is a consultant for equipping and training leaders in the local church. She has served on staff at Precept Ministry, Chattanooga, Tennessee as a student leader, teaching youth how to inductively study the Bible.

Linda V. Callahan received her MA in marriage and family therapy with a specialization in child and adolescent counseling from Psychological Studies Institute, Chattanooga, Tennessee. She provides in-home counseling for children, adolescents, and families as a therapeutic care manager with Family Menders of Chattanooga.

Jane Carr, PhD, is Associate Professor of Christian Education and Program Director of the Masters of Arts in Christian Education at Talbot School of Theology in La Mirada, California. In addition, she has served for nineteen years on the pastoral staff at Yorba Linda Friends Church in Southern California where her primary focus has been children's ministry and leadership development. She is the founder of CMPros, an online e-group that networks children's ministry professionals around the world. Her doctoral research explored issues related to job satisfaction among children's ministry professionals. She speaks and provides consultation to churches both nationally and internationally.

Mara Lief Crabtree, DMin, Wesley Theological Seminary; MPS, Loyola University of New Orleans; DASD, San Francisco Theological Seminary; MA Regent University; is Associate Professor of Spiritual Formation and Women's Studies at Regent University School of Divinity in Virginia Beach, Virginia. Ordained with the Communion of Evangelical Episcopal Churches, she serves as a chaplain in the International Order of St. Luke.

Karen Crozier, PhD, is an adjunct professor at Claremont School of Theology in the religious education department. She is a former assistant professor of practical theology at Azusa Pacific University in the Haggard School of Theology, and early childhood educator for Fresno Unified School District. Rev. Dr. Crozier is ordained with the Church of God, Anderson, Indiana, and National Baptist Convention, Inc., and she serves as an associate minister at New Hope Missionary Baptist Church in San Bernardino, California.

James Riley Estep Jr., PhD, Trinity Evangelical Divinity School, D.Min., Southern Baptist Theological Seminary, is Professor of Christian Education at Lincoln Christian Seminary in Lincoln, Illinois. He is the chairperson of the Christian Education Study Group for the Stone-Campbell Journal Conference, and has published or presented over forty pieces on Christian education and related fields.

Jeffrey E. Feinberg, PhD, is leader of Etz Chaim Congregation in Lincolnshire, Illinois. He is also Executive Secretary for the Union of Messianic Jewish Congregations, an international body of Messianic Jewish congregations. His publications include several Messianic Jewish devotional commentaries including *Walk with Genesis* and *Walk with Exodus*, published by Lederer/Messianic Jewish Publishers. Dr. Feinberg and his wife, Pat Feinberg, have authored Messianic Jewish curriculum materials for all age levels. Through FLAME Foundation, they post a reading calendar, which integrates Torah Readings ("Parashiot") with New Testament selections.

Stephanie Goins, MA in psychology, wrote her master's thesis on forgiveness. She practiced counseling for a period of time before going into missions full time. She, along with her husband J., joined Youth With a Mission (YWAM) in 1989 and have spent several years in Africa and Europe. She is currently working on her doctoral thesis through Oxford Centre for Mission Studies/University of Wales. Her contribution for this book is taken from her field research.

Judy Harris Helm, EdD, West Virginia University, assists early childhood and elementary schools in integrating research and new methods through her consulting and training company, Best Practices, Inc. Dr. Helm is past state president of the Illinois Association for the Education of Young Children. Her latest of seven books, *Building Support for Your School: Using Children's Work to Show Learning*, was released in August 2006. The Chicago Children's Museum developed an exhibit based on her work, *The Power of Documentation: Children's Learning Revealed* which is now touring the country. Her work has been translated into five languages and she provides consultation and training throughout the country and internationally.

Dana Kennamer Hood, PhD, is Chair of Department of Curriculum and Instruction at Abilene Christian University. She teaches courses in early childhood and elementary education. Dr. Hood has presented papers at numerous regional, national, and international conferences on topics related to children's spiritual development and nurture. She is co-author of *Let All the Children Come to Me: A Practical Guide to Including Children with Disabilities in Your Church's Ministry*. She serves on the children's ministry leadership team of her church where she has taught Sunday School for over twenty years. Her Sunday school class includes children with various disabilities including autism and Down Syndrome. Dr. Hood's doctoral dissertation explores children's perceptions of God from a contextualist perspective.

Sungwon Kim, PhD, Southwestern Baptist Theological Seminary, has a master's degree in Christian education, an MDiv from Chongshin University, Seoul, Korea, and an MA in early childhood education. She has served in Korean churches as a preschool minister for eleven years and has had previous experience as a kindergarten teacher.

Kevin Lawson, EdD, is Professor of Christian Education and the director of the PhD and EdD programs in Educational Studies at Talbot School of Theology, Biola University. He is also the editor for the *Christian Education Journal*, published by Talbot in cooperation with the North American Professors of Christian Education. He is chair of the Children's Spirituality Conference planning team, author of *How to Thrive in Associate Staff Ministry*, and he has also contributed to a number of edited books on Christian education and children's ministry, as well as publishing articles in a number of journals in the field of Christian education.

Scottie May, PhD, is an assistant professor in the department of Christian Formation and Ministry at Wheaton College. She earned her master's degree from Wheaton College and doctoral degree from Trinity Evangelical Divinity School. She co-authored *Children Matter: Celebrating their Place in the Church, Family and Community* with Catherine Stonehouse, Beth Posterski, and Linda Cannell. She also wrote "A Contemplative Model of Children's Ministry," a chapter in *Perspectives on Children's Spiritual Formation: Four Views*, and a chapter with Donald Ratcliff, "Brain Development and the Numinous Experiences of Children," in *Children's Spirituality: Christian Perspective, Research, and Applications*.

Marcia McQuitty, PhD, is Associate Professor of Childhood and Parent Education Studies in the Human Growth and Development Division in the School of Education Ministries at Southwestern Baptist Theological Seminary. She also serves as faculty liaison/advisor for the Naylor Children's Center, a lab school for persons pursing a career in preschool ministries in the local church. She has written curriculum materials and training manuals and has led church, state, and national conferences for the Southern Baptist Convention.

Heidi Schultz Oschwald graduated with her bachelor's degree in Children and Family Ministries from John Brown University in 2007. She currently teaches children at the Lollipop Learning Tree in Salem, Oregon. Her research paper for the course, "Children's Spiritual Development," with Dr. Allen contributed to the chapter in this book.

Donald Ratcliff, PhD, is the Price-LeBar Professor of Christian Education in the Formation and Ministry Department at Wheaton College in Wheaton, Illinois. He has studied children's religious and spiritual development for more than twenty-five years, and has edited several books related to this topic including *Children's Spirituality: Christian Perspectives, Research, and Applications*, and five books for Religious Education Press. He has developed extensive web pages related to children's spirituality (http://childspirituality.org/don/) as well as qualitative research (http://don.ratcliffs.net/qual). He is a charter member of the planning team for the Children's Spirituality Conference: Christian Perspectives, and is an academic supervisor for the Search Institute's Center for Spiritual Development in Childhood and Adolescence, as well as a research consultant for the Oxford Centre for Missions Studies.

Pam Scranton, MEd, is an adjunct professor at Bradley University and is the curriculum coordinator at Northminster Learning Center. Ms. Scranton is in her eighteenth year as an early childhood educator. She taught at Valeska Hinton Early Childhood Education Center and in the Woodford County Special Education Bright Beginnings program, before coming to the Northminster Learning Center to teach the Discovery Preschool program. She is a frequent presenter in school districts on topics such as engaging children in project work, authentic assessment, and developmentally appropriate practice. She is a contributing author of *The Power of Projects* and co-author of *Teaching Your Child to Love Learning* and *Teaching Parents to Do Projects at Home*.

Timothy A. Sisemore, PhD, Fuller Theological Seminary, is clinical professor of counseling and psychology at the Psychological Studies Institute (PSI) in Chattanooga, Tennessee and directs PSI's Chattanooga Bible Institute Counseling Center. His practice and teaching focus on children and adolescents. Dr. Sisemore has written four books, two of which focus on biblical views of children. His most recent, *World-Proof Your Kids:*

Raising Children Unstained by the World, critiques current culture as it conflicts with promoting the fruit of the Spirit in the lives of children.

Catherine Stonehouse, PhD, is Orlean Bullard Beeson Professor of Christian Discipleship and Dean of the School of Practical Theology at Asbury Theological Seminary. Her research focuses on the spirituality of children. She is the author of *Joining Children on the Spiritual Journey: Nurturing a Life of Faith*, co-author of *Children Matter: Celebrating their Place in the Church, Family, and Community*, and has contributed chapters in several books. In the classroom she addresses the disciple ministries of the church with special attention to the spiritual nurture of children and their families.

La Verne Tolbert, PhD, Talbot School of Theology, is adjunct professor at Haggard School of Theology and Biola University. Dr. Tolbert is founder of Teaching Like Jesus Ministries, a consultation and teacher-training ministry dedicated to equipping volunteers in the local church utilizing the principles from her book, *Teaching Like Jesus: A Practical Guide to Christian Education in Your Church* and its Spanish version *Enseñemos Como Jesus*. She writes curriculum for children's church/Sunday school and is the director of Christian education ministries at Crenshaw Christian Center in Los Angeles. Her latest book, *Keeping Your Kids Sexually Pure: A How-To Guide for Parents, Pastors, Youth Workers and Teachers* highlights her dissertation research on school-based clinics. Dr. Tolbert is a planning team member for the Children's Spirituality Conference.

T. Wyatt Watkins, MDiv, Christian Theological Seminary, Indianapolis, also holds a bachelor of violin performance from Indiana University. He is pastor of Cumberland First Baptist Church in Indianapolis, and a charter member of the Indianapolis Chamber Orchestra. Watkins's titles include *Gospel, Grits, and Grace: Encountering the Holy in the Ridiculous, Sublime, and Unexpected*, *How Sweet the Sound: Stories Inspired by the Hymns We Love*, *The Promise Restored: Rediscovering the Ten Commandments in an Uncertain World*, *What Our Kids Teach Us About Prayer*, and *Praying the Parables*.

John H. Westerhoff III, EdD, retired professor of theology and Christian nurture at Duke University, and most recently a visiting professor of Christian Ethics and Moral Theology at General Theological Seminary in New York, is the author of the classic *Will our Children Have Faith?* In addition, he has authored many other books, articles, and chapters on Christian formation. He currently serves as a priest associate and theologian at St. Anne's Episcopal Church in Atlanta.